Employment Tribunal Claims

tactics and precedents

Naomi Cunningham was called to the Bar in 1994 and worked at a number of London law centres before joining the Free Representation Unit (FRU) as employment caseworker in 2000. She has written for the *Industrial Law Journal* (OUP) and *Adviser* (Citizens Advice), and is one of the contributing editors of *Employment Court Practice* (Sweet & Maxwell, 2007). She practises as a member of the employment team at Farrar's Building.

Michael Reed was called to the Bar in 2003. He currently works as the employment caseworker at FRU where he appears regularly for claimants in the employment tribunals and the EAT and has responsibility for training and supervising a large number of volunteers. He is a director of the Discrimination Law Association.

The Legal Action Group is a national, independent charity which promotes equal access to justice for all members of society who are socially, economically or otherwise disadvantaged. To this end, it seeks to improve law and practice, the administration of justice and legal services.

Employment Tribunal Claims

tactics and precedents

SECOND EDITION

Naomi Cunningham and Michael Reed

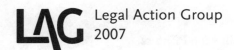

Legal Action Group
2007

This second edition published in Great Britain 2007
by LAG Education and Service Trust Limited
242 Pentonville Road, London N1 9UN
www.lag.org.uk

First edition 2005
Revised first edition 2006

While every effort has been made to ensure that the details in this text are correct, readers must be aware that the law changes and that the accuracy of the material cannot be guaranteed and the authors and the publisher accept no responsibility for any loss or damage sustained.

British Library Cataloguing in Publication Data
a CIP catalogue record for this book is available from the British Library.

ISBN   978 1 903307 55 7

Typeset and printed by Hobbs the Printers,
Totton, Hampshire SO40 3WX

Foreword to the first edition

The Hon Mrs Justice Cox DBE

When, as a law student, I first developed an interest in the law governing employment relationships, that law was to be found secreted away in the standard contract textbooks under the quaint heading: 'The Law relating to Master and Servant'. The right not to be unfairly dismissed had yet to enter the statute books; and the process of revolutionising what had hitherto been an entirely contractual relationship was just about to begin.

Now, some 35 years later, employment law is threatening to drown us all in the sea of case law and legislation, both domestic and European, that it has become. Employment tribunals too have moved well away from their original concept as a straightforward, cost-free system for the speedy resolution of employment disputes, to the modern, sophisticated arena they have become for determining what are often cases involving inordinate factual and legal complexity. There are now new and complex procedural regulations governing the conduct of the increasing number of cases which come before them.

Yet, as we struggle to keep up with all this, we can lose sight of the fact that the art of running a claim in the tribunal, and knowing how best, tactically, to prepare for and conduct a hearing, involve skills which are just as important as a sound knowledge of the substantive law and procedure. Given our adversarial process, they are skills which can make all the difference to winning or losing a case. Intimate knowledge of how tribunals work, the art of writing good letters, where to look for the relevant law, how and when to press for disclosure, effective use of the questionnaire procedure, deciding which witnesses to call or, sometimes more importantly, not to call, knowing how to present good arguments in closing a case, negotiating a beneficial settlement, settling grounds of appeal from an adverse decision – the list is endless; and each of them is a vital component in the weaponry of an employment adviser.

How useful therefore, to be able to reach for a book like this and find, all in one place, sensible and realistic guidance on every conceivable aspect of employment litigation. This text, as its title suggests, marks a change from the Legal Action Group practitioner texts now so familiar to those who work in the various LAG specialist areas. It concentrates on the practical and the tactical and, in my view, neatly fills a gap in the employment adviser's library, where information and advice of this kind, on this scale and in this format has not previously been accessible.

The author observes that this book is aimed primarily at those unqualified or part-qualified employment advisers; but it will in my view be extremely attractive to a far wider audience, including the busy, the newly qualified and indeed the not so newly qualified employment practitioner, when advising or appearing for either employees or employers.

The real value of this text lies in the straightforward and comprehensive advice it provides; and in its success in demystifying the legal process and lawyers' jargon. We lawyers, so familiar with the terminology of our discipline, tend to forget how perplexing it can be to those outside our sheltered world. A tribunal Chairman, once giving directions to unrepresented litigants on how to prepare for a hearing and referring to the need for 'skeleton arguments' was met, predictably, by the question from one of them, 'do you mean thin?'

Most useful of all perhaps is the comprehensive collection of precedents, those important documents which have already stood someone in good stead and can therefore confidently be used by the novice, the busy or the less experienced adviser, to whom they will become real friends.

The author is to be congratulated for producing what will undoubtedly become a most helpful, informative and well-used resource for those working in one of the most dynamic and fascinating areas of the law.

Laura Cox
Royal Courts of Justice
February 2005

Introduction

This book grew out of a file of precedents created for volunteers at the Free Representation Unit (FRU) in London where we have both worked as caseworker with responsibility for training and supervising volunteer employment tribunal representatives.[1] We have both also at different times been FRU volunteers ourselves. FRU volunteers are typically postgraduate law students, pupil barristers or trainee solicitors who come to the organisation with little or no prior knowledge of employment law and practice. They found a broad collection of precedents reassuring when taking their first steps in employment tribunal litigation, and that suggested that a similar collection might be of use as well to other non-specialist, unqualified or part-qualified advisers and to lay people representing themselves in the employment tribunals.

The book was conceived as very little more than the original collection of sample documents, supported by footnotes and short sections of explanatory text. The explanatory text expanded greatly in the writing of the first edition. Much of this, too, reflects experience drawn from FRU. Volunteers grappling with a difficult legal problem would have a wealth of specialist law reports, text books and articles to rely on. Guidance on softer questions – questions about the 'feel' of the process, how a tribunal is likely to react to a particular application, how to go about structuring a cross-examination, where to pitch the next offer in a negotiation, etc – is much harder to find in written form. One of the main aims of this book is to fill that gap. The book does not set out the substantive or procedural law except to the minimum extent necessary to place the precedents and tactical guidance in their context.[2]

---

1   Naomi Cunningham from August 2000 to April 2004; Michael Reed from January 2005 to date.
2   For accessible guides to employment law and employment tribunal procedure, see Tamara Lewis, *Employment Law: an adviser's handbook* (ELAH 7) (7th edn, Legal Action Group, 2007) and McMullen, Tuck and Criddle, *Employment Tribunal Procedure: a users' guide to tribunals and appeals* (ETP 3) (3rd edn, Legal Action Group, December 2004); for a much more detailed and technical treatment, see *Harvey on Industrial Relations and Employment Law* (Butterworths, Looseleaf). *Butterworths Employment Law Handbook* (15th edn, Butterworths, 2007) edited by Peter Wallington is a comprehensive collection of employment legislation.

Although the book is primarily written with claimants acting for themselves and unqualified or part-qualified advisers in mind, we hope that it will also prove useful to lawyers who only occasionally practise employment law, and to specialist employment lawyers early in their careers. The focus of the book, true to its origins, is on the conduct of proceedings by or on behalf of employees. Most of the text is applicable to both sides, however, and many of the precedents could be used with minor adaptations by employers and their advisers.

The collection of precedents deliberately makes no attempt at comprehensiveness. Its aim is to demonstrate techniques and tactics through examples rather than to provide a precedent for every occasion. For this reason it is both broader and shallower than its closest comparators. It is shallower in that it offers a relatively small range of examples of formal employment tribunal pleadings and makes no attempt to illustrate all the kinds of complaint that can be brought to an employment tribunal.[3] It is broader in that it does offer a greater range of kinds of documents – correspondence with the respondent and the tribunal, written submissions, cross-examination notes, chronologies, draft directions, etc, as well as formal employment tribunal pleadings – than is usual. The intention in this is not to persuade users that they should depend on a precedent for every need: on the contrary, the intention is to provide varied enough examples to give users the confidence to draft their own documents flexibly and responsively. Precedents – like water-wings – cannot be said to have done their job until their users discard them.

Many of the precedents in this book are loosely based on documents drafted for real disputes, so they are not simplified textbook cases: some of them raise problematic legal arguments or tactical decisions. They are offered as demonstrations of the kinds of documents that claimants or their advisers may need to draft at various stages of the dispute rather than as templates to be followed closely.

The book is divided into chapters that broadly follow the sequence of employment tribunal proceedings. Each chapter aims to give clear practical guidance on the stage of proceedings discussed, to alert users to unwritten rules, conventional practice and pit-falls, and to give them insights into the likely thought processes of the tribunal and the other parties. Sample pleadings, letters and other documents appear through-out each chapter to illustrate the points made. These are given numbers

---

3   See ETP 3 pp22–30 and *Harvey on Industrial Relations and Employment Law* (Butterworths) division U.

that correspond to the preceding paragraph number: so, for example, a precedent following paragraph 3.7 will be P3.7; if two precedents follow one after the other at that point, they will be numbered P3.7.1 and P3.7.2. Occasionally where it seems useful to show the structure of the document before giving a sample, there will be what we have called a 'document outline'. These are numbered similarly.

Employment tribunals and the lawyers who appear in them have their own habits and expectations. Chairmen can behave as if these were self-explanatory when, to an outsider or a beginner, they are not.[4] One particular source of difficulty for the non-lawyer operating in employment tribunals comes – ironically – directly from efforts to make the process informal and non-legalistic. The tribunal system is supposed to provide a quick, cheap and informal process; procedure rules are expressed in non-technical language, and everything is supposed to be plain and straightforward.

The problem with this is that the whole structure is still dominated by lawyers. Employment tribunal chairmen are trained lawyers, as are very many of those who represent claimants and respondents before them. The employment tribunal rules are in many ways a simplified version of the rules that apply in the ordinary courts, many of which have literally centuries of development and case law behind them. The result is that the employment tribunal procedure rules look very different from the perspective of a non-lawyer who simply reads the words and tries to work out what they mean, than from the perspective of a lawyer who instinctively compares them to the rules he or she is familiar with in other legal contexts. Tribunal chairmen may throw up their hands in horror at what they see as a basic failure of good practice or tribunal etiquette, and claimants acting in person or inexperienced advisers can sometimes be made to feel that the process – for all its supposed informality – is in fact a minefield of obscure unwritten rules and embarrassing unexpected howlers.[5]

A key aim of this book is to alert users to the unwritten rules and guide them in the art of staying on the right side of the decision-making body. A subsidiary aim is to encourage inexperienced advisers

4   'Chairman' is the term used in the legislation and is not intended to be gender specific.

5   For example: in one hearing, the chairman was heard to bark at an unrepresented employer, repeatedly and with rising irritation, 'Don't lead the witness!' The employer clearly had no idea what this meant, but was too rattled to ask – and so carried on asking leading questions until the claimant's representative intervened to suggest that it might be better if the chairman explained what he meant by 'leading' and why it was unhelpful.

not to let the occasional 'telling off' from the tribunal alarm them unduly: although the adviser who is constantly in hot water with the tribunal is probably doing something wrong, the adviser who never makes him or herself unpopular with a tribunal is probably not serving his or her clients well either. Beginners in the field should also take courage from the thought that all practitioners learn by their mistakes. Where we warn against any specific error, there is a good chance that one of us has road-tested it.

All names are fictional, and where documents are adapted from real cases, other details have been changed to preserve anonymity. Letters are written in the names of Natalie Cummings and Malcolm Rhodes, fictional alter-egos of the authors, who practise employment law from the imaginary North London Law Centre. Curiously, all the respondents with whom Ms Cummings and Mr Rhodes deal are represented by the same George Bean of Carrot & Marrow Solicitors in Islington; even more curiously, a series of computer glitches in the tribunal service have assigned all their cases the same number, 123456/2006. As for the perennial problem of a neutral pronoun, we have chosen to use 'she' and 'he' in alternate chapters. Both should be taken to mean 'he or she.'

Acknowledgements

We are both indebted to countless FRU volunteers whose questions and problems have taught us as much as we have taught them, and whose courage and enthusiasm are a constant source of inspiration. We are grateful too to Michael Gleeson, (a barrister and former FRU volunteer) and Nigel Duncan (Principal Lecturer at the Inns of Court School of Law, City University), who provided invaluable comments during preparation of the first edition; and most of all to Tim Pitt-Payne, who first suggested the book and whose experience and insights have informed it throughout. Any remaining errors are our own.

Naomi Cunningham
Michael Reed
London
August 2007

Dedication

for FRU, of course

Contents

Table of precedents

Chapter 5

Chapter 6

Chapter 13

Table of cases

Table of statutes

Table of statutory instruments

Abbreviations

ACAS	Advisory, Conciliation and Arbitration Service
BPBU	Bar Pro Bono Unit
CAB(x)	Citizens Advice Bureau(x)
CCJ	County Court Judgment
CEHR	Commission on Equalities and Human Rights
CFA	Conditional fee agreement
CMD	Case management discussion
CPR	Civil Procedure Rules
CRE	Commission for Racial Equality
DCA	Department of Constitutional Affairs
DDA 1995	Disability Discrimination Act 1995
DDP	Dismissal and disciplinary procedure
DPA 1998	Data Protection Act 1998
DRC	Disability Rights Commission
EA 2002	Employment Act 2002
EA(DR)R 2004	Employment Act 2002 (Dispute Resolution) Regulations 2004 SI No 752
EAT	Employment Appeal Tribunal
EDT	Effective date of termination
ELAAS	Employment Lawyers Appeals Advice Scheme
ELAH 7	*Employment Law: an adviser's handbook* (7th edn, Legal Action Group, 2007)
EOC	Equal Opportunities Commission
EqPA 1970	Equal Pay Act 1970
ERA 1996	Employment Rights Act 1996
ETP 3	McMullen, Tuck and Criddle *Employment Tribunal Procedure* (3rd edn, Legal Action Group, December 2004)
FOIA 2000	Freedom of Information Act 2000
FRU	Free Representation Unit
GP	Grievance procedure
HR	Human resources
ICR	Industrial Case Reports
IRLR	Industrial Relations Law Reports
NCIS	National Criminal Intelligence Service
PHR	Pre-hearing review
POCA 2002	Proceeds of Crime Act 2002
REC	Racial Equality Council
RNIB	Royal National Institute for the Blind
RNID	Royal National Institute for the Deaf

Glossary

The purpose of this glossary is to provide non-technical working definitions for the terms in common use in the employment tribunals that are most likely to give non-lawyers difficulty. Many of these terms are explained at greater length in the main text of this book; some are defined by statute, and this glossary is no substitute for considering the language of the statutory definition.

ACAS
Advisory, Conciliation and Arbitration Service: the statutory body that has a duty to attempt to bring about the settlement of employment tribunal disputes; see *conciliation*.

actual dismissal
Dismissal where the employer has terminated the contract of employment: contrasted with *constructive dismissal*, where the employee has resigned in response to the employer's fundamental breach of the contract of employment.

additional information
Further details of the *claim or response* provided at the request of the opposing party.

adjournment
A hearing is said to be adjourned if after it has begun it is put off to another day, or to later in the same day.

affidavit
A formal sworn statement used in legal proceedings. An affidavit has to be sworn in front of a solicitor or barrister.

affirm
1. An employee is said to affirm her contract of employment if, after the employer has committed a fundamental breach of contract, she acts in a way that implies that she intends to keep the contract alive. This deprives her of the right to resign and complain of *constructive dismissal*.
2. Before giving evidence a witness must either swear an oath to tell the

truth (on the appropriate holy book), or affirm, that is, make a solemn non-religious promise to tell the truth.

appellant
The party – whether the employer or the employee – who appeals against a decision.

attendance note
A file note recording what was said at a meeting or in the course of a telephone conversation.

authorities
Previously decided cases relied on by a party in support of its arguments.

bundle
The papers prepared for use at a hearing – for example, a bundle of documents, a bundle of authorities, etc – usually paginated, indexed, and held together securely (for example, in a lever arch file).

burden of proof
The party that has the job of persuading the tribunal that its assertions on any issue are correct is said to bear the *burden of proof* on that issue. For example: a claimant who says that she was dismissed for raising health and safety issues must show that this was the reason for her dismissal if she is to succeed in her unfair dismissal claim, and so if the tribunal cannot decide what was the reason for her dismissal she fails. If her employer says that she has failed to take reasonable steps to *mitigate* her loss, however, it is for the employer to show that that is true: it is not for her to show that she has done everything she reasonably could.

case management discussion
A hearing before a chairman at which procedural arrangements for the hearing are made.

case law
Previously decided cases that establish points of principle; law derived from that source as opposed to *legislation*.

cast list
A list of the individuals involved in the events on which the claim is based.

chairman
The lawyer who presides over an employment tribunal hearing; see also *wing member*.

chronology
A list of key events, with dates, in date order.

claim
1. The document by which the claimant starts employment tribunal proceedings. 2. The subject-matter of the claimant's case.

claimant
The individual who brings the claim to the employment tribunal.

comparator
In a discrimination case, the claimant may say that the employer treated someone else more favourably than him or her in comparable circumstances. This other person is referred to as the *comparator*. Comparators may be actual or hypothetical: often the allegation is not that a real other person was better treated, but that another person with the same characteristics as the claimant except for his or her race (or sex, or religious belief, etc) *would have been* better treated.

conciliation
The attempt (usually by ACAS) to bring about a negotiated settlement of the claim.

consolidate
To link two (or more) related cases so that they are heard together.

constructive dismissal
Resignation in response to a fundamental breach of contract by the employer, which is treated as dismissal for the purposes of unfair dismissal protection. Compare *actual dismissal*.

contributory fault
Culpable conduct by an employee that has contributed to his or her dismissal, relied on as a reason to reduce compensation.

costs order
An order that one party should pay the other a sum of money representing some or all of the legal fees that the second party has incurred in the case (expenses order in Scotland). See also *preparation time order.*

COT3
The form on which an ACAS officer records a settlement.

cross-examination
Questioning of a witness in order to undermine the case of the party who called the witness, or to discredit the witness's evidence.

culpable
Deserving blame.

declaration
A *remedy* that may be given by a court or tribunal. A declaration is a formal, binding statement about the legal rights of a party.

direct discrimination
Treating a person unfavourably on a prohibited ground, for example, because of his or her race, sex, etc. See also *indirect discrimination.*

directions hearing
The old term for a *case management discussion.*

directions
Orders issued by the tribunal as to the procedural aspects of the case – for example, as to disclosure of documents, exchange of witness statements, bundles of documents, etc.

disclosure
The process by which one party tells the other party what relevant documents it has, and/or provides copies of them.

discovery
The old term for *disclosure*.

discretion
A decision-maker is said to have a discretion if it has a choice between different courses of action that is not governed by a fixed rule but instead requires consideration of all the circumstances. For example, a tribunal that has found that an employer has made unauthorised deductions from the claimant's wages must order the employer to pay the sum deducted – it has no discretion as to whether or not to do so. By contrast, a tribunal that considers that a claimant's case was *misconceived* has the power to order him or her to pay some or all of the respondent's costs: but it has a wide discretion whether to make a costs order, and if so how much to order the claimant to pay.

discrimination by way of victimisation
Treating an employee unfavourably because he or she has made a complaint of discrimination (or helped another person to do so). For example, it is *discrimination by way of victimisation* to dismiss a woman because she has complained of sex discrimination. To an employment lawyer, 'victimisation' is a technical term meaning this kind of discrimination. Hence a claim that uses the word in its non-technical sense of bullying or harassment is likely to prompt a request for additional information seeking confirmation that no form of discrimination is alleged.

distinguish
An argument that the tribunal need not follow a previously decided case because it is different in some material respect from the case before them is referred to as *distinguishing* the earlier case: see paragraph 1.35.

effective date of termination
The day on which the employment terminated, often important for calculating time limits for presenting a claim.

Employment Appeal Tribunal
The body that hears appeals from the employment tribunals.

ET1
The form (otherwise referred to as the *claim*) by which the claimant starts tribunal proceedings.

ET3
The form (otherwise referred to as the *response*) on which the respondent responds to the claim.

evidence in chief
The main body of evidence given by a witness – usually by way of a witness statement – before cross-examination by or on behalf of the opposing party.

examination in chief
Asking questions of one's own witness.

expeditious
prompt

extempore
Reasons or a judgment are said to have been given extempore if given straight away at the end of the hearing; compare *reserved*.

floating
Sometimes, on arrival at tribunal on the hearing day, the parties are told that the starting time for their hearing has not been fixed but that their case will be heard once a tribunal or chairman becomes free. In this situation the case is said to be *floating*.

further particulars
The old term for *additional information*.

hearsay evidence
Evidence given by a witness of a statement made by another person, given for the purpose of establishing the truth of the statement.

indirect discrimination

In general, applying a rule or practice that is on its face neutral as between different groups, but that imposes a disproportionate disadvantage on members of one race, sex, etc. Applying the same minimum height requirement to male and female job applicants, for example, would usually be unlawful on grounds of indirect discrimination, unless justified by the requirements of the job. Where discrimination is prohibited, indirect discrimination is prohibited unless unlawful.

inference

A conclusion drawn from established facts.

interlocutory

Preliminary and/or procedural.

issues

The questions on which the parties disagree, and which the tribunal will have to adjudicate on.

judgment

The tribunal's final determination of an issue or the issues in the case.

leading question

A question that indicates the answer expected. Leading questions are generally allowed in *cross-examination* but not – except on uncontroversial matters – in *examination in chief*. Hence, representatives may be told by the tribunal not to 'lead' their own witnesses.

Legal Services Commission

The body that administers public funding for legal advice and representation.

legalese

Unnecessarily obscure or pompous language used by lawyers to enhance their importance/mystery/fees.

legislation
Law that is set out in Acts of Parliament or regulations (or European Instruments) as opposed to being derived from previously decided cases.

liability
What courts or tribunals have to decide is often divided into questions about liability – that is, whether a legal wrong has been done to the claimant – and questions about *remedy* – that is, what is to be done about it.

limitation period
The period within which a claim must be brought.

liquidated damages
A sum agreed between the parties to a contract to be payable in the event of breach (or a certain defined breach) by one party, provided that the sum represents a genuine attempt to value the loss or damage that would be caused to the innocent party by the breach. If it is simply an arbitrary sum intended to coerce full compliance with the terms of the contract, then it is a *penalty clause* and unenforceable.

listing
The process of fixing a date for a hearing.

misconceived
Having no foundation, or no reasonable prospect of success.

mitigation
The process by which a claimant reduces the amount she has lost (by reason of dismissal, discrimination, etc) by her own efforts – for example, by getting another job.

notice of appearance
The old term for the *response* or ET3.

open
Correspondence or a meeting is said to be open if it is not *without prejudice* (see below).

order
An instruction by the tribunal that requires a person or party to do something.

organogram
A chart showing an organisation's structure.

originating application
The old term for the *claim or ET1*.

party
A claimant or respondent: the persons whose rights and obligations are to be decided in the proceedings.

penalty clause
A clause in a contract that imposes a disproportionate financial penalty on one party for breach of the contract in order to coerce that party into strict compliance: for example, a clause in a contract of employment that provided that an hour's pay would be docked for every five minutes by which the employee arrived late. Penalty clauses are unenforceable, but see *liquidated damages*.

pleadings
The old term for *statements of case*.

postponement
Putting off a hearing to another date.

precedent
1. A decided case that establishes a point of principle to be followed in other cases in the future. 2. A document intended as an example of how to draft documents of the particular kind demonstrated.

pre-hearing review
A hearing that takes place before the main or substantive hearing, usually before a chairman alone, in order to decide preliminary matters.

prejudice
Disadvantage. Exercises of the tribunal's case management discretion – e.g. whether or not to postpone a hearing – will often

depend partly or wholly on the 'balance of prejudice' between the parties. For example, whether the disadvantage to Party A in having the hearing put off is greater or less than the disadvantage to Party B in having to go ahead without a particular who cannot attend on the date originally set.

preparation time order

An order that one party pay the other a sum of money representing the time they have spent preparing the case, available in place of a costs order if the receiving party has not been legally represented.

privilege

A document is said to be privileged if it does not have to be disclosed to the other party despite being relevant. The rule that the content of *without prejudice* negotiations must not be disclosed to the tribunal is also a variety of privilege.

pro bono

Short for 'pro bono publico' (Latin): for the public good. Where a lawyer is acting *pro bono* he or she is acting without charging the client a fee.

promulgate

Legalese for 'send out'.

protected disclosure

A disclosure made by an employee for which by virtue of the Public Interest Disclosure Act 1998 she must not be dismissed or subjected to a detriment.

quantum

Latin for 'how much', used as legal shorthand for the amount that the claim is worth. See also *liability*, remedy.

questionnaire

A list of questions that a claimant or potential claimant in a discrimination case can serve on the other party.

re-engagement

A remedy for unfair dismissal: the claimant must be re-employed in a job comparable to his or her old job.

reinstatement
A remedy for unfair dismissal: the claimant must be given his or her old job back.

remedy
What the claimant gets from the respondent if she is successful in her claim. By far the most common remedy awarded by employment tribunals is compensation, but other remedies are available in some cases: for example, a declaration, reinstatement or re-engagement.

repudiation
Fundamental breach of contract: an employer or employee who has acted in fundamental breach of the contract of employment is said to have *repudiated* it.

reserved decision
A decision that is not given on the day of the hearing but at a later date.

respondent
1. The party against whom a claim is made. 2. In an appeal, the party resisting the appeal.

response
The respondent's answer to the *claim*.

review
The process by which the tribunal may revisit its own decision and, if it thinks fit, revoke or vary it.

serve
If a document is required to be 'served' on someone, it must be sent or given to them.

skeleton argument
A written summary of the arguments that a party will put forward at a hearing.

statement of truth
An assertion, contained in a witness statement, that the contents of it are true.

statements of case
In the employment tribunals, the claim and response (often still referred to as pleadings).

statute
Another term for an Act of Parliament.

subject access request
a request under the Data Protection Act 1998 for personal data.

submissions
The points made by a party or his or her representative to persuade the tribunal to find in his or her favour.

substantive
Relating to the substance of the claim, rather than to procedural or *interlocutory* matters.

'Tomlin' order
An order staying proceedings while the terms of a settlement are put into effect.

whistleblowing
The familiar name for making a *protected disclosure*.

wing member
An employment tribunal is made up of a *chairman*, who is legally qualified, and two *wing members*. The wing members need not be, and are usually not, legally qualified, but they will have relevant experience, for example, as trade unionists or personnel managers.

without prejudice
The phrase used to indicate that a letter or conversation is directed to achieving a settlement and is therefore not to be disclosed to the tribunal.

witness statement
The written account of the evidence given by a witness. In England and Wales it forms the basis of that witness's *evidence in chief* and may be read aloud by the witness or taken as read. In Scotland, witness statements are not used: *evidence in chief* is given orally.

CHAPTER 1

Preliminary matters

Sources of employment law advice and representation

1.1 This book is partly aimed at individuals representing themselves in employment tribunal claims. The employment tribunal process is intended to be accessible to people without specialist knowledge, and many individuals do represent themselves. Nevertheless, most individual claimants will prefer to have representation if they can find it, and in most cases representation will improve their chances of a successful outcome.[1]

1.2 It is suggested that claimants who cannot afford to pay substantial sums of money for representation should consider the possibilities of free or affordable representation in this order:

- their trade union, if they belong to one;
- their household, credit card, car (etc.) insurance;
- a voluntary sector advice centre or one of the statutory Commissions;
- high street solicitors;
- employment consultants.

Trade unions

1.3 A claimant who is a member of a trade union should normally expect to be represented by the union in a dispute with his or her employer. Unions have different rules about which cases they will support, and some will withdraw support (sometimes shortly before the hearing) if the claimant refuses to accept what the union's lawyers advise is a good offer of settlement. Claimants considering relying on union assistance should make sure that they have been given clear information about the circumstances in which the union will withdraw its assistance.

Household insurance

1.4 Household (and other) insurance policies include legal expenses insurance surprisingly often. This tends to be a neglected source of assistance for claimants for the simple reason that many do not realise that they

---

1 The claimant is the individual complaining to an employment tribunal of a breach of his or her employment rights. Until October 2004 the correct term was 'applicant' and this term is likely still to be used occasionally. The other party – usually the employer – is called the respondent.

have the cover. It can be extraordinarily good value: the insurance may cover all legal expenses, including specialist representation at the hearing, with no claw-back even if the claimant recovers a large award. It is important to investigate this at an early stage in the dispute, however, because a claimant who has already taken steps in employment tribunal proceedings without the advice of an insurer-approved lawyer may find that she has invalidated her insurance.[2]

Voluntary sector advice agencies

1.5   There are various kinds of voluntary sector advice agencies that may be able to offer free advice and/or representation. Almost all of them are badly over-stretched, and many claimants will spend fruitless hours telephoning advice agencies only to be told that no-one can help. However, some agencies will deliver an exceptional service that rivals the best that private practice solicitors can offer, so (within limits) it is worth persevering. The process may well be frustrating, but anyone seeking free representation should try not to let the frustration show. Mostly 'we cannot help' means just that – the organisation simply has no spare capacity, or does not do this sort of work. If there is any flexibility, human nature is as it is and charm almost always gets further than aggression.[3]

1.6   Most voluntary sector advice agencies belong to an umbrella organisation, and that organisation's website will often be the best starting point for finding local services. The main umbrella organisations and their website addresses:

Law Centres:	Law Centres Federation: www.lawcentres.org.uk
Citizens' Advice Bureaux:	Citizens Advice: www.citizensadvice.org.uk
Other advice agencies:	AdviceUK (formerly the Federation of Independent Advice Agencies): www.adviceuk.org.uk

2 It is also worth checking motor insurance and any policy attached to credit cards, and any other membership that might include insurance. Even membership of a football club has been known to provide this type of benefit.

3 There is a practical insight of wide application here. Even when – as sometimes – aggression may be effective, charm should always be tried first. The reason is that if charm does not work, aggression is still available as a last resort. Starting with aggression and then trying to backtrack to charm is futile.

Law Centres®

1.7   Law Centres® are, in effect, not-for-profit solicitors' practices that specialise in what is broadly defined as 'social welfare law' – typically housing, immigration, employment and welfare rights. Most, if not all, law centres operate a catchment area policy and will only advise those who live (or sometimes work or worked) in their area. Many will only accept clients who are financially eligible for public funding, and the rest are likely to impose some kind of means test on access to their services. Most employ an employment lawyer or specialist adviser. The website of the umbrella body, the Law Centres Federation, lists 60 law centres, roughly half of them in Greater London and most of the rest in substantial town or city centres.

Citizens Advice Bureaux

1.8   Citizens Advice Bureaux (CABx) tend to offer a generalist service, and only some employ a specialist employment adviser. CABx do not generally have a catchment area policy and will advise anyone who approaches, subject to availability of advisers. CABx do not generally means-test their clients except for Legal Services Commission funded work. There are around 460 CABx in the UK providing advice from over 3,000 locations: any sizeable town centre is likely to have one. The umbrella group is called Citizens Advice (formerly more intelligibly known as the National Association of Citizens Advice Bureaux).[4]

Racial Equality Councils

1.9   Racial Equality Councils (RECs) are specialist advice agencies that serve their local area but will deal only with claims that involve an element of race discrimination.

4 www.citizensadvice.org.uk

The Free Representation Unit and the Bar Pro Bono Unit

1.10   In London, the Free Representation Unit (FRU) can sometimes provide representation at employment tribunals, but it does not deal direct with members of the public. Cases must be referred, after a hearing date has been fixed, by a solicitor, law centre, CAB or other advice agency.[5] Claimants in London who are receiving advice and assistance for case preparation, but whose adviser is not able to represent them at a hearing should make sure their cases are referred to FRU as soon as a hearing date is set to have the best chance of representation. Most FRU volunteers are student or trainee lawyers who work under the supervision of a specialist employment lawyer. They choose their own cases, rather than having cases assigned to them, so FRU can never guarantee representation in any given case until a particular volunteer has offered to take the case on.

1.11   The Bar Pro Bono Unit (BPBU) is a charity funded by the Bar Council and others that matches clients in need of free representation with barristers willing to give their time. Because the kind of work barristers are permitted to do is restricted, BPBU is best able to assist clients who are represented by a solicitor's firm or advice agency that is willing to retain conduct of the case and instruct the barrister to do defined pieces of work – to draft a document, for example, or appear at the hearing. Like FRU, BPBU will only accept referrals from an advice agency it will not deal direct with members of the public. Unlike FRU, BPBU puts applications for assistance through a careful sift to decide whether or not to offer help, so an application to BPBU should always be made as early as possible. BPBU itself is located in London, but its services are potentially available throughout England and Wales. As with FRU, the fact that BPBU has accepted a referral is no guarantee that it will be able to assist. The Unit's website is www.barprobonounit.org.uk.

---

5   FRU only accepts referrals from solicitors and advice agencies that are signed up with the organisation and pay an annual subscription; for further details, and a list of subscribing agencies, see www.freerepresentationunit.org.uk

LawWorks

1.12   LawWorks is a solicitors' pro bono organisation.[6] Like the Bar Pro Bono Unit and FRU, it accepts applications for assistance only through advice agencies. Like BPBU, it applies both means and merits tests before offering assistance. An application form can be downloaded from its website.

Specialist charities

1.13   Some of the larger disability charities, including RNIB (Royal National Institute for the Blind), RNID (Royal National Institute for the Deaf), and the Disability Law Service employ specialist advisers who can advise and sometimes represent in disability discrimination cases. Public Concern at Work provides a helpline on whistleblowing issues but does not undertake casework. The Terence Higgins Trust provides helpline advice on HIV-status employment issues, and may be able to refer on to other agencies for casework. The Andrea Adams Trust provides advice and information on bullying at work.[7]

1.14   This is not a comprehensive list, and policies and personnel can change rapidly, so it is always worth investigating carefully whether there is a specialist charity that may be able to help.

The Commission for Equality and Human Rights

1.15   From 1 October 2007 the three statutory commissions, the Equal Opportunities Commission (EOC), Commission for Racial Equality (CRE) and Disability Rights Commission (DRC) will be replaced by the Commission for Equality and Human Rights.[8] The CEHR will be responsible for all aspects of equality law, including those like age and sexual orientation not covered by on of the original commissions.

1.16   The existing commissions have provided helpline advice and website guidance on tribunal claims. In rare cases they were able to provide representation for a case where the result would impact a large number

---

6   www.lawworks.org.uk

7   The websites of these organisations are at www.rnib.org.uk., www.rnid.org.uk, www.dls.org.uk, www.pcaw.co.uk, www.tht.org.uk and www.andreaadams.org

8   See www.eoc.org.uk, www.cre.gov.uk, www.drc.org.uk and www.cehr.org.uk

of other individuals. The CEHR is likely to take a similar approach. Early indications are that it is unlikely to provide representation in more than a dozen cases each year, and these will be test cases chosen for their strategic importance.

Private practice solicitors

1.17   Claimants who are eligible for Legal Services Commission funding (those who are dependent on means-tested benefits, or are on very low incomes) may be able to find a solicitor who can advise and assist with preparation of the case. There is no public funding (in any but the most exceptional cases) for representation at the tribunal hearing, so claimants who take advantage of this scheme are likely to find that they either have to represent themselves at tribunal or pay privately for a solicitor or a barrister to represent them. In London, some solicitors will be able to refer the case to the Free Representation Unit at this stage, so before choosing a solicitor it may be worth finding out whether they subscribe to FRU's service.

1.18   The decision to pay privately for employment law advice should be approached with caution. Lawyers' fees can mount up frighteningly fast, and the total value of an employment tribunal claim is often too small to justify them. Some solicitors offer 'no win no fee' agreements, but the drawback to these is that, because the solicitor is taking a risk of not being paid at all, the fee if the case is successful will normally be higher than it would otherwise have been. There can also be sums that the client has to pay anyway, such as fees for medical or other experts' reports or barristers' fees. Occasionally this will be the best, or the only practical, way of running an employment tribunal claim, but a claimant considering taking this course should make sure she or he has had a very clear explanation of the 'worst case' outcome before making a decision. It is also worth asking solicitors to advise, as a preliminary matter, on whether any insurance policy the claimant has is capable of covering legal expenses.

Employment consultants

1.19   There are no restrictions on who may appear as a representative in the employment tribunals, and a number of firms of employment consultants offer their services in this area. Some of these market their services aggressively to claimants and respondents in employment tribunal cases. They vary in quality, and although some can provide a good and relatively cheap service, others are worse than useless. Unlike barristers and solicitors, they are not regulated by a professional body. It is suggested that claimants should do their research carefully before using the services of these organisations. One question to ask is how many costs orders have been made against clients of the organisation in the past year, compared to the total number of clients represented. Costs orders are still rare in the employment tribunal, and they tend – though not invariably – to suggest bad advice or poor conduct of the case by the representative. Costs orders running at 1% or more of cases handled by a particular consultancy would give cause for concern.[9] It is also worth asking whether any wasted costs order have ever been made against the organisation: wasted costs orders are very rare indeed, and even one against a particular consultancy can be taken as a warning.

Whether to bring a claim

1.20   For a lawyer, the question whether a claim should be brought is normally approached by way of three questions: (i) what are the prospects of success? (ii) how much compensation will be awarded (or what other benefit will it bring) if it succeeds? and (iii) what will it cost to run?

1.21   For a claimant, the third question needs to be considered carefully from all angles. The question how much money will need to be spent on the claim is, of course, an important one. Even if you are acting for yourself or are lucky enough to have free representation, there will be some financial costs telephone calls, postage, photocopying, fees for expert reports, etc. However, the non-financial costs of running a case against your former employer should be looked in the eye too.[10]

---

9 In 2005–06, 86,083 employment tribunal cases were settled, withdrawn or disposed of by the tribunal. Of those cases, around 20,000 of which would appear to have gone to a hearing, costs were awarded against the claimant in only 148 cases: Employment Tribunal Service Annual Report for 2005–06, available at www.ets.gsi.gov.uk

10 Most employment tribunal cases concern, one way or another, the termination of the employment relationship, so the 'former employer' is referred to here although can be and occasionally are brought against a current employer.

1.22   The first thing to notice here is just how important the employer/employee relationship can be for the employee. Obviously this varies: the 25-year-old graduate in her third job in the last four years will feel much less attachment to her employer than the fifty-something who has been with the same employer since leaving school at 16. But in many cases, losing your job doesn't just mean losing an income: it may also means losing much of your reason for getting up in the morning, daily contact with people with whom you have a common experience and circle of acquaintance, your status, your self-esteem and in some cases of long-standing employment, much of your social life as well.

1.23   The second point to note is that the importance of the employment relationship is not symmetrical. Most employees have a considerable emotional investment in their jobs. Employers do not as a rule have any particular emotional attachment to their employees.[11] Although the bodies – the companies, public authorities, charitable trusts, unincorporated associations or partnerships – that employ staff act through human beings, and those individual human beings can be kind and well-meaning, the body itself does not, whatever its mission statement or staff handbook may say to the contrary, 'care'. It is incapable of caring; it simply lacks the equipment with which caring is done.

1.24   Both factors can make litigation tempting. Being an employee can have something in common with being the child of a psychopathic parent: you have a large emotional investment in a relationship with something that does not care about you at all. Litigation can seem like the only way to shout loudly enough to force the psychopath to pay attention. A significant proportion of all employment tribunal cases are motivated at least as much by personal feelings of rejection and betrayal as by a realistic or well-judged expectation of winning sufficient compensation to justify the cost of the claim.[12]

1.25   This is not a good basis on which to litigate. Because the employ-ment relationship is so important to an employee, its termination often causes significant distress, and not infrequently depression. One of the consequences, ultimately, of an employment tribunal claim may be that the employer has to pay the former employee some money. Occasionally this will be a large sum of money, but more often it will

11 The authors apologise for any shattered illusions.
12 This is a wholly unscientific observation, but the authors have between them seen a lot of employment tribunal claims and believe it to be broadly true.

be modest.[13] Very rarely, the employer is ordered to reinstate or re-engage the employee; even more rarely such an order is obeyed.[14]

1.26 The price that the employee will pay for these uncertain benefits is a long period in which she must dwell on the events surrounding the termination; study all the correspondence and associated documentation in detail; give a statement to an adviser or solicitor (or write it herself); draft or approve the claim to the tribunal; read and comment on the employer's response; correspond with the employer or its solicitor; and ultimately, unless the claim settles, undergo hostile cross-examination and listen to the employer justify its conduct in the course of the hearing. The net effect is that the employee must keep some kind of relationship going with the former employer, and must allow the events surrounding or preceding the termination of employment to dominate her thoughts – and very likely her dreams too – over a period of many months, or even a number of years.

1.27 For these reasons, if the employment has ended in stress and depression for the employee, litigating about it will almost certainly exacerbate both effects. Claimants often say something to the effect 'If I had known what this was going to be like, I would never have begun.' Here another mechanism comes into play. Litigation is a form of gambling, and gambling is notoriously addictive. Losses are part of the reason: you may wish you had never begun, but the heavier the losses you have sustained to date, the more painful and difficult it is to admit that they have been suffered for nothing. From this point it is an easy path to obsession. Litigation can seriously damage your mental health, and social lives and marriages can suffer or crumble under the strain.

1.28 The conclusion to all of this is that litigation – even in the relatively informal and low-risk environment of the employment tribunals – is almost always a bad idea once you have taken into account the factors that lawyers do not concern themselves with as well as those that they

---

13 The median award for unfair dismissal in 2005–06 was £4,228; the median awards for race, sex and disability discrimination were respectively £6,640, £5,546 and £9,021. Awards exceeding £50,000 were made in only 2.6% of unfair dismissal cases, and 6.8%, 2.4% and 11.8% of race, sex and disability discrimination cases: Employment Tribunal Service Annual Report for 2005–2006, available at www.ets.gsi.gov.uk

14 In 2005–06 the tribunals made eight orders for reinstatement or re-engagement, that is in only 0.23% of unfair dismissal cases that were upheld after a hearing.

do.[15] It is sensible to litigate (a) if you have to; or (b) if there is a fairly clear probability that the costs – emotional as well as financial – will be justified by the benefits; or (c) where you have a point you want to make, but the outcome is not of enormous personal importance to you, and the financial costs are borne by someone else.[16] One point to keep clearly in mind when making this decision is that on the whole, the angrier you feel about the way your employer has treated you, the higher will be the emotional costs and risks of fighting the case.

1.29   A middle way can be to make the decision to commence proceeding purely in order to achieve a settlement, while resolving that it will be withdrawn if not settled during the early stages.[17] This is like gambling with a set budget. It may require considerable firmness of purpose to stick to your original intention about how much effort and money you will commit before cutting your losses, but if you can do that it is worth considering.

Outline of the employment tribunal process

1.30   Strictly speaking an employment tribunal case begins with a formal claim on form ET1 (see chapter 3 below), but since the introduction of the statutory dispute resolution procedures, an internal grievance procedure is now a necessary first step in many cases. Broadly, there is a distinction between complaints of dismissal (other than constructive dismissal) and other complaints (including constructive dismissal).[18] An employee whose complaint is about dismissal (other than constructive dismissal) is not required to bring a statutory grievance, but may proceed direct to a complaint to the employment tribunal.

---

15 This is no criticism of lawyers. It is as reasonable to expect your lawyers to help you decide whether the emotional costs of litigation are worth incurring as to expect your priest or therapist to provide legal advice; their expertise is elsewhere.

16 You have to litigate, in effect, if you face a threat that your children will be taken away from you or you will be sent to a country where you will be tortured and murdered. Necessity of this sort rarely if ever arises in the employment context.

17 The resolution has to be made privately of course: it will be wholly futile if the employer is aware of the strategy.

18 For an explanation of this term see glossary; for more detail, see ELAH 7 para 6.33.

1.31   In very broad outline, then, the process falls into four stages: (1) internal grievance process; (2) the employee's formal claim and the employer's response, presented on forms ET1 and ET3 respectively; (3) requests by each side for information and documents, and requests to the tribunal for orders if these requests are not voluntarily complied with; (4) preparation by each side of all the documents that will be required for the hearing: the witness statements, an agreed bundle of all relevant documentary evidence, any written representations, chronologies, lists of issues, etc; and (5) the hearing itself. There may be negotiations at any of these stages. The parties are normally referred to as the claimant (the employee who brings the claim) and the respondent (the employer, who responds to it).

1.32   In the more detailed outline that follows, the players are referred to as C (for claimant) and R (for respondent), and T (the employment tribunal). A complaint of a discriminatory failure to promote is taken as an example, and it is assumed that the case goes all the way to a decision by the employment tribunal. There could be different outcomes at many points: this example should be seen as one of the possible paths through a fairly complicated flow-chart rather than a recipe for what must happen in every case.

R tells C that his application for promotion has been unsuccessful.

C presents a grievance complaining of race discrimination.

R invites C to a hearing to consider the grievance.

R rejects C's grievance.

C appeals, and at the same time serves on R a questionnaire.[19]

R invites C to an appeal hearing

R gives C a decision on the appeal

C is dissatisfied and completes and presents formal claim to tribunal on form ET1

T accepts the ET1[20]

T sends ET1 to R

R responds by completing form ET3

T accepts the ET3 and forwards it to C[21]

T lists the case for a directions hearing or T issues directions without a hearing

C sends request for additional information and disclosure of documents to R

19 Note that the questionnaire can be served at any time from the notification of C that he has not been promoted until 21 days from the presentation of a claim to the tribunal.

20 If T considers that the claim does not include all the required information, the statutory grievance procedure has not been followed, or it does not have jurisdiction to consider the claim – or, from 6 April 2005 (but see paras 1.63–1.64 below), if it has not been presented on the required form – it will reject the claim. In that case it may be necessary either to redraft the claim and try again, or to appeal the decision to reject the claim or seek a review.

21 Again, there are grounds on which the ET3 may be rejected.

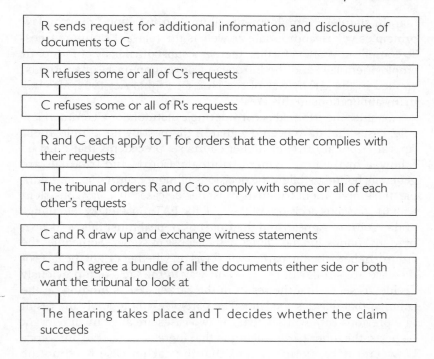

R sends request for additional information and disclosure of documents to C

R refuses some or all of C's requests

C refuses some or all of R's requests

R and C each apply to T for orders that the other complies with their requests

The tribunal orders R and C to comply with some or all of each other's requests

C and R draw up and exchange witness statements

C and R agree a bundle of all the documents either side or both want the tribunal to look at

The hearing takes place and T decides whether the claim succeeds

Sources of employment law

1.33   Much of employment law is contained in legislation, but it must be remembered that at the heart of the employment relationship is the contract of employment. Non-lawyers should also remember that legislation is far from static. Most of the major employment statutes have been regularly updated since they came into force. This means that some care needs to be taken to ensure that you are referring to the current law.[22]

1.34   Contract law is what is called a common law subject: that is, its main principles are to be found in previously decided cases rather

---

22 The *Butterworths Employment Law Handbook* by Peter Wallington is a comprehensive (and annually updated) collection of employment statutes which most lawyers will take with them to the tribunal, and the tribunal will always have available for its own use at the hearing. The government has recently created www.statutelaw.gov.uk, an online database of legislation. This will also be updated, but was still being brought up-to-date at time of writing.

than in statutes.[23] Employment tribunals must apply common law principles where appropriate as well as the relevant statutory rules. To complicate matters further, there is a substantial body of European employment law; and the European Convention on Human Rights, applied in the UK by way of the Human Rights Act 1998, also has many applications in this area.

1.35   Whether the tribunal is considering a statutory or a common law rule, cases that have been decided in the past by the Employment Appeal Tribunal (EAT) or higher courts set precedents that must be followed by the employment tribunals. Courts and tribunals are generally bound to follow the decisions of higher courts: so, for example, the employment tribunals must decide cases in a way consistent with the previous decisions of the EAT, the EAT must follow the rulings of the Court of Appeal, and the Court of Appeal must follow its own previous rulings and the rulings of the House of Lords.[24] Sometimes the argument between the parties will focus on whether or not the facts of the case are similar in the relevant way to the facts of a previously decided case, so that the result in the earlier case is binding on the tribunal that decides the later. The party seeking to apply the result in a previous case will say that the two cases are alike in all relevant respects; the other party will argue that there is a material difference between the cases that means that the earlier case need not be followed.[25]

1.36   The only way to gain a proper understanding of this process of reasoning is to read reports of cases. Employment cases are reported in two monthly series, the Industrial Case Reports (ICR) and the Industrial Relations Law Reports (IRLR), both of which should be available in any law library.[26] The standard method of referring to a

---

23   The standard practitioners' textbook is *Chitty on Contracts*, 29th edn, Sweet & Maxwell, 2004. Chitty is very comprehensive, but is likely to be forbiddingly technical for anyone without a legal training. The important point, for non-lawyers, is simply to be aware that there are two different kinds of law operating in this field.

24   Unlike the Court of Appeal, the EAT is not technically bound by its own previous rulings, but will normally be reluctant to depart from them.

25   The latter kind of argument is often referred to as 'distinguishing' the earlier case.

26   In London, the Hammersmith, Holborn and Westminster Public Libraries maintain a specialist law collection, and the Supreme Court Library at the Royal Courts of Justice on the Strand is open to the public. Any university law school will have a law library and some will allow members of the public to use reference facilities in some circumstances: inquiries should be made of the local law school.

case reported in one of these, or similar, series follows the pattern: *Party v Other Party* [2004] IRLR 382. This indicates that the report of the case will be found at page 382 of the 2004 volume of the Industrial Relations Law Reports. In addition, more recent decisions of the Employment Appeal Tribunal, the Court of Appeal and the House of Lords are all available online.[27] Two volumes, M Rubenstein, *Unfair dismissal: a guide to relevant case law* and M Rubenstein and Y Frost, *Discrimination: a guide to the relevant case law on sex, race and disability discrimination and equal pay* provide helpful quick reference to the case law in those two areas.[28]

Books

1.37 A great many books are published on employment law, and the following represent a tiny sample of what is available. Lewis, *Employment Law: an adviser's handbook* (ELAH 7) is an excellent and accessible short guide to the substantive law, and McMullen et al *Employment Tribunal Procedure* (ETP 3) gives a detailed explanation of tribunal procedure (Legal Action Group, 7th edn, 2007 and Legal Action Group, 3rd edn, 2005). *Harvey on Industrial Relations and Employment Law*, published by Butterworths, is a large loose-leaf publication in several volumes that explains the law in great detail and is updated regularly throughout the year.[29] It is likely to be dauntingly technical for anyone without a legal training, but if a difficult question arises to which the answer cannot be found in one of the shorter books it will be worth consulting. Similar comments apply to *Employment Court Practice* (Sweet & Maxwell, 2007) which deals with procedure in employment tribunals and appeals to EAT and Court of Appeal.

Key employment cases

1.38 There are certain decided cases that determine points of such fundamental importance to employment law that all those advising in the area need to be aware of them, and preferably to have read them.

27 Key websites are BAILII (British and Irish Legal Information Institute) at www.bailii.org, the EAT website at www.employmentappeals.gov.uk and the Court Service website at www.hmcourts-service.gov.uk

28 LexisNexis Butterworths, 25th edn, 2007 and LexisNexis Butterworths, 20th edn, 2007.

29 It is also available as an online subscription service.

No two employment lawyers would compile the same list, and the decision whether to list 10, 50 or 100 cases is arbitrary. With those reservations, the following is offered as a selection of some of the fundamental cases – divided into broad subject areas – that advisers should be familiar with.

Unfair dismissal

Iceland Frozen Foods v Jones [1983] ICR 17, EAT
Post Office v Foley [2000] ICR 1283, CA

Conduct dismissal

Burchell v British Home Stores [1980] ICR 303, EAT
Linfood Cash & Carry Ltd v Thomson [1989] IRLR 235, EAT

Procedural fairness

Polkey v AE Dayton Services [1987] IRLR 503, HL[30]

Redundancy dismissal

Williams v Compair Maxam [1982] ICR 156, EAT
Murray v Foyle Meats [1999] ICR 827, HL
W Devis & Sons Ltd v Atkins [1977] IRLR 314, HL

Constructive dismissal

Western Excavating v Sharp [1978] ICR 221, CA

---

30 The effect of this decision has been altered since 1 October 2004 by the Employment Rights Act 1996 s98A, but it has been such an important part of the landscape for employment lawyers for so long that it is still helpful to be familiar with it.

Trust and confidence term

Eastwood v Magnox Electric plc [2004] ICR 1064, HL

Who is an employee

Ready Mixed Concrete v Minister of Pensions [1968] 2 QB 497, CA
Carmichael v National Power [1999] ICR 1226, HL

Discrimination

Igen v Wong [2005] ICR 931, [2005] IRLR 258.
Shamoon v Chief Constable of the Royal Ulster Constabulary [2003] ICR 337, HL
King v Great Britain-China Centre [1992] ICR 516, CA
Nagarajan v London Regional Transport [1999] IRLR 572, HL
Chief Constable of West Yorkshire Police v Khan [2000] ICR 1169, HL
Glasgow City Council v Zafar [1998] ICR 120, HL
Vento v Chief Constable of West Yorkshire [2001] IRLR 124, EAT

Transfer of Undertakings (Protection of Employees) Regulations

Litster v Forth Dry Dock & Engineering Co Ltd [1989] ICR 341, HL
Suzen v Zehnacker Gebaudereinigung GmbH Krankenhausservice [1997] ICR 662, ECJ

Mitigation of loss

Wilding v British Telecom [2002] IRLR 524, CA

Appeals

Anya v University of Oxford [2001] ICR 847, CA
Meek v City of Birmingham District Council [1987] IRLR 250, CA
Kumchyk v Derby City Council [1978] ICR 1116, EAT
Yeboah v Crofton [2002] IRLR 634, CA

The tribunal's powers

1.39   The tribunals operate under the Employment Tribunals (Constitution and Rules of Procedure) Regulations 2004, and in particular under Schedule 1 to these Regulations, the Employment Tribunal Rules of Procedure.[31] These are referred to throughout this book simply as the 'procedure rules'.

1.40   It is worthwhile for any claimant or adviser with limited experience in this area to read the Regulations and the procedure rules at an early stage in proceedings so as to be broadly familiar with the scope of the tribunal's powers. Particular provisions to note are the interpretation provisions at regulation 2, the overriding objective at regulation 3 and the guidance on calculation of time limits at regulation 15. Rules 1 to 48 of the Procedure Rules are the main rules that govern most types of proceedings, and rules 10 (case management), 11 (applications), and 37 to 48 (costs and preparation time orders) are of particular practical significance.

1.41   The President of the employment tribunals has power to issue practice directions giving detailed guidance about how cases should be conducted.[32] At the time of writing no employment tribunal practice direction has been issued under the new rules, and there is no proposal to issue any in the near future.

1.42   As stated above, the procedure rules will not be the only material informing the tribunal in its procedural decisions. Tribunals are very often guided – sometimes, but not always, consciously – by principles and procedures that operate in the ordinary courts, often drawn from the Civil Procedure Rules (CPR) which apply there. If the tribunal criticises a claimant for some failure to observe 'obvious common sense' or 'basic good practice' in some aspect of the conduct of proceedings on which neither the claimant's own common sense nor the procedure rules provide any guidance, the chances are that this is what is going on. The chairman has absorbed principles from the CPR or rules of conduct or etiquette in the ordinary courts, and is treating them as self-evident.

1.43   For this reason, some familiarity with the CPR is, although not essential, certainly helpful for employment advisers – partly so that they are not taken by surprise when the tribunal borrows from the

---

31   SI No 1861.
32   Compare the EAT Practice Direction of 2004.

CPR, and partly so that they are in a position either to warn the tribunal against automatic adherence to rules devised for a more formal (and unequivocally adversarial) setting, or sometimes to propose that the manner of dealing with particular practical problems set out in the CPR should be adapted for the employment tribunal.[33] The CPR can sometimes provide helpful insights into the thinking behind the tribunal procedure rules. In many instances, the latter are a simplified version of the former; sometimes, on the other hand, it is clear that a deliberate distinction has been made between the tribunal rules and the CPR.[34]

1.44 The up-to-date CPR can be found on the Ministry of Justice website.[35] This should be regarded as a recommendation only for advisers who will run a substantial number of cases for clients, however: grappling with the fairly forbidding CPR will rarely, if ever, be the best use of time for a claimant representing him or herself in a single case.

General note on correspondence

1.45 Much of a party's correspondence with the tribunal or the other side will have a secondary tactical motive as well as the purpose it has on its face. It should be remembered that any correspondence may in some circumstances be read by the tribunal, so it is advisable always to maintain a calm and co-operative style. This will not invariably be reflected by the respondent or its advisers but it will almost always be in the client's interests to resist any temptation to be abrasive or sarcastic.[36] This can be particularly important if there is a costs application by either side. If there is unavoidable delay, or if there has been a

33 Legal systems are often divided into 'adversarial' systems where the judge's only task is to listen to the case put by each side and to make a decision based on what the parties have put before him or her; and 'inquisitorial' systems where the decision-maker has a duty to investigate. Employment tribunal hearings are broadly adversarial, but because parties are not necessarily expected to be represented, the tribunal also has an inquisitorial role expressed in the duty at rule 14(3) of the procedure rules to make such enquiries of persons appearing before them and of witnesses as they consider appropriate. Once again, because tribunals are dominated by lawyers who are used to a wholly adversarial system, this duty often gets overlooked.

34 For an example, see *Kopel v Safeway Stores plc* [2003] IRLR 753, EAT.

35 www.justice.gov.uk/civil/procrules_fin/index.htm

36 Correspondence from the other side may well reflect the adviser's wish to demonstrate to their own client that they are conducting the litigation vigorously.

misunderstanding, apology costs nothing and can help avoid unnecessary conflict with the other party. A well placed and graceful apology may even help tip the tribunal away from making a costs award if otherwise there are grounds for one.

1.46   There are good reasons in any event to keep relations with the respondent as calm as possible. Many aspects of the preparation of the case will go more smoothly if there is co-operation between the parties.[37] Both sides are likely to encounter certain difficulties along the way, and will sometimes need the other side's indulgence when they are unable to meet deadlines, etc. If the tone of the proceedings has been quarrelsome from the start, each side may waste a great deal of time (and in some cases their client's money too) scoring every possible point off the other. It is far better to be pragmatic and flexible about things that do not matter, and to conserve energy for the few battles that will win or lose the case. For a claimant acting in person against a represented employer, it is worth making a real effort to remember that the lawyer on the other side is simply doing the job he or she is paid to do in representing the respondent's interests, and is not a personal enemy of the claimant's.[38]

1.47   Letters should make their point in plain language and as few words as possible. Fancy type-faces should be avoided. Inexperienced advisers and lawyers sometimes feel that they ought to act the part and write legalese. This is never a good idea. Opening and closing gambits like 'I write further to our conversation [/my letter] of [date]' or 'I write in relation to the above-mentioned matter and refer to your letter of [date]' or 'I look forward to hearing from you at your earliest convenience and thank you for your attention' are redundant. The heading indicates the subject-matter of the letter, and 'thank you for your letter of [date]' is ample to provide the link to the letter being answered. If there is a particular need for an urgent answer, it is sensible to spell that out, but otherwise there is not normally any need to ask for a reply.

1.48   Many solicitors still routinely duplicate faxed or e-mailed correspondence by post. This is unnecessary and causes the tribunal and the other party additional work. If the other party finds it at all

---

37 Litigation is very like a formal game with a serious outcome. To win any game, it is necessary to co-operate sufficiently with the other player to complete it. Angry squabbling about when exactly witness statements should be exchanged, who prepares the bundle for the hearing, whether the hearing is likely to last for three days or four etc is as futile and as little likely to affect the outcome as a dispute between two chess players about whether the 12 inch or the 18 inch chessboard should be used.

38 This is good advice for lawyers too.

difficult to deal with correspondence (by reason of a visual impairment, for example, or dyslexia) it is particularly unhelpful and time-wasting. The tribunals positively request that parties should not do it. If it is essential to ensure that a document arrives by a certain date, the sensible thing is to fax it and then follow the fax with a telephone call to confirm arrival. An attendance note of that conversation, identifying the person spoken to, should be ample proof of delivery if the point arises subsequently.

1.49   E-mail is a fast and efficient method of communicating with the other party or the tribunal, and is perfectly acceptable. If a plain text e-mail does not seem to give the right degree of formality, a letter can be attached as a separate document. The main danger of using e-mail for this purpose is that the speed of e-mail exchanges can escalate a difference of views into a quarrel very quickly, and e-mails leave a permanent record that may later be shown to the tribunal. E-mails need to be drafted with the same care as any other correspondence, and should always be calm and reasonable. It is sensible to get into the habit of removing information about previous drafts, etc from any e-mailed attachment. This can be most simply done by selecting and copying the text and pasting it into a new document before attaching to an e-mail. Sending a witness statement to the respondent with recoverable information about previous drafts could be very damaging.

1.50   All letters to the tribunal (apart from requests for witness orders: see para 5.40) should be copied to the respondent. Many advisers will routinely copy all correspondence with the other side, other than 'without prejudice' correspondence, to the tribunal, but this is unnecessary.[39] It is preferable to copy correspondence to the tribunal only if it is relevant to something that the tribunal is being asked to do. So, for example, it is not necessary to copy a request for additional information to the tribunal when it is first made; but if the respondent refuses to comply with the request, then it should be copied to the tribunal with the request for an order. If there has been an extended wrangle between the parties over some aspect of case preparation, the tribunal will only need to see the relevant correspondence if and when it is asked to arbitrate on the wrangle, or if one party seeks costs on grounds of the other party's unreasonable conduct. At that point the whole correspondence can be copied to the tribunal, or collated into a bundle to support a costs application at the hearing.

---

39   See glossary for 'without prejudice'.

1.51   Thought should be given at all stages to the convenience of both the other party and the tribunal. A history of conspicuously considerate letters will be one of the best defences against a costs order if there is an application for costs at any stage. So, for example, if the claimant is unable to meet a deadline that has been set by the tribunal or agreed between the parties, the tribunal and/or the other side should be informed of the difficulty as soon as the claimant is aware of it, and a realistic revised timetable should be proposed. If the claimant seeks to amend his or her claim, then it is likely that the respondent will need time to amend their response to deal with the new points: the letter requesting permission to amend should recognise this and propose suitable arrangements.

1.52   It is conventional to address letters sent to the tribunal to 'the Regional Secretary', with a request, where appropriate, to refer the letter or the application to a chairman for his or her attention. The regional secretaries are the administrative heads of the employment tribunals; the regional chairmen are the judicial heads. Similarly, correspondence with the Employment Appeal Tribunal is addressed to the Registrar, who is the administrative head of the EAT. At the time of writing the Registrar at the EAT and many, possibly the majority, of the regional secretaries are women. The examples in this book use the salutation 'Dear Madam' throughout.

1.53   Letters are drafted in the first person in this book because this gives the writer personal responsibility for the content. 'We' is too often an excuse for pomposity. The form of address 'Dear Sirs' is still in common use but can cause irritation, so letters are either addressed to the individual with conduct of the case ('Dear Mr Bean', 'Dear Ms Marrow', 'Dear Madam') or else solicitors' firms and other organisations are addressed by name – as for example 'Dear Carrot & Marrow', 'Dear NaffTat plc', 'Dear Camden Council'.

1.54   Documents other than letters are given formal headings showing the parties' names, the tribunal, the case number and the title of the document laid out in a conventional pattern.[40]

1.55   These headings are not compulsory and are far from universal in employment tribunal litigation; it is largely a matter of personal taste whether or not to use them. They may, marginally, help to convey a sense of competence and professionalism to the tribunal and the other party.

---

40   See for example P3.11.1 on page 65 below.

Telephone calls

1.56 The choice between writing a letter and making a telephone call to the tribunal or the respondent will often be obvious. Self-evidently a formal request for disclosure of documents or an application for permission to amend the claim or postpone the hearing must be made in writing. If the respondent has faxed a letter part of which is illegible, then equally clearly the only sensible thing is to pick up the telephone to them straight away and ask them to re-send it.

1.57 Between these extremes there will be many communications for which either a letter or a telephone call will do. To a large extent the choice will be a matter of personal preference, although those who are not used to conducting litigation probably tend to make their task harder than necessary by dealing with almost everything by letter. For this reason it is worth suggesting that as a rule claimants should keep letters to a reasonable minimum and use the telephone instead where possible.[41] This will save time and energy, and will also tend to encourage practical co-operation between the parties.

1.58 It is also worth remembering that both tribunal staff and lawyers acting for the respondent can be a valuable source of background information about how things are usually done or what the tribunal's expectations will be, and this kind of information is much easier to tap into in a fairly informal telephone conversation than in an exchange of letters.[42]

File and diary management

1.59 Running an employment tribunal case requires habits that are second nature to solicitors, and to many others whose normal work requires them to handle correspondence files over months or years. For others they will be unfamiliar and will need to be learned.

---

41 Provided clear file notes are made promptly after all conversations and filed with the rest of the papers.

42 Note too that the forces that encourage professional representatives to write quarrelsome letters – see note 37 above – do not operate in the same way when they speak on the telephone. This explains the solicitor who writes consistently abrasive letters but is charming and co-operative on the telephone: it is not a fiendish plot to disorientate the claimant, just a consequence of the fact that he sends his client copies of his letters but not tapes of his telephone calls.

1.60   The first point is that the papers relating to the case should be kept together in a ring-binder, lever-arch file or cardboard wallet file. Probably a wallet file is the most convenient. Copies of all documents sent out should be filed, and all documents received should be filed. Hand-written originals should be retained on the file even if subsequently typed up. A brief attendance note should be made promptly of any telephone conversation or meeting. The question 'was that phone call worth recording?' does not arise. If the conversation was short and seemingly trivial, the time taken to decide whether or not there could be any circumstances in the future in which it might be important to have a record of it will be greater than the time taken to record it. If it was of any length, it is bound to need a record. In case of a subsequent application for a costs or preparation time order, it is also sensible to record the time spent.[43]

P1.60 Attendance note

Attendance notes do not need to follow any particular format, and a hand-written note (provided it is legible) is perfectly adequate.

Client: Davis

Date: 28 September 2007

T/C[44] to client to discuss schedule of loss. The figure of £500 p/w is gross, but without overtime pay. She will look out payslips for last 6 months of employment and send them. Will also send all payslips for temp work since dismissal.

Explained need for evidence of mitigation.[45] Client will collect all rejection letters and copy applications that she has retained so far into a file, and will start to keep notes of any inquiries and copies of all applications.

10 minutes

1.61   Papers should be subdivided into logical categories. The following categories are suggested: (i) correspondence and attendance notes, held together with a treasury tag, with the most recent item on the top; (ii) statements of case and orders – the claim, the response, any directions from the tribunal, the decision; (iii) documentary evidence;

---

43 See ETP 3 Chapter 3.
44 Telephone call.
45 See glossary and para 10.29.

and (iv) statements. These sub-files can be enclosed in a folded sheet of paper to keep them separate from each other, or separated in a ring binder or lever arch file with tabbed divider cards. A running list of the telephone and fax numbers of all the people who may need to be contacted in connection with the case on the outside cover of the file is a useful time-saving device. It is also a good idea to keep a prominent note of key dates somewhere on the file cover.

Time recording

1.62 Because (since October 2004) the tribunals have power in certain circumstances to make 'preparation time orders' to compensate parties for the time they have spent preparing the case, it is prudent for claimants and their advisers.[46] to get into the habit of keeping a running record of the time they spend on the case. Preparation time can mount up to a surprising extent: it is much easier to demonstrate this convincingly by showing the Tribunal a record of this kind than by looking back at the work done weeks or months after the event and trying to estimate long after the event how long it would have taken. Claimants who are representing themselves should remember to record time that a lawyer might not have to spend – such as time travelling to a library or to a local print shop to fax a document. A note of any expenses, and itemised telephone bills, should also be kept.

1.63 Probably the simplest method of keeping a rough account of the time spent on a file is to keep a sheet or two laid out along the lines of the following precedent at the front of the file, and to try to remember to complete it at the end of each telephone call or session of work on the case.

---

46 Including advisers acting for free: there is a standard hourly rate of £27 at the time of writing (see note 10 on page 322) that does not depend on showing that any charge has been made.

P1.63 Time sheet

Date	Activity	Time spent	expenses
4/10/07	t/c to EOC helpline	20 mins	
4/10/07	Trip to library for research (incl travel)	4 hours	£1.40 fare £5.20 copying
5/10/07	t/c to EOC helpline	5 mins	
5/10/07	Drafting grievance letter	1 hour	
24/10/07	Considering E's response	20 mins	
8/11/07	Trip to library for research	3½ hours	£1.40 fare £2.00 copying
9/11/07	Drafting ET1	3 hours	
9/11/07	t/c to EOC helpline	20 mins	
9/11/07	Redrafting ET1 in light of advice	1½ hours	
9/11/07	Trip to print shop to fax ET1	40 mins	£2 fare £1.20 fax
13/11/07	Drafting questionnaire	2 hours	
13/11/07	T/c to ACAS	5 mins	
13/11/07	Reading letter from E's solicitor	20 mins	
13/11/07	t/c to CAB	5 mins	
14/11/07	Drafting letter to E's solicitor	30 mins	

Key dates and time limits

1.64   It is particularly important to establish a rigid habit of noting key dates in such a way that it is impossible to forget them. There are many ways of setting up automatic reminders, though an old-fashioned diary will still be the most effective for many people. Whatever method is chosen, there is a pit-fall to be avoided at each end of the process. The first is to forget to make the initial entry. An adviser who is busy when first consulted by a new client may be tempted to postpone the task of calculating and noting key dates until a calmer moment. This is always a mistake: a calm moment may not present itself for some time, and by the time it does the task may have been forgotten. An adviser who does not have time to calculate and record key dates at once does not have time to take on a new case.

1.65 The second pit-fall is to set up the reminder, but then to fail to register it when it falls due. There is no point noting key dates in a diary that is rarely opened, or setting up a reminder on an e-mail account that is not accessed every day. It is far better to link reminders to existing habits than to try to establish completely new habits: someone who already checks an e-mail account daily will do better to set up an automatic reminder on their e-mail package than to resolve to buy a desk diary and look in it every day. Someone who already has and constantly uses a desk diary will be better served by an entry in that.

1.66 It is beyond the scope of this book to discuss time limits in detail, but two calculations need to be second nature to employment advisers.[47] The first is the end of the normal time limit for presentation of the claim, which for the great majority of claims over which the tribunal has jurisdiction is three months less one day from the date of dismissal (in complaints about dismissal) or from the act complained of (in the case of most other complaints).[48] Discrimination complaints can present difficulties as there will often be allegations of a number of discriminatory acts on different dates. Sometimes it will be possible to argue that these all form part of the same continuing act, but this argument can be complicated. The safest course is to treat the normal time limit as expiring 3 months after the earliest of the acts complained of. Often this will be impossible because the client will have put up with mistreatment for weeks, months or sometimes even years before seeking advice; in that case the claim should be presented as soon as it can be drafted, subject to compliance with the dispute resolution procedures.[49]

1.67 The second crucial calculation is the last day for presentation of an appeal to the Employment Appeal Tribunal, which is 42 days from the date when the employment tribunal's judgment or order is sent to

---

47 For a detailed discussion of time limits, see ELAH 7, paras 20.27–20.35. 22.47, 21.13–21.35.

48 For details, see ETP 3, Chapter 3.

49 See chapter 2 below.

the parties. This means that if the judgment is sent to the parties on Thursday 12 April 2007, then the notice of appeal together with forms ET1 and ET3 and a copy of the judgment appealed must be received by the Employment Appeal Tribunal before 4pm on Thursday 24 May 2007.

1.68   In either case, it is essential – especially if the deadline is close – to make sure that the document has arrived, and was complete on arrival. This last cannot be over-emphasised: there is no method of delivery that is 100% fool-proof, and a missed deadline for presenting a claim or an appeal is the kind of error most likely to get an adviser sued for negligence.[50] If a claim or appeal in the last few days is unavoidable, the best course is to fax the document, print and retain a transmission confirmation on the file, telephone the tribunal to check that each page has arrived and is complete, and to make and retain on the file a note of this conversation and the name of the individual spoken to. This is in fact good practice even where the expiry of a time limit is not imminent: if a new claim is posted four weeks before the deadline but lost in the post, the deadline may have passed by the time the claimant or adviser wonders why no acknowledgement has yet been received from the tribunal. A document lost in the post will not usually provide a sufficient excuse for a late claim or appeal, so advisers should either make a diary note to chase if no acknowledgement is received within a reasonable time (but still within the limitation period); or else – which is probably easier – simply fax the document and double-check safe arrival at once.

Adjustment of time limits for the purposes of the dispute resolution procedures

1.69   With effect from 1 October 2004, the whole subject of time limits in the employment tribunals became immensely more complicated. Detailed consideration of the relevant provisions is beyond the scope of this book, but a practical guide to tribunal litigation would fail its users if it did not lay down a clear warning that the rules about presentation of claims are now extremely treacherous for claimants and their advisers.

---

50 Not even hand-delivery: for a cautionary tale see *Gdynia American Shipping Lines v Chelminski* [2004] IRLR 725, CA. See also *J R Beasley v National Grid* UKEAT/0626/06 in which a claim delivered 88 seconds late was held to be out of time.

Note first, however, that the dispute resolution procedures were almost universally condemned by employment lawyers, including employment tribunals and the Employment Appeal Tribunal, and are at the time of writing the subject of proposals for very substantial amendment.[51]

Outline of the effect on time limits

1.70   For a fuller account of the regime implemented by the Employment Act (EA) 2002 and the Employment Act 2002 (Dispute Resolution) Regulations (EA(DR)R) 2004 see ETP 3 paras 3.3–3.15. In very broad outline, this legislation does three things:

- It requires employers to go through a statutory procedure (a dismissal and disciplinary procedure (DDP)) before dismissing or disciplining any employee, and provides that a dismissal in the absence of those procedures is unfair.
- It requires employees to raise an internal grievance through a statutory grievance procedure (GP) and then wait 28 days before making a complaint to the tribunal about anything[52] other than a dismissal.
- It provides for adjustments up or down of awards to claimants in cases where DDP or GP (as the case may be) has not been completed: the award will be adjusted upwards if it is the employer's fault that the procedure was not completed, down if it was the employee's fault.

1.71   These provisions have the effect that employees cannot always present their claims immediately when they arise, and for that reason the time limits for presentation of claims is sometimes but not always extended by three months.

1.72   The rules governing these extensions of time are at EA(DR)R 2004 reg 15. Again a broad outline of the effect of them is necessary here. For complaints about grievances, the extension of time is gained by doing one of two things:

- raising a grievance; or
- presenting a claim to the tribunal that is premature either because no grievance has been raised, or because 28 days have not yet passed since the grievance was raised.

---

51 See the review, 'Better Dispute Resolution' by Michael Gibbons, published DTI March 2007, available on the DTI website: www.dti.gov.uk. For further developments, see the blog that supports and updates this book, www.etclaims.co.uk

52 Almost anything: see ELAH 7, para 22.55.

1.73   For complaints about dismissal, the additional three months is available in one situation only:

- if at the time the normal time limit for the complaint expired the claimant had reasonable grounds for believing that there was an ongoing disciplinary or dismissal procedure.

1.74   Note that it is not the case that a claimant must always wait for the outcome of an internal appeal against dismissal or against the outcome of his or her grievance before presenting a claim to the tribunal. Note too that time will not always be extended to six months.

Multiple claims

1.75   Multiple claims (in the sense of cases where the claimant has a number of different complaints against the employer) are very common: they are probably the rule rather than the exception. Most complaints about dismissal are accompanied by a wages claim, or a contract claim; many are accompanied by a discrimination claim as well. Discrimination claims may be against both the employer and the individual colleague who has discriminated.

1.76   The dispute resolution regime means that careful thought has to be given to what the relevant limitation period is for each claim separately. Sometimes the periods will coincide or overlap, but that is not to be assumed. Note in particular the danger of missing the deadline for a complaint against an individual respondent in respect of acts for which the employer is also liable.

Example

Tanya Waters is employed as a semi-skilled machinist in a factory. All the other machinists in her department are men. Her male colleagues are often offered overtime work at busy times. She is only rarely offered overtime. On 5 October 2007 the factory receives a large order with a tight deadline and several of her colleagues are given two hours overtime a night that day and for the whole of the following week, ending 12 October. On 12 October, Tanya complains to her department supervisor about this and says that she thinks she is being left out because she is a woman. The supervisor, Mo, tells her she is a nuisance and always moaning about something, and tells her to get a life.

On 25 October Tanya is handed a letter inviting her to a disciplinary meeting on 27 October to discuss her persistent lateness. She went through a bad patch for time-keeping a few months earlier because of child-care difficulties and was given a written warning, but her time-keeping had been mostly good for the last couple of months: she has only been late on two or three occasions since the beginning of August, and nothing was said at the time. At the end of the meeting on 27 October she is dismissed with immediate effect, but with pay in lieu of notice. She appeals the dismissal on Monday 30 October. The appeal is heard on 5 November and dismissed.

Towards the end of November Tanya gets an appointment with her local CAB. She is advised that she has potential claims of sex discrimination in the allocation of overtime, and also of unfair dismissal and sex discrimination by way of victimisation in relation to the dismissal. She is told that she can bring complaints against her employer, and against Mo. She is advised to raise a grievance about the overtime complaint, but because of money worries arising from the loss of her job she does not get around to it until 4 January 2008.

Tanya was dismissed on 27 October 2007, so the normal period for presentation of her unfair dismissal complaint and her complaint that her dismissal was discriminatory ends on 26 January 2008. The last unfair allocation of overtime ended on 12 October 2007, so the normal period for presenting that complaint ends on 11 January 2008. Because she raised a grievance about the overtime allocation on 4 January 2008 – inside the normal period for presentation of the claim – she has the benefit of a three month extension, so her sex discrimination claim in relation to that must now be presented to the tribunal by 11 April 2008.[53] That claim cannot be presented until 1 February 2008, because she must wait 28 days after raising her grievance. For her unfair dismissal claim and her complaint that the dismissal was an act of victimisation, on the other hand, she does

---

53 Or, according to the EAT in *Bisset v (1) Martino and (2) Castlehill Housing Association* UKEAT/0023/06, 12 April 2008. The authors respectfully doubt that *Bisset* was correctly decided, it remains safer to assume that the last date for presenting a claim subject to a three month normal limitation period and three month extension is six months less one day from the act complained of.

> not get a three month extension on the normal time limit. This
> is because her appeal was concluded back in November: she
> does not have reasonable grounds to believe that there is an
> ongoing DDP. For her complaint about overtime against Mo,
> no grievance is required, and so there is no opportunity to earn
> a three month extension. This complaint must therefore be
> brought within three months of 12 October 2007, that is on or
> before 11 January 2008.
>
> This means that Tanya has separate, non-overlapping win-
> dows of opportunity in which to present her claims. She must
> present her discrimination claim against Mo on or before 11
> January 2008. She must present her unfair dismissal and vic-
> timisation claims on or before 26 January 2008. She must pres-
> ent her sex discrimination claim against the employer on or
> before 11 April 2008, but she may not present it until 1 February.

The tribunal's duty to reject incomplete claims

1.77   The 2004 procedure rules insist that certain 'required information'
must be included on all claims, and that claims must be presented
on the prescribed form. Because the tribunals have a duty to reject
claims that do not comply with these requirements, this is a further
source of potential difficulty in presenting a valid claim within the relevant time limit. There is no automatic extension of time in a case
where a claim is presented within the applicable time limit but rejected,
although in some cases tribunals may be amenable to the argument
either that it was not reasonably practicable to present the claim in
time or that an extension should be granted on just and equitable
grounds.[54]

1.78   The Employment Tribunal Service has adopted an extremely strict
policy in relation to the prescribed form, rejecting claims unless they
are made on the online or pdf forms (both available from the employment tribunal service website); or on the official paper form, available
from Job Centres, CABx or on request to the employment tribunals'
public inquiry line, 08457 959775. Claims presented on a re-typed or
scanned version of the form, or on a copy taken from a reprint of the
official form in a textbook, have been rejected. A number of cases

---

54 Depending which test applies: see ETP 3 paras 3.28–3.29.

illustrate both the strictness of the rules and the willingness of the EAT to mitigate their effects. In *Butlins Skyline Ltd v Beynon*,[55] the EAT overturned the rejection of a claim where the faxing process had reduced the form in size, usefully confirming at the same time that a rejection is subject to both review and appeal; see also *Grant v In 2 Focus*.[56] In *Cummings v Scholarest* UKEAT/0625/06, rejection of a claim for failing to identify the claimant where her name had been mis-spelled on the form was overturned by the EAT.

1.79   If an employee presents a complaint near the end of the limita-tion period, and the tribunal rejects it as incomplete, or because it is not presented on the prescribed form, the employee may by the time she knows her claim has been rejected either be too late to correct her claim and resubmit it, or have a very limited time indeed in which to do so. For this reason it is important to present the claim as soon as pos-sible in order to have time to correct and present again in the event of rejection.

Whether to present the claim or wait for the outcome of the statutory procedure

1.80   Complaints about grievances may not be presented until 28 days have elapsed since the grievance was raised, but it is important to be aware that aside from that there is no requirement for employees to wait a rea-sonable period, or any period, for their employers to complete statutory procedures before presenting a tribunal claim. The Employment Act (EA) 2002 s31 provides for the reduction of awards where non-com-pletion of the statutory procedure is attributable to a failure by the employee either to comply with a requirement of the procedure, or to exercise a right of appeal, but those are the only two circumstances in which the employee will be blamed for non-completion of the process. It follows that there should be no penalty for presenting an appeal (against dismissal, or against an unsatisfactory outcome to a grievance) and immediately presenting a claim.

1.81   The risk of having the claim rejected as incomplete on the first attempt means that the safest course is:

---

55 [2007] ICR 121.
56 [2007] UKEAT 0310/06.

- to present a complaint about dismissal as soon as possible after the effective date of termination;[57]
- to present a complaint about a grievance as soon as possible once 28 days have elapsed after the presentation of the initial grievance.

1.82   Employees who are very confident that they know when the relevant limitation period expires and can present a valid claim on the first attempt might sometimes to get a tactical advantage by waiting for a period after presenting an internal appeal before presenting the claim. The reason for this is that giving the employer the opportunity to deal with the appeal before presenting the claim also gives the employer the opportunity to fail to deal with the appeal within a reasonable time, and that can give rise to an enhanced award of compensation.

1.83   If the employee presents a claim a day or two after appealing, the employee will not suffer a reduction of his award by reason of the non-completion of the procedure because EA 2002 s31(2)(c) gives only two situations in which non-completion of the procedure will be treated as the employee's fault and this is not one of them.[58] However, if non-completion of the statutory procedure is attributable to the employer's failure to deal with an appeal within a reasonable time, then any award made to the employee should be adjusted upwards.

1.84   It follows that in some cases a tactical pause (probably for 28 days or so, time limits permitting) after appealing the employer's internal decision and before presenting a claim to the tribunal may result in an enhanced award for the claimant. However, this tactic should be used, if at all, with great caution: the most important thing is to ensure the claim is presented in time.

---

57 See glossary.

58 The two situations are where the employee has failed to comply with a requirement of the procedure, or where he or she has failed to exercise a right of appeal.

Before the claim

Introduction

2.1   As touched on in chapter 1, statutory dispute resolution procedures were created with effect from 1 October 2004 by the Employment Act (EA) 2002 and the Employment Act 2002 (Dispute Resolution) Regulations (EA(DR)R 2004. The dispute resolution regime makes it compulsory in many circumstances for employees to present their employers with a written grievance and give them 28 days to deal with it before they are allowed to make a complaint in relation to the same matter to an employment tribunal.

2,2   The regime was misconceived at the policy level: it is more likely to intensify and prolong disputes and increase reliance on lawyers than to lead to early and informal resolution. At the level of detail it is even worse: the rules are obscure, cumbersome and over-complicated, and raise many difficult practical problems for both employees and employers. The regime has been widely condemned by lawyers and the Employment Appeal Tribunal, and the Gibbons Review has recommended repeal. Unfortunately this will not be done until 2009 at the earliest. This chapter aims to provide a broad overview of the procedures; for the detail see the Act and Regulations themselves and ELAH 7 chapter 22.

2.3   One crumb of comfort for employees is that the grievance procedures themselves are straightforward. The complexities arise in working out when they are compulsory, whether or not they have been complied with (and if not, whose fault it is), and what the consequences are of any non-compliance. While those questions are important for claimants, they fall to be answered in the end by tribunals. Claimants should focus on raising a grievance where necessary and then following the process through to the end.

2.4   This chapter deals with grievances because they are a step that the employee must take in many cases before being allowed to present a claim to the employment tribunal. Where there has been an actual (as opposed to constructive) dismissal, the employer is under duties to follow statutory disciplinary and dismissal procedures that are in many ways parallel to the employee's duty to raise a grievance. The statutory disciplinary procedures are not dealt with in this book since the duties under them fall primarily on the employer, and a failure to comply with them does not prevent an employee from presenting a claim to the employment tribunal.

The two types of grievance procedure

2.5 The EA 2002 provides for 'standard' and 'modified' grievance procedures. Each procedure is, as mentioned above, straightforward in itself.

Standard grievance procedure

2.6 The standard procedure has the following six stages:

1. A written statement of the grievance, which the employee must give or send to the employer.
2. A meeting, which the employer must arrange and the employee must take all reasonable steps to attend, to discuss the grievance.
3. Notification to the employee of the employer's response to the grievance. The employee must also be notified of his or her right of appeal.
4. Notification by the employee that he or she wishes to appeal.
5. An appeal meeting, which the employer must arrange and the employee must take all reasonable steps to attend.
6. The employer's decision on the appeal.

2.7 The process should normally be followed through to the end, even if the employee does not have any confidence that his employer will deal with the grievance in good faith. The requirement to comply with the grievance procedures before presenting a tribunal claim does not apply if, for example, it is not reasonably practicable to raise a grievance, or if there are reasonable grounds for thinking that raising a grievance will lead to a threat to a person or property or a continuation of harassment. However, these exemptions are strictly defined, and it will be difficult to predict in advance when the tribunals will be prepared to accept that they apply. On the rare occasions that an employee genuinely believes that raising a grievance will expose him or her to personal risk, that consideration must obviously outweigh the danger of damaging a subsequent tribunal claim. Otherwise, it is suggested that employees should make all possible efforts to comply with the procedures.

The modified procedure

2.8   The modified procedure applies if the employment has ended and the employer and employee have agreed in writing that the modified procedure should apply.

2.9   The modified procedure leaves out the meetings and the appeal stage and consists of two steps:

1. A written statement of the grievance, including the basis for the grievance, which the employee must give or send to the employer.
2. The employer's written response to the grievance.

2.10   An employee whose employment has ended and who wishes to raise a grievance will need to decide whether to propose the modified procedure. It is suggested that this will often be preferable: grievance meetings are likely to be stressful for the employee, and the longer standard process presents the employee with more stages to complete and therefore more stages, potentially, to be blamed by the tribunal for failing to complete. However, the modified procedure can only be adopted with the employer's agreement, so if the employer declines to run the modified procedure and proposes a meeting, the employee should attend and then complete the full standard procedure.

The initial statement of grievance

2.11   Section 32 of the EA 2002 provides:

(2) An employee shall not present a complaint to an employment tribunal [of one of the specified kinds] if–
   (a) it concerns a matter in relation to which the requirement [to follow a grievance procedure] applies, and
   (b) the requirement has not been complied with.

2.12   Employees, therefore, are generally prohibited from presenting complaints to employment tribunals concerning 'matters' in relation to which they have not previously raised as grievances with their employers.

> **Example**
> Suppose Anwara Begum feels aggrieved about how much she is being paid by her employers and about their refusal to vary her working day to ease problems with her childcare arrangements. She presents a formal grievance that says:
>
> > 'I do not think it is fair that I am paid less than John Kandler.
> > I have mentioned this on several occasions and you have promised to do something about it each time but you have never done anything, and now I have discovered that John got a 7% pay rise last April. I did not even get a pay rise to keep pace with inflation because you said the company was going through a difficult time.
> > I also think it is unfair that you have refused my request to work at home for part of the week in order to ease the terrible difficulties I have been suffering with childcare.'

2.13 Her employers fail to resolve her grievance to her satisfaction and, having taken advice, she presents complaints to the tribunal of sex and race discrimination, under the Equal Pay Act (EqPA) 1970 and under the flexible working provisions of the Employment Rights Act (ERA) 1996. Before it decides whether or not to accept the formal claim, the tribunal must decide whether these matters have been raised in Ms Begum's grievance. In her grievance, Ms Begum has complained of the facts that she is unhappy about, that she is paid less than a colleague, and that she has not been allowed to work at home for part of the week, but she mentioned nothing about her specific rights under EqPA or ERA.

2.14 This means that grievances must be drafted with some care. If a claim has not been raised in a grievance a claimant be barred from pursuing her claim. There is, however, a wide recognition in the system that claimants should not be barred from bringing a claim because of minor technical deficiencies in their grievance. Provide a grievance is clear enough that the respondent can understand what the claimant is complaining about the requirement of the standard procedure should be satisfied.[1] A grievance letter does not need to be in a specific form or style.

2.15 If the modified procedure is used, claimants must be careful that they do set out the basis for their grievance fully. This is a step beyond

---

1 *Shergold v Fieldway Medical Centre* [2006] ICR 304.

setting out the grievance itself and means that the facts surrounding the complaint should be set out in more detail.[2]

2.16   The prudent course must be to take care to ensure that the factual basis of all the complaints that the employee may subsequently wish a tribunal to consider are raised in the internal grievance. The approach taken here is to spell out the legal basis for the complaints in terms little, if at all, different from what would be included in the narrative sections of a formal claim. In effect this means that employees who are considering an internal grievance are likely to need legal advice at this stage. This runs contrary to the intention with which the rules appear to have been drafted, but it seems nevertheless to be the only safe course.

2.17   It is sensible for the employee to state in the grievance letter any practical steps that she thinks the employer ought to take to resolve the grievance, but it is probably not appropriate to ask for a specified sum in compensation at this stage.

P2.17.1 Written grievance

Seamus McNally
McNally & Sons
26 Lower Street
London
N19 2PQ

20 October 2006

Dear Mr McNally

Statement of grievance

I would like to ask you to consider my grievance about two matters.

1. I do not think it is fair that I am paid less than John Kandler. We have the same job title and we do almost exactly the same work and cover for each other's absences, but he is paid nearly £4,000 per year more than me. I believe that this is a breach of my right to equal pay under the Equal Pay Act 1970 and/or not to suffer discrimination on racial grounds under the Race Relations Act 1976.

2 *Bradford MDC v Pratt* [2007] IRLR 192.

I want you to agree to pay me the same as Mr Kandler from now on. I also want to discuss how much back pay you should pay me.

2. You have refused to consider the request that I made in my letter of 18 September for a change in my working arrangements so that I can pick my daughter up from her kindergarten. I have a right under Part VIIIA of the Employment Rights Act 1996 to have this request properly considered at a meeting. I also believe that your refusal to let me work at home for part of the week constitutes indirect discrimination on grounds of sex.

I want you to hold a meeting to discuss the practicalities of my working at home for two days each week.

I hope to hear from you shortly with a proposed date for a grievance meeting about these matters.

Yours sincerely

Anwara Begum

P2.17.2 Written grievance – Unauthorised deductions from wages complaint and possible future constructive dismissal[3]

Ms P Denny
Supaclean Ltd
14 Hartwell Way
Croydon
Surrey CR0 1AB

7 December 2007

Dear Ms Denny

Enhanced wages for weekend work

I have worked for Supaclean for 12 years now, first as a cleaner and since March 1999 as a cleaning supervisor. I have always been paid time

---

3 In this case the standard procedure must apply because the employment is on-going.

and a half for hours worked between 6 pm on Friday and 8 am on Monday.

On 15 October 2007 I received a letter from Andy Parsons, the cleaning manager at the Celtic Bank where I work, telling me that from the following week I would not get extra pay for weekend work any more, and I have received reduced pay for all seven weeks since the week beginning 18 October.

I think this is unfair. Please treat this letter as starting a grievance under the statutory grievance procedure.[4]

I think this is a fundamental breach of my contract of employment, and I reserve the right to resign in response if you do not resolve my grievance satisfactorily.

Yours sincerely

Sufiya Halai

Dispute resolution procedures and 'without prejudice' communications

2.18   A problem that is not directly addressed in the legislation is the question whether in any circumstances a statutory grievance procedure will take on the character of without prejudice negotiations.[5]

2.19   As a matter of principle the distinction between an open statutory grievance procedure and without prejudice negotiations depends on whether or not there is a live dispute between the parties which they are attempting to settle: see *BNP Paribas v Mezzotero*.[6] If compromise of a live dispute is contemplated, then the process, whatever it is called and irrespective of whether the parties state that their letters and/or meetings are 'without prejudice,' is privileged.

2.20   It will often be a difficult question whether the process does represent an attempt to settle a live dispute. In *BNP Paribas* the EAT held that the fact that a grievance had been raised did not mean that

---

4 It is not essential, but is probably prudent, to refer directly to the statutory procedure.

5 See para 6.11 below and glossary.

6 [2004] IRLR 508.

there was a live dispute between the parties, and consequently the employee was allowed to give evidence about what had been said at a grievance meeting that the employer had sought to label 'without prejudice.'

2.21 In *Arnold Clark Automobiles Ltd v (1) Richard G Stewart (2) Barnetts Motor Group Ltd* EAT(SC) [2005] UKEAT 0052 the EAT held that a letter before action sent by the employee's solicitors and marked 'without prejudice' was a sufficient step 1 grievance letter. It does not appear to have been argued, however, that this was something that the tribunal had no right to see or take into account by reason of its 'without prejudice' nature. For the moment the authors consider that this point remains obscure.

Constructive dismissal and grievance procedures

2.22 An employee who has resigned in response to his or her employer's fundamental breach of contract is deemed by virtue of ERA 1996 s95(1)(c) to have been dismissed. This is widely referred to (although the term does not appear in the Act) as 'constructive dismissal'.[7]

2.23 Constructive dismissal has always been a tactical minefield for employees and those who advise them. Timing is important, because an employee who does not resign reasonably promptly after the employer's fundamental breach may be said to have 'affirmed' the contract and lost the right to treat the breach as terminating the contract.[8] At the same time, if the employer's conduct is not yet sufficiently definite, the employee may be said to have resigned prematurely – for example, where an employer has threatened but not yet committed a fundamental breach of the contract of employment. The compulsory grievance procedures complicate matters further.

2.24 In some ways, constructive dismissal is the mirror image of dismissal for gross misconduct: one party to the employment contract has done something so bad that the other party cannot be expected to continue the relationship. A key difference, however, is that the employee, unlike the employer, has no obligation to act fairly, to conduct a fair investigation or to consider alternatives before resigning: if the employer has committed a fundamental breach of contract, the

---

7 See glossary; for a fuller explanation see ELAH 7 chapter 6.
8 See ELAH 7 paras 6.39–6.42.

employee may simply walk out and complain of constructive dismissal.

2.25   The statutory dispute resolution procedures do not change this. This is important: the definition of constructive dismissal is not altered by the introduction of statutory grievance procedures. The obligation to raise a grievance and wait 28 days before presenting a tribunal complaint does not bring with it any duty to 'give the employer a fair hearing' before resigning. It is no doubt intended (if naively) to have the result that in some cases the resignation or the tribunal complaint may be headed off, but the actual obligations it imposes on the employee are purely formal. Some tribunals may need to be specifically warned against this error of treating the employee as bound to act reasonably.

2.26   An employee who considers that they have been constructively dismissed must now raise a statutory grievance and wait 28 days for the outcome before they may present a claim to an employment tribunal, but they may resign before, after, or at the same time as they raise their grievance. Employees who wish to attempt to resolve the problem by way of the grievance procedure before resigning should expressly reserve the right to resign in reliance on the employer's breach.[9]

2.27   There is a possible argument that under the EA(DR)R 2004 and the EA 2002, an employee who raises a grievance and then resigns when the grievance is not satisfactorily resolved must present a further grievance about the constructive dismissal itself before presenting a complaint of constructive dismissal to the tribunal. As yet this point has not been clarified by case-law.

2.28   The best way of dealing with this is to combine the letter of resignation with the letter of grievance and complain of both the breach of contract and that it has lead to the resignation. The EAT has confirmed that a resignation letter can also act as a grievance letter.[10]

2.29   This advice is likely to mean that the raising of the grievance is an empty gesture, designed solely to comply with the procedure. It is unlikely that, once an employee has resigned, their grievance can be resolved satisfactorily. This does not mean that it is not worth attempting to resolve the problem with the employee before resigning, only that the statutory procedure is unlikely to be the best way of doing so. Employees who want to sort things out with their employees will do better to take whatever action seems most likely to persuade their employer to improve the situation, without worrying about the statu-

---

9 See ELAH 7 para 6.40.
10 *Canary Wharf Management Ltd v Edebi* [2006] ICR 719.

tory procedure, while remembering that the grievance procedure will need to be gone through before they reach tribunal. Employees must, however, be cautious not to be seen to affirm the contract through delay.

P2.29 Constructive dismissal – combined resignation & grievance

Philip Badger
Bubbles Packaging Ltd
Handley Lane Industrial Estate
Ashford
Kent AS12 3AB

23 October 2006

Dear Mr Badger

Resignation

Your behaviour towards me over the last several months has been increasingly abrupt and undermining. This Monday's incident is beyond what I am prepared or can be expected to tolerate, and I resign with immediate effect.

Grievance

On Monday 16 October at around 4pm I was in the middle of a conversation with Tina, my PA, about this month's sales report when you stormed into my office holding a copy of my draft strategy report to the Board. In the hearing of Tina and three other managers in my department you shouted, 'Can't you get anything right, you useless fuckwit?' I asked Tina to leave and closed the door of my office, and then asked you if you had anything more constructive to say. You dropped the report in the wastepaper basket and said, 'It's hopeless. I'll just have to do it myself.' You then returned to your office.

You have treated me with increasing contempt over the last 3 or 4 months. You have had an increasing tendency throughout that period to sigh loudly, raise your eyes heavenwards or mutter 'Really!' when I have addressed you, you have used curt e-mails copied to my subordinates to communicate with me on many occasions when it would have been more convenient and more courteous to speak to me direct, and in the last couple of weeks you have avoided any eye contact with me and ignored me when I have greeted you. I consider that your brusque and undermining conduct towards me over recent months, culminating in your outburst on Monday last week, constituted a fundamental breach of the implied term of trust and confidence that is part of my contract of employment. I have therefore been constructively dismissed, and I believe that my dismissal was unfair. I wish to raise a formal grievance about these matters.[11]

Because my employment has come to an end, there is a choice to be made between the standard and the modified grievance procedures as set out at Chapters 1 and 2 of Part 2 of Schedule 2 to the Employment Act 2002. My view is that the modified procedure is appropriate. Please confirm in writing, by return, your agreement that the modified procedure should apply.

Yours sincerely

Amanda Kulpa

Borderline cases of constructive or actual dismissal

2.30   A further complication will arise in cases falling on the borderline between constructive and actual dismissal.

Example
Suppose Mike works as a florist, making up bouquets. He likes this work and is good at it, but his time-keeping is hit-or-miss. His employer, Rob, gets impatient with this, and says 'If you don't buck your ideas up I'll put you on deliveries and we'll see how you like that.' The next Monday morning, Mike is 20 minutes late again, and his employer says, 'Right. I warned you. You're on deliveries this week. If your timekeeping improves over the next few weeks we'll think about putting you back in the shop. Here's

---

11   It is advisable to make it clear that the grievance is about both the manager's conduct, and about the constructive dismissal itself.

> your list of drops – the van's already loaded and you know where it is.' Mike objects that he is not employed as a driver, but Rob says, 'Here's the list – it's your choice, you can either do the deliveries or you can bugger off and not come back.' Mike leaves.

2.31   Mike has either resigned in response to his employer's breach of contract, or he has been summarily dismissed – without any disciplinary process – for refusing to obey an order; but it is not entirely clear which it is. He would probably prefer to argue that he has been actually dismissed, but he had better commence a grievance in case a tribunal subsequently takes the other view. At the same time, he should make it clear from the outset that he takes the view that there has been an actual dismissal so that his grievance letter is not able to be treated as evidence that he has resigned.

P2.31.1 Conditional grievance in a borderline constructive/ actual dismissal case

Rob Selassie
Flower Power
44 Broadway Lane
Camden
London WC1X 1AB

20 November 2006

Dear Rob

Last Monday you ordered me to carry out delivery work instead of my usual floristry work, and you said that I could either do that or 'bugger off and not come back.' I was employed as a florist and I do not believe you were entitled to make me work as a delivery driver instead. In the circumstances, I believe that you have dismissed me from my job as a florist, and I intend to complain to an employment tribunal of unfair dismissal.

Without prejudice to my assertion that your conduct last Monday amounted to actual dismissal, I invite you to treat this letter as starting a formal grievance under the statutory grievance procedure. Because my employment has already come to an end, if the grievance procedures apply at all, there is a choice to be made between the standard and the modified grievance procedures as set out at Chapters 1 and 2 of Part 2 of Schedule 2 to the Employment Act 2002. My view is that if any grievance procedure is needed, it is the modified procedure that is appropriate. Please confirm in writing your agreement that the modified procedure should apply.

Yours sincerely

Mike O'Donnell

P2.31.2 Written grievance relating to sex discrimination

Jane Slough
Personnel Department
Fencemarket plc
212-220 Station Approach
Manchester M1 2BA

17 July 2007

Dear Ms Slough

Grievance: sex discrimination

I have worked in the Manchester branch of Fencemarket for the last six years. I work four hours a day, from 8am to 12 noon. I became pregnant early this year and announced my pregnancy to my line manager on 6 April. I am due to start my maternity leave on 2 October.

When I told my line manager that I was pregnant, she said, 'You'll have to stay on the tills from now on, then.' I asked her why, and she said, 'We can't have you waddling about the shop in your condition. The aisles are too narrow. I wouldn't answer for the consequences.' She has taken me off all duties apart from checkout since 9 April. I get very tired and bored sitting on the tills all day and my head aches. I used to like the variety of doing different duties.

I think the way I am being treated is sex discrimination. I am only being treated this way because I am pregnant. I want my manager to be told that I must be allowed to return to the full range of duties until I start my maternity leave.

[If the employee might wish to resign over this issue, a paragraph here asserting that the treatment amounts to a fundamental breach of contract and reserving the right to resign in response should be included.]

Yours sincerely

Elaine Brown

P2.31.3 Appeal against unsatisfactory outcome of grievance[12]

Mrs Alison Parker
Supaclean Ltd
14 Hartwell Way
Croydon
Surrey CR0 1AB

11 January 2008

Dear Ms Parker

Grievance: enhanced wages for weekend work

I enclose copies of my previous correspondence with Ms Denny, and minutes of the grievance meeting that was held last week. I wish to appeal Ms Denny's decision on my grievance.

I do not accept that Supaclean is entitled to change my terms and conditions of employment by giving me a month's notice. I have never been given a written contract to sign, and it has never previously been suggested to me that Supaclean has this right.

---

12 See the grievance at P2.17.2; Ms Denny has responded to the grievance by making up four weeks' enhanced pay but asserting that after four weeks the company has the right to impose the change.

Please let me know when you can hear my appeal. I still reserve the right to resign in response to this fundamental breach of my contract of employment if you do not satisfactorily resolve my grievance.

Yours sincerely

Sufiya Halai

Questionnaires

2.32   Since the point of questionnaires is to get information out of the employer, this subject is dealt with more fully at Chapter 4 below. However, it is important to note in the context of what can or should be done before a claim starts that in discrimination cases, a potential claimant may wish to serve a questionnaire on the employer before taking the final decision whether to make a claim to the employment tribunal. Employees or unsuccessful job applicants who are considering a discrimination claim should read ETP 3 paras 4.17–4.22 at an early stage and think about whether they wish to serve a questionnaire before presenting a claim to the employment tribunal.

Note that a questionnaire does not double as a grievance for the purpose of statutory dispute resolution procedures: *Holc-Gale v Makers UK Ltd* [2006] ICR 462.

CHAPTER 3

The claim and the employer's response

The formal claim

3.1   A complaint to the employment tribunal is made on form ET1. Much of the form is concerned with general information, such as the name and address of the parties and the dates of employment. The main narrative part of the complaint will be the content of boxes 5.1, 6.2, 7.1, 8.3 and 9.1. This is the claimant's opportunity to set out, briefly, the story of what her employer did that she considers unlawful. If the complaint is straightforward, this can simply be written or typed in the box provided, but it is also acceptable – and common practice – to write 'see attached' in the relevant box and provide a separate document headed 'details of complaint'.

3.2   The purpose of the formal claim is to explain to the tribunal, and the other party, what it is that the employee complains of and why she says that it was unlawful.[1] There is no need to set out the evidence in great detail at this stage, or to argue the law, but it is necessary to give the employer enough information that it knows what factual allegations it has to meet and what the legal nature of the complaint is. It is important to make explicit all the complaints that the employee wishes to raise at the initial stage: employment tribunal time limits are strict, and an amendment raising a new complaint will often be treated, for the purposes of the time limits, as a separate claim.[2]

3.3   How much detail is enough for the formal claim is a question of judgement in each case. It is always possible to tell a story in more detail: the length of a story can increase infinitely, like the length of a coastline, depending on the degree of magnification through which it is observed. 'I was dismissed and it was unfair and discriminatory' is clearly inadequate: the employer will need to know whether actual or constructive dismissal is alleged, whether the claimant complains that the reason for dismissal was inadmissible, or of the procedure adopted in dismissing or the substantive decision to dismiss or both, what kind of discrimination – sex, race, disability, sexual orientation, religion – is complained of and whether direct or indirect, and so on. On the other hand, a claim that gives verbatim accounts of conversations and

---

1   This used to be called the 'originating application'; it is now simply called 'the claim'. This attempt at plain English confusing as it blurs the distinction between the subject or subjects of complaint and the formal document that sets it out. In this book the expression 'the formal claim' is used to signify the document that starts employment tribunal proceedings and to distinguish the document from the subject-matter of the case.

2   See ETP 3, paras 7.3–7.8.

quotes at length from the company handbook or minutes of meetings is probably going into a great deal of detail that could safely be left to the witness statements.[3] A comparison between precedents P3.11.2 and P5.28.1 below illustrates the difference between the formal claim and the claimant's witness statement.

3.4   The following example is drawn from life:

> **Example**
> 'On or about July 2007 the Respondent unfairly instructed the Claimant to sign a document without arranging for an interpreter to inform the claimant of the meaning of the document that he was being asked to sign. The respondent unreasonably informed the claimant that if he did not sign the document he would not be paid his wages. The Claimant contends that the Respondent's actions are contrary to the RRA. The Claimant has suffered loss and damage due to the Respondent's actions.'

3.5   This is so vague and inexplicit as to be meaningless. What document was the Claimant asked to sign? Precisely how did this amount to race discrimination? What loss and damage has the Claimant suffered?

3.6   Always bear in mind that the claim form is the first thing the tribunal will read. When they read it, they will know nothing about the case. It is important to give them enough information for them to understand your claim and begin to be convinced by it.

3.7   A good way of testing whether a draft claim has included all the essentials is to ask the question: if we prove everything we have asserted here, will we win the case? Or will the tribunal have to make other assumptions or find facts that we have not asserted in order to give the claimant an award? If the tribunal cannot make an award to the claimant without finding facts that the claimant has not asserted in the formal claim, then the claim has not included everything it should have. So for example to make an award for unauthorised deductions from wages, the tribunal will need to be satisfied: (i) that the employee was entitled under her contract of employment be paid certain amounts; (ii) that the employer paid her less than the amount to which she was entitled on one or more occasions; (iii) that she had not authorised the deduction(s) in writing; (iv) that there was no statutory or contractual authority for the deductions. All of these elements must be present as assertions in the formal claim.

---

3   If not just left out.

The employment tribunal form

3.8   The current version of the form is compulsory for all claims. It is called the ET1, and it is nine pages long. Forms are available from tribunal offices, job centres and CABx. There is also an online version, which can be completed on the tribunal web-site.

3.9   Most of the information asked for on the form should simply be written or typed on the form itself, and in simpler cases it will be possible to write all the necessary information on the form. However, where there is a story to tell that is at all complicated, it remains more convenient to attach separate sheets to the form. Any attached sheets should show clearly which sections of the form they relate to. It is suggested that claimants should write a note at box 10 ('Other information') indicating how many additional sheets are attached to the form.

3.10   The claim is likely to be rejected for any failure to provide compulsory information. Even if the claim in not rejected, missing information can cause problems later in proceedings. Questions marked * on the form must be answered in all cases. Questions marked * and ● must be answered if relevant. If separate sheets are attached dealing with certain sections of the form, care should still be taken to ensure that any necessary tick-boxes or specific questions at those sections have been dealt with.

3.11   The first precedent opposite shows the entire form completed for a disability discrimination claim. The subsequent precedents only show the additional pages that would be attached to the form, but not the form itself.

P3.11.1 ET1 – disability discrimination

1 Your details

1.1	Title:	Mr ☐ Mrs ☐ Miss ☐ Ms ☑ Other
1.2*	First name (or names):	Pauline Cecilia
1.3*	Surname or family name:	Phelps
1.4	Date of birth (date/month/year):	27 / 9 /53 Are you: male? ☐ female? ☑
1.5*	Address:	14 Strawberry Field, Gotherington, Cheltenham, Gloucestershire
		Postcode GL52 1AB

You do not need to answer 1.6 and 1.7 if you have appointed a representative (see section 11).

1.6	Phone number **(where we can contact you during normal working hours)**:	
1.7	How would you prefer us to communicate with you?	Post ☐ Fax ☐ E-mail ☐
		Fax:
		E-mail address:

2 Respondent's details

2.1*	Give the name of your employer or the organisation or person you are complaining about (the respondent).	Gentleman, Sharpe & Co Solicitors
2.2*	Address:	2 Abbey Close, Tewkesbury, Gloucestershire
		Postcode GL20 5AB
2.3	If you worked at an address different from the one you have given at 2.2, please give the full address.	
		Postcode

2.4● If your complaint is against more than one respondent please give the names, addresses and postcodes of additional respondents.

3   Action before making a claim

3.1* Are you, or were you, an employee of the respondent?   Yes ☑️   No ☐
If 'Yes', please now go straight to section 3.3.

3.2 Are you, or were you, a worker providing services to the respondent?   Yes ☐   No ☐
If 'Yes', please now go straight to section 4.
If 'No', please now go straight to section 6.

3.3● Is your claim, or part of it, about a dismissal by the respondent?   Yes ☐   No ☑️
If 'No', please now go straight to section 3.5.

3.4● Is your claim about anything else, in addition to the dismissal?   Yes ☑️   No ☐
If 'No', please now go straight to section 4.
If 'Yes', please answer questions 3.5 to 3.7 about the
non-dismissal aspects of your claim.

3.5● Have you put your complaint in writing to the respondent?

Yes ☑️ Please give the date you put it to them in writing.   **9 / 5 /2007**
No ☐

If 'No', please now go straight to section 3.7.

3.6● Did you allow at least 28 days between the date you put your   Yes ☑️   No ☐
complaint to the respondent and the date you sent us this claim?
If 'Yes', please now go straight to section 4.

3.7● Please explain why you did not put your complaint in writing to the respondent or,
if you did, why you did not allow at least 28 days before sending us your claim.
(In most cases, it is a legal requirement to take these procedural steps. Your claim
will not be accepted unless you give a valid reason why you did not have to meet
the requirement in your case. If you are not sure, you may want to get legal advice.)

4 Employment details

4.1 Please give the following information if possible.

When did your employment start? **17** / **6** / **82**

When did or will it end? / /

Is your employment continuing? Yes ☑ No ☐

4.2 Please say what job you do or did. **Secretary**

4.3 How many hours do or did you work each week? ...**35**...hours each week

4.4 How much are or were you paid?

Pay before tax **£18,750** each **year**

Normal take-home pay (including overtime, commission, bonuses and so on) **£15,688** each **year**

4.5 If your employment has ended, did you work (or were you paid for) a period of notice? Yes ☐ No ☐

If 'Yes', how many weeks or months did you work or were you paid for? ....weeks ....months

5 Unfair dismissal or constructive dismissal

Please fill in this section only if you believe you have been unfairly or constructively dismissed.

5.1 • If you were dismissed by your employer, you should explain why you think your dismissal was unfair. If you resigned because of something your employer did or failed to do which made you feel you could no longer continue to work for them (constructive dismissal) you should explain what happened.

please see attached sheet

5   Unfair dismissal or constructive dismissal continued

5.1 continued

5.2   Were you in your employer's pension scheme?   Yes ☑   No ☐

5.3   If you received any other benefits from your employer, please give details.

5.4   Since leaving your employment have you got another job?   Yes ☐   No ☑
If 'No', please now go straight to section 5.7.

5.5   Please say when you started (or will start) work.

n/a

5.6   Please say how much you are now earning (or will earn).   £   each

5.7   Please tick the box to say what you want if your case is successful:
   a To get your old job back and compensation (reinstatement)   ☐
   b To get another job with the same employer and compensation (re-engagement)   ☐
   c Compensation only   ☐

6   Discrimination

Please fill in this section only if you believe you have been discriminated against.

6.1 ● Please tick the box or boxes to indicate what discrimination (including victimisation) you
are complaining about:

Sex (including equal pay)	☐	Race	☐
Disability	☑	Religion or belief	☐
Sexual orientation	☐		

6.2 ● Please describe the incidents which you believe amounted to discrimination, the dates of
these incidents and the people involved.

please see attached sheet

7   Redundancy payments

Please fill in this section only if you believe you are owed a redundancy payment.

7.1 • Please explain why you believe you are entitled to this payment and set out the steps you have taken to get it.

8   Other payments you are owed

Please fill in this section only if you believe you are owed other payments.

8.1 • Please tick the box or boxes to indicate that money is owed to you for:

unpaid wages?   ☐
holiday pay?   ☐
notice pay?   ☐
other unpaid amounts?   ☐

8.2   How much are you claiming?

Is this: before tax? ☐   after tax? ☐

8.3 • Please explain why you believe you are entitled to this payment. If you have specified an amount, please set out how you have worked this out.

9   Other complaints

Please fill in this section only if you believe you have a complaint that is not covered elsewhere.

9.1 ● Please explain what you are complaining about and why.
Please include any relevant dates.

10 Other information

10.1 Please do not send a covering letter with this form.
You should add any extra information you want us to know here.

5 additional sheets are attached to this form

11 Your representative

Please fill in this section only if you have appointed a representative. If you do fill this section in, we will in future only send correspondence to your representative and not to you.

11.1 Representative's name:	Natalie Cummings
11.2 Name of the representative's organisation:	North London Law Centre
11.3 Address:	14 Border Street, Shoreditch, London
	Postcode EC2A 1AB
11.4 Phone number:	020 7123 4567
11.5 Reference:	NC/PP/0123
11.6 How would they prefer us to communicate with them?	Post ☐ Fax ☐ E-mail ☑ Fax: E-mail address: ncummings@northlondonlaw.org.uk

Please sign and date here

Signature: *Natalie Cummings*   Date: 20 / 6 / 2007

Data Protection Act 1998. We will send a copy of this form to the respondent(s) and Acas. We will put some of the information you give us on this form onto a computer. This helps us to monitor progress and produce statistics.

P3.11.1 ET1 – constructive dismissal and disability discrimination

IN THE EMPLOYMENT TRIBUNAL   Case No _____ [4]
BRISTOL

BETWEEN

PAULINE PHELPS

Claimant

and

SHARPE, GENTLEMAN & CO SOLICITORS

Respondent

DETAILS OF CLAIM
ET1 SECTION 5.1

---

1. The claimant suffers from depression and agoraphobia and has a facial disfigurement. She has suffered from these conditions for all of her life. She has a disability within the meaning section 1 of the Disability Discrimination Act 1995.

2. The claimant was first employed by Sharpe, Gentleman & Co as a secretary in June 1984. It was a fundamental term of her contract of employment that the respondent would not act in a manner calculated to destroy the trust and confidence that should exist between employer and employee.[5]

3. The claimant was interviewed for the post by Alistair Gentleman and his then secretary, Margaret Church. At the interview she explained that because of her facial disfigurement she was shy with new people and would prefer to work somewhere quiet where she would not have to deal with the public. Mr Gentleman assured her that that would not be a problem. Before she started work she filled in a form for the Respondent about her general health. On the form she indicated that she had suffered from severe depression in the past, but that she was not at that time receiving any treatment.[6]

---

4 The case number is assigned by the tribunal once the claim is received, so the number cannot be given here because it is not known yet.

5 This is an implied term of every contract of employment. Where it is to be relied on it should preferably be spelled out like this.

6 This is included because it is important to establish that the respondent was aware of the claimant's disability.

4. The claimant worked for Mr Gentleman until his retirement in July 2006. She was happy in the role and Mr Gentleman made it clear that he was very satisfied with her work. She sat in an inner office adjoining Mr Gentleman's room on the third floor of the building where she never encountered clients. During the 22 years she worked for Mr Gentleman the claimant never took a day's sick leave. Her depression recurred from time to time and she took anti-depressants for three periods of a year or two each during this time, but she was able to continue working on each occasion. Mr Gentleman was aware of her condition and was understanding if she was depressed or tearful at work.

5. At the time of Mr Gentleman's retirement there were four partners in the firm, 10 further fee-earners, nine secretaries and two part-time receptionists. The claimant and another three secretaries each worked full-time for the four partners, and the other six formed a pool that shared the work generated by the 10 assistant solicitors. The appointment of one of the assistant solicitors, Madeleine Grey, as a new partner had been announced to take effect from September 2006.

6. Mr Sharpe told the claimant that he wanted her to join the pool of secretaries. Members of the pool worked in a large open-plan office on the ground floor of the building and they had to pass through the public waiting room to enter or leave the building or to get to the kitchenette or the toilet. The claimant told Mr Sharpe that she would find this difficult and stressful, but he refused to consider her suggestion that she should work full-time for Miss Grey.

7. The claimant started work in the pool on 16 August 2006. She found it very stressful from the first day. All of the other members of the pool were in their twenties, so at 50 the claimant was the eldest by more than 20 years. The working environment was noisy and the claimant found the other secretaries' conversations distracting. She also became convinced that they disliked her. During the week beginning 16 August, four different temporary secretaries worked in the pool for a day or two each.

8. On 23 August the claimant went to see Mr Sharpe to ask him to move her to a different room. She was distressed and in tears at several points during his meeting. She explained that the environment in the room used by the pool was very difficult for her and was affecting her ability to concentrate on her work, that she had recently started to have difficulty sleeping and that she was worried about the effect on her health. She said that she was afraid she would get depressed again. Mr Sharpe told her that he knew it was a big change

for her but that she had shown herself to be a survivor in the past and he was sure she would get used to it in time.

9. The claimant continued to work for the next few weeks, but became increasingly depressed and anxious. Finally on 20 October 2006 she had a panic attack on the way to work and was picked up by the police shaking and crying at the wheel of her car. She was admitted to hospital for two nights and was then signed off work for 12 weeks by her GP, who also prescribed anti-depressants.

10. When the claimant returned to work on 8 January 2007, the other members of the secretarial pool welcomed her warmly. They had arranged between them to place her desk in a corner partly screened from the rest of the room by pot plants, and she became aware that they were making a real effort to keep noise levels in the room down. The claimant felt better able to cope, but she continued to find the working environment stressful. She was often tearful by the end of the day, and she had difficulty sleeping. She started to work additional hours in the evenings to catch up on work that she felt she should have been able to do during the day.

11. On 16 February 2007 the claimant's GP wrote to Mr Sharpe explaining that the claimant's mental health was suffering from the conditions in which she was working and asking him to consider moving her to a different room. He explained that the claimant was taking anti-depressants and that he did not think it was likely that she would be able to stop taking them unless her work situation improved considerably. Mr Sharpe did not reply to this letter.

12. At the end of February 2007 one of the respondent's receptionists started a period of maternity leave and it was announced that her position would be covered during her absence by the pool secretaries on a rota. When the first rota was circulated on 1 March 2007, the claimant was horrified to see her name on it. She went to see Mr Sharpe in tears and told him that she could not possibly sit at the front desk dealing with members of the public. He told her that it would not be fair on the other secretaries if he took her off the rota and said that it would probably be good for her. He said that as she was obviously upset she should go home straight away that day and get a good night's sleep. He said he hoped she would feel calmer in the morning.

13. The claimant went to see her GP the next day and was signed off sick for 8 weeks.

14. The claimant sent the respondent a written statement of grievance on 9 May 2007 and a letter of resignation on 10 May 2007.

15. The respondent was in breach of the trust and confidence term of the claimant's contract of employment in the following ways:
    (i) in refusing to consider her suggestion that she might work full-time for Miss Grey, despite being aware of the reasons why she was bound to find the secretarial pool a difficult working environment;
    (ii) in refusing on 23 August 2006 to consider moving the claimant to work in a different room despite her evident distress;
    (iii) in failing to reply to the letter of 16 February 2007 from her GP;
    (iv) in imposing on her on 1 March 2005 the requirement that she provide reception cover on a rota despite knowing that this was bound to cause her extreme distress and was likely to be injurious to her health.

16. In presenting her resignation on 10 May 2007 the claimant has accepted the respondent's repudiation of her contract of employment and is therefore constructively dismissed.

17. The respondent's dismissal of the claimant was unfair, and the claimant seeks a basic award and compensation for unfair dismissal.

DETAILS OF CLAIM
ET1 SECTION 6.2

18. The following provisions, criteria or practices adopted by the respondent placed the claimant at a substantial disadvantage in comparison with persons who were not disabled:
    (i) the requirement from August 2006 that the claimant work as a 'pool' secretary instead of being assigned to a specific fee-earner or fee-earners;
    (ii) the requirement from August 2006 that the claimant work in the open-plan office shared by members of the pool;
    (iii) the requirement that she provide reception cover on a rota from March 2007.
19. It was the duty of the respondent to take such steps as it was reasonable in all the circumstances for it to have to take in order to prevent these matters from placing the claimant at a disadvantage. The respondent did not take any such steps and has accordingly discriminated against the claimant contrary to the Disability Discrimination Act 1995.
20. The claimant claims compensation for disability discrimination including damages for injury to feelings and interest.

Natalie Cummings
North London Law Centre
20 June 2007

P3.11.2 ET1 – Whistleblowing dismissal

IN THE EMPLOYMENT TRIBUNAL   Case No _____
LONDON CENTRAL

BETWEEN

SAIFUR RAHMAN

Claimant

and

SAINT JULIAN'S HOSPITAL NHS TRUST

Respondent

PARTICULARS OF CLAIM
ET1 SECTION 5.1

1. The claimant started working for the Hospital as a porter in December 2002. His job was to transport patients and equipment from one part of the hospital to another, as instructed by medical staff.
2. The claimant was employed on an initial probationary period of six months. In about May 2003 he attended a probationary review meeting at which his line manager, Mark Bowland, congratulated him on his performance and told him that his employment would be confirmed. He was given a letter confirming this the next day.
3. There were no further formal appraisals, but the claimant was never given any reason to believe that there were any concerns about his performance, and in November 2003 he was promoted to the position of supervising porter.
4. On 7 May 2007, the claimant was sent to Coventry Ward, a geriatric ward, to collect a patient for physiotherapy. As he reached the ward he heard the Ward Sister, Lorraine Winston, say to a junior nurse 'Give him some Somnex, it's the only way we'll get any peace round here. Don't put it on his chart or the doctor will create.' When the Sister saw that he had heard her she looked embarrassed and said 'Only joking.'
5. The claimant was concerned about this. He knew that Somnex was a powerful prescription sedative, and he thought it sounded as if a patient was being given it without a prescription to keep him quiet. He reported his concerns to Mr Bowland, but Mr Bowland refused to take any action.

6. On 11 May the claimant wrote to the Chief Executive of the Hospital about what he had overheard. This was a protected disclosure within the meaning of section 43A of the Employment Rights Act 1996.

7. On 17 May the Chief Executive replied promising that his allegation would be looked into, and on 24 May the claimant received a letter from Martin Ogunfowora, a human resources manager at the hospital, saying that his allegation had been thoroughly investigated and no evidence of unauthorised medication had been found.

8. On the same day, when the claimant visited the Coventry Ward to collect Mrs Goody for another physiotherapy session, Sister Winston said to him, 'You're toast.' He said 'What do you mean?' but she just said, 'You're toast. Just you wait.'

9. On 28 May 2005 the claimant received a letter dated 25 May from Maisie Lee, another human resources manager. The letter said that he had been accused of swearing at a Sister in the presence of patients and junior nurses and he was suspended with immediate effect and invited to a disciplinary hearing at 10.30 on 4 June 2005. It enclosed copies of statements from Sister Winston and two other nurses from the Coventry Ward. All the statements said that when Sister Winston had asked him why he was late to collect a patient on 22 May he had shouted, 'I've had enough of your fucking nagging. Why don't you take the fucking patient yourself if you're in such a hurry?' The statements said he had then wheeled the patient's pushchair out of the ward so fast that the patient had cried out in alarm, and slammed the door behind him.

10. At the disciplinary hearing on 4 June 2005 the panel refused to believe the claimant when he said that this allegation was completely untrue. When he tried to tell them about the concern he had raised about medication of a patient in the Coventry Ward the chairman of the panel insisted that that was a completely separate matter that had been investigated already and had no relevance to the disciplinary proceedings. When he asked them if they had spoken to Mrs Goody, one member of the panel said that that would have been completely inappropriate.

11. The chairman of the panel asked the claimant if he would apologise to Sister Winston if they decided not to dismiss him. The claimant said that he would not, because the allegation was a complete fabrication.

12. At the end of the disciplinary hearing the claimant was dismissed for gross misconduct. When he asked about an appeal, the chairman told him that the only way an appeal could succeed was if he offered to apologise to Sister Winston. The claimant was not prepared to admit untrue allegations, so when he received the dismissal letter he did not appeal.

13. When the claimant told Penny Short, a student nurse he was friendly with, about his dismissal, she told him that she had seen him collect the patient on 25 May and could have confirmed that he had collected Mrs Goody quietly and without incident. She said that no-one had asked her what she had seen or heard.

14. On 11 June 2007 the claimant started to look for advice on a potential unfair dismissal claim against the Hospital. Between 11 and 15 June he telephoned eight different advice agencies, most of which could not offer him an appointment at all. Finally the Care Workers' Advice Project (CWAP) offered him an appointment on 9 July 2005. He attended that appointment, but on arrival he was told that the adviser he was due to see was off work that day. He was not able to get another appointment until 23 July 2007. On 23 July, the adviser at the CWAP told him that he would have to appeal the decision to dismiss him and wait 28 days before he could present a claim. He was also told that he had until 3 December to present his claim to the tribunal.[7] The adviser also told him that public interest disclosure cases were very complicated and he ought to see a solicitor. She made an appointment for the claimant to see a solicitor at the North London Law Centre at 4pm on 10 September 2007.

15. Accordingly the claim is eight days' out of time. The claimant asserts that it was not reasonably practicable for him to present his claim by 3 September and that he has presented it promptly as soon as he was aware that it was late.

16. The reason or principal reason for the claimant's dismissal was that he had made a protected disclosure and his dismissal was therefore unfair.

17. Further or alternatively the claimant's dismissal was unfair because:
    (i) the respondent did not adequately investigate the allegations against the claimant, and in particular failed to make inquiries of either Mrs Goody or Penny Short;
    (ii) the disciplinary panel was not provided with full information about the reason why Sister Winston might have a grudge against him;
    (iii) he was denied an effective right of appeal.

18. The claimant seeks compensation for unfair dismissal.[8]

North London Law Centre
10 September 2007

---

7 This adviser has clearly heard something about the Employment Act 2002 (Dispute Resolution) Regulations 2004, but has misunderstood them very badly.

8 As Mr Rahman has been dismissed without notice for something that he has not done, he also has a claim for dismissal in breach of his contractual right to notice. This should be included at section 8 of the ET1 form.

P3.11.3 ET1 – race and sex discrimination

IN THE EMPLOYMENT TRIBUNAL   Case No _____
LONDON CENTRAL

BETWEEN

ABOSEDE OJO

Claimant

and

EAST LONDON RIGHTS SHOP

Respondent

PARTICULARS OF CLAIM
ET1 SECTION 6.2

---

1. The claimant is a UK citizen of Nigerian national and ethnic origin. She is a qualified solicitor, admitted in January 2005, and she has worked both before and after qualifying as an immigration adviser. Since March 2006 she has worked full time as an immigration caseworker for the Haringey Refugee Centre, where she earns £21,800 per year.

2. The respondent is a charity that provides free legal advice in immigration, housing, welfare rights, and employment.

3. On 6 February 2007 the respondent's advertisement for an immigration solicitor appeared in the Guardian. The advertisement stated that the minimum requirements for the post were (i) qualification as a solicitor; (ii) at least three years' experience of immigration advice and casework. The advertised salary was £29,200. The closing date for applications was 2 March and interviews were to be held on 12 March.

4. The claimant felt that the job was ideally suited to her, and it was within walking distance of her home. She also felt that in terms of her career development it was time for her to move on to a job that required a qualified solicitor. She requested an application pack, and on 1 March 2007 she hand-delivered her application to the respondent.

5. By 12 March, the claimant had heard nothing further from the respondent, so she concluded that she had been unsuccessful in her application. She was very disappointed not to have been short-listed. On 14 March, she telephoned the respondent to ask for feed-

back on her application. The man she spoke to was abrupt, but told her that her application was badly written and the panel had not found her account of her experience convincing. When she asked him to specify what they had not believed, he said that he was not prepared to continue the conversation. The claimant found this conversation extremely humiliating.

6. Towards the end of March 2007, the claimant met David Burn by chance. The claimant had known Mr Burn when he had worked for her as a volunteer at the Haringey Refugee Centre between April 2005 and May 2006. She discovered in conversation that he had been the successful candidate for the post for which she had applied with the respondent.

7. Mr Burn was only admitted as a solicitor in January 2007 and has not previously worked full-time, paid or unpaid, as an immigration adviser or caseworker.

8. The claimant has substantially more experience of immigration advice and casework than Mr Burn. The claimant believes in failing to shortlist and/or appoint her to the post the respondent has discriminated against her on grounds of race or national or ethnic origin and/or on grounds of sex.

9. The claimant seeks compensation for race and/or sex discrimination, including damages for injury to feelings.

Natalie Cummings
North London Law Centre
20 July 2007

P3.11.4 ET1 – minimum wage

IN THE EMPLOYMENT TRIBUNAL   Case No _____
LONDON CENTRAL

BETWEEN

MICHAEL CHART

Claimant

and

JACK-IN-A-BOX OPERA LIMITED

Respondent

PARTICULARS OF CLAIM
ET1 SECTION 8.3

---

1. The claimant is a singer. On 11 October 2006 he auditioned for a production of *The Pirates of Penzance* put on by the respondent. At the end of the audition, the respondent's artistic director, Peter Jake, offered the claimant a part in the chorus for an initial six week run with the possibility of extension. The claimant accepted this offer.

2. Mr Jake explained that as a chorus member the claimant would be required for six evening performances and two matinees a week. Each performance would last for two hours, and the claimant would be paid £6 per hour.

3. The claimant was told to come to the theatre each afternoon of the week beginning 23 October 2006 for rehearsals. Performances would start on Monday 30 October. The claimant inquired about payment for rehearsals and Mr Jake said that there were separate arrangements for rehearsals which the theatre manager, Martin Joseph would explain.

4. The claimant attended rehearsals during the week beginning 23 October from 2pm until 5pm on Monday to Wednesday. On Thursday and Friday he was required to attend at 12.30 for make-up and costume because these were dress rehearsals.

5. Mr Joseph was not present for the rehearsals until Friday. On Friday the claimant asked him what he would be paid for rehearsal time. Mr Joseph told the him that it was not company policy to pay for rehearsals.

6. At the end of the week all members of the cast were told that they were required at the theatre from 6pm for a 7.30pm call and on Thursdays and Saturdays from 1pm for a 2.30pm call. The performance would last for two hours plus a 20 minute interval. They would be paid £12 per call.

7. The claimant sang in the production throughout the six week run, which was not extended. He usually left the theatre after an evening performance at about 10.05 or 10.10pm, and never earlier than 10pm. He was not free after the matinees until at least 5pm so he worked at least 32 hours each week of the run. He was paid £96 for each week, so he was paid £3 per hour. During the rehearsal week he was required to work 18 hours for no pay.

8. The claimant was entitled to be paid a minimum of £5.35 per hour throughout his working hours in accordance with the National Minimum Wage Act 1999 and Regulations under it. He did not at any time give the respondent written permission to make deductions from his wages, and he has accordingly suffered unauthorised deductions from his wages contrary to section 13 of the Employment Rights Act 1996.

9. The claimant seeks an order that the respondent repay the sums deducted, namely:

Rehearsals
18 hours × £5.35 = £96.30

Performances
32 hours × (£5.35 − £3) = 32 hours × £2.35 = £75.20 per week
£75.20 × 6 weeks = £451.20

Total: £547.50

North London Law Centre
25 December 2007

P3.11.5: ET1 – sex discrimination

IN THE EMPLOYMENT TRIBUNAL   Case No _____
LONDON CENTRAL

BETWEEN

YASMIN CREASEY

Claimant

and

BRISTOL ADVOCACY PROJECT

Respondent

PARTICULARS OF CLAIM
ET1 SECTION 6.2

1. The claimant was employed by the Bristol Advocacy Project (the respondent) as a receptionist and filing clerk. She was told on starting work that she was on a nine month probationary period from 16 April 2007, but no arrangements were made for appraisal or review.
2. On 15 June 2007, the claimant told her line manager, Mary Smiling, that she was four months pregnant.
3. As far as the claimant was aware, her work was satisfactory. All her colleagues seemed friendly towards her and no-one made any complaints.
4. The claimant started her maternity leave on 5 November 2007. On Friday 2 November, her last day at work, her colleagues gave her a card and a bunch of flowers. Mrs Smiling wished her good luck and said 'See you next year.'
5. On 7 January 2008, the claimant received a letter dated 5 January from Reuben Fitzwell, Director of the respondent, informing her that as her performance during her probationary period had been unsatisfactory, her employment would not be confirmed and would accordingly come to an end on 15 January.
6. The respondent discriminated against the claimant on grounds of her sex in that the reason or the principal reason for her dismissal was that she was absent on maternity leave.
7. Alternatively the respondent discriminated against the claimant on grounds of her sex in that, by reason of her absence on maternity

leave, it assessed her probationary performance over the first 7 months of her employment instead of over the full 9 months.[9]

8. The claimant seeks compensation for sex discrimination including damages for injury to feelings and interest.

ET1 SECTION 5.1

9. The claimant's dismissal was automatically unfair in that the reason or the principal reason for her dismissal was her absence on maternity leave.

10. The claimant seeks compensation for unfair dismissal.

North London Law Centre
24 March 2008

---

9   Ms Creasey has no need to lodge an internal grievance in relation to her complaint that the dismissal itself was discriminatory, because the grievance procedures do not apply to dismissals. This alternative complaint is that an act other than dismissal was also discriminatory, so she will have had to present a grievance in relation to that and wait 28 days before presenting her claim to the employment tribunal.

P3.11.6 ET1 – equal pay

IN THE EMPLOYMENT TRIBUNAL   Case No _____
LONDON SOUTH

BETWEEN

ANNE COOPER

Claimant

and

THE BIG OFFICE SUPPLIERS LIMITED

Respondent

DETAILS OF CLAIM
ET1 SECTION 6.2
---

1. The respondent is a supplier of stationery and general office equipment by mail order.
2. The claimant has been employed by the respondent as Manager of their Office Furniture Department since January 1996.
3. The claimant is employed on like work with Andrew Blight, her predecessor.
4. Alternatively the claimant is employed on work of equal or greater value to that performed by:
   • Marcus Plange, Manager of the respondent's Stationery Department;
   • Andrew Sharpe, Marketing Department; and
   • Timothy Carter, a member of her staff employed part-time in the Office Furniture Department and part-time in the Stationery Department.
   • Andrew Blight, Marcus Plange, Andrew Sharpe and Timothy Carter are referred to collectively as 'the comparators' in this document.
5. The claimant's contract of employment must be deemed to include an equality clause having the effect that if any term of her contract of employment is less favourable than the corresponding term of any of the comparators' contracts, her contract is deemed to be modified so as not to be less favourable.

6. The claimant complains of contraventions of the equality term in relation to each of the four comparators.
7. The claimant was at the time of her appointment as Manager offered £20,800 per annum;
8. the claimant believes that OP, AS and JB were all paid in the region of £25,000 per annum around the time of her appointment;
9. the claimant believes that TC, a member of her staff, has been paid more than her since his appointment to her department in about May or June 1997;
10. Mr S had a company car when he worked for the respondent, but the claimant has at no time been offered a car;
11. From 2000 until 2004, the respondent refused to pay the claimant's mobile telephone bills although it paid bills in comparable circumstances for all four comparators.
12. The claimant will provide further particulars of these comparisons after disclosure of documents.

North London Law Centre
17 January 2008

Rejection of the claim

3.12   The tribunal will reject a claim in four circumstances:

- in all claims presented on or after 1 October 2005 where the claim is not presented on the prescribed form (ET 1);
- where any of the required information has not been included (that is, where any question marked * on the form has not been answered, and where any relevant question marked l has not been answered);
- where the tribunal does not have power to consider the claim; or
- if a grievance procedure is required to be followed before the claim is presented, where either no grievance has been sent to the employer or the claim is made before 28 days have elapsed since the grievance was presented.

3.13   The potential rejection of a claim means that it is very important to present claims as early as possible, subject to the need in some cases to wait 28 days after sending the employer a written statement of grievance. If a claim is rejected as premature because the claimant has not presented a grievance or has not waited 28 days after doing so, rejection will not be disastrous: the claimant will simply have to lodge a grievance and then present the claim again in due course, and the premature presentation of the claim will have had the result of extending time for a further three months from the normal time limit for the claim.

3.14   The requirement that the claim be presented on the prescribed form can cause unexpected difficulty. A good deal of emphasis has been placed on the forms being the correct size.[10] This means that photocopies from forms reproduced in books are no longer acceptable. It has also resulted in at least one claim being rejected on the grounds that the forms had supposedly 'shrunk in the fax'.[11] It is safest to submit only on an original form or electronically through the tribunal web-site.

3.15   Rejection on the grounds that the tribunal does not have power to consider the claim need not be fatal either: if the tribunal's entitlement to consider the claim is in doubt, then that question will have to be considered at some point, so there is no particular disadvantage to the claimant in having it made the subject of a decision at a preliminary stage. If the claimant believes that the claim has been wrongly rejected on this ground, she should apply for review of the decision under rule 34 of the Procedure Rules, and if necessary appeal to the Employment Appeal Tribunal.

10 Presumably to facilitate digital scanning by the tribunal.
11 Although overturned on appeal: *Grant v In 2 Focus Sales Development Services Ltd* [2007] UKEAT/0310/06.

P3.15 Application for review of the decision to reject a claim

In Mr Rahman's unfair dismissal case, the tribunal has rejected his claim as being presented late.[12] He applies for a review of that decision because although he admits that the claim is late, he says that it was not reasonably practicable for him to present it in time.

The Regional Secretary
London Central Employment Tribunal
19–29 Woburn Place
London WC1X 0LU
My ref NC/ir123

Your ref 123456/04

FAX ONLY 020 7273 8686

27 September 2007

Dear Madam

Saifur Rahman v St Julian's Hospital NHS Trust

Thank you for your letter of 26 September 2007.[13]

I wish to apply for a review of the decision to reject the claim on the grounds that it was wrongly made as a result of an administrative error and/or that the interests of justice require a review.

Administrative error
The narrative section at box 5.2 of the form ET1 explains that Mr Rahman was unable to present his claim in time because of difficulty, despite his strenuous efforts, in getting prompt and accurate advice. He asserts that in the circumstances it was not reasonably practicable for him to present his claim in time. It seems likely that the explanation given by Mr Rahman for the lateness of his claim on his ET1 form was simply overlooked when the decision was made to reject the claim on the ground that the tribunal lacked jurisdiction to hear it.

---

12 See P3.11.2 above.
13 The notification that the claim was rejected.

The interests of justice

The account given by Mr Rahman of the reasons why his claim was presented late is credible and convincing. The question whether it was reasonably practicable for him to present his claim is one that cannot fairly be resolved against him without hearing his oral evidence on the subject. In the circumstances it is suggested that the interests of justice require a review in order for this question to be properly explored.

Yours faithfully

Natalie Cummings

Rejection for lack of relevant required information

3.16 The potential for rejection on the ground that the form does not contain all the relevant required information is the most troubling ground of rejection for claimants. A failure by simple oversight to include one piece of required information can have the result that the claim is rejected. If the claim has been presented close to the deadline, it may be too late to correct an error of this nature by the time the tribunal has communicated its decision to reject.

3.17 This means that the form has to be completed with very great care, with particularly close attention paid to each question marked * or ●. Where the claimant is in any doubt whether a particular question marked ● is relevant, she should answer it to the best of her ability in case the tribunal takes the view that it is. If at all possible, claim forms should be presented to the tribunal several weeks before the expiry of the relevant deadline so as to allow time for presentation of a corrected claim within time if the original claim is rejected.

3.18 If, despite these efforts, a claim is presented without the necessary information, the omission may not be fatal. The tribunal should consider whether an ET1 makes it clear that a right that the tribunal has jurisdiction over has been breached. If this is clear, the form is sufficient.[14] Although this approach appears to relax the rule to near irrelevance, it is of course preferable to ensure that all the required information is included and avoid any need to argue about the scope of the rule.

14 *Grimmer v KLM Cityhopper UK* [2005] IRLR 596.

3.19   If a claim is rejected on this ground close to the deadline with the result that the corrected claim is inevitably late, it may sometimes be possible to persuade the tribunal that in all the circumstances (especially if the claimant was not receiving any advice at the time of the first attempt) it was not reasonably practicable to present the claim, or that it is just and equitable to extend time.[15] Again, it is better to avoid these arguments.

Amendment of the claim

3.20   Sometimes it becomes clear, after a claim has been started, that the original claim form does not adequately explain the basis of the claim, or that additional claims need to be added. The tribunal has power under rule 10(q) of the Procedure Rules to permit amendment of a claim or response. There is a significant amount of case law on the question of whether and in what circumstances the tribunal should permit a claimant to amend his or her claim. The detail of that is beyond the scope of this book, but some tactical points are worth making here.[16]

3.21   Broadly, amendments close to the hearing will be harder to secure than amendments made soon after the claim was started, and more substantial amendments will be harder to secure than minor ones. If a claim has to be presented in a hurry because the time limit is close, it is legitimate to draft the bare bones of the claim in order to present it in time, but if this is done, an amendment fleshing out the claim should be forwarded to the tribunal as soon as possible. In these circumstances a note should be included in box 10 explaining that further details will follow shortly, and possibly suggesting that the respondent should not be required to present its response until after that step has been taken.

3.22   This tactic should only be used if there is genuine urgency. Where it is used, the claim, however brief, must still make it clear what is the nature of the complaint. Some employee advisers believe that if a client presents with a complaint about discrimination, a claim merely alleging 'race discrimination' or 'sex discrimination', etc, should always

15   For some claims (for example, unfair dismissal) it is necessary to persuade the tribunal that it was not reasonably practicable to present the claim in time if time is to be extended; in other cases (for example, discrimination claims) it is only necessary to persuade the tribunal that in all the circumstances it is 'just and equitable' to extend time.

16   See ETP 3 chapter 7 for the detailed rules.

be faxed to the tribunal the same day, with a promise of 'full details to follow,' to guard against the possibility that the time limit in respect of any particular act may be about to expire. This is probably futile, and certainly dangerous. A claim that gives no clue as to what is the nature of the discrimination alleged is at risk of being rejected outright as invalid, and will do nothing to preserve the claimant's position. What it may do is give the claimant or adviser a false sense that there is now no urgency for a properly pleaded claim.

3.23   If the claim really has to be presented in a great hurry (for example, where the claimant comes to a law centre for advice on the last day of the limitation period), it may be very short, but it should not lack content altogether. The following words in boxes 5.1 and 6.2 of the claim form should be sufficient to start Mrs Creasy's claim.[17]

> **5.1**
> I was dismissed on 14 January 2005, during my maternity leave. I believe that the reason for my dismissal was that I was on maternity leave, so my dismissal was automatically unfair.
>
> **6.2**
> I believe that the reasons for my dismissal was that I was on maternity leave, so my employer's conduct in dismissing me amounted to sex discrimination.

This, on the other hand, is inadequate.

> **5.1**
> Unfair dismissal: full details to follow.
>
> **6.2**
> Sex discrimination: full details to follow

17 See P3.11.5 above.

Late amendments

3.24   The main danger with a late application for amendment is that it will be refused on the basis that there is insufficient time before the hearing for the respondent to deal with the changes. The other danger is that it will be granted, but that the case will be postponed or adjourned in order to allow the respondent to deal with the changes.[18] In these circumstances a costs or preparation time order may be made in favour of the respondent.

3.25   Under rule 40 of the Procedure Rules, the tribunal has power to order one party to pay to the other side the costs incurred by reason of a postponement or adjournment, and in contrast to the general power to award costs, there is no requirement that the tribunal should be satisfied that the paying party has behaved unreasonably or improperly before making such an order. Tribunals have been slow to make costs orders except against parties they consider to have been at fault in some way, but this is a reason for particular caution when applying for permission to amend.

3.26   An amendment to add a completely new claim is likely to run into time limit difficulties and may well require a postponement of the hearing in order to permit the respondent to deal with the new allegations.[19] The claimant should be realistic about this: the best chance of heading off a costs application in these circumstances will lie in a co-operative approach.

3.27   A worse complication that could now be caused by an amendment to add a new claim is the possibility that it will give rise to the need to raise a fresh grievance and wait 28 days before seeking the amendment. It is to be hoped that faced with this kind of situation tribunals will be prepared to take a broad view of the question whether a particular 'matter' has been raised by way of a grievance and will not insist on proceedings being held up while a fresh grievance procedure runs its course, but this cannot be guaranteed. If the amendment constitutes a large proportion of the total claim, it may be better to raise the difficulty and invite the tribunal to deal with it at an early stage than to run the risk that the respondent thinks of it just before the

---

18   A hearing is usually said to have been 'postponed' if it has been put off to a later date before it started; if the parties attend on the hearing date and it is then decided either before the hearing starts or part-way through it that it needs to be put off to another day, it is said to have been 'adjourned'.

19   See ETP 3 paras 7.4–7.7.

hearing – or even during it – and this causes delay and inconvenience on all sides.

3.28   An application to amend that changes the way the claimant puts her case without starting a fresh complaint should address if possible both the reasons why the amendment could not have been made sooner, and the impact it will have on the respondent's preparation.

DOCUMENT OUTLINE: Application for permission to amend to change the basis of the claim

Identification of the nature of the application – that is, application for permission to amend under rule 10(q) of the Procedure Rules

Terms of amendment sought

Explanation why the claim could not have been/was not pleaded in this way originally and/or why the amendment could not have been sought earlier

Reason(s) why the application should be granted including explanation of how this will enable the tribunal to deal with the case efficiently and fairly

Any consequential matters – for example, request for consequential postponement, or suggestion if appropriate that the respondent should have extra time for some step it needs to take

Instructions for the respondent on when and how to oppose the application

P3.28.1 Application for permission to amend the basis of the claim

The claimant here has applied unsuccessfully for a job with the respondent. She believes that she is better qualified than the successful male candidate, and she has already presented a claim form complaining of direct sex discrimination. She has now discovered that the respondent has a policy that gives internal candidates preferential treatment over external candidates. The Department employs far more men than women in positions from which they could realistically apply for a post of the relevant kind, so she now seeks to amend her claim to include a complaint of indirect discrimination.

The Regional Secretary
London Central Employment Tribunal
Ground floor, Victory House
30-34 Kingsway
London
WC2B 6EX

My ref: NC/ir 123
Your ref: 123456/06

FAX ONLY 020 7273 8686

22 January 2008

Dear Madam

Annabel Firsk v Department for Administrative Affairs

1. Request for permission to amend the claim

I should be grateful if you would put before a Chairman my request for permission under rule 10(q) of the Employment Tribunal Rules of Procedure to amend this claim to insert at the end of the narrative at box 6.2 the following:[20]

'The minimum requirements for the post of Senior Operational Officer were (a) at least two years' relevant experience and (b) a postgraduate qualification in Administrative Policy.

---

20   Or the text of the amendment could be attached as a separate sheet or sheets.

The respondent's Recruitment and Retention Policy states, at 6.1:

> 'All posts will be advertised internally and externally. Internal candidates will be considered first. Any internal candidate will be considered on the basis of his written application together with the comments of his line manager and one other internal referee at the candidate's option. Interviews may be held. If the Recruiting Manager is satisfied that the needs of the Department will be met by the appointment of an internal candidate, he will appoint an internal candidate without considering external candidates. In this event external candidates will be informed that their applications have been unsuccessful.
>
> If no appointment is made from among internal candidates, the Recruiting Manager will proceed to consider external candidates. External candidates will be considered on the basis of their written application and their performance at interview. References will be taken up only after a provisional decision to appoint has been made.'

Of those already in the respondent's employment capable of meeting the minimum requirements for the post, 100% were men at the material time. It follows that the respondent's policy of preferring internal over external candidates was a provision, criterion or practice which was such that it was to the detriment of a considerably larger proportion of women than of men, and it was to the detriment of the claimant because it meant that she was not permitted to compete on equal terms with internal candidates, and the respondent's policy was therefore indirectly discriminatory against the claimant on grounds of sex.[21]

It was not possible for the claimant to plead her complaint in this way when she presented her original claim because she was not aware of the respondent's preferential treatment of internal candidates until 12 January 2007 when she received a copy of the respondent's recruitment procedure.

This amendment will assist the tribunal in dealing with the case efficiently and fairly because (i) it clarifies the issues between the parties; and

---

21 It is not completely clear that it does follow, but it is arguable.

(ii) the prejudice to the claimant from a refusal of the application and depriving her of a significant part of her claim would be less than any prejudice to the respondent flowing from permitting the amendment.[22]

2. Request for consequential postponement

If this amendment is permitted, it is clear that the respondent will need time to make consequential amendments to its response, and both parties will have to reconsider what evidence they should call. In the circumstances I suggest that the hearing listed for 11-15 February 2008 should be postponed. It might be helpful to list the case for a directions hearing instead on the first day of that appointment.

3. Objection by the respondent[23]

This letter is copied to the respondent. The respondent should note that if it objects to the application, it must write to the tribunal within seven days of receiving this letter, or before the date of the hearing (whichever date is the earlier) explaining the reasons for its objection, and should copy that letter to me.[24] Rule 11 of the Procedure Rules has been complied with in relation to this application.

Yours faithfully

Natalie Cummings

---

22 Rule 11(3) of the Procedure Rules requires a statement of 'how the application will assist the chairman or tribunal in dealing with the case efficiently and fairly' to be included in every interlocutory application. The provision is illjudged, and inevitably invites bland and formulaic treatment. This statement or something very like it will be adequate for most if not all amendment applications.

23 This paragraph, or something to the same effect, is required by rule 11 if the claimant is legally represented, and desirable in any event.

24 This quotes rule 11(4)(b). The rule is unsatisfactory, because it is not clear whether the alternative date to 'within seven days of receiving' the letter is merely 'before the hearing' or 'seven days before the hearing'. However, the party applying for an order cannot be faulted for giving the respondent ambiguous instructions if the ambiguity is the ambiguity of the rules themselves. The instruction should be to copy the objection to all other parties if there are more than two.

P3.28.2 Application for amendment to add an alternative basis for the claim

The Regional Secretary
London Central Employment Tribunal
Ground floor, Victory House
30-34 Kingsway
London
WC2B 6EX

My ref: NC/ir 123
Your ref: 123456/06

FAX ONLY 020 7273 8686

15 March 2007

Dear Madam

Michael O'Donnell v Robert Selassiee t/a Flower Power

I should be grateful if you would put before a Chairman my request for permission to amend the claim in this case to delete the contents of box 5.1 and substitute the following:[25]

1. The claimant started work as a florist at the respondent's shop on 5 March 2007.
2. There was no written contract, but it was a fundamental term of the oral contract, alternatively an implied term, that the claimant was employed to work as a florist in the shop. His duties were making up bouquets and wreaths, selling flowers, advising customers on their purchases, unpacking and displaying new deliveries and ordering flowers from wholesalers. He enjoyed the work and was good at it.
3. It was an implied term of the claimant's contract of employment that the respondent would not conduct himself in a way calculated to destroy the mutual trust and confidence that should exist between employer and employee.
4. The claimant travels to work by Tube on the Northern Line, which is often subject to delays. The respondent was mostly understanding about this, but during the week beginning 14

---

25 It will often be possible simply to add a paragraph or two to the existing text, but sometimes the end result will be clearer if the whole claim is rewritten.

November 2006 the claimant was delayed on four out of five days. When the claimant arrived 10 minutes late for work on Thursday 17 November, the respondent complained about his time-keeping and threatened to put him on deliveries if he did not improve.

5.   On Monday 21 November the claimant left home half an hour earlier than usual in order to be sure to be at work on time, but his train was held up in a tunnel for 45 minutes because of a bomb alert. When he arrived at work 20 minutes late, the respondent told him that he was on deliveries this week. The claimant objected, and the respondent said 'You can either do the deliveries or you can bugger off and not come back.' The claimant was not prepared to be employed as a delivery driver, so he collected his coat and went home.

6.   In the circumstances the respondent summarily dismissed the claimant from his job as a florist without any prior formal warnings and without following any disciplinary procedure. The dismissal was accordingly unfair.

7.   Alternatively, in ordering the claimant to work for as a delivery driver, the respondent was in breach of the terms of the claimant's contract of employment referred to at paragraphs 2 and 3 above. In leaving the premises on 21 November and not returning, the claimant resigned in response to the respondent's fundamental breach of his contract of employment and was accordingly constructively dismissed. The dismissal was not preceded by any formal warnings or any disciplinary procedure and was accordingly unfair.

8.   The claimant seeks basic and compensatory awards for unfair dismissal.

It was not possible to make this amendment earlier because the claimant presented his claim without the benefit of legal advice. His belief was that he had been constructively dismissed. It was not until he instructed me, at our first appointment on 16 January 2007, that I was in a position to advise him that his case is probably better characterised as actual dismissal.

The facts alleged by Mr O'Donnell are simple. These facts, if proved, are on any view close to the borderline between actual and constructive dismissal. The factual allegations appeared in full in the original claim. The respondent has denied that Mr Selassie issued an ultimatum and claims that he simply asked Mr O'Donnell, as a favour, to cover the deliveries that day but made no attempt to insist that he should do so. According to the respondent, Mr O'Donnell lost his temper for no obvious reason and stormed out.

The amendment, if permitted, will make little or no difference to the manner in which the respondent puts its case or the witnesses it needs to call. In the circumstances I suggest that although the hearing is only three weeks away, there can be no need for a postponement or for any consequential amendment of the respondent's response.

This amendment will assist the tribunal in dealing with the case efficiently and fairly because it would be unfair to the claimant if the claim were defeated by reason of a technical failure to characterise the dismissal correctly at the outset.

This letter is copied to the respondent. The respondent should note that if it objects to the application, it must write to the tribunal within seven days of receiving this letter, or before the date of the hearing (whichever date is the earlier) explaining the reasons for its objection, and should copy that letter to me.[26] Rule 11 of the Procedure Rules has been complied with in relation to this application.

Yours faithfully

Natalie Cummings

---

26 See note 23 above.

CHAPTER 4

Getting information from the other side

Introduction

4.1 There are essentially four tailor-made ways of getting information from the other side in the context of employment tribunal proceedings, plus two other mechanisms of wider application that may occasionally be of use in this context.

4.2 Of the first four, three come from the employment tribunals' general powers under the tribunal rules of procedure[1]. The fourth, available in discrimination cases only, is the service of a questionnaire. The fifth is a subject access request under the Data Protection Act 1998. A sixth, of which claimants may occasionally be able to take advantage is a request under the Freedom of Information Act (FOIA) 2000, in force from 1 January 2005. A claimant cannot demand personal information about him- or herself under the FOIA 2000, but it is possible to imagine circumstances in which an FOIA 2000 request could assist with, for example, a claim under the public interest disclosure ('whistleblowing') provisions of the Employment Rights Act (ERA) 1996.[2]

4.3 This chapter starts with general guidance about the first three of these taken together before considering disclosure of documents, requests for additional information and requests for written answers separately. Requests for orders for all three categories of information are then taken together. The last two sections of the chapter deal with questionnaires and the Data Protection Act (DPA) 1998 and then providing information to the respondent.

The tribunal's powers

4.4 The relevant powers of the tribunal are contained at rule 10(2)(b),(d) and (f) of the Procedure Rules, which give the tribunals specific powers to order a party to provide additional information, to disclose documents or information to another party, or to provide written answers to questions put by the tribunal.

---

1 Schedule 1 to the Employment Tribunals (Constitution and Rules of Procedure) Regulations 2004.

2 See the *Law of Freedom of Information* by John Macdonald QC and Clive Jones (OUP, 2003); *Information Rights* by Philip Coppel (Sweet & Maxwell, 2004); and Part IV of *Computer Law: The Law and Regulation of Information Technology* edited by Chris Reed and John Angel (OUP, 2007).

4.5   The term 'additional information' at rule 10(2)(b) replaces the expression 'further particulars' in earlier versions of the rules. This is presumably an attempt at 'plain English,' but an unfortunate one because it blurs a distinction that was useful. The distinction is between what used to be called 'further particulars' on the one hand, and written answers to questions put by the tribunal on the other.[3] A request for further particulars of a formal claim or the respondent's response was a request that the other party clarify some assertion that they have made in their document. A request for written answers was a free-standing request that they provide relevant information. In other words, the former was a question whose gist was 'When you say XYZ, what do you mean?' The latter was a question that did not refer to or seek clarification of something the other party had already said.

4.6   The power to order written answers to questions remains at rule 10(2)(f) of the Procedure Rules, so presumably the distinction was intended to persist. In practice it will rarely if ever matter very much whether a request is expressed as a request for additional information or written answers: what does matter is that it is clear what information is sought.

Requests generally

4.7   Requests for documents, additional information and written answers should be kept to what is relevant to something in dispute between the parties. Long requests of questionable relevance will be liable to be refused by the respondent, and the tribunal is unlikely to grant an order. The temptation to cross-examine by correspondence should be resisted,[4] as should the temptation to seek an unnecessary level of detail. Requests drafted by solicitors tend to be sprinkled with expressions like 'with full particularity,' 'giving the precise time of each meeting', 'giving the exact words used' and so on, but this is often futile. It is rare that witnesses will remember the exact words of an oral exchange or the precise time of anything; and rarer still that this level of detail will matter.

---

3 The rule refers to questions put by the tribunal, but this power is most often used at the request of one party or the other: the tribunal puts questions to one party at the request of the other.

4 See para 4.12.

4.8   Questions and requests should be asked one at a time and numbered (not bulleted), so that if the respondent gives adequate answers to some but not others it is easy to identify, in asking the tribunal to order the respondent to answer, which questions have yet to be dealt with. Questions should be put one at a time, and should be short, clear and concrete. Often the aim will be to force a respondent whose ET 3 is drafted in vague generalisations ('an incident occurred', 'steps were taken', 'the claimant was abusive' and so on) to be specific about who did what, when, and what the consequence was. It is helpful to keep the different kinds of request separate: then the application for an order can refer to the correct sub-paragraph of rule 10 of the Procedure Rules in relation to each request or group of requests.

4.9   The letter should specify a date by which responses are required, and should warn that an order will be sought from the tribunal if that deadline is not met. If there is no particular reason for a longer or shorter period, 14 days is a standard period to allow. If the request is made close to the hearing date, a shorter period may be inevitable. If the request is for information or documents which is likely to cause the respondent and/or their advisers substantial work, it is sensible to allow a longer period if possible. The closer the hearing, and the more extensive the requests, the less likely the tribunal is to grant an order, so these requests should always be made as soon as possible after the response is received and carefully limited to what is genuinely relevant.[5]

4.10   Sometimes a late request is unavoidable. If the claimant's adviser realises four weeks before the hearing that a substantial request is called for, there may be a tension between giving the respondent a realistic time to comply, on one hand, and still being in a position to ask the tribunal for an order if they refuse, on the other. The best solution is probably to ask the respondent for an indication by return if it is unwilling to answer any of the requests. Then if it does so, the claimant's adviser can seek an order straight away. If it does not, but the answer when it comes is incomplete, the claimant's adviser may be able to persuade the tribunal to make a last minute order on the grounds that it is the respondent's fault that the application is made late.

---

5   One of the authors once asked the Royal Mail for a year's sickness records for 'all employees,' forgetting to limit the request to comparable employees at the depot at which the claimant was employed. The response was an amused 'How many articulated lorry-loads do you think that will be?'

Deciding what to ask for

4.11   The best starting point for a request for disclosure, additional information and/or written answers is the response. It is a useful exercise
to go through the ET3 line by line, checking for ambiguous or incomplete statements and documents that may or must exist. The following precedent is an employer's response to a claim annotated with
thoughts about the requests or questions that it suggests: see P4.23.2
below for the resulting request. A similar exercise can be done with the
formal claim and any other relevant documents the claimant already
has. It is convenient to deal with requests for documents, and requests
for additional information and written answers together at this stage:
often there will be both a question to ask and a document that may
exist. The exercise is also likely to throw up questions that do not need
to be put to the respondent because the client can answer them, and
other questions that are better saved for cross-examination than asked
in advance in correspondence. See para 4.12 below for how to approach
the choice between these two.

**P4.11 Employer's response to claim annotated for disclo-
sure requests**

IN THE EMPLOYMENT TRIBUNAL   Case No 123456/06
LONDON SOUTH

BETWEEN

CLAUDIA CHAMPION

Claimant

and

THE MINISTRY OF TRUTH

Respondent

_____

GROUNDS OF RESISTANCE

1. Paragraphs 1 and 2 of the claim are
    admitted.

2. In or around May 2005 the respondent's senior management team decided that for operational reasons it was desirable to merge the Croydon and Guildford Area Managers' Offices.

> Who took the decision? Written proposals, discussion papers, memos, agendas and minutes of relevant meetings; all email correspondence leading up to the decision, etc.

3. Detailed consultations took place with all staff who were likely to be affected by the proposed reorganisation. The claimant told James Petrie, the Regional Administrator in a meeting on 30 June 2005, that she had for some time been hoping for an operational position, ideally as Department Manager of the Central London Information Unit. She specifically said that she did not want to continue working in the Area Manager's Office after the reorganisation.

> Who was consulted? When, how, and by whom? All documentation of consultation process.

> Any note or minute of that meeting.

4. Suitable arrangements were made to locate a suitable post at the claimant's grade into which to transfer her. Mr Petrie consulted colleagues and formed the view that the claimant needed to improve her skills before being ready to be appointed to an operational post.

> Who did what? When? With what results?

> minutes of any meetings, file notes of any conversations, any email traffic.

> What skills did she need to develop?

5. The respondent identified as suitable a post at the Croydon Information Centre, but the claimant told Mr Petrie that she was not prepared to work at that location. To try to resolve the situation, Mr Petrie arranged to meet with the claimant on 28 September 2005 for a discussion of the remaining options. In the course of that meeting, Mr Petrie told the claimant that it was his view, shared with other members of the Management Team, that she would

> Any note or minute of that meeting.

not be ready for a Department Manager post until she had been through a re-training programme.

6. Mr Petrie met with the claimant again on 19 October 2005 Mr Petrie told the claimant what arrangements had been made for training to equip her to take up an operational post, and he promised her that in March 2006 he would take a final decision as to her permanent redeployment.

> Any note or minute of that meeting; Mr Petrie's diary entry.

> What training?

7. The respondent denies that the claimant was at any time redundant. She was employed in a post from which she could have been redeployed anywhere in the UK. There were vacant positions at her level in several different locations to which she could have been appointed had she requested redeployment.

8. The respondent denies that it acted in breach of the claimant's contract of employment as alleged or at all.

Written requests and cross-examination

4.12 There are always decisions to be taken about whether to seek information before the hearing by way of a request for further particulars or written answers, or to save it for cross-examination. The best way of approaching this is to think about what the question is for, and how the answers will differ depending on the circumstances in which the question is asked. For example: the question 'How many of the staff of grade C3 and above are women?' asked in cross-examination may elicit the answer 'Well of course I don't have exact figures, but I'd say about half.' This will be very difficult for the claimant to challenge during the hearing unless she herself can list the staff at that level. A request in advance for a list of all staff, showing grade and sex, makes it much more difficult for the employer to give anything but a straight and truthful answer.

4.13 On the other hand, if the question is put in correspondence 'What factors did the dismissing manager consider before deciding to dismiss?' the likely answer will be a textbook account, drafted by a lawyer, of all the relevant and proper considerations that the manager should have had in mind. By the time of the hearing, the manager in question, having read this, may well have persuaded herself that she did indeed have all those things in mind. The same question put to the manager for the first time in cross-examination may produce a floundering (and therefore extremely helpful) demonstration that she did not have a clue what she ought to consider, and did not – for example – give the claimant any credit for his long unblemished service, or trouble to acquaint herself with his performance and past appraisal records.

4.14   As a rule of thumb, if the question is designed to get hard information that the claimant does not know without asking, it is probably best to make it the subject of a request for additional information or written answers. If the claimant does not know the answer, and it could be damaging to his case, then it should almost certainly be asked, if at all, in correspondence. If the aim is to embarrass a witness or get them to make a useful admission, or give them an opportunity to say something foolish, it is best to save it for cross-examination.

4.15   When requesting further detail of something that has been said in the employer's response, it is conventional – and helpful – to quote the relevant part so that the request can be read as a single self-contained document: that is, the reader can see what each question is getting at without having to refer back to the response. See P3.47 for an example of how a request can be laid out.

Disclosure of documents[5]

4.16   There are two distinct ways in which the tribunal may approach disclosure of documents. One is to follow the practice that is prescribed by the Civil Procedure Rules in the ordinary courts. Here each party first provides the other (or others) with a list of all documents in its power or possession that are relevant to any of the questions to be resolved in the proceedings, and says which of those documents are privileged[7] and exempt from disclosure. This is followed either by provision of copies

---

6   Disclosure was called 'discovery' in previous versions of the rules, and practitioners are likely to continue to use the two terms interchangeably for some time.

7   See para 4.29.

of those documents that the other party does not already have or the opportunity to view them and take copies.[8]

4.17   Alternatively, the tribunal may simply direct that each party must send the other copies of all of the documents on which it intends to rely at the hearing. This is simpler and cheaper for the parties as it does not require them to conduct a search for relevant documents, draw up long lists, and admit to the existence of documents they do not particularly wish to disclose. The downside, especially for the employee (since in most employment cases the great bulk of relevant documents will be in the hands of the employer), is that the simpler process may fail to turn up relevant and helpful documents because the employer, having no intention of relying on them at the hearing itself, is not obliged to and does not choose to disclose them. It is suggested, therefore, that claimants' advisers should get into the habit of asking the respondent for all relevant (non-privileged) documents in their possession or control, and asking the tribunal to make an order in those terms if the respondent refuses.

4.18   If an order for general disclosure has been made, then both parties have a serious obligation to comply with it fully and honestly, and in particular not to suppress relevant documents which they regard as embarrassing or harmful to their case. The tribunal can be expected to take a dim view of any failure to make full disclosure that emerges at the hearing, especially by a party that has been professionally represented, and legal representatives have their own duty to ensure that their clients understand and have complied with the duty of disclosure. See 4.65 below on the claimant's duty of disclosure.

4.19   Even if an order for general disclosure has been made, the claimant's adviser should never assume that the duty has been properly complied with on the other side. The duty is poorly understood by non-lawyers, and often inadequately explained by lawyers to their clients. It will almost always be necessary to make specific requests for documents that the respondent does not deem relevant, or to whose relevance it has not turned its mind.

4.20   If no order for general disclosure has been made, there is no reason why the claimant should not nevertheless ask the respondent to carry out a search for all relevant documents, and ask it to confirm that it has done so.

---

8 The latter is inconvenient, and it is fairly rare for parties to choose to do it: normally parties simply send each other copies of the relevant documents in their possession.

Checklist for disclosure request

4.21   All organisations document their work differently, so there could be no comprehensive list of the kinds of documents that it might be helpful to request. The following lists may serve as a helpful reminder of some of the possibilities, however. Again, requests for documents and requests for information are closely related, and sometimes one will suggest the other.

General

- company or staff handbook
- contract of employment
- statement of particulars of employment
- claimant's personnel file
- requests from managers for human resources (HR) advice
- HR advice on conduct of interview, consultation or disciplinary meeting[9]
- letters
- memos
- file notes
- e-mails
- minutes of disciplinary or appeal meetings (including any hand-written notes taken at the time)
- minutes of other relevant meetings
- appraisal records
- reports
- discussion papers
- diary entries (including electronic diaries)
- log-books
- timesheets
- rotas
- pay records
- sales records
- receipts
- accounts
- bank statements

9 Employers may wish to claim privilege in respect of internal personnel or HR advice. Communications with in-house lawyers are privileged, but advice from personnel professionals who are not qualified lawyers is not and should be disclosed: see para 4.33 below.

- clocking records
- tacograph records
- insurance claims
- accident book
- order book
- telephone bills
- call logs (some organisations log each telephone call received in a book held at reception)
- text messages
- 'history' or 'statistics' files associated with any suspect document[10]

Redundancy

- redundancy policy
- redeployment policy
- personnel records of other employees[11]
- redundancy selection criteria
- written records of process leading to decision to make redundancy
- other employee's score sheets from the redundancy section[12]

Discrimination (especially recruitment discrimination)

- application forms, including the application forms of other candidates for the post
- job advertisements (it may also be useful to find out where the advertisements were placed)

---

10 see paras 4.27–4.28 below.
11 Employers will often be reluctant to provide this on 'confidentiality' grounds; sometimes they will refer to the Data Protection Act 1998. Sometimes identifying details can be deleted from confidential documents, but if information about another employee is important then the tribunal should be willing to order discovery even if the employee says it is 'confidential'. The Data Protection Act 1998 does not prevent disclosure of relevant documents in legal proceedings and is irrelevant: employers who seek to rely on it for this purpose should be asked to quote the specific provisions they rely on. If necessary, the tribunal has power to hold a hearing in private for the purpose of hearing evidence that has been communicated to the witness in confidence: Procedure Rules r16.
12 There is likely to be a tussle for these, which the employee will often lose. Claimants should read *British Aerospace plc v Green* [1995] IRLR 433, CA and be ready to deal with the argument that the score sheets of other candidates are not relevant. There will be a better chance of obtaining them if very specific allegations can be made of the respects in which certain other employees must have been scored over-generously.

- person specification
- job description/role specification
- interview notes and/or score sheets
- written guidance for interview panel
- equal opportunities policy

4.22 The employee himself will usually be an excellent source of information about the kind of question it is useful to ask, and the kind of documents her employer may have. The trick, for an adviser, is to harness your own knowledge of how to get information out of an employer with the claimant's knowledge of his employer's working practices. One technique is simply to remember to ask questions like 'How can we prove that?' and 'What records does the employer keep?' at intervals while taking the statement. Another is to give the client a first draft request for discovery, etc, find out if they know any of the answers already or have copies of the documents themselves, and ask them for ideas about what else it might be useful to ask for.

4.23 Email correspondence is particularly important, and is still often overlooked or partially overlooked. Much that a few years ago would have been the subject of a quick phone call is now dealt with by e-mail. People tend to express themselves informally and candidly by e-mail, and they are more likely to forget that their e-mails may come under scrutiny. Often they will say in an e-mail things that they would not dream of putting in a letter or even a formal memo. For this reason, e-mail correspondence can be extremely revealing. Mobile phone text messages may also be revealing, but a printed list of such messages may or may not be in the 'control' of the sender or recipient depending on the nature of the agreement with the mobile phone company. This is relevant because a document is only subject to the duty of disclosure if it is in the possession or control of a party.

P4.23.1 Request for discovery of documents – redundancy dismissal

Mike Allen was dismissed for redundancy, but he believes that there was no genuine redundancy situation, and that the real reason for his dismissal was a personality clash with a senior manager. He was employed as 'Engineering Process Manager'. Shortly after his dismissal, the company appointed an 'Engineering Design Manager'. Mr Allen believes that this is his post in disguise.

George Bean
Carrot & Marrow Solicitors
21 Lower St
Islington
London N12 3AB

Our ref: NC 1234/2007
Your ref: GB/ar 6789

27 July 2007

Dear Mr Bean

Mike Allen v ADAL Ltd

REQUEST FOR DISCOVERY OF DOCUMENTS

Please provide copies of the following:
1. All appraisals from the claimant's personnel file done in the years 2005, 2006 or 2007.
2. Monthly engineering department order summaries for the months January 2006 to May 2007 inclusive.
3. All documentation of the process that led to the respondent's decision to make the post of Engineering Process Manager redundant, including:
    (a) minutes of any meetings;
    (b) file notes recording any telephone conversations;
    (c) any reports, letters, memos or e-mails.
4. Any notes or minutes taken at the consultation meeting held between the claimant on 24 March 2007 and Ben Ledgerman.
5. Any notes or minutes taken at the meeting of 30 March 2007 between Ben Ledgerman and the claimant.

6. Any notes or minutes taken at the appeal meeting on 11 April 2007.
7. All documentation of the process that led to the respondent's decision to create the new post of Engineering Design Manager in May 2007, including:

   (a) minutes of any meetings;
   (b) file notes recording any telephone conversations;
   (c) any reports, letters, memos or e-mails.

8. All documentation of the recruitment process that led to the appointment of Terry Seaman as Engineering Design Manager in May 2007, including:

   (a) job description;
   (b) person specification;
   (c) notes or minutes of interview or any informal discussion between Mr Ayers and more senior management;
   (d) letter offering the new post;
   (e) contract of employment.

9. The report presented by Ben Ledgerman to the respondent's Board of Directors in summer 2006 concerning the company's potential for growth over the following five years.

Please list any other documents in your possession or control that are relevant to any issue between the parties, saying in respect of which documents you claim privilege. Please confirm that your client has carried out a reasonable search for relevant documents.[13]

Please provide these documents by 12 noon on Friday 10 August[14], failing which I shall apply to the tribunal for an order.

Yours sincerely

Natalie Cummings

---

13 This request echoes the requirement of a 'disclosure statement' by rule 31.10 of the Civil Procedure Rules. This is not compulsory, or even common practice, in the employment tribunals but there is no reason why the claimant should not ask for it.
14 It is much clearer to name the day than to say 'within 14 days of today'.

P4.23.2 Request for disclosure of documents – constructive dismissal

George Bean
Carrot & Marrow Solicitors
21 Lower St
Islington
London N12 3AB

Our ref: NC 1234/2006
Your ref: GB/ar 6789

3 August 2007

Dear Mr Bean

Claudia Champion v Ministry of Truth ET/123456/06

REQUEST FOR DISCLOSURE OF DOCUMENTS

Please provide copies of the following documents:

1. Any minutes of Area Management Board meetings containing any reference to the claimant or her post during the 18 months from 1 May 2004.
2. All documents retrievable from Dawn Morvern's computer mentioning the claimant or relating to her or her circumstances created between 1 May 2004 and 31 June 2006, together with their associated statistics files.
3. The business plan mentioned by Simon Maltby during the meeting with area Higher Executive Officers (HEOs) on 15 April 2005.
4. All documentation of the process leading to the decision to create a third HEO post at the London Area Office including memos, reports, minutes of meetings, file notes, e-mails or any other documents.
5. Any minutes or other record of any meeting that took place between Sean McKitterick and James Petrie in accordance with Mr McKitterick's letter to Mr Petrie of 15 March 2006.

Please list any other documents in your possession or control that are relevant to any issue between the parties, saying in respect of which documents you claim privilege. Please confirm that your client has carried out a reasonable search for relevant documents.[15]

Some of these requests may take some time to meet, so I should be grateful for your response within the next 28 days[16], that is by close of business on 31 August. I shall be grateful of course if you are able to respond earlier. Please let me know promptly, however, if you are unwilling in principle to comply with any of these requests so that if necessary I can apply for an order without delay.

Yours sincerely

Natalie Cummings

Faked documents

4.24   Claimants' advisers should not disregard the possibility that the respondent or some of its witnesses have created after the event the documents that they think will assist them in defending the case. This is not an allegation that should be made lightly simply because a document is damaging, but if there are real grounds for thinking that it may have been done then it should be investigated. A point to bear in mind in this context (as in many others) is that organisations are made up of a number of different individuals who do not all have the same information or interests. The middle manager who dismissed may have faked documents – unknown to the more senior manager who confirmed the dismissal on appeal – as much to protect himself from criticism as to defend the employer from unfair dismissal proceedings. A faked document certainly does not mean that the employer's whole approach to the proceedings is dishonest, less still that their lawyers are in on the conspiracy.

4.25   Creating a convincing back-dated document is surprisingly difficult, and if a document is under suspicion the first step is obviously to examine it carefully for internal evidence that it is not what it purports to be. For example: a hand-written document that is said to have

---

15 See note 13 above

16 14 days is a more usual time limit, but a claimant who is aware that his or her request is on the heavy side will be well advised, if possible, to allow a more generous time limit.

been created over a period by different individuals may be suspiciously uniform, giving the impression that it was in fact written by one person, using the same scratchy ball-point pen, in a single sitting. Notes supposedly taken in the course of a heated meeting by one of the participants may be implausibly perfect and complete. A writer recording what is supposed to have been the present when the document was written may inadvertently use a past tense, or betray knowledge of information that was not available until later than the purported date of the document. Dates may be wrong. If the document is one that is supposed to have been given to the applicant at the time, the applicant may even have a different version.

4.26   Three specific techniques for testing the genuineness of suspect documents are worth keeping in mind. First, any typed document put forward as a contemporaneous record of a meeting or telephone call will almost certainly have been typed up from hand-written notes. These should be requested as well, so that comparisons can be made.[17]

4.27   Secondly, documents created on a computer will have an associated 'history' or 'statistics' file showing when the document was created, edited and printed. If the respondent discloses what the claimant believes are fake documents, it can be helpful to make a supplementary request for the statistics file. This too may be faked, of course, if the respondent has the know-how and the will to do so, but if the request is dealt with by someone who believes the document to be genuine, or does not understand or bother to read the statistics file, or indeed by anyone who takes the disclosure duty seriously, information that seriously damages the credibility of the original document may be disclosed. Alternatively, if the respondent makes thin excuses for failing to disclose it, this in itself may usefully damage their credibility.

4.28   Finally, if a document is sufficiently important, it may in rare cases be proportionate to call in a forensic computer expert to examine the computer, or to have the original document analysed by an expert in techniques such as electro-static document analysis (a method of recovering faint imprints on paper from the pages above them, suitable for hand-written documents under suspicion).[18]

---

17 If the respondent claims that the hand-written notes were discarded once the typed document had been created, this can be pursued in cross-examination. Any reasonably sophisticated manager can be expected to know – especially if he has ever been through tribunal proceedings before – that original documents should be filed alongside the typed transcripts as a matter of course.

18 See paras 5.61–5.67 below on how to find and instruct an expert witness.

Privilege

4.29   A document is said to be 'privileged' if, although relevant, it is exempt from disclosure or cannot be relied on as evidence. There are three kinds of privilege that commonly affect employment tribunal proceedings. The are the 'without prejudice' rule, legal advice privilege, and litigation privilege. The first relates to communications in the course of negotiation and is dealt with at para 6.11 below. The last two are superficially similar, but it is important to understand the differences between them.

Legal advice privilege

4.30   Legal advice privilege protects all communications passing between a lawyer her client in connection with giving and receiving legal advice, whether or not there are current or contemplated legal proceedings. This means, for example, that the claimant has no right to see a letter from the employer to its solicitor seeking advice on the best way to dismiss the claimant, or the solicitor's reply. Similarly, the respondent has no right to see communications between the claimant and her solicitor.

4.31   However, what the rule does not cover is at least as important as what it does cover. Some employers may try to claim privilege in respect of every document they do not wish to disclose because they regard it as confidential, but legal advice privilege is defined more narrowly than that.

4.32   Legal advice privilege does not extend to advice given before proceedings are contemplated to either the employer or the employee by a person who is not a lawyer, even if that person is acting in a role that is very similar to a lawyer's role. So, for example, advice given by the employer's human resources department to a manager on how to conduct a disciplinary hearing, how to approach a capability or sickness procedure, how to select for redundancy, etc, will not normally be privileged.[19] Similarly, legal advice privilege does not extend to advice from external personnel consultants if they are not legally qualified,[20] nor to communications in the course of a disciplinary process between the

---

19 Although the situation is different if the advice comes from an in-house lawyer.
20 *New Victoria Hospital v Ryan* [1993] ICR 201.

claimant and his or her union representative. These kinds of communications should be disclosed by each side.[21]

4.33   This is widely misunderstood by both employers and employees. Employers especially will often assume that they cannot be expected to show the claimant what they regard as 'confidential' human resources advice to managers. They may refer to legal advice privilege in arguing that they should not have to disclose this material; or they may simply omit it from their list of documents altogether because they believe that it is none of the claimant's business. Claimants who believe that this kind of material exists will often have to make a considerable fuss before they get it. The fuss is worth making, because if at the time the advice was sought and given both the manager and the human resources adviser believed that what they said to each other would not come out in tribunal proceedings, the communications between them will be unguarded and may contain material that is very helpful for the claimant.

Litigation privilege

4.34   Litigation privilege protects from disclosure any document that was created for the purposes of current or future litigation, and it protects communications between unqualified advisers and their clients as well as between lawyers and their clients.

4.35   The key distinction to understand, therefore, is between: (a) documents that were created at the time of the acts or processes that have since become the subject of employment tribunal litigation; and (b) documents that have come into existence because of, and for the purpose of, the litigation itself. Documents in class (a) will only be privileged if they are communications between a qualified lawyer and his or her client for the purpose of legal advice. Documents in class (b) will always be privileged.

4.36   It is worth observing here that notes of a hearing taken by one party or its legal or other advisers are not privileged.[22] This will most often be relevant if there is an appeal for which notes of evidence are

---

21 The sharp distinction between communications with qualified lawyers, and communications with unqualified advisers whose role is very similar to that of a lawyer has been the subject of some criticism, but until the Court of Appeal or the House of Lords revisits the question the distinction stands.

22 Because they are a record of what has taken place at a public hearing – and this by definition, cannot be confidential. See *Lambert v Home* [1914] 3 KB 86, CA; and *Comfort v Lord Chancellor's Department* UKEAT/0137/05.

needed, or a remitted hearing after an appeal at which the claimant wishes to rely on evidence given previously by the respondent.[23] However, if a hearing is not completed in the time allotted and has to be adjourned for some weeks or months before it can be finished, then a party who has not been able to take accurate notes of the hearing may wish to seek discovery of the other party's notes. This is an application that both the tribunal and the respondent may find surprising, but there is no reason in principle why it should not succeed.[24] The claimant should remind the tribunal that the overriding objective at regulation 3 of the Employment Tribunals (Constitution and Rules of Procedure) Regulations 2004[25] requires, among other things, 'ensuring that the parties are on an equal footing'. Where the claimant has represented herself and the respondent has attended with counsel and a solicitor (and larger legal teams are not uncommon) the justice of this should be evident.

Requests for additional information

4.37 These are requests of the general form 'When you said XYZ in your response, what did you mean?' It will almost always be necessary to request disclosure of documents from the respondent, but there is no need to assume that a request for additional information is required unless there is something about the response that leaves them in genuine doubt about what it is the respondent is alleging. Unnecessary requests could leave you at risk of a costs order.

---

23 Where, for example, one of the respondent's witnesses made helpful admissions under cross-examination.

24 Any user of this book who makes such an application is invited to notify the authors of the outcome by way of the blog that updates and supports the book at www.etclaims.co.uk.

25 SI No 1861.

P4.37 Request for additional information

George Bean
Carrot & Marrow Solicitors
21 Lower St
Islington
London N12 3AB

Our ref: NC 1234/2004
Your ref: GB/ar 6789

18 May 2007

Dear Mr Bean

Claudia Champion v Ministry of Truth ET/123456/04

REQUEST FOR ADDITIONAL INFORMATION

Under paragraph 3:
Of: *It is admitted that in or around May 2005, a decision was taken to merge the Croydon and Guildford Area Managers' Offices.*

1. Please say who took the decision to merge the Croydon and Guildford Area Managers' Offices.

Of: *As part of the implementation, all staff affected were consulted in order to take into account, where possible, the wishes of individuals in re-allocating posts.*

2. Please say who was consulted.
3. Please say in each case who carried out the consultation.
4. Please say when and where the consultation took place.
5. Please say whether the consultation was carried out by way of meetings, by correspondence or otherwise.

Under paragraph 4:
Of: *It was considered by the respondent that the claimant needed to develop the required skills before being able to take up an operational post.*

6. Please say what skills it was thought the claimant needed to develop before being able to take up an operational post.

Of: *Accordingly, arrangements were made to find her another post at her grade.*

7. Please say what arrangements were made.
8. Please say who made them.

Please provide this information by 12 noon on 1 June 2007, failing which I will apply to the tribunal for an order.

Yours sincerely

Natalie Cummings

Requests for written answers

4.38   The comments at para 4.7 above on requests for additional information apply here too: the tribunal has power to order written answers to questions, but it does not follow that in every case a request for written answers must be made.

Applying for an order for disclosure, additional information or written answers

4.39   An application for an order should normally be made as soon as the deadline set for voluntary compliance with the request has passed. If the respondent requests extra time, that request should be granted if it is reasonable and can be granted without jeopardising the claimant's chances of getting an order from the tribunal if the respondent fails to meet the new deadline. So, for example, if a request is made with a 14-day time limit seven weeks before the hearing and the respondent asks for another week to comply, there is no reason not to agree: the tribunal will not hesitate to make an order four weeks before the hearing if it turns out in the end that it is needed. On the other hand, if the request is made four weeks before the hearing with a 14-day time limit, it will be prudent to request the order as soon as the time limit has expired even if the respondent is promising imminent voluntary compliance.[26] An application that is received in the last seven days before the hearing is unlikely to be granted.

4.40   The application should explain briefly the relevance of the documents or information sought, and say how granting the application will help the tribunal deal with the case efficiently and fairly. It should also contain the usual instructions for the respondent about how and when to oppose the application, and it must of course be copied to the respondent. Sometimes the relevance of the request is self-evident, in which case the request for an order can be brief. In other cases, the need for the requested documents or information will require careful explanation, or if the respondent has put in a reasoned objection to complying this may need to be dealt with at some length.

DOCUMENT OUTLINE: Applying for an order for disclosure

Identify the order sought, and refer to (and enclose) the letter of request

Explain the relevance of the requests

Deal with the respondent's objections, if any

Explain how an order will help the tribunal to deal with the case efficiently and fairly[27]

Give the respondent instructions for opposing the request[28]

---

26 It does not hurt in these circumstances to explain to the respondent that the application is made protectively and will be withdrawn if the respondent complies voluntarily in the meantime.

27 This is required in order to comply with rule 11 of the Procedure Rules.

28 This is required in order to comply with rule 11 if the claimant is legally represented, but it will save time in any case since the alternative is for the tribunal to give the other party those instructions after receiving the application.

P4.40.1 Request for an order for discovery – unfair redundancy (straightforward)

The Regional Secretary
London Central Employment Tribunal
19–29 Woburn Place
London WC1H 0LU

Your ref: 123456/2007
My ref: NC/1234

13 August 2007

Dear Madam

Mike Allen v ADAL Ltd

I should be grateful if you would put before a Chairman my request for an order that the respondent comply with my requests for disclosure of documents as set out in my letter of 27 July, of which I attach a copy. I have received no reply.

A central issue between the parties is whether there was a genuine redundancy situation affecting Mr Allen's post. The relevance of the appointment of Mr Seaman as Engineering Design Manager is that Mr Allen believes that the new post of Engineering Design Manager was in reality the same as the post of Engineering Process Manager from which he had been dismissed.

In the circumstances disclosure of the requested documents will clarify the matters in dispute between the parties and will assist the tribunal in dealing with the case efficiently and fairly.

This letter is copied to the respondent. The respondent should note that if it objects to the application, it must write to the tribunal within seven days of receiving this letter, or before the date of the hearing (whichever date is the earlier) explaining the reasons for its objection, and should copy that letter to me. Rule 11 of the Procedure Rules has been complied with in relation to this application.

Yours faithfully

Natalie Cummings

P4.40.2 Request for an order for discovery – constructive dismissal (more complex)

The Regional Secretary
London Central Employment Tribunal
19–29 Woburn Place
London WC1H 0LU

3 September 2007

URGENT PLEASE

Dear Madam

Claudia Champion v Ministry of Truth ET/123456/07

I should be grateful if you would put before a Chairman my request for an order that the respondent comply with my requests for discovery of documents as set out in my letter of 3 August, of which I attach a copy together with the reply received today.

The respondent has refused to provide items 1 and 2. The claimant asserts that her wish to return to an operational post, and in particular the post of Department Manager in the Central London Information Unit, was realistic and had previously been discussed with management as a feasible medium-term option. She believes that Area Management Board Meeting minutes from the period before the reorganisation will support this contention. She further believes that Area Management Board Meeting minutes from the period around and immediately after the reorganisation will show that the respondent had no coherent plan for her redeployment after the reorganisation.

As to item 2, Dawn Morvern is James Petrie's personal assistant and would have typed the notes of the meetings in September and October 2003 which James Petrie has put forward as his contemporaneous notes of those meetings. The claimant does not accept Mr Petrie's account of the meeting and does not believe that the notes were typed up at the time. She believes that the notes were created some time after the event. For this reason item 2, including statistics files showing when each document was created, edited and printed, are highly relevant.

The requested documents are relevant to important issues between the parties, and granting this application will therefore assist the tribunal in dealing with the case efficiently and fairly.

I am sorry that this request is made close to the hearing date. In my letter of 3 August I asked the respondent to notify me at once if it objected in principle to providing any of the disclosure sought so that I could apply for an order in good time if necessary. I received no reply to that letter until today, when the respondent complied with my requests 3–6 but refused to comply with requests 1 and 2. In the circumstances I suggest that there is no unfairness to the respondent granting the order sought.

This letter is copied to the respondent. The respondent should note that if it objects to the application, it must write to the tribunal within 7 days of receiving this letter, or before the date of the hearing (whichever date is the earlier) explaining the reasons for its objection, and should copy that letter to me. Rule 11 of the Procedure Rules has been complied with in relation to this application.

Yours faithfully

Natalie Cummings

Questionnaires

4.41   The questionnaire procedure is unique to discrimination claims. In any discrimination claim, the claimant may, either before or after commencing proceedings, serve on the respondent (or potential respondent) a list of questions. The respondent is not obliged to answer the questions, and the tribunals have no power to order replies to a questionnaire; but the tribunal that hears the case will have regard to the questionnaire and any reply and may draw inferences from a failure to reply or from evasive or incomplete replies.

4.42   Before 1993, the employment tribunals had no general power to order a party to give written answers to questions: it could order further particulars (what is now called 'additional information') of an employer's response to the claim, and it could order disclosure of documents already in existence; but it could not order a respondent to provide specific information such as statistics on the make-up of its workforce, or lists of employees dismissed in the last year or so broken down by reason for dismissal and ethnic origin.

4.43   This meant that before 1993 the questionnaire procedure was very important indeed. The tribunal's power to draw inferences from inadequate replies provided a sanction to encourage – although not compel – employers to respond. After the 1993 Rules came into force the importance of the questionnaire procedure diminished somewhat: general questions aimed at casting light on how an employer treats ethnic minority staff, or women, for instance, can be put as requests for written answers, and if the tribunal thinks the question is relevant it can order the employer to respond.

4.44   However, there are three significant respects in which the questionnaire procedure can still provide real tactical benefits. The first is that it is available before proceedings start, and can be used by an employee thinking of making a claim to help decide whether or not the claim is well founded. This can be particularly useful in recruitment cases, where an applicant for a job may have an uneasy feeling that he or she may have suffered unlawful discrimination, but very little hard information about the employer or its practices or even about the successful candidate for the job. In those circumstances, the decision whether to proceed with a claim may well depend on the reply to a questionnaire: if the employer gives a convincing and legitimate explanation for its failure to recruit the aggrieved candidate, that may be the end of the matter.

4.45   The second strength of the questionnaire procedure lies in the fact that the tribunal has no power to order replies to a questionnaire. Ironically, this may make the questionnaire in one way a more powerful weapon in the hands of the claimant. An employer faced with a list of requests for discovery of documents or written answers which it considers excessively long and detailed, or questionably relevant, can say to the claimant 'We consider that your requests are irrelevant and oppressive, and we are not prepared to answer them without an order from the tribunal.' The decision whether the questions are relevant is then left to the tribunal. If the tribunal refuses to order answers because it does not regard the questions as relevant, or because it considers them excessive, it is difficult subsequently to criticise the employer for failing to respond. In other words, by this means the employer can pass to the tribunal the decision whether or not the questions need to be answered.[29]

4.46   Faced with a long and detailed questionnaire, the employer does not have this option. It cannot pass the decision about whether or in how much detail it should reply to the tribunal: it must make the judgement itself. This means it will, if it is well advised, play safe. It will normally be better for an employer to give more information than would ever have been ordered than to risk giving the claimant the opportunity to invite the tribunal to draw adverse inferences from incomplete answers. Questionnaires, therefore, will often be a way of digging up more information than a tribunal would be likely to order an employer to disclose.

4.47   This is deliberate. It is recognised both in the way the legislation is drafted[30] and in discrimination case law[31] that discrimination cases are difficult to prove and the relevant information will often be elusive. The standard case law on disclosure makes it clear that 'fishing expeditions' will not be permitted.[32] Discrimination is an exception: in discrimination cases, claimants are provided with line and hook.

4.48   The third strength of the questionnaire procedure is that it can elicit from the respondent, before disclosure, assertions which the claimant can prove to be false using documents that the Respondent does not know she has in her possession.

The form for the questionnaire

4,49   Links to the official forms for the various discrimination questionnaires can be found on the blog that supports and updates this book at www.etclaims.co.uk. Hard copies should be obtainable from a Job Centre or Citizens Advice Bureau. Each of the questionnaires appears as part of the statutory instrument that gives it its effect.

4.50   Each form includes a number of standard questions that must be completed in all cases. Each (with the exception of the equal pay questionnaire) follows a very similar pattern. The claimant gives his or her

---

29 However, see *'Dattani'* for a suggestion by the Employment Appeal Tribunal that inferences can be drawn in discrimination cases from failure to respond to requests for disclosure or written answers as well as questionnaires.

30 Especially the partially reversed burden of proof at, for example, Sex Discrimination Act 1975 s63A.

31 See, for example, *King v Great Britain–China Centre*, [1992] ICR 516, CA.

32 See *British Aerospace plc v Green* [1995] IRLR 433.

name and address and the name and address of the person or body whose conduct is the subject of complaint, and sets out the substance of the complaint: this is at box 2 of the race, sex and disability questionnaires, and box 1.2 of the religion or belief and the sexual orientation questionnaires.[33] Claimants' advisers almost invariably repeat here the whole of the complaint as it appears in the claim to the tribunal.[34]

4.51   At box 3 there is a standard statement: 'I consider that this treatment may have been unlawful because' and a box for the insertion of the reasons why the treatment complained of is considered unlawful.[35] Most advisers routinely cross out 'because' and leave the box blank. This is sensible. The legal basis of the claim will need to be made clear in the claim form submitted to the tribunal, but as that is in a different format there is no need to take on the extra work of re-drafting it for the questionnaire.

4.52   There then follow two standard questions which the claimant need not alter, and at box 6 there is space for further specific questions.[36]

4.53   Box 6 is the point at which the real work of drafting the questionnaire is done. It can be tempting to assume that it is good to ask as many questions as possible at this point; or that a brief questionnaire is somehow inadequate. Neither assumption is justified. There is no necessity to dream up questions for the sake of making the questionnaire look substantial. In some cases it will not be necessary to serve a questionnaire at all. If you cannot think of any useful questions to ask at this stage it is better not to serve a questionnaire than to serve a questionnaire putting a number of questions that either do not help the case or positively hinder it. Moreover, including a lot of unnecessary detail can be an effective way of engaging the sympathy of the tribunal on the side of the respondent and damaging its willingness to draw inferences from failures to answer any good questions.

4.54   The advice at para 4.12 above on making a careful choice between questions to put in writing and questions to save for cross-examination applies here too. A claimant will not be restrained by the tribunal from attempting to cross-examine on paper by means of the questionnaire

---

33   References to box numbers in what follows are for simplicity references to the numbering of the sex discrimination questionnaire alone.

34   See chapter 3 above. It is not obvious that this is really necessary, but as it is nearly universal practice and has been for many years it is probably as well to conform.

35   This appears at box 1.3 in the case of sexual orientation and religion or belief.

36   The box is small, and claimants will almost always need to attach their box 6 questions as a separate sheet or sheets.

procedure, but it does not follow that this is a good thing to do. If the case is strong enough, demonstrating to the employer by way of a questionnaire that there are difficult and pointed questions to which they do not have good answers can help to lever a settlement out of them without going to tribunal, but this is a high risk strategy. If the case does still proceed to a hearing, much of the benefit of effective cross-examination will be lost if the respondent is given the chance to deal with the hardest questions at leisure and with the advice of its lawyers.

4.55   It is common practice to request documents as part of the questionnaire procedure. The legislation permits tribunals to draw inferences from a failure to reply to questions, or from evasive or incomplete replies to questions. It is not obvious that this also applies to a failure to provide documents on request: probably an employer is entitled simply to say 'Here are my answers to your questions; if you wish for disclosure of documents, you must deal with that after you have presented a claim under the tribunal's power to order disclosure.' However, requests of these kind can operate as an effective bluff: the only way for an employer to find out for sure whether the tribunal will draw adverse inferences from its decision to withhold documents is to withhold them. Most employers will not take the risk, so requests for documents in a questionnaire are worthwhile.

Checklist of subjects to cover in a questionnaire

4.56   As usual with checklists in this book, this is not and could not be exhaustive. It is intended to suggest ideas and give claimants an idea of the kinds of questions that it can be useful to ask. In this list, for simplicity in illustrating the ideas, examples are restricted to sex and disability discrimination, and in the former case it is assumed that the victim of discrimination is a woman. These topics can easily be adapted to fit complaints of discrimination on grounds of race, sexual orientation, or religion or belief.[37]

---

37 For more extensive lists of sample questions, see the Commissions' websites; Tamara Lewis's excellent booklets RRA Questionnaires (Central London Law Centre, 2003); DDA Questionnaires (Central London Law Centre, 2001); SDA and Equal Pay Questionnaires (Central London Law Centre, 2005) and Discrimination Questionnaires (Central London Law Centre, 2004); and Disability Discrimination Claims: an adviser's handbook by Catherine Casserley and Bela Gor (Jordans, 2001).

- the respondent's equal opportunities policy, what it covers, when and how often staff have been trained on it;
- the respondent's workforce profile – that is, the proportions in which women/people with disabilities are found in the organisation, and what levels of seniority;
- the proportion of applicants for the job in question or similar jobs over a defined period who were female or had disabilities;
- if the complaint is about an allegedly discriminatory provision, criterion or practice (that is, indirect discrimination) the relative proportions of male and female employees who were adversely affected;
- whether the respondent has been the subject of any previous complaints of sex/disability discrimination or whether a particular individual has previously been accused of sexual harassment;
- what adjustments to the workplace/the claimant's job description/working practices/the recruitment process have been considered to deal with the claimant's disability;
- the reasons why the claimant was treated in the way that he or she is complaining about;
- the reasons why other individuals have not been treated in the same way as the claimant;
- who made the decision to treat the claimant in the way that he or she is complaining about;
- the manner in which other employees have been treated, and if different the reasons why;
- in a recruitment or promotion case, the qualifications of the successful candidate;
- in a reasonable adjustments case, the cost of any adjustments the claimant says should have been made and the employer's resources; it may sometimes be productive to explore the employer's expenditure on non-essentials if the employer is pleading poverty.[38]

---

38 See glossary for an explanation of reasonable adjustments.

P4.56.1 Questionnaire – sex discrimination

These answers follow the format of the SDA 1975 questionnaire which is available from the Equal Opportunities Commission website (www.eoc-law.org.uk) and a copy of which is reproduced at appendix B.

To: Bristol Advice Project
Of: 2 Hillock Way, Clifton, Bristol B2 1AB

1. I   Yasmin Creasey

   of   23A St Matthew's Hill, Bristol, B1 2CD

2. consider that you may have discriminated against me contrary to the Sex Discrimination Act 1975.

> (i) I was employed by the Bristol Advice Project as a recep-
> tionist and filing clerk. I was told on starting work that I was
> on a nine month probationary period from 19 April 2006, but
> no arrangements were made for appraisal or review.
> (ii) On 15 June 2006, I told my line manager, Mary Smiling, that I
> was four months pregnant.
> (iii) As far as I was aware, my work was satisfactory. All my col-
> leagues seemed friendly and no-one made any complaints.
> (iv) I started my maternity leave on 6 November 2006. On Friday
> 3 November, my last day at work, my colleagues gave me a
> card and a bunch of flowers. Mrs Smiling wished me good luck
> and said 'See you next year.'
> (v) On 8 January 2007, I received a letter dated 5 January from
> Reuben Fitzwell informing me that as my performance during
> my probationary period had been unsatisfactory, my employ-
> ment would not be confirmed and would accordingly come
> to an end on 15 January 2007.

3. I consider that this treatment may have been unlawful because:

(Questions 4 and 5 are standard questions printed on the form.)

6.   Other questions (if appropriate):

> (i) Does the respondent have an equal opportunities policy? Please provide a copy.
> (ii) Does the respondent have a maternity leave policy? Please provide a copy.
> (iii) When was the decision taken that I was not to be confirmed in post?
> (iv) Who took the decision?
> (v) What information did he or she rely on? Please provide copies of any written information relied on.
> (vi) How many new employees have you recruited in the last five years? In each case please specify:
> > (a) whether the recruit was male or female;
> > (b) the date of recruitment;
> > (c) whether he or she was subject to a probationary period, and if so of what duration;
> > (d) what appraisals or progress reviews were conducted during the probationary period; and
> > (e) whether the recruit was confirmed in post, and if not, the date when the decision not to terminate the employment was taken.

P4.56.2 Questionnaire – disability discrimination

In this precedent only the questions at part 6 of the form are reproduced. The claimant is Pauline Phelps of P3.11.1 above, and the statement of the basis for her belief that she has suffered discrimination would closely follow the statement at box 6.1 of her claim form.

6.   Other questions (if appropriate):
   (i)   Do you have an equal opportunities policy? Please provide a copy.
   (ii) Have any of your partners or staff received training on the Disability Discrimination Act 1998? Please give names and dates.
   (iii) Do you accept that I am disabled for the purposes of the Disability Discrimination Act 1998 in that (a) I have a facial disfigurement and (b) I suffer from depression and agoraphobia?[39]

---

39 It is worth asking this now in order to have advance notice of whether there is any need for medical evidence on either point.

(iv) Who made the decision that I should go to work in the pool of secretaries after Mr Gentleman's retirement in July 2006?

(v) What alternatives, if any, were considered?

(vi) Why was my suggestion that I should work full-time for Miss Grey from August 2006 rejected?

(vii) What adjustments did you consider making from August 2006 to prevent the arrangements for working in the pool of secretaries from placing me at a substantial disadvantage compared to persons who were not disabled?[40]

(viii) What steps were taken to investigate my condition or to assess what adjustments might helpfully be made to prevent working in the pool of secretaries from placing me at a substantial disadvantage?

(ix) Why was there no reply to my GP's letter of 16 February 2007?

(x) Who took the decision that morning reception should be covered during the maternity leave of Alison Sheppard by members of the pool?

(xi) Who took the decision that I should be included on the reception rota?

(xii) What arrangements did you consider making to prevent the arrangements for morning reception cover from placing me at a substantial disadvantage compared to persons who were not disabled?

Data Protection Act requests

4.57 The Data Protection Act (DPA) 1998 provides a means by which individuals may require disclosure of certain kinds of information held about them by any person or body. In many cases the employment tribunal's power to order disclosure of relevant documents will be an adequate means of getting hold of information for an employment

---

40 This question is deliberately broad. A series of detailed questions at this stage about whether the employer considered this or that specific adjustment may prompt to the employer to claim that each was considered and think of convincing reasons why each was rejected. If they are not going to answer the questionnaire honestly, a question in this form at least leaves them to do the work of thinking of the adjustments they could or should have considered at the time. It will be difficult for them to claim at any later stage that they considered any adjustment that they do not mention in answer to this question.

tribunal case, but a DPA 1998 request will occasionally be helpful, particularly where the employee wants the information (for example, for the purposes of an internal grievance) before employment tribunal proceedings have started.

4.58   The two main limitations on what an employer (or other body) can be compelled to disclose under the DPA 1998 concern (a) the manner in which the information is held and (b) the nature of the information. Since a ruling of the Court of Appeal in *Durant v Financial Services Authority* in 2003 a restrictive view has been taken of both.[41]

4.59   Information is only covered by the DPA 1998 if it is either held on a computer or as part of a sufficiently structured paper filing system.[42]

4.60   The effect of the judgment of the Court of Appeal in *Durant* is that information held in paper filing systems will not come within the right of access provided by the DPA 1998 unless the filing system is sophisticated enough that it can be readily discovered whether personal data are held in relation to a particular individual, and if so, where in the files specific information about specific individuals will be found. Paper files will not be covered unless the information in them is similarly accessible to computerised files. This means that only highly structured and well-organised paper files are subject to the right of access.

4.61   The other limitation is the kind of information that is covered. The right of access is not to every piece of information held on a computer or a sophisticated paper file that mentions the individual making the request: the information has to be about the individual in question, or to have him or her as its focus. Suppose, for example, Mark Bowland of P3.11.2 above makes a subject access request to the Hospital, and the Hospital keeps computerised personnel records. A search of those records by reference to Mr Bowland's name will turn up his own personnel file, but also Mr Rahman's and no doubt several others, because he line-manages Mr Rahman and has been mentioned in the latter's

---

41 [2003] EWCA 1746.

42 Claimants who are employees of a public body who find limb (e) of the definition of 'data' at section 1 of the Act may be led to think that this means that they are entitled to a much broader category of information from their employers than other employees, but the impression is misleading. Section 33A(2) excludes employment-related data from this definition, and the net result is that public employees are entitled to the same amounts and kinds of information from their records about themselves as any other employees. Other information held by their employers may be accessible under the Freedom of Information Act 2000, and in this respect they may be better-placed than private sector workers: see note 1 above.

employment tribunal claim against the Hospital. Mr Bowland's own personnel file is clearly about Mr Bowland and he can demand to see it. Mr Rahman's file only mentions him in passing, and he is not entitled to see it or even the parts of it that mention his name.

4.62   Under the DPA 1998, the person seeking information about him or herself is called the 'data subject' and the body holding (or believed to be holding) information is the 'data controller'.

Making a request under the DPA 1998

4.63   Despite these limitations, a request for information under the DPA 1998 may have its uses. The data subject does not have to know what kind of information is held about him or her, or where or how it is held: the data controller must reveal its existence when asked.[43]

4.64   The data controller may charge a fee of up to £10 for providing the information, and must provide the information within 40 days of receiving the request and the fee. The sensible course is to enclose £10 with the request.

P4.64 Data Protection Act 1998 request to employer

Sarah Feldman has worked for Glad Rags plc, a national retail clothing chain, for 15 years. Her career progressed well for most of that time, but for the last five years she has made a series of unsuccessful applications for promotion. She has not been able to discover why her progress has suddenly stopped, although she is now one of a small number of women at her level of seniority and she has started to wonder if she has reached a 'glass ceiling'. However, a manager recently told her that he thought it ought to be obvious to her why she has stopped making progress. He said that there were certain kinds of things on a person's record that would always stop them from reaching the highest levels. Ms Feldman was completely baffled by this and demanded to know what he meant. He refused to explain, saying only that she 'must be realistic in all the circumstances'.

---

43   A request for information under the DPA 1998 is known as a 'subject access request'.

The Legal Department
Glad Rags plc
25 Budgerigar Wharf
London E1 7QB

5 April 2007

Dear Madam/Sir

Data Protection Act 1998: subject access request

Please provide me with the following information, to which I am entitled under section 7 of the Data Protection Act 1998:

1. A description of what personal data is held by Glad Rags plc of which I am the data subject.
2. The purposes for which these data are being processed.
3. To whom these data are or may be disclosed.
4. The information constituting any personal data of which I am the data subject.
5. Any information available to Glad Rags plc as to the source of that information.[44]

I enclose £10 and look forward to hearing from you as soon as possible, and in any event within 40 days.

Yours faithfully

Sarah Feldman

The claimant's disclosure of documents

4.65   The claimant is under the same duty as the respondent to comply properly with whatever order the tribunal has made for disclosure of documents – that is, to disclose all relevant documents in his possession or control, or to disclose all documents on which he proposes to rely at the hearing as the case may be (see paras 4.16–4.20 above). Claimants in employment tribunal disputes will typically have far less to disclose than respondents as normally it is the employer that holds

---

44   These five categories are parallel to the relevant subsections of section 7.

the great bulk of the relevant documentary evidence, but advisers should be careful to ensure that claimants have understood the scope of the duty to disclose. The idea that there might be a duty to show a former employer personal diaries, private letters or e-mails, bank statements, telephone bills, etc will come as a surprise to many claimants.

4.66   Again, attention needs to be paid to the form of the tribunal's direction (if any) on disclosure: if disclosure of all relevant documents in each party's power or control is ordered, then the claimant as much as the respondent must comply with it fully. The tribunal is likely to react badly if it becomes clear in the course of the hearing that the claimant has relevant documents that she has not disclosed.

4.67   The safest course in fact will normally be to disclose all relevant documents (other than privileged documents, as to which see paras 4.29–4.36 above) whichever order the tribunal has made. A decision to withhold a particular document because the claimant does not wish to rely on it and does not wish the respondent or the tribunal to see it needs to be approached with great caution. The parties and their advisers have a duty not to mislead the tribunal, so it will never be permissible to withhold a document that flatly contradicts an assertion in the witness statement. There may be a relevant document in the claimant's possession that gives a misleading impression, but even so it will normally be better to disclose and explain it than to attempt to suppress it.

4.68   Moreover, because there is always a duty of full disclosure in litigation in the ordinary courts (with which the chairman at least is likely to be familiar), the tribunal itself cannot necessarily be relied upon to understand that the same duty does not automatically apply in the employment tribunal. A claimant who has withheld a relevant document because she considers it misleading may find herself in hot water with the tribunal if she is subsequently forced to admit to its existence. If this happens, the adviser should be ready to argue that in the absence of a specific direction by the tribunal, there can be no duty of general disclosure in employment tribunal proceedings because there is nothing in the rules to impose it, but even if this is accepted the claimant's credibility is likely to have been damaged.

4.69   P4.10 is a letter explaining this to a client. Bear in mind too that the term 'document' is not confined to material that already exists in paper form: computer files, e-mails, etc should be disclosed if relevant.

P4.69.1 Letter explaining disclosure duty to the claimant

Claudia Champion
3 Conifer Way
Croydon
Surrey CR10 8RY

9 July 2007

Dear Claudia

Case management order

I enclose a copy of the case management order from the case management discussion last week. As you see, the next step is that the parties are required to disclose to each other all documents in their power
or possession relevant to the case.

I probably have most of your relevant documents in my file already, but
please think carefully about whether you have any other papers relating
to the events leading up to your resignation. For instance, did you keep
your own notes of any of the meetings? Did you keep a diary? Did
you send or receive any letters or e-mails about the way you were
being treated at the time? We do not need to show the other side
communications between you and qualified legal advisers, but letters
to or from the CAB or your Trade Union rep may need to be included.
If you are unsure about any particular document, please send me a
copy and I will advise on whether or not it should be disclosed.

It is important that we disclose everything relevant at this stage as late
or incomplete disclosure will annoy the tribunal at best, and at worst
could damage our credibility and/or give rise to a costs order.

I hope you had a good time in Cornwall and Tuckey[45] has recovered
from his adventure with the milk jug.

Yours sincerely

Natalie Cummings

45   'Tuckey' is the claimant's cat. Obviously this last sentence is just friendly
noise. But litigation is stressful enough, and the rest of this letter could feel a
bit starchy to an anxious client.

P4.69.2 Claimant's list of documents

The claimant worked for a small local charity. An e-mail dispute with the chair of the management committee, Tony Byrd, about her workload escalated to the point that she went sick with stress and then resigned. The full e-mail correspondence with Tony Byrd and other management committee members is clearly relevant and should be disclosed – although it is almost certainly in the respondent's possession already. What may come as a surprise to the claimant is that her contemporaneous e-mails about the dispute to her friend Carol Parker and her husband, David Manley, and any relevant diary entries, also have to be disclosed.

IN THE EMPLOYMENT TRIBUNAL
LONDON CENTRAL

BETWEEN

BELINDA MANLEY

Claimant

and

LOCAL ACTION PROJECT

Respondent

CLAIMANT'S LIST OF DOCUMENTS

Date	Description
21 Aug 06	e-mail BM/Tony Byrd (TB)
21 Aug 06	e-mail TB/BM
21 Aug 06	e-mail BM/David Manley (DM)
21 Aug 06	e-mail BM/TB
22 Aug 06	e-mail TB/BM
22 Aug 06	e-mail TB/Carol Parker
22 Aug 06	e-mail BM/DM
22 Aug 06	e-mail DM/BM
22 Aug 06	BM's personal diary page
25 Aug 06	e-mail TB/BM, cc management committee (MC)
25 Aug 06	e-mail BM/TB, cc MC
25 Aug 06	BM's personal diary page
25 Aug 06	e-mail Tola James (TJ) /BM

25 Aug 06	e-mail BM/TJ
25 Aug 06	e-mail TJ/BM
28 Aug 06	e-mail BM/MC
28 Aug 06	e-mail TB/BM, cc MC
4 Oct 06	e-mail BM/MC
5 Oct 06	e-mail TJ/BM, cc MC
11 Oct 06	BM's notes of meeting with TB and TJ
11 Oct 06	BM's personal diary page
11 Oct 06	e-mail BM/DM
13 Oct 06	letter BM/TJ, cc MC
18 Oct 06	memo TJ/BM
12–30 Oct 06	extract from BM's itemised phone bill
20 Oct 06	GP's certificate
20 Oct 06	letter TJ/BM
9 Nov 06	letter of resignation
Nov 06 – Jan 07	privileged correspondence with the CAB

Responding to requests for additional information

4.70   Some solicitors, when acting for respondents, will invariably make a request for additional information, however much detail the claimant has put in the claim. Normally it will be more economical for the claimant simply to answer unnecessary questions than to get into a debate about whether or not they are legitimate at this stage. Occasionally the claimant will refuse to answer questions on the grounds that they are requests for evidence or an attempt to conduct a written cross-examination. Broadly, questions that seek additional detail on what it is the claimant alleges are legitimate; questions that explore why the claimant thinks the tribunal ought to believe his or her allegations are not.

4.71   It is helpful to repeat each request before answering it so that the letter is a self-contained document that the tribunal can understand without constantly referring back to the letter of request.[46] If there have been reasonably co-operative dealings with the respondent, it is sensible to ask for the request letter to be e-mailed so that this can be done by cutting and pasting the relevant portions of the request.

46 This can usefully be generalised: letters and documents generally will very often do their job better if they are self-contained than if they can only be properly understood by reference to other documents.

P4.71 Letter responding to requests for disclosure and additional information

George Bean
Carrot & Marrow Solicitors
21 Lower St
Islington
London N21 3AB

29 September 2007

Dear Mr Bean

James Dodd v Pineapple Plant Hire Ltd

Thank you for your letter of 31 August to the Citizens' Advice Bureau. I apologise for the delay in responding to your requests, which has been caused by the transfer of the case from the CAB to the Law Centre.
RESPONSE TO REQUEST FOR ADDITIONAL INFORMATION

1. Request
Of: *My GP warned that for a couple of weeks I might suffer side effects*

Please state:

(a) when the claimant's GP advised him that he would suffer side effects;
(b) the nature of the side effects.

1. Response
(a) 13 December 2006, the day on which the medication was changed.
(b) That it would take two weeks for his body to adjust to the new medication and that in that period he was liable to suffer hyperglycaemic episodes.

2. Request
Of: *I advised management and others at Pineapple accordingly*

Please state:

(a) whom the claimant advised at Pineapple;
(b) when the claimant allegedly advised the management and others.

2. Response
(a) The claimant told his manager Sue Slight.
(b) 14 December 2006.

Yours sincerely

Natalie Cummings

CHAPTER 5

The role of witnesses

The role of witnesses

5.1   Witnesses are needed by the tribunal wherever there is a dispute about what happened: the witnesses on one side tell their story, and then the witnesses on the other side say something between 'No, it wasn't quite like that, it was like this', and 'That is a complete pack of lies from beginning to end. What really happened was this ... ' Once in a while the employment tribunal is called upon to decide a case where the parties are in complete agreement about what happened, and disagree only as to the legal consequences. For example: there is a written contract of employment that says something ambiguous about the circumstances in which the employee will receive sick pay. The parties are agreed that the claimant was sick for a certain period in certain circumstances, and that she received no sick pay; all they disagree about is whether in those particular circumstances the contract entitled her to sick pay. In those cases, it may be possible to dispense with witnesses; to the extent that the tribunal needs to be given some factual background, the parties may be able to agree a factual account.

5.2   These cases will be fairly rare: witnesses are called in the great majority of substantive hearings to tell the tribunal what happened.

Deciding what witnesses to call

5.3   In very many employment tribunal cases, the claimant gives evidence herself, but calls no other witnesses, whereas the respondent calls several witnesses. This is not surprising: most claims are, one way or another, about dismissal, and in most workplaces it takes several managers to dismiss an employee, but only one employee to be dismissed. Moreover, employment tribunal claims are almost exclusively about events that have taken place in a workplace. The people who have firsthand knowledge of those events will predominantly be those employed in that workplace; and employees are understandably reluctant to make themselves unpopular with their employers by giving evidence against them in the employment tribunal.[1]

5.4   Claimants often feel that this stacks the odds against them: if the respondent has five witnesses, they feel that they too ought to be able to field a comparable team. This is usually a mistake. First, most tribunals can be trusted not to decide disputes of fact on numbers

---

1   This can be disappointing standing up to your employer over an injustice to a colleague is not perhaps at the high end of heroism but it is a rare thing nevertheless.

alone. If Sister Winston (of P6.11.2) and two other nurses say that Saifur Rahman shouted 'I've had enough of your fucking nagging' etc, but Mr Rahman can provide no witnesses to support his denial, Mr Rahman is very little if at all worse placed than if the evidence against him on this point were Sister Winston's alone. Whether it is Mr Rahman against three nurses or Mr Rahman against one nurse, the tribunal will have to decide whom to believe. It will not be surprised that none of his former colleagues is willing to support him at the tribunal, so it will not hold this against him.

5.5   In fact, calling two or more witnesses to give what is basically the same evidence (e.g. that Mr Rahman swore at Sister Winston, or that he did not) is a dangerous tactic for either side, particularly if the witnesses are likely to face expert cross-examination. Making the truth sound truthful under skilful cross-examination can be difficult. Sustaining a consistent lie under the same conditions is extremely so. Some witnesses are clever enough to emerge from cross-examination unscathed even when they are not telling the truth, but calling three witnesses to give essentially the same evidence gives the other side three shots at doing serious damage to the story in cross-examination.

5.6   Witnesses in addition to the claimant are sometimes helpful, of course. A colleague may, exceptionally, prove willing to risk the employer's displeasure by giving evidence about what took place in the workplace, and if the colleague can give relevant evidence about something that the claimant has no first hand knowledge of, this can be very powerful. A relative or spouse may be able to give evidence about the emotional effects of discrimination. A former colleague may have relevant evidence to give. Sometimes expert evidence is necessary. In general, witnesses should only be called if they have genuinely relevant evidence about the central incidents. Claimants often want to put in character evidence, or references from previous employers, but this kind of material is almost never worthwhile.

5.7   Occasionally the claimant may be disappointed to learn that the respondent does not plan to call a particular witness whom she was hoping to cross-examine. Generally it will be preferable for the claimant to seek to capitalise on the witness's absence than to try to secure her attendance, but if you believe that the reason why the respondent has decided not to call a particular individual is that it expects her to be a disastrous witness who will either agree with anything that is suggested to her, lose her temper or be caught out lying (or ideally all three), you may wish to try to secure her attendance.[2]

---

2 For how to go about this, see para 5.46 below.

The role of witness statements

5.8   Witness statements are expected in England and Wales.[3] There will normally have been a direction to exchange statements with the other side some days or weeks before the hearing, but even if this is not the case the tribunal will expect to see typed witness statements on the day. Some tribunals will refuse to hear from a witness for whom no written statement has been prepared, or will order an adjournment (with the risk of costs) in order for this to be done.

5.9   The witness statement will normally be read aloud by the witness, who will then be questioned by the respondent's advocate and the tribunal. If time is short, the statements are long or there is some reason why a particular witness will find it difficult to read aloud, the tribunal may take time at the beginning of the hearing to read the statements. Then when the witnesses come to give evidence they can simply be asked to confirm that the statement is theirs and is true, and cross-examination can begin.

5.10   The aim in drafting a witness statement is to give, clearly and in a logical (usually chronological) order, the whole of the story the witness has to tell. When it comes to the hearing, however, there is very often a need to expand orally on the witness statement, either because the statement is not as complete as it should have been or because the witness wishes to comment on allegations that have been made for the first time in the respondent's witness statements. Tribunals should always permit supplementary questions in chief to deal with matters raised for the first time in the other side's witness statements.[4]

5.11   Tribunals will often also permit an advocate to ask supplementary questions even where the additional information sought could have been included in the original statement, but it is unwise to rely on this. The statement should therefore be drafted to include all the detail that the party wants the tribunal to hear. Sometimes in complex cases the tribunal will direct the parties to exchange supplementary witness statements after the main statements have been exchanged. Again, if this is done it is important to include the whole of the claimant's comment on the respondent's statements in the supplementary statement:

---

3   Curiously, the practice is different in Scotland, where witnesses give their evidence by way of examination-in-chief: that is, the advocate on their side asks them a series of questions – which should not be leading questions – aimed at giving them the chance to tell their story.

4   That is, questions from the claimant or her advocate.

if supplementary statements have been permitted, there is a real risk that supplementary questions in chief will be strictly limited.

Relevance

5.12   Relevance is difficult. What the witness thinks is important may be very different from what the tribunal considers relevant. Material is relevant if it is directly about the subject-matter of the complaint, or if it tends to suggest that the claimant's central allegations are true.

> **Example**
> The claimant complains of a number of separate instances of sex discrimination. She feels that she has been undervalued for years, and has a series of complaints against a number of different managers about failures to promote on a number of different occasions. She has had particular difficulties at work since returning from a period of maternity leave two years ago.
>
> Most of the individual acts are more than three months before her complaint, but the tribunal has agreed to extend time for events over the last two years because they concern the same individuals and are connected. The claimant is still very aggrieved about what happened when she worked for a different branch of the same employer four years ago, but the tribunal has refused jurisdiction to hear those complaints. The claimant may still want to talk about what happened four years ago, and may feel that it is all part of the same pattern. If it involves different individuals at a different workplace, the tribunal will almost certainly say that this story has no bearing on whether or not they should believe the claimant's more recent allegations.
>
> If on the other hand the claimant says that the same manager who failed to promote her also bullied a colleague into resigning shortly after her return from maternity leave, this is plainly relevant. It is not part of the claimant's complaint, but it tends to suggest that this manager has a bad attitude to new mothers.

5.13   A significant part of the adviser's task in drafting the claimant's witness statement is to exclude irrelevant material, and at the same time to explain to the claimant why it is irrelevant. If this is not handled sensitively, the claimant may feel she has been stifled and prevented from telling the full story, and may be keen to put that right under cross-examination. Most tribunals will be tolerant up to a point, but if they are presented with a large volume of irrelevant material they are likely to become impatient and to start imposing strict limits on what they are prepared to listen to. It is far better for the claimant to have her adviser make carefully-judged decisions before the hearing about what to include and what to leave out than to have a tired, bored and impatient tribunal make those decisions in haste.

5.14   As well as excluding irrelevant material, the statement must cover the relevant material in full. This advice is easier to give than to follow. It is necessary to have a clear idea of what conclusions the tribunal will have to come to if the claimant is to succeed, and then to ensure that the claimant (or her witnesses) give evidence in support of each.

Example

Saifur Rahman (of P3.11.2 above and P5.28.1 below) complains of unfair dismissal. He will succeed if the tribunal concludes that the reason for his dismissal was that he made a protected disclosure. He will also succeed if the tribunal concludes that although the employer's belief in his misconduct was genuine, that was not a belief for which they had reasonable grounds and/or there were procedural faults with the dismissal.

Mr Rahman's evidence therefore needs to establish the following key points:
- that he made a public interest disclosure – so he needs to tell the story of his complaint about what he heard Sister Winston say;
- that it was Sister Winston whose complaint about him got him into trouble;
- that her complaint was untrue;
- that the disciplinary panel dismissed him because of what Sister Winston had said;
- that the panel did not investigate the complaint against him properly;
- that he was not given an effective right of appeal.

Hearsay

5.15   Hearsay is a much misunderstood concept, but there is no real mystery to it. Evidence is not hearsay evidence just because the witness is reporting what someone else said: in P5.28.1 below, Saifur Rahman's allegation that he heard Lorraine Winston say 'Give him some Somnex' is not hearsay. Hearsay evidence is evidence of a statement of another person given for the purpose of proving the truth of that statement. 'Give him some Somnex' is not a statement at all and is not capable of being true or false. Saifur's assertion that Penny Short had told him that no-one had asked her what she had seen or heard of the alleged incident is hearsay: the purpose of telling the tribunal that Penny said this is to persuade the tribunal that no-one had asked Penny what she had seen or heard. Clearly the best witness of this is Penny, not Saifur, and it is for that reason that there has always been a suspicion of this kind of second-hand evidence.

5.16   There are procedural rules in the ordinary courts that have to be satisfied if hearsay is to be admitted. These do not apply in the employment tribunal, which is entitled to hear any evidence it considers relevant. Nevertheless, it is fair for the tribunal to be sceptical of hearsay evidence unless there is some good reason why the maker of the statement in question could not herself be called to give evidence.

5.17   The claimant in an employment tribunal case may be at a tactical advantage here. If Saifur Rahman failed to call Penny Short, he might be criticised for that by the hospital's counsel, who would say that the tribunal should place little weight on this evidence because Penny was not there to be cross-examined. However, if Saifur has failed to persuade Penny to attend and give evidence because she is still employed by the hospital, he has a good answer to this: 'I cannot persuade Penny to attend because she is worried about souring relations with her employer. You are her employer, so if you say I am misquoting her, or her statement is untrue, why have you not called her?'

5.18   If a claimant wants to rely on hearsay evidence, it may be a useful tactic[5] to alert the respondent to this in advance and invite them to call the witness themselves. It will be difficult for the respondent to protest that the tribunal should place little weight on the statement of a witness who is not available for cross-examination if it is the respondent's own fault that the witness is not available. The letter should be copied to the tribunal.

---

5 Inspired by the Civil Procedure Rules: see rule 33; and on the relevance of the CPR generally, see para 1.42 above.

P5.18 Letter notifying respondent of intention to call hearsay evidence

Carrot & Marrow Solicitors
2 Lower Street
Islington
London N12 3AB

17 January 2007

Your ref: GB/ar 6789
Our ref: NC 1234/2006

Dear Mr Bean

Saifur Rahman v St Julian's Hospital NHS Trust

You will note when witness statements are exchanged that Mr Rahman will give evidence that a care assistant at the Hospital, Penny Short, has told him that although she was present on the Coventry Ward when the incident for which he was dismissed was alleged to have taken place, no-one asked her what she had seen or heard. If asked, she would have confirmed that Mr Rahman's collection of Mrs Goody had passed without incident.

Because Ms Short still works for the Hospital, it has not been possible to persuade her to attend the hearing to give evidence for Mr Rahman. It is of course open to you to call her if you wish.

Yours sincerely

Natalie Cummings

cc the Employment Tribunal

Evidence distinguished from argument

5.19   The witness statement is not the place for legal argument, which should be dealt with in submissions at the end of the hearing. For example, Alice Fearon[6] describes the treatment she has suffered and how it has affected her, but she does not go on in her statement to say why she thinks it amounts to sex discrimination: that is argument, which she or her representative will put in closing submissions to the tribunal. If the respondent's witness statements contain legal argument, the claimant's representative should resist the temptation to cross-examine on it. If in doubt, there is no reason why an adviser should not check with the chairman that she agrees that a particular assertion is legal argument and a matter for submissions on both sides rather than cross-examination.[7]

Example

An employer says 'The Claimant refused an offer of the same job only four miles away from her home. All my other staff agreed to the move, and they all lived more than four miles from the new office. I offered to pay her bus fares and change her hours so that she did not have to travel at lunch-time, but she refused everything and insisted she had to be within 10 minutes' walk of home in case her mother needed her. I know her mother is old and frail, but I am running a business and I do not have to make a good worker redundant just because she refuses to commute a short distance to work.'

The first three sentences here are assertions of fact, and if the claimant agrees that they are accurate then the employer need not be cross-examined on them. The final sentence is a statement of opinion as to the law. It is wrong, but there is no need for the claimant's adviser to take this up with the respondent in cross-examination.

---

6   See P5.28.2 below.

7   Chairmen can be unhelpful when faced with a question of this nature, and say something like 'It is a matter for you what questions you want to put to the witness.' Qualified lawyers and advisers acting for a fee or employed by an advice agency have to take this. A claimant acting in person, or an unqualified person acting for a friend or relative on a one-off basis may wish to point out that she does not have legal expertise, and the chairman does: part of the chairman's function is to provide this sort of guidance.

The style of writing

5.20   The statement is a formal document, and where lawyers are involved it will normally have been drafted by a lawyer. It is worth making sure that the witness is aware that this is standard practice. Sometimes a witness is asked in cross-examination: 'Did you write this yourself?' and the witness, suddenly fearing that it will be thought improper for her to have signed a document drafted by someone else, may be rattled enough to answer 'Yes' when it is obvious that cannot be true.

5.21   The aim in drafting a witness statement should be to write a clear, logical and reasonably formal account, but using words that are within the witness's own vocabulary. A balance must be struck between attempting a close imitation of the witness's natural speaking style – which in most cases will be excessively informal – and drafting a document parts of which, because of complex vocabulary or syntax, the witness cannot comfortably read aloud or even does not understand. The witness's credibility will be severely damaged if it turns out in the course of questioning that she does not understand the meaning of some of the words used in her 'own' statement: although there is no expectation that she has written it herself, she certainly should have read it carefully and made sure that she was happy to swear to it. It is important to remember that the statement will have to be read under the stress of the tribunal hearing. If in doubt, it is probably better to err on the side of informality.

5.22   It is important to make the statement concrete and specific. If the claimant is a kitchen assistant whom the chef has victimised by allocating her to all the dirtiest and most unpleasant jobs, her statement should not say 'The chef treated me unfairly in the allocation of kitchen tasks' – it should say 'From [approximate date when the victimisation started] the chef started allocating me only to the pot-wash, cleaning the chip-fryers, and filling the pig bins. These were all hot, smelly and unpleasant tasks, and everyone hated them. I was never put on floor mopping, wiping the kitchen surfaces or table clearing, which were the end of service tasks that everyone preferred.' Similarly, if the claimant's manager called her a 'useless fuckwit,' her statement should not say 'My manager shouted and swore at me' – it should spell out the allegation in full. Sometimes claimants are hesitant to quote abusive language in the formal setting of a tribunal; they can be assured that the members of the tribunal are used to hearing such stories, and will want to know exactly what was said in any relevant exchange.

5.23   Tribunals have different preferences when it comes to referring to individuals by name, and no approach will please all tribunals. Here each individual's full name is used when she is first mentioned; subsequently she is referred to in whatever manner is habitual with the witness, thus: 'The next day I found a note on my desk from my line manager, Jennifer Bennett (Jenny) telling me that I was not to work from home in the future without her express permission. Jenny was not in that day ...'

5.24   If a statement mentions 'Jennifer Bennett' once and then refers consistently to 'Ms Bennett' it will be confusing for the tribunal if the witness, in answer to questions, speaks of 'Jenny.' It is easier to make the statement conform to whatever name comes naturally to the witness than to expect the witness, under the stress of cross-examination, to remember to refer to the person she knows as Jenny as 'Ms Bennett' or 'Jennifer Bennett'.

5.25   A statement should be set out in numbered paragraphs, double spaced so that there is space for notes. The 'statement of truth' is a formality that has become common in the employment tribunals because it is required in the ordinary courts. There is no technical necessity for it in an employment tribunal, but there is no harm in conforming either.

Accuracy

5.26   The accuracy of the statements is extremely important. The adviser should make sure that the claimant (or other witness) understands very clearly that the statement is her statement, not the adviser's, and she must be sufficiently sure that it is all true to be willing to swear to it. It is essential that the witness has had a sufficient opportunity to check the statement for accuracy before it is signed. If possible, it is preferable to send the witness away with a draft to read at leisure rather than asking her to read it in an interview room while the adviser waits: many people simply cannot give the task the attention it needs if they are conscious that someone busy is waiting for them to finish.

5.27   It is necessary to remember that giving evidence in a tribunal is a once-in-a-lifetime experience for most people, and witnesses are often confused about exactly what their role is. One of the most heart-sinking things that can happen for a representative listening to her witness give evidence is to hear the employer's advocate say 'The statement at paragraph 24 is not true, then?' and the witness reply 'No, it's not'.

There is worse to come. The next question goes, 'So why did you put it in your statement?' and the witness answers 'Because Miss Cummings told me to.'

5.28   Of course Miss Cummings did not think she was telling the witness what to say. She drafted a witness statement that she believed reflected what the witness had told her. What she failed to do was make it sufficiently clear to the witness that ultimate responsibility for the contents of the statement lay with the witness, not with the adviser; and that the task she was attempting was to draft a true account of what the witness told her, and not to tell the witness what she ought to say.

DOCUMENT OUTLINE: Witness statement

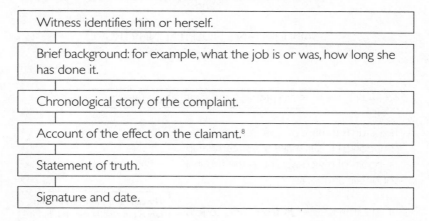

Witness identifies him or herself.

Brief background: for example, what the job is or was, how long she has done it.

Chronological story of the complaint.

Account of the effect on the claimant.[8]

Statement of truth.

Signature and date.

---

8   If it is clear by the time the statement is drafted that there will need to be a separate remedy hearing, this can go in a separate statement for the purpose. It should not be assumed that remedies will be dealt with separately unless the tribunal has said so.

P5.28.1 Witness statement – unfair dismissal for whistle-blowing

IN THE EMPLOYMENT TRIBUNAL   Case No 123456/07
LONDON CENTRAL

BETWEEN

SAIFUR RAHMAN

Claimant

and

SAINT JULIAN'S HOSPITAL NHS TRUST

Respondent

STATEMENT OF SAIFUR RAHMAN

I, Saifur Rahman, of 25a Pepper Lane, London E11 2LL, make this statement in support of my complaint to the tribunal of unfair dismissal:

1. I came to the UK from India to join my wife and baby son in July 2000. After a short period working for a family business, I applied for a job at the Hospital as a porter and started working there in December 2002. My job was to transport patients and equipment from one part of the hospital to another, as instructed by medical staff.

> *The claimant's immigration history is not strictly relevant, but it sets the scene.*

2. I was employed on an initial probationary period of six months. In about May 2003 I attended a probationary review meeting with my line manager, Mark Bowland (Mark). Mark congratulated me on

my performance. He said that he had heard very good things from all the medical staff I had worked with, and he said that the patients liked me because I was gentle and respectful with them. He said my employment would be confirmed. I got a letter from Mark confirming me as a permanent employee the next day. I did not have any other formal appraisals, but it continued to be clear that Mark and the medical staff I worked with were very happy with my work. I also got on well with patients.

The point of paragraphs 2, 3, 4 and 5 is to establish Mr Rahman as a good, reliable and caring employee whose employers think well of him this is directly relevant because it suggests that Sister Winston's allegations are inherently implausible and the Hospital should have regarded them with scepticism and investigated them more carefully than they did.

3. In November 2004 I was promoted to the position of supervising porter.

4. Sometime in January or February 2007 I had a conversation with one of the Sisters, who asked me about my career intentions. She said she thought I was wasted as a porter and seemed to be picking up a lot about the patients and their care. She asked me if I had ever thought about getting qualified as a nurse. I had not thought about that before, but I discussed it with my wife that evening and began to think about it seriously. I did not know this Sister's name except that I think she was known as Shaz, but she was in charge of the ENT ward until about the end of March 2006.

5. On 7 May 2006 I was sent to Coventry Ward, a geriatric ward, to collect a patient, Lisa Goody (Mrs Goody), for physiotherapy. Mrs Goody was well into her eighties and frail and quite deaf, but she was still mentally very sharp. She greeted

Mrs Goody's mental acuity is relevant, because her age notwithstanding she could and should have been asked what had happened.

me by name and said 'How's my favourite boy nurse?' She knew I was not a nurse, but she liked to tease.

6. As I reached the ward I heard the Ward Sister, Lorraine Winston, say to a junior nurse 'Give him some Somnex, it's the only way we'll get any peace round here. Don't put it on his chart or the doctor will create.' I think she was referring to a patient I knew as Roy. Roy was quite far gone with dementia and could be bad-tempered and difficult. Lorraine then looked up and saw that I had heard what she had said. She looked flustered, and said 'Only joking. You'd have to be a saint not to be tempted with some of them.'

7. I was very worried about this. I knew about Somnex because my mother-in-law, who is in her eighties, suffered a serious stroke last year while she was on the drug. It is a powerful prescription sedative, and it is dangerous for old people. I did not believe that Lorraine had been joking, and I was afraid that what I had heard meant that Roy was being given Somnex, without a prescription or proper record-keeping, to keep him quiet. I knew Roy was on a low salt diet, and I thought that might mean he was thought to be at risk of a stroke, so I was worried that Somnex might be particularly dangerous for him.

8. I reported what I had heard to Mark. I did not tell him about my own family experience of Somnex because I am not an expert, but I thought it was bad if a patient was

> *Again, helping to establish that Mr Rahman is habitually kind to patients. 'She liked to tease' shows that the 'boy nurse' comment does not mean she is not on the ball.*

> *Paras 7 and 8 explain the subject-matter of the public interest disclosure allegation: Mr Rahman is explaining what he heard and why it troubled him. It is important to establish that his disclosure was made in good faith.*

being given prescription drugs without the doctors' knowledge. Mark refused to take any action. He said 'Don't worry, Lorraine's been at the Hospital forever. She would never do anything like that.' When I pressed him he said, 'What do you know about drugs?'

9. On 11 May 2007 I wrote to the Chief Executive of the Hospital about what I had overheard.

10. On 17 May 2007 the Chief Executive replied promising that my allegation would be looked into, and on 24 May I had a letter from Martin Ogunfowora, a human resources manager, saying that my allegation had been thoroughly investigated and no evidence of unauthorised medication had been found.

11. That afternoon, I went to Coventry Ward to collect Mrs Goody for another physiotherapy session. Sister Winston was on the desk doing paperwork. She looked up and said to me, 'You're toast.' I asked her what she meant, but she just repeated, 'You're toast. Just you wait.'

12. On 26 May 2007 I got a letter dated 25 May from Maisie Lee, another human resources manager. The letter said that I had been accused of swearing at a Sister in the presence of patients and junior nurses. It said I was suspended with immediate effect, and there would be a disciplinary meeting at 10.30am on 4 June 2007.

13. Enclosed in the letter were copies of written statements signed by Lorraine and two other nurses from

As this does not seem to have resulted in any action, it is not the relevant disclosure itself, but it is relevant to explain that Mr Rahman started by raising his concerns at the appropriate level and did not go straight to the Chief Executive.

This is the disclosure.

This explains, implicitly, how Sister Winston became aware of the allegation.

This is not hearsay: Mr Rahman does not quote it in order to persuade the tribunal that he is toast, but to persuade them that Sister Winston had it in for him.

the Coventry Ward, Sharon Foster and Michelle Brown. All the statements said that when Lorraine had asked me why I was late to collect a patient on 24 May 2007 I had shouted, 'I've had enough of your fucking nagging. Why don't you take the fucking patient yourself if you're in such a hurry?' The statements said I had then wheeled Mrs Goody's wheelchair out of the ward so fast that she had been frightened and had cried out, and that I slammed the door behind me.

These two paragraphs are centrally relevant: they deal with what Sister Winston did to victimise Mr Rahman for his complaint.

14. I was shocked and astounded by these allegations. I have never sworn at work in my life, and I would never shout at a nurse. I do not think I was late to collect Mrs Goody, and I am sure Lorraine did not accuse me of being late at the time. I am always careful to move patients gently so that they are not frightened. I am especially careful with elderly patients because I know hospital can be very frightening for them. I always try to treat elderly patients as I would like my own parents to be treated.

This emphasises again why the employer should have found Sister Winston's allegations implausible.

15. I thought, and I still think, that the only possible explanation for the accusation was that this was what Lorraine meant when she said 'You're toast'. She meant that she was intending to make up a story to get me sacked.

16. I went to the disciplinary hearing on my own because although the letter had said that I could ask a colleague to accompany me I did not want to tell a colleague about these horri-

Strictly speaking Mr Rahman's opinion on this subject is not relevant, but this explains the basis for his complaint of automatically unfair dismissal.

ble accusations. I thought it would be all around the hospital if I told anyone and I was afraid some people might believe it. I arrived for the hearing at 10.10 because I was anxious not to be late, but the meeting did not start until 10.45. No-one told me why it was starting late or apologised. They just called me in at 10.45 and started the meeting.

This is of marginal relevance, but it bolsters Mr Rahman's insistence that it would be completely out of character for him to behave as alleged.

This shows a cavalier attitude to proceedings by the employer.

17. I told the panel that the allegations against me were completely untrue. I said that Mrs Goody would remember if anything like this had happened. One of the panel said it would be completely inappropriate to ask a geriatric patient that sort of question, and anyway there were three witnesses who all said the same thing. This was the elder of two women on the panel: I think it must have been Elaine Watson. They seemed to think that because there were three nurses saying one thing and only me saying the other, the nurses must be telling the truth.

18. I tried to tell the panel that I thought this was Lorraine's way of getting back at me for writing to the Chief Executive about her giving Somnex to an elderly patient. The chairman of the panel said this was a completely separate matter that had been investigated already. He said it was not relevant. Another member of the panel started to ask me a question about this, but the chairman stopped her and said again that it was a separate matter and had been dealt with. The panel member who wanted to ask the question

In other words, the employer was alerted to the fact that Sister Winston might have an axe to grind ...

... but refused to take this into account.

looked very much the youngest member of the panel. She seemed quite nervous and blushed when the chairman spoke to her. From the paperwork I have seen since I think she was Leah Tuckey.

19. Towards the end of the meeting the chairman of the panel said that this was a very serious allegation and they would be bound to consider dismissing me. He asked me if I would apologise to Lorraine if they decided not to dismiss me. I did not see how I could apologise for something that I had not done, and I told them that.

20. At about 11.20am they told me to go outside and wait while they decided what to do. I was given a cup of tea by someone in the personnel office, but I had hardly started it when they called me back in. I do not think I can have waited more than 5 minutes. When I went back in, the chairman told me that they had decided to dismiss me without notice for gross misconduct. I asked if there was a right of appeal, but the chairman said 'It is all in the letter, but there's not much point appealing unless you are prepared to apologise.' I remember that this is exactly how he put it because I thought it was a bit odd that he referred to the dismissal letter as if it already existed. I did not think they had had time to write anything.

21. I was sent outside again. The chairman told me to wait while he wrote the dismissal letter, but the personnel officer who had made me a cup

> *That is, there was a member of the panel who was sympathetic to Mr Rahman, but she was powerless.*

> *It is always a good idea to pin time estimates to concrete events in this way if possible.*

of tea brought it almost at once. I had the impression that they must have had it ready before the meeting began. The letter said that I had a right of appeal and could exercise it by writing to the Director of Human Resources. I did not appeal because of what the chairman had said. I could not apologise to Lorraine because I was not prepared to admit to having behaved in a way that was inconceivable.

It will be argued for Mr Rahman that in this way he was effectively denied any right of appeal. Even if this is not accepted, it is important to explain why he has not exercised his right of appeal in order to avoid being penalised for that failure if and when the tribunal comes to consider.

22. I left the Hospital in a state of shock and went home to tell my wife what had happened. She was very upset and cried on and off all afternoon and evening.

Strictly irrelevant, but might help the sympathy vote along.

23. My wife and I are friendly with Penny Short, a care assistant at the Hospital. She lives close by and has a young daughter at the same nursery as our son, and we baby-sit for each other sometimes. When she heard that I had been dismissed she came round for tea. She told us that she had seen me arrive to collect Mrs Goody on 27 May and she could have confirmed if she had been asked that I had collected her quietly and without incident. She said she knew it was 27 May because that was her first day back from leave. She said to me that no-one had asked her about the allegations that had been made against me.

It might be said by the employer that Penny is only supportive because she is a friend, so it is better to admit to the friendship up front than to give the impression that she is a purely neutral onlooker.

This is hearsay: Mr Rahman seeks to establish that no-one did ask her about the allegation.

24. I have not yet been able to find another job, although I have made many applications. I have had a lot of interviews, but employers always

want to know what my last job was and why I have left it. When I tell them I do not hear from them again. I am now wondering if I should apply to do the nursing diploma course full-time as there is no point in studying part-time if I do not have a job.

> *This explains the level of Mr Rahman's loss, set out more fully in his schedule of loss.*

25. This statement is true to the best of my knowledge and belief.

Signed _____ Dated _____

P5.28.2 Witness statement – sex discrimination[9]

IN THE EMPLOYMENT TRIBUNAL   Case No 12345/2005
LONDON NORTH WEST

BETWEEN

ALICE FEARON

Claimant

and

NAFF TAT PLC

Respondent

_____
STATEMENT OF ALICE FEARON
_____

I, Alice Fearon of 2 Pond Lane, Hackney London N17 2BD make this statement in support of my complaint to the employment tribunal:

1. On 5 April 2007 I was interviewed for a job as a sales assistant at the Naff Tat on Tottenham High Road. The interview was set up by

---

9   The story makes it clear that the employee had been treated badly, but the argument that the treatment amounted to sex discrimination is far from clear-cut.

Helen Wale (Nell), my Disability Employment Adviser at the Tottenham Job Centre. I have a learning disability.

2. I was offered the job, and I started work the next day.

3. There were several things about the new job that I was a bit worried about. I was told that Sunday working on a rota was compulsory. I did not really want to work Sundays because I am a regular member of a local church, but as I had been out of work for three years I accepted the job. I was also worried once I started work about some safety issues. I was expected to climb a wobbly ladder to ceiling level, and some of the fire exits were blocked. I tried to talk to my manager, James Barfield (James) about these worries, and I also told him that I was not happy about being made to stay at work sometimes after 6pm when I was supposed to finish. He just said I could take the job or leave it.

4. I was particularly unhappy about the company's insistence on searching me every time I left the premises, up to four times a day. A manager did the search in the public area of the shop, asking me to lift up my top and my trouser leg showing my bare skin to demonstrate that I was not stealing any of the company's goods. These searches were almost always carried out by a male manager or supervisor. The only time the search was done by a woman was on my last day when the regular manager was not there and the relief manager was a woman.

5. I found this search procedure extremely humiliating. I would have found it unpleasant if the search had been conducted in private by a woman, but I found it particularly upsetting to be searched like this by a man in public. I talked to Nell about it, and she contacted the company's head office and was told that it was company policy to conduct searches and to insist on Sunday working. She also came to see James at the shop, and he demonstrated to her how the search was done.

6. On 19 and 20 April I had two days off, and I went to see Nell at the Job Centre. She contacted the Naff Tat head office and spoke to someone who promised that in future the searches would be done by a woman and away from the public area of the shop. I do not believe that they can have intended to keep this promise because most days I worked in the shop there was no female manager or supervisor present.

7. On 21 April for the first time there was a female relief manager. I went to see Nell in my lunch break. I was searched on my way out, as usual in the public area of the shop. I told Nell that I had decided that I was not going to put up with the searches any more. I asked her to be there with me when I told the manager this.

8. A little while after I got back from lunch, Nell came into the shop. I told the relief manager in front of her that I was not going to let them search me any more. The relief manager said it was company policy and she would make me. Nell asked her how she intended to do this, and I said she could call the police if she wanted.

9. The relief manager telephoned Michael Sugar, the regional manager after Nell had left. He came at about 5pm, looking very angry. He called me upstairs and said that I was on a trial period and they were dismissing me because my work was unsatisfactory. I asked him to put the reason for my dismissal in writing, but he said it was not company policy. He then escorted me off the premises.

10. Before my dismissal no-one had criticised my work in any way. I am convinced that I was dismissed because I refused to submit to the searches.

11. I found the searches extremely upsetting. I had been very excited when I was offered the job at Naff Tat and asked to start work the next day because I had been out of work for so long. I was happy to have a job at last and I was looking forward to earning a wage and having some money to spend. This meant that I was particularly upset when the job did not work out. For the fortnight that I worked at Naff Tat I cried most days because I was so upset about the searches, and I only put up with the situation for as long as I did because I was not confident about my chances of getting another job. I put on weight while I was at Naff Tat because I was so unhappy that I went to McDonald's every day for lunch to cheer myself up. The whole situation made me feel very low and damaged my confidence.

12. When I was dismissed by Naff Tat, I was worried that I would be out of work again for a long time. I thought any other employer would want to know why I had been dismissed from my previous job.

13. This statement is true to the best of my knowledge and belief.

Signed _____ Dated _____

Preparing witnesses: how far can you go?

5.29   Witnesses must not be coached. That is to say, they must not be told
what answers to give, or rehearsed in their manner of giving them.
If you are an adviser, it is sometimes necessary to spell this out to the
claimant: some will want to be told what they ought to say. The only permissible answer to 'What should I say if they ask me XYZ?' is 'You
must tell the truth'.

5.30   However, although it is unacceptable – and for a lawyer, professional misconduct – to coach a witness, that does not mean that witnesses must be sent completely naked into battle. There are various
steps that can quite properly be taken to make it easier for the witness to give her evidence in a helpful and convincing manner. Managers
and personnel officers giving evidence for the respondent will often
have appeared as witnesses before or seen their colleagues giving evidence in other proceedings. They may even have been sent on special witness training courses. There is nothing wrong with trying to level
the playing field a little. In the paragraphs below it is assumed that
the claimant is represented, although the advice given here can also be
followed by a claimant intending to represent herself.

Attending a hearing

5.31   The claimant (and any other witness who is willing) should be encouraged to attend an employment tribunal hearing in order to get an idea
for the feel of the process and in particular how cross examination is
conducted. If the respondent is legally represented, the claimant should
try to see a hearing (or part of one) in which the respondent is represented.

Getting familiar with the bundle

5.32   The claimant should be provided with a complete copy of the hearing
bundle as soon as it is available, and should become as familiar with it
as possible. The reason for this is that suggestions may be made to
her in cross-examination which she could show to be wrong by reference to a document in the bundle if she could find it in time. In a document-heavy case, it may also be worth pointing out before she has
begun to give her evidence that if in the course of cross-examination she
is sure there is a document that proves she is right but cannot immediately find it, there is no reason why he should not say so and ask to

be taken to it.[10] She is entitled to assume that the lawyer cross-examining him knows the bundle better than she does.

The oath or affirmation

5.33   Each witnesses will be asked how she wishes to give her evidence that is, whether she wishes to swear to tell the truth on the Bible or the Koran or another holy book, or make a solemn non-religious promise, called an affirmation.[11] Occasionally, when asked this by the Chairman, a witness will say something to the effect 'I don't mind'. This is probably the only available bad answer to the question, and can give the impression that the witness takes a casual approach to the oath, but a surprising number of witness give it. It is a good idea, therefore, to warn witnesses that they need to make up their mind about whether they will swear or affirm, and if they will swear, on which holy book.[12] There is no rule that witnesses with a religious affiliation must swear rather than affirm: it is a purely personal choice that will not be questioned by the tribunal.

The truth, the whole truth, and nothing but the truth

5.34   Whatever its form, the promise is to tell the truth, the whole truth and nothing but the truth. This is not only a solemn commitment that the witness is required to make: it is also the best single piece of advice to any witness about how to convince the tribunal. Leaving aside any question of moral judgement, telling lies is a very effective way to help win the case for the other side. Trying to add 'spin' to the story is nearly as effective. If a damaging admission has to be made, it is far better to make it readily and candidly than to have it wrung out of you after a lot of hesitating and hedging.

---

10   She must not be given this or any other advice once she has begun to give her evidence. Once a witness has been sworn, she must not speak to anyone about the subject-matter of the case or her evidence until she has been released.

11   Most commonly this is established by the clerk before the hearing or the relevant day's evidence begins, but sometimes the chairman will ask immediately before the witness sits down at the witness table.

12   Not knowing which is the applicable holy book can probably be taken as a sufficient indication that the more appropriate choice is to affirm.

5.35   Moreover, trying to sustain a lie or a series of lies is to enter into a demanding contest with the lawyer conducting the cross-examination, which the witness is likely to lose. Most witnesses giving evidence and responding to cross-examination will be doing something they have never done in their lives before, under high pressure and in unfamiliar surroundings. Most lawyers cross-examining witnesses are doing something they have been carefully trained to do, and in which they have practised and honed their skills over large number of previous hearings. The contest is an unequal one. The witness's eagerness to give the 'right' answer (that is, the answer that is the most beneficial rather than the most truthful) is a weakness that can be exploited.[13]

5.36   For an advocate, the most disappointing kind of witness to cross-examine is one who simply gives a short, clear, calm and truthful answer to every question.

Translated witness statements

5.37   Sometimes the claimant or a witness does not have good enough English to give evidence in English. An interpreter will be needed for the hearing, and in most cases for the purposes of drafting and approving the statement as well. This calls for particular caution. Suppose the claimant is a Bengali speaker with very limited English. The adviser speaks no Bengali, so interviews the claimant through an interpreter and then drafts the witness statement from her notes of that interview. The finished document, being written in English, is not something that the claimant can read and check for herself, so until it has been translated back to her she cannot properly be asked to swear to the tribunal that it is true. It is almost certainly not completely true: drafting a completely accurate witness statement from a set of notes of an interview is rarely possible on the first attempt even when adviser and client share a mother tongue.

5.38   The best course in these circumstances is to arrange a second interview with the interpreter present at which the interpreter reads and translates the statement sentence by sentence and corrections can be made. The statement of truth should then say something like 'I have had this statement translated to me and its contents are true to the best of my knowledge and belief.'

13 For example, the traps demonstrated at para 8.60 simply do not work if the witnesses resist all temptation to 'spin'.

5.39   In these circumstances it will be impractical for the witness to read her statement aloud to the tribunal. The normal course is for questions to be asked to establish that the statement has been translated for her and that she swears to its truth and then the tribunal to read it to themselves.

Witness orders

5.40   The tribunal has power under rule 10(c) of the Procedure Rules to order the attendance of witnesses. The power is mainly exercised on the application of a party, most often in circumstances where the witness is willing to give evidence but is concerned that without an order her employer may not give her time off to attend the hearing. An application for a witness order is made by writing to the tribunal. The letter should explain briefly the relevance of the witness's evidence and the reason why an order is needed – for example, that the witness is unwilling to attend without an order, or that the witness is afraid her employer will not give him or her time off. The letter should also give the full name and address of the witness.

5.41   Rule 11 of the Procedure Rules states that any application to the tribunal must say how the order will assist the tribunal in dealing with the proceedings efficiently and fairly. In the case of a witness order, that follows from the fact that the witness has relevant evidence to give, so it is suggested that this should be included.

5.42   An application for a witness order is the only interlocutory application to a tribunal that need not be copied to the respondent with instructions about how and when to object if they wish to. A witness order is a private matter between the party seeking it, the witness and the tribunal, and will not be disclosed to the other party.

DOCUMENT OUTLINE: Application for a witness order

Request for an order against X
Brief explanation of the relevance of X's evidence
Statement that X is unwilling to attend without an order (with reason if known)
Witness's full postal address

P5.42 Application for a witness order

The Regional Secretary
Employment Tribunals (London South)
Montague Court
101 London Rd
West Croydon CRO 2RF

Your ref: 12345/2007
Our ref: NC/1234/07

15 December 2007

Dear Madam

Mr R Rahman v St Julian's Hospital NHS Trust

I should be grateful for an order for Ms Penny Short to attend the hearing as a witness in this case at the hearing listed for 12–14 January 2008.

Ms Short's evidence will assist the tribunal in dealing efficiently and fairly with the case because she was present on the occasion on which the respondent alleges that Mr Rahman was guilty of the misconduct for which he was dismissed. Ms Short will give evidence that the alleged misconduct did not take place, and that she had no involvement in the respondent's investigation into the allegation.

Ms Short's address is 123 Rodney Road, London N17 9EQ. She works for the respondent as a care assistant and is unwilling to attend unless ordered to do so.

Ms Short is due to sit an examination at 10am on the first day of the hearing. I propose to call the claimant first, and I think it is most unlikely that his evidence will be completed until after lunch, so I should be grateful if Ms Short could be ordered to attend from 2pm only.

Yours faithfully

Natalie Cummings

Tactical considerations on witness orders

5.43   The difficulty for the claimant in an employment tribunal case is that witnesses who might be able to give helpful evidence will more often than not be employees of the respondent. They may well be unwilling to give evidence because – rightly or wrongly – they fear victimisation by the employer. There is only a limited amount of comfort the claimant's adviser can give such a witness: it is not accurate to say 'Your employer cannot dismiss you or victimise you for giving evidence.' The employer can do either, and some will. Dismissal for such a reason would give the witness a strong employment tribunal claim of her own, and victimisation on this basis would be actionable in its own right, but most employees will feel that keeping their job or not being victimised is preferable to having good grounds for a claim to the employment tribunal.

5.44   A witness who is genuinely unwilling to attend the hearing and give evidence presents a difficult problem. There are two kinds of unwilling witnesses a claimant might seek to call. The more common kind is someone who is (or is believed to be) essentially supportive of the claimant, but is unwilling to be involved in tribunal proceedings, often out of concern for her own employment position. Sometimes a witness will first agree to give evidence, and provide a statement, but then change her mind; sometimes she will simply refuse to give a statement at all. It is risky to apply to the tribunal for an order even if the witness has previously provided a statement: a judgement will need to be made whether the witness will stick to her statement if forced to attend against her will. If the witness has not provided a statement and refuses to do so, the risks are even greater: the claimant has no way of knowing what she will say.

5.45   More rarely, a claimant may wish to seek a witness order compelling the attendance of someone she knows will wish to support the respondent's case, but whom she wishes to cross-examine. Both situations are potentially difficult.

Hostile witnesses

5.46   If the claimant calls a witness whom she believes to be supportive, but who effectively changes sides at the hearing, the claimant may wish to cross-examine her. It may, for example, be necessary to ask her why she has changed her story, or suggest to her that the employer has put pressure on her.

5.47 Here the claimant may well find herself up against another of the unwritten rules of the employment tribunals: 'This is your witness', she may be told, 'so you cannot cross-examine her'. This will be news to most non-lawyers, and it is nowhere to be found in the Procedure Rules. It reflects the practice in the ordinary courts, and it is a practice that, broadly speaking, it is useful to follow in the employment tribunals.

5.48 A very large part of cross-examination is asking a series of leading questions. If parties were routinely allowed to cross-examine their own witnesses, the evidence obtained that way would be of little use. If the adviser asks the claimant 'Did so-and-so happen?' and 'So then you did so-and-so?' and 'That was because you felt ... so-and-so?' the tribunal will not feel it has heard the story from the claimant at all. Instead they will have heard the claimant obediently agreeing to everything her adviser has suggested.

5.49 On the other hand, if a witness is clearly unwilling to give evidence helpful to the party that has called her, then it does need to be open to that party to cross-examine. In those circumstances, if the cross-examination is effective, the evidence wrung out of the witness may be telling.

5.50 In the ordinary civil and criminal courts there is a body of rules, drawn from both legislation and decided cases, on the circumstances in which a party is to be permitted to cross-examine her own witness. In the tribunals there are no comparable established rules, but it is clearly within the tribunal's general case management powers under rule 10 to permit cross-examination of a hostile witness if necessary. Any assertion (from the tribunal or the other side) that the tribunal has 'no power' to do so is simply wrong: if necessary the tribunal can be reminded of rule 14(2) of the Procedure Rules:

> 'So far as it appears appropriate to do so, the chairman or tribunal shall seek to avoid formality in his or its proceedings and shall not be bound by any enactment or rule of law relating to the admissibility of evidence in proceedings before the courts.'

5.51 Slightly different questions arise in relation to the witness, known to be supportive of the employer's case, whom the claimant wishes to cross-examine but whom the respondent does not propose to call.[14] The best way of securing the attendance of such a witness, if it works, is to pressurise the respondent into calling her. It is perfectly fair to warn

---

14 This will only very rarely be advisable.

a respondent that if they do not call a particular witness who plainly has relevant evidence to give, the claimant will make much of this failure in submissions and ask the tribunal to draw inferences from that witness's absence. If the respondent buckles under pressure and calls the witness the goal is achieved.

5.52   If the respondent refuses to call the witness, there are various options. The claimant can simply carry out the threat and draw the tribunal's attention to the letter. Most tribunals will see the point.[15]

5.53   A second possibility is to request a witness order, but invite the tribunal to call the individual as its own witness. Since the tribunal has power to exercise any of its rule 10 case management powers on its own initiative, it is clear that it must have power to order the attendance of a witness who is not identified as either the claimant's or the respondent's witness. If the witness is known or firmly expected to be hostile, it is advisable to make it clear that the purpose of the request is to allow the claimant to cross-examine the witness.

5.54   A third possibility is to ask the tribunal to order the witness to attend for cross-examination by the claimant. In the ordinary courts, where one party relies on hearsay evidence, for example, there is a procedure under the Civil Procedure Rules for the other to apply to the court for an order that the maker of the statement relied upon should attend for cross-examination on the statement.[16] The powers of employment tribunals to order the attendance of witnesses are broad enough to allow them to do this without a specific rule and there is no reason in principle why they should not adopt this procedure in an appropriate case where it seems clear that there is a witness who has highly relevant evidence to give but who has not been called by either party.

---

15 Although on one occasion known to the authors when a FRU volunteer took this course, he returned from the hearing to report that the chairman had told him it was outrageous to suggest that inferences could be drawn from a particular witness's absence: if he thought that the witness had relevant evidence to give, he could have applied for a witness order. This illustrates something of a catch-22: if some tribunals will take this line, others will refuse to contemplate permitting the claimant to cross-examine her 'own' witness. It is suggested that an adviser in this situation should stand firm, insist that there is nothing improper about inviting the tribunal to draw inferences in these circumstances, and if the effect of the tribunal's refusal to do so is sufficiently important, appeal.

16 See paras 1.42–1.44 above.

P5.54 Application for an order for a witness to attend for cross-examination

The Regional Secretary
London Central Employment Tribunal
Ground floor, Victory House
30-34 Kingsway
London
WC2B 6EX

Your ref: 123456/2007
My ref: NC/1237

14 December 2007

Dear Madam

Rahman v St Julian's NHS Trust

I should be grateful if you would put before a Chairman my application for an order for the attendance of Sister Lorraine Winston at the hearing of this case on 12–14 January 2008.

Sister Winston is the nurse who the claimant alleges made false accusations of misconduct against him. The respondent has indicated that it does not intend to call her. It is clear that Sister Winston has relevant evidence to give, and it is also clear that she will not be a willing or co-operative witness for the claimant. In the circumstances the tribunal is asked to order her attendance as its own witness, and to make her available for cross-examination by either party.

Sister Winston's professional address is:

Coventry Ward
St Julian's Hospital
Commerce Way
London E11 1LL

Yours faithfully

Natalie Cummings

Absent witnesses

5.55   From time to time the claimant will want the tribunal to receive evidence from a witness who has given a statement but who is unable (or unwilling) to attend the hearing. Tribunals will normally be willing to read the statement, but its weight will be severely limited by the fact that the witness is not available for cross-examination by the other party. Evidence from an absent witness should only be used if it is clearly relevant and important, and in that case the claimant should be ready with a clear and full explanation for the witness's inability to attend. Some claimants may prefer to put in an affidavit, but there is probably little real advantage in an affidavit over an ordinary signed statement: either way, the problem remains that the witness is not available for cross-examination.[17]

Expert witnesses

5.56   Sometimes it is necessary to instruct an expert witness in an employment tribunal case. This arises most often in disability discrimination cases where the claimant's disability is in issue, or in other discrimination cases where it is said that the claimant's health has suffered as a result of the discrimination. In an unfair dismissal there may be disputes about the extent of the illness of an employee dismissed for medical incapacity, or about what steps it was reasonable for the claimant to take to mitigate her loss.[18]

5.57   Medical experts are not the only kind of expert it is ever necessary to call in the employment tribunal. If there is a dispute about the extent of a pension loss, then if the claim is large enough it may be necessary to instruct an actuary. A computer expert may be needed if there is a dispute about the implications of computer files or records. A handwriting or document analyst may be needed if there is a sufficiently important dispute about the genuineness of a document.

5.58   The only reference in the Procedure Rules to expert witnesses is at rule 10(2)(t): 'Examples of orders which may be made under paragraph (1) are orders ... (t) as to the use of experts or interpreters in the proceedings.'

---

17 See glossary for an explanation of 'affidavit'.
18 For mitigation, see glossary and para 10.27.

5.59   As so often, the seeming simplicity of the rule is treacherous, and puts non-lawyers at a disadvantage. Expert evidence is an area in which employment tribunals have a particularly strong tendency to conduct proceedings as if they were bound by the provisions of the Civil Procedure Rules. For this reason a claimant who thinks that a report from a medical or other expert is or may be necessary should always look at Part 35 of the CPR.[19]

5.60   The Employment Appeal Tribunal has also given guidance on expert evidence in the employment tribunals in *De Keyser v Wilson*.[20] The main points are as follows:

- A party seeking to rely on expert evidence should ask the tribunal for guidance and/or directions as to whether expert evidence will be acceptable and what arrangements are to be made.
- A joint expert is normally to be preferred.[21]
- If a joint expert is used, the parties should agree how the costs of the evidence are to be divided.
- If one party is unable to contribute to the cost, then the other party may reasonably choose their own expert. Even if this is the case, the tribunal may attach more weight to the evidence if the other party has been asked to approve or at least comment on the proposed letter of instruction to the expert before it was sent.
- The letter of instruction should tell the expert what questions she is required to answer.
- The letter should not take sides between the parties, but should ask the questions in a neutral form, and should emphasise that the expert's main duty is to the tribunal rather than to either party.

19 Reproduced at the end of this chapter; and see www.justice.gov.uk
20 [2001] IRLR 324, EAT.
21 However, where medical evidence is needed the claimant will often have a strong preference to use an existing medical adviser – often a consultant – who already knows her medical history. The respondent will rarely agree to appoint the claimant's own consultant as a joint expert, so separate experts will often be unavoidable.

P5.60 Letter requesting directions for medical evidence

The Regional Secretary
Bristol Employment Tribunal
FAX ONLY 0117 925 3452

Your ref: 123456/2007
Our ref: NC ir/123

8 August 2007

Dear Madam

Pauline Phelps v Sharpe, Gentleman & Co Solicitors

I should be grateful if you would put before a Chairman my request for a direction for a medical report in this case.

Ms Phelps' complaint against the respondent is of discrimination on grounds relating to her disability. Ms Phelps has suffered from occasional bouts of moderate to severe depression throughout her adult life, and she has a serious facial disfigurement. The respondent in its notice of appearance denies that Ms Phelps suffers from a disability within the meaning of section 1 of the Disability Discrimination Act 1995.

In the circumstances, I suggest that medical evidence regarding Ms Phelps' condition will be essential to allow the tribunal to deal with the case efficiently and fairly.

Ms Phelps has for the last eight years been under the care of Mrs Roberta Toms, a consultant psychiatrist at St Matthew's Hospital, Bristol. Mrs Toms has indicated that she is willing to provide a report. I should be grateful for the Tribunal's order that the claimant should be permitted to rely on expert evidence from Mrs Toms on the question of the claimant's disabilities, and I suggest that it would be helpful to list the case for a case management conference to discuss detailed arrangements for this together with any other case management issues that arise.[22]

---

22 An alternative would be to propose detailed directions in this letter – especially if it has been possible to agree them in principle with the respondent first – but a case management discussion (CMD) will more often be necessary in a Disability Discrimination Act 1995 case.

My unavailable dates[23] during August and September are:
Week beginning 13 August
Week beginning 20 August
6, 14 and 21 September

Yours faithfully

Natalie Cummings

Choosing an expert

5.61   In the case of medical evidence, the choice of expert will often be obvious: the consultant who has been treating the claimant is likely to be best-placed to give evidence about her condition. In some cases it may be sufficient to ask the claimant's GP for a report. If the claimant is not under the care of a consultant, the claimant may need to contact her local hospital for a list of specialists in her condition; alternatively the Disability Rights Commission or a specific disability charity may be able to help.

5.62   If these sources fail to locate a suitable expert – or if a non-medical expert is required – two helpful websites that will put claimants in touch with experts in a wide variety of fields are www.jspubs.com and www.theexpertwitnessdirectory.co.uk.

Paying for the report

5.63   If a chairman orders a medical report in a disability case, the tribunal service will normally pay for it, subject to certain limits.[24] The claimant should first enquire how much the doctor will charge for a report, and then ask the tribunal to confirm that it will pay the fee. The claimant may need to pay the expert before recovering the money from the tribunal. Where an adviser is acting, instructions should not be sent to an expert without making sure that the claimant is willing, if necessary, to pay.

---

23   It is obviously preferable to tell the tribunal unavailable dates at this stage than to wait for a CMD to be listed and then ask for it to be postponed because it is inconvenient.

24   See the leaflet 'Expenses and allowances payable to parties and witnesses attending an Employment Tribunal' available on the Employment Tribunal Service website at www.employmenttribunals.gov.uk

5.64   For other non-medical expert evidence, the parties will normally each have to pay the cost of their own experts, or share the cost of a joint expert. If the claimant cannot afford to share the cost of a joint expert, the respondent should be reminded of the suggestion in *de Keyser* that the evidence is likely to carry more weight if the instructions are agreed between the parties.

Drafting the letter of instruction

5.65   The letter should start with a short, clear summary of what the case is about and why expert evidence is needed. The questions on which the expert's opinion are sought should be spelled out, and the letter should end with guidance on what needs to be included in the report. It is helpful to enclose a copy of the Practice Direction that accompanies Part 35 of the CPR.[25]

5.66   The most important – and difficult – part of the task is drafting the questions for the expert. The starting point must be a clear understanding of what it is that the claimant needs to prove in order to succeed in her claim. For example, in a Disability Discrimination Act (DDA) 1995 case where it is disputed that the claimant is disabled for the purposes of the Act, the claimant will typically have to show:[26]

- that she suffers from a physical or mental impairment;
- that the impairment affects mobility, manual dexterity, physical co-ordination, continence, ability to lift, carry or otherwise move everyday objects, speech, hearing, eyesight, memory, ability to concentrate, learn or understand or perception of the risk of physical danger;[27]
- that the impairment has an effect on her ability to carry out normal day-to-day activities;
- that the effect is substantial;
- that the effect has lasted or is likely to last at least 12 months.[28]

---

25 Reproduced at the end of this chapter.
26 The rules for what exactly the claimant has to show are complicated: see generally ELAH 7 chapter 15.
27 The DDA 1995 makes meeting this requirement part of the definition of having an effect on the ability to carry out normal day-to-day activities: see DDA 1995 Sch 1, para 4. The result, for practical purposes, is that the claimant needs to prove both that the impairment affects one of these specific abilities and that it has a substantial and long-term effect on her ability to carry out normal day-to-day activities.
28 An effect that is likely to recur is treated as continuing for these purposes.

5.67 The questions for the expert should be confined to matters on which she can be expected to have an opinion by virtue of her particular expertise. So, for example, a medical expert can sensibly be asked what the condition is, how long it is likely to last, what its effects are or can be expected to be on the claimant's ability to do specific things. She should not be asked whether the claimant is disabled within the meaning of the DDA 1995, however, because that is a question for the tribunal to decide by applying the correct legal test to the facts as it finds them.[29]

DOCUMENT OUTLINE: Letter of instruction to expert

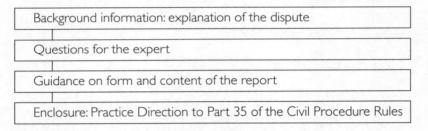

Background information: explanation of the dispute

Questions for the expert

Guidance on form and content of the report

Enclosure: Practice Direction to Part 35 of the Civil Procedure Rules

---

29 See for example *Abadeh v British Telecommunications plc* [2001] IRLR 23.

P5.66 Letter of instruction to medical expert

Roberta Toms
St Matthew's Hospital
St Matthew's Hill
Bristol BS1 2BZ

3 September 2007

My ref: NC ir 1234

Dear Mrs Toms

Ms Pauline Phelps DOB 27.9.59

INSTRUCTIONS FOR MEDICAL REPORT

BACKGROUND

Ms Phelps has made a complaint to the employment tribunal of constructive dismissal and discrimination contrary to the Disability Discrimination Act (DDA) 1995. She relies on depression and her facial disfigurement and she says that working practices imposed on her by her employer have placed her at a substantial disadvantage compared to workers who are not disabled.

Ms Phelps' former employer does not accept that she has a disability for the purposes of the DDA 1995.

QUESTIONS

I should be grateful if you would provide a medical report dealing with the following questions about the depressive illness for which I understand you are currently treating Ms Phelps:

1. What is Ms Phelps' current condition? How serious is it?

   This will show whether or not she has a mental impairment.

2. What are the causes of Ms Phelps' depression?

   This may not be strictly relevant, but if depression has clear and comprehensible causes that is likely to help the tribunal to believe that it is real and substantial.

3. What treatment is Ms Phelps receiving for her depression?

4. Does it affect any of the following:
   (i) Her mobility: i.e., does it affect her ability to go to work, visit friends, go shopping, etc?
   (ii) Her memory?
   (iii) Her ability to concentrate?
   (iv) Her ability to learn?
   (v) Her ability to understand?
   (vi) Her perception of the risk of physical danger?

5. If Ms Phelps is affected by her depression in any of these respects, please say to what extent in your opinion she is affected.

6. To what extent would Ms Phelps' ability to do any of the things listed at question 2 be affected if she were not receiving any treatment for her depression?

7. Has Ms Phelps suffered from depression in the past? Please give a brief account of her medical history in this respect, including any treatment.

8. How long do you expect Ms Phelps' current depression to last?

> *The effects of medical treatment are disregarded for the purposes of assessing the seriousness of the effects of an impairment, so it may be important to know what treatment is being received and what the condition would be without it, see question 6 below.*

> *The question deals only with the categories from schedule 1 that are relevant to Ms Phelps' case.*

> *It is important to show that the effects are 'substantial,' but the expert's view will carry more weight if she has not been prompted in the letter of instructions by a question of the form 'Would you describe the effects as substantial?' or similar. See paras 5.2 and 5.33 above on leading questions.*

> *See the comment on question 3 above.*

> *This is relevant to whether the effects are long-term.*

> *As is this.*

FORM AND CONTENT OF REPORT

I attach guidance on the form and content of expert evidence from the applicable practice direction. Please note in particular that the report must contain the following two statements:

'I understand my duty to the Tribunal in writing this report and I have complied with that duty and will continue to comply with it.'

and

'I confirm that insofar as the facts stated in my report are within my own knowledge I have made clear which they are and I believe them to be true, and that the opinions I have expressed represent my true and complete professional opinion.'

My client will of course be responsible for your reasonable fee for this report.

Yours sincerely

Natalie Cummings

Civil Procedure Rules (CPR), Part 35

5.68   Part 35 of the Civil Procedure Rules and the accompanying Practice Direction are reproduced here because, although not technically applicable, they are essential reading for anyone considering calling expert evidence in the employment tribunal.

Civil Procedure Rules (CPR), Part 35

Part 35 of the Civil Procedure Rules and the accompanying Practice Direction are reproduced here because, although not technically applicable, they are essential reading for anyone considering calling expert evidence in the employment tribunal. See para 5.44 above.

Duty to restrict expert evidence
35.1   Expert evidence shall be restricted to that which is reasonably required to resolve the proceedings.

Interpretation
35.2   A reference to an 'expert' in this Part is a reference to an expert who has been instructed to give or prepare evidence for the purpose of court proceedings.

Experts – overriding duty to the court
35.3   (1) It is the duty of an expert to help the court on the matters within his expertise.
(2) This duty overrides any obligation to the person from whom he has received instructions or by whom he is paid.

Court's power to restrict expert evidence

35.4 (1) No party may call an expert or put in evidence an expert's report without the court's permission.

(2) When a party applies for permission under this rule he must identify –

(a) the field in which he wishes to rely on expert evidence; and

(b) where practicable the expert in that field on whose evidence he wishes to rely.

(3) If permission is granted under this rule it shall be in relation only to the expert named or the field identified under paragraph (2).

(4) The court may limit the amount of the expert's fees and expenses that the party who wishes to rely on the expert may recover from any other party.

General requirement for expert evidence to be given in a written report

35.5 (1) Expert evidence is to be given in a written report unless the court directs otherwise.

(2) If a claim is on the fast track, the court will not direct an expert to attend a hearing unless it is necessary to do so in the interests of justice.

Written questions to experts

35.6 (1) A party may put to –

(a) an expert instructed by another party; or

(b) a single joint expert appointed under rule 35.7, written questions about his report.

(2) Written questions under paragraph (1) –

(a) may be put once only;

(b) must be put within 28 days of service of the expert's report; and

(c) must be for the purpose only of clarification of the report, unless in any case –

(i) the court gives permission; or

(ii) the other party agrees.

(3) An expert's answers to questions put in accordance with paragraph (1) shall be treated as part of the expert's report.

(4) Where –
    (a) a party has put a written question to an expert instructed by another party in accordance with this rule; and
    (b) the expert does not answer that question, the court may make one or both of the following orders in relation to the party who instructed the expert –
        (i) that the party may not rely on the evidence of that expert; or
        (ii) that the party may not recover the fees and expenses of that expert from any other party.

Court's power to direct that evidence is to be given by a single joint expert

35.7 (1) Where two or more parties wish to submit expert evidence on a particular issue, the court may direct that the evidence on that issue is to be given by one expert only.

(2) The parties wishing to submit the expert evidence are called 'the instructing parties'.

(3) Where the instructing parties cannot agree who should be the expert, the court may –
    (a) select the expert from a list prepared or identified by the instructing parties; or
    (b) direct that the expert be selected in such other manner as the court may direct.

Instructions to a single joint expert

35.8 (1) Where the court gives a direction under rule 35.7 for a single joint expert to be used, each instructing party may give instructions to the expert.

(2) When an instructing party gives instructions to the expert he must, at the same time, send a copy of the instructions to the other instructing parties.

(3) The court may give directions about –
    (a) the payment of the expert's fees and expenses; and
    (b) any inspection, examination or experiments which the expert wishes to carry out.

(4) The court may, before an expert is instructed –
    (a) limit the amount that can be paid by way of fees and expenses to the expert; and

(b) direct that the instructing parties pay that amount into court.

(5) Unless the court otherwise directs, the instructing parties are jointly and severally liable (GL) for the payment of the expert's fees and expenses.

Power of court to direct a party to provide information

35.9 Where a party has access to information which is not reasonably available to the other party, the court may direct the party who has access to the information to –

(a) prepare and file a document recording the information; and

(b) serve a copy of that document on the other party.

Contents of report

35.10 (1) An expert's report must comply with the requirements set out in the relevant practice direction.

(2) At the end of an expert's report there must be a statement that –

(a) the expert understands his duty to the court; and

(b) he has complied with that duty.

(3) The expert's report must state the substance of all material instructions, whether written or oral, on the basis of which the report was written.

(4) The instructions referred to in paragraph (3) shall not be privileged (GL) against disclosure but the court will not, in relation to those instructions –

(a) order disclosure of any specific document; or

(b) permit any questioning in court, other than by the party who instructed the expert,

unless it is satisfied that there are reasonable grounds to consider the statement of instructions given under paragraph (3) to be inaccurate or incomplete.

Use by one party of expert's report disclosed by another

35.11 Where a party has disclosed an expert's report, any party may use that expert's report as evidence at the trial.

Discussions between experts

35.12 (1) The court may, at any stage, direct a discussion between experts for the purpose of requiring the experts to –
  (a) identify and discuss the expert issues in the proceedings; and
  (b) where possible, reach an agreed opinion on those issues.

(2) The court may specify the issues which the experts must discuss.

(3) The court may direct that following a discussion between the experts they must prepare a statement for the court showing –
  (a) those issues on which they agree; and
  (b) those issues on which they disagree and a summary of their reasons for disagreeing.

(4) The content of the discussion between the experts shall not be referred to at the trial unless the parties agree.

(5) Where experts reach agreement on an issue during their discussions, the agreement shall not bind the parties unless the parties expressly agree to be bound by the agreement.

Consequence of failure to disclose expert's report

35.13 A party who fails to disclose an expert's report may not use the report at the trial or call the expert to give evidence orally unless the court gives permission.

Expert's right to ask court for directions

35.14 (1) An expert may file a written request for directions to assist him in carrying out his function as an expert.

(2) An expert must, unless the court orders otherwise, provide a copy of any proposed request for directions under paragraph (1) –
  (a) to the party instructing him, at least 7 days before he files the request; and
  (b) to all other parties, at least 4 days before he files it.

(3) The court, when it gives directions, may also direct that a party be served with a copy of the directions.

Assessors

35.15 (1) This rule applies where the court appoints one or more persons (an 'assessor') under section 70 of the Supreme Court Act 1981(1) or section 63 of the County Courts Act 1984(2).

(2) The assessor shall assist the court in dealing with a matter in which the assessor has skill and experience.

(3) An assessor shall take such part in the proceedings as the court may direct and in particular the court may –

   (a) direct the assessor to prepare a report for the court on any matter at issue in the proceedings; and

   (b) direct the assessor to attend the whole or any part of the trial to advise the court on any such matter.

(4) If the assessor prepares a report for the court before the trial has begun –

   (a) the court will send a copy to each of the parties; and

   (b) the parties may use it at trial.

(5) The remuneration to be paid to the assessor for his services shall be determined by the court and shall form part of the costs of the proceedings.

(6) The court may order any party to deposit in the court office a specified sum in respect of the assessor's fees and, where it does so, the assessor will not be asked to act until the sum has been deposited.

(7) Paragraphs (5) and (6) do not apply where the remuneration of the assessor is to be paid out of money provided by Parliament.

Practice Direction Supplementing CPR Part 35

Part 35 is intended to limit the use of oral expert evidence to that which is reasonably required. In addition, where possible, matters requiring expert evidence should be dealt with by a single expert. Permission of the court is always required either to call an expert or to put an expert's report in evidence.

EXPERT EVIDENCE – GENERAL REQUIREMENTS

1.1 It is the duty of an expert to help the court on matters within his own expertise: rule 35.3(1). This duty is paramount and overrides any obligation to the person from whom the expert has received instructions or by whom he is paid: rule 35.3(2).

1.2 Expert evidence should be the independent product of the expert uninfluenced by the pressures of litigation.

1.3 An expert should assist the court by providing objective, unbiased opinion on matters within his expertise, and should not assume the role of an advocate.

1.4 An expert should consider all material facts, including those which might detract from his opinion.

1.5 An expert should make it clear:
   (a) when a question or issue falls outside his expertise; and
   (b) when he is not able to reach a definite opinion, for example because he has insufficient information.

1.6 If, after producing a report, an expert changes his view on any material matter, such change of view should be communicated to all the parties without delay, and when appropriate to the court.

FORM AND CONTENT OF EXPERT'S REPORTS

2.1 An expert's report should be addressed to the court and not to the party from whom the expert has received his instructions.

2.2 An expert's report must:
   (1) give details of the expert's qualifications;
   (2) give details of any literature or other material which the expert has relied on in making the report;
   (3) contain a statement setting out the substance of all facts and instructions given to the expert which are material to the opinions expressed in the report or upon which those opinions are based;
   (4) make clear which of the facts stated in the report are within the expert's own knowledge;
   (5) say who carried out any examination, measurement, test or experiment which the expert has used for the report, give the qualifications of that person, and say whether or not the test or experiment has been carried out under the expert's supervision;

(6) where there is a range of opinion on the matters dealt with in the report—
(a) summarise the range of opinion, and
(b) give reasons for his own opinion;
(7) contain a summary of the conclusions reached;
(8) if the expert is not able to give his opinion without qualification, state the qualification; and
(9) contain a statement that the expert understands his duty to the court, and has complied and will continue to comply with that duty.

2.3 An expert's report must be verified by a statement of truth as well as containing the statements required in paragraph 2.2(8) and (9) above.

2.4 The form of the statement of truth is as follows:

'I confirm that insofar as the facts stated in my report are within my own knowledge I have made clear which they are and I believe them to be true, and that the opinions I have expressed represent my true and complete professional opinion.'

2.5 Attention is drawn to rule 32.14 which sets out the consequences of verifying a document containing a false statement without an honest belief in its truth.
(For information about statements of truth see Part 22 and the practice direction which supplements it.)

INFORMATION

3   Under Rule 35.9 the court may direct a party with access to information which is not reasonably available to another party to serve on that other party a document which records the information. The document served must include sufficient details of all the facts, tests, experiments and assumptions which underlie any part of the information to enable the party on whom it is served to make, or to obtain, a proper interpretation of the information and an assessment of its significance.

INSTRUCTIONS

4   The instructions referred to in paragraph 2.2(3) will not be protected by privilege (see rule 35.10(4)). But cross-examination of the expert on the contents of his instructions will not be allowed unless the court permits it (or unless the party who gave the instructions consents to it). Before it gives permission the court must be satisfied that there are reasonable grounds to consider that the statement in the report of the substance of the instructions is inaccurate or incomplete. If the court is so satisfied, it will allow the cross-examination where it appears to be in the interests of justice to do so.

QUESTIONS TO EXPERTS

5.1 Questions asked for the purpose of clarifying the expert's report (see rule 35.6) should be put, in writing, to the expert not later than 28 days after receipt of the expert's report (see paragraphs 1.2 to 1.5 above as to verification).

5.2 Where a party sends a written question or questions direct to an expert, a copy of the questions should, at the same time, be sent to the other party or parties.

5.3 The party or parties instructing the expert must pay any fees charged by that expert for answering questions put under rule 35.6. This does not affect any decision of the court as to the party who is ultimately to bear the expert's costs.

SINGLE EXPERT

6   Where the court has directed that the evidence on a particular issue is to be given by one expert only (rule 35.7) but there are a number of disciplines relevant to that issue, a leading expert in the dominant discipline should be identified as the single expert. He should prepare the general part of the report and be responsible for annexing or incorporating the contents of any reports from experts in other disciplines.

ASSESSORS

7.1 An assessor may be appointed to assist the court under rule 35.15. Not less than 21 days before making any such appointment, the court will notify each party in writing of the name of the proposed assessor, of the matter in respect of which the assistance of the assessor will be sought and of the qualifications of the assessor to give that assistance.

7.2 Where any person has been proposed for appointment as an assessor, objection to him, either personally or in respect of his qualification, may be taken by any party.

7.3 Any such objection must be made in writing and filed with the court within 7 days of receipt of the notification referred to in paragraph 7.1 and will be taken into account by the court in deciding whether or not to make the appointment (section 63(5) of the County Courts Act 1984).

7.4 Copies of any report prepared by the assessor will be sent to each of the parties but the assessor will not give oral evidence or be open to cross-examination or questioning.

CHAPTER 6

Negotiation and settlement

Introduction

6.1   Most employment tribunal complaints end in settlement, and for good reason. Hearings are stressful and expensive, and often the claimant can achieve by negotiation a benefit that is more important than anything the employment tribunal could order. A favourable reference is the most common example of this: tribunals have no power to order an employer to provide a reference, but often an agreed reference is the key consideration for a dismissed employee keen to get back to work. From the employer's side, the costs of a hearing can often be considerably higher than the value of the claim, and the employer will only rarely recover any of its costs after an employment tribunal hearing. Even if the employer thinks the claim is completely without merit, it may be cheaper to settle than to fight.

6.2   The psychology of a negotiation is often more complex than this. It is always worth remembering that the practical and financial interests of the two opposing sides are not the only significant factors affecting the outcome. Where the employer is an organisation, the individual who is taking decisions about the tribunal case may be more concerned to protect his own position than to achieve the best outcome for the respondent. A manager who has no option but to authorise payment to the claimant if the tribunal makes an award may feel that it is safer to let this happen than to take the decision to settle the case. The question 'Why did you pay Poppy Snook all that money?' can be laid very firmly to rest by the answer 'I had to because that was what the tribunal ordered'. The answer 'because I thought we would probably lose the case and anyway it was cheaper than paying our lawyers' locates responsibility for the decision with the manager.

6.3   The manager taking decisions about the case may be the same person who decided on dismissal, or upheld the dismissal on appeal. Here 'I thought we were likely to lose' would be very little different from 'I thought I had messed up'. The manager may prefer to expose the company to the risk of a large payment after which he can grouse companionably to colleagues and superiors about the inherent employee bias in the tribunal system than to limit the financial damage to the company by implicitly admitting fault.

6.4   The question of loss of face can have a profound effect on negotiations, and the party who is aware of this can be at a significant advantage. Making the employer eat dirt may sometimes be a tempting thought, but making them feel that they are striking a hard bargain is much more likely to be an effective way of getting the best possible deal for the claimant. Your aim as a negotiator is to make it as easy and painless as possible for the other side to do what you want them to do. This is why it is normally advisable to open negotiations in an optimistic position: if you ask for £15,000 and ultimately agree to settle for £5,000, the respondent can congratulate itself that it beat you down to 1/3 of what you wanted. That in itself may help the lawyer on the other side to sell the deal to his client or the personnel officer to sell it to the CEO.[1] On the other hand, if you open negotiations at £5,000 and then refuse point blank to budge, the respondent can only settle by humiliatingly giving you everything you asked for. Similarly, if you produce a first draft for an agreed reference, it is prudent to build in some elements that you are willing to concede if pushed.

The lawyers' role

6.5   Lawyers and advisers add another layer, of course. Once negotiations have reached a point where settlement is looking more probable than not – and especially if negotiations are complex and are taking up a lot of time in themselves – it is very difficult for lawyers to remain fully focused on preparation for the hearing. This gives negotiations an added momentum: the closer the hearing approaches with a settlement in prospect, the more nightmarish it will be for both sets of lawyers if the deal falls through.

6.6   Claimants' advisers should be aware of this for two reasons. One is that there is the possibility of being badly caught out: the deal always can fall through at the last minute, and there is a limit to how much pressure it is proper or fair to put on a client to accept a settlement that the adviser considers good. In the end, it must be remembered that it is the client's case, not the adviser's, and the point of the whole exercise is to provide a result that the client can live with. If fighting a losing battle in the tribunal gives the client a better sense of 'closure' than accepting a modest settlement, then the battle should be fought. There is also the theoretical risk that the other party's apparent willingness to negotiate is pure sham, intended to disrupt the claimant's preparation for hearing. This is a distant risk, but it is wise to proceed as if it could be the case if only because settlement is never certain until a deal is done.

---

1   As a rule, both parties to a settlement will tell themselves that they have struck a good bargain. In most cases only one of them is right.

6.7   The other reason to be wary of the momentum towards settlement is that, especially if most of the negotiation has focused on the financial side of the deal, it can put the claimant in a weak position when it comes to non-financial aspects. This is best headed off first by taking instructions carefully about what the client cares most about; and then by making sure to open with a clear statement of what, other than money, he is looking for.

> **Example**
> Suppose a reference is the key issue for the claimant, but the employer has an invariable policy of not providing references for employees they have dismissed. There is a long negotiation about money that finally produces a figure, the day before the hearing is due to begin, that is acceptable to both sides. Only then does the claimant's adviser ask for a reference. The danger here is that by now both sides are behind with hearing preparation, and either side (depending which has stronger nerves) may be forced into a deal that is not genuinely satisfactory. Alternatively, the deal falls through and precious preparation time has been wasted on both sides negotiating about something that was not the key issue.

Withdrawing free assistance

6.8   The position of voluntary sector advisers can be complicated by a need to focus services where they are most needed. This is a legitimate concern, and it is perfectly proper for an adviser to warn a client early in proceedings that representation will be withdrawn if the client refuses an offer of settlement that the adviser considers good.[2] Provided the client has time to make alternative arrangements it is fair to act on that warning. It is not fair, however, to withdraw representation on this basis within a few days of the hearing: by this time it will be far too late for the client to make any alternative arrangements, or to prepare adequately to represent himself. If settlement negotiations break down shortly before the hearing, even if the reason for that is unreasonableness on the part of the claimant, then an adviser who has previously promised to represent should not back out.

---

2   Subject to applicable rules of professional conduct: barristers and solicitors should have regard to their respective codes.

6.9   It is suggested that advisers who wish to impose this kind of limit on free services might for tie the threat to the statutory conciliation period:[3] a sensible rule might be that if the adviser advises acceptance of an offer received within the conciliation period, and the claimant fails to accept it before the end of the period, then the adviser may cease to act. If it became known that voluntary sector advisers commonly applied this rule, that in itself would be a powerful incentive for respondents to make realistic offers within the conciliation period.

External factors

6.10   Finally, the potential power of seemingly wholly irrelevant factors should not be forgotten. If the hearing is listed for a day on which England is due to play Argentina in the World Cup, the party who is not a football fan and is represented by a lawyer who is not a football fan will be at a very significant advantage over a party who is – or whose lawyer is – keen to see the match.

'Without prejudice' communications

6.11   Statements made – whether orally or in writing – in the course of negotiations cannot be referred to in front of the tribunal. This is what is known as the 'without prejudice' rule. Letters dealing with a proposed settlement are often headed 'without prejudice,' and lawyers may preface a conversation on the subject with a request for agreement that what is said should be 'without prejudice'. There is no magic in the words: whether or not they are used, settlement negotiations are exempt from disclosure to the tribunal. The purpose of this rule is to allow parties to litigation to lower their guard for the purposes of negotiation without weakening their position in the event that negotiations fail. Sometimes letters are headed 'without prejudice save as to costs'. This means that although the contents of the letter and any response cannot be shown to the tribunal before or during the substantive case, one or other party may refer to these discussions after the case has been decided in the context of a costs application.

---

3   See ELAH 7 para 20.57.

What should be included in a settlement?

6.12 The parties can make any lawful agreement to settle their dispute. The fact that a settlement can achieve a result that a contested hearing could not is often one of the key factors that persuades the parties to negotiate. Usually – but by no means always – the most important aspect of the settlement is financial, but very often a reference will be important too. In many cases these two will be the only or main benefits in return for which the claimant agrees to drop his claim. It is important, however, to have an open mind to more creative solutions in a suitable case.

What the employee may want included

6.13 The following list is not – and could never be – exhaustive: it is intended only to suggest lines of thought:

- money
- a reference
- a confidential apology
- an apology published in the employer's newsletter
- an admission of liability[4]
- to be allowed to stay for a defined period in tied accommodation
- a commitment by the employer to change some aspect of its employment practices for the future
- a promise that some of the respondent's staff will be required to undergo some form of equal opportunities training
- a promise to adopt and publicise an equal opportunities policy, or re-draft its existing policy
- different hours of work
- a promise to send the claimant on a particular course
- a promise to move the claimant to a different department or office
- a promise to move a colleague (e.g., in a harassment case the harasser) to a different department or office

---

4 See for example para 6.16 and P6.69.2 below.

- a promise to short-list the claimant for the next vacant post of a certain description
- reinstatement to the claimant's old job or re-engagement to a different job.[5]

6.14   In the very rare cases where it is possible to agree reinstatement or re-engagement of a dismissed employee, this should be done by way of a 'compromise agreement' or a form COT3, or ordered by consent by the tribunal.[6] An informal agreement to withdraw on terms, although adequate in many cases, may fail to preserve continuity on reinstatement or re-engagement.[7] If continuity is not preserved, the resumed employment may be very insecure because it will be a year before the claimant has statutory protection from unfair dismissal.

What the employer may want included

6.15   There are certain familiar elements that employers often want to see included in an agreement.

'Without admission of liability'

6.16   Employers rarely want to admit liability. Unless there is a practical reason why the claimant needs an admission of liability, this should probably be conceded without too much fuss. But bear in mind that there are circumstances where an admission of liability is important. There are two common situations where this may arise. If the respondent is on the verge of insolvency and cannot or may not be able to meet its liabilities for redundancy pay, the employee will need either an admission that he has been made redundant or a tribunal finding to the same effect to claim his redundancy pay from the National Insurance Fund. Similarly, if the employee has insurance that will cover his mortgage repayments in the event that he is made redundant (but not if he is dismissed for reasons relating to capability or conduct), it will be important to insist on an admission that redundancy was the reason for the dismissal.

---

5   If this is a real possibility in a misconduct dismissal, the employer may wish to substitute a final warning for the decision to dismiss. There is no reason why this should not be agreed in a suitable case.

6   See para 10.15 below for explanations of these terms.

7   See Harvey, notes to R1036.

Confidentiality

6.17   Employers tend to want to keep the settlement confidential either because they do not want to give any encouragement to other employees who might consider making a similar claim in the future, or simply to avoid loss of face. Often this is not objectionable in principle to the claimant, but the confidentiality clause should not promise too much: claimants will invariably tell their spouse or immediate family about the settlement, so it is futile to ask them to sign an agreement that prohibits this.

Repayment of the settlement sum as a debt if the claimant acts in breach of the confidentiality clause (or other requirement)

6.18   This is a clause that rolls off the word-processors of many respondents' solicitors. It is included in order to frighten the claimant into compliance with the confidentiality (or other) clause, and it will almost always be unenforceable as a 'penalty clause'.[8] On one view this is a reason why claimants should sign up to it with a light heart: it is not worth the paper it is written on. However, it is suggested that this kind of clause should be resisted, because in reality the effect is likely to be to cause the claimant needless anxiety.

Settlement of any other claim that the claimant may have against the employer arising out of the employment or its termination or (sometimes) otherwise

6.19   These are very common, and some respondents will refuse point blank to settle a case without a general clause of this nature. These clauses are difficult to draft correctly and are often ineffective.[9] If there is in fact no other potential claim, then there is nothing to be lost, and in these circumstances they are unobjectionable; the question whether they are effective is therefore unlikely to arise. However claimants should

---

8   See glossary and *CMC Group PLC & ors v Michael Zhang* [2006] EWCA Civ 408.
9   *Hinton v University of East London* [2005] IRLR 552.

give the question whether another claim could arise some thought, because if they do have another claim against the employer there is a risk that they will have signed it away. If this kind of clause is included, it is standard practice to qualify it with something along these lines: 'For the avoidance of doubt, nothing in this agreement affects any rights the claimant may have in respect of personal injury or accrued pension rights.'

6.20   The latter may be difficult to negotiate if the original claim has a personal injury element – if, for example, the claimant has alleged that harassment at work has made him ill. In that case, the solution may be to include in the settlement any personal injury of which the claimant is aware at the time, but not any latent injury. It is important that if, for example, the claimant falls ill years later from the delayed effects of some chemical he was exposed to at work, he should not be prevented from suing his employer for that.

What is a good settlement?

6.21   This very much depends on what you mean by 'good'. In the end a good settlement is one that the claimant is happy with. But this defi-nition is not very useful in practice. Claimants often feel they need advice about what is a good settlement before they can decide what will satisfy them. At the same time, advisers often work hard to per-suade their clients that it is prudent to accept a sum that the client considers disappointing.

6.22   In general terms, a good settlement is one that accurately reflects the likely outcome of the hearing. It needs to do so in two ways. First, it must reflect how likely the claimant is to win. Long shot claims are not worth much compared with strong claims. Second, it must take account of how much the claimant will receive if they do win. High value claims are worth more than low value claims.

6.23   In theory this is a simple analysis. A client with a near certainty of winning a fixed sum would be foolish to accept much less than they anticipated receiving from the tribunal. A client who has no realistic chance of winning should accept whatever they can get. In practice, however, things are more complex. In anything more than the simplest case it is difficult to assess what the chances of winning are. And, should the claimant win, he might win more or less, depending on the tribunal's decision on compensation. Claimants may win one part of a case, but not another. Or the respondent may have brought a counter-claim that needs to be considered. These factors makes the calculation more difficult, but the same basic approach applies.

> **Example**
> Ms Jones has brought an unfair dismissal claim and race discrimination case against her employer. Her adviser considers that her unfair dismissal claim is very strong (approximately 80% chance of success). If she wins the unfair dismissal she will almost certainly recover £10,000 and, depending on the tribunals findings has a 50% chance of getting a further £5,000. Her race discrimination claim, however, is weak with only a 10% chance of success. If she wins the discrimination claim she will receive an injury to feelings award of approximately £5,000.
>
> Therefore, a reasonable settlement figure will be:
>
> **(80% x £10,000)+(80% x 50% x £5,000)+(10% x £5,000)=£10,500**

6.24   The level of uncertainty, both of the chances of success and the amount of compensation will determine the range of acceptable settlements. In cases with a high level of certainty the range of acceptable offers will be very small. Where matters are very uncertain the range of acceptable settlements will be wide.

6.25   It is important to remember that this is a way of thinking about settlement, not a precise method of calculation. In practice the decision to settle and for what sum will be based on many factors that have little to do with the merits of the case. For example, a client with debt problems may be well advised to settle a good claim for less than he might have achieved in tribunal, because settlement will get him the money when he needs it, and certainly rather than probably. Similarly, a respondent facing a claim which is likely to attract unfavourable publicity may be willing to pay more to get rid of it, even if the chances of losing it are small.

References

6.26   References are sometimes treated by advisers as a side issue, to be tacked on to an agreement if possible at the last minute but not to be made a deal-breaker once a sum of money has been agreed. This can be a great mistake. The most serious concern of an employee who has been dismissed will very often be to get another job. A recent dismissal by an employer who is not prepared to provide a favourable reference will be a great handicap in the labour market, and an agreed reference will often be the most important aspect of the deal. It is often helpful to include an agreement that reference requests will be dealt with by a named individual at the previous employer, particularly if there is a suitable manager whom the claimant trusts.

6.27　　The value of open references should not be underestimated. Many employers, particularly of low-paid workers, will expect job applicants to bring references with them to the interview, and will not themselves go to the trouble of taking up references from named referees.[10] An agreement to provide a number of open references should be included as a matter of course. Similarly, a terse and uninformative reference may be more useful than it initially appears. Many employers do not produce detailed references, even for employees who don't bring tribunal claims against them. Particularly in low paid jobs, a few lines may be all that is expected. An over-elaborate reference for an unskilled manual worker could ring alarm bells with a potential employer.

6.28　　Respondents' attitudes to references vary widely. Some will simply refuse to provide any reference at all for employees they have dismissed for reasons of misconduct or poor performance, but many will be willing to give a factual reference in these circumstances.

Drafting a reference

6.29　It is a good idea for the claimant to take the initiative in providing the first draft of a reference, and, as tends to be the case in any negotiation, it is advisable to aim reasonably (but not absurdly) high and include more than you think the other side is likely to accept. In other words, it is sensible to build in some points for the respondent to win on that the claimant is prepared to concede.

6.30　　Drafting a reference for a dismissed employee that sounds satisfactory without being untruthful is something of an art. The model to follow is the over-priced boxed salad from a sandwich shop: three prawns, a crabstick and a squirt of pink salad cream carefully arranged on top of a large quantity of iceberg lettuce may fool the careless buyer into thinking he has bought a 'seafood salad' worth £4.95. Similarly, a bland account of job title, dates of employment, duties made to sound

10　See P Toynbee, *Hard Work: Life in Low-pay Britain*, Bloomsbury, 2003.

as extensive and responsible as possible, topped off with an endorsement of whatever can be honestly endorsed, can appear to the careless reader to be a good reference. Employers can be surprisingly flexible about this: even if the employee was dismissed for serious misconduct it is sometimes possible to secure a reference that talks up his few good points and draws a charitable veil over his misconduct or incompetence.

6.31   If the question of a reference looks set to become a deal-breaker, the claimant should take careful stock. What needs to be remembered is that the tribunal cannot order a reference. Claimants sometimes assume that a positive tribunal finding will somehow 'clear their name' and may therefore help them get another job without a reference. Nothing could be further from the truth: if 'I was dismissed from my previous job' looks like bad news to a potential employer, 'I was dismissed from my previous job but I took my employer to an employment tribunal and won' is even worse.

6.32   It follows that if the money offered is as much or more than the claimant can realistically hope to get at a hearing, it is futile to let the settlement founder on the employer's refusal provide a reference. It is sensible to let this happen only if the sum of money offered is independently unacceptable: in other words, if an agreed reference would be a sufficient benefit to persuade the claimant to settle the case at what is otherwise an undervalue.

6.33   The document outline below suggests the questions that a reference might cover, in a logical order. Obviously it is better to leave a subject out altogether if the only truthful statement that can be made about it is damaging.

DOCUMENT OUTLINE: References

Heading – ex-employee's name
Job title and dates of employment
Responsibilities at termination
Performance and any promotions
Attendance, time-keeping, conduct, likeability

P6.33.1 Reference: genuinely good

Jane Close

Jane Close was employed by the company's Payroll Section for two periods separated by maternity leave and career break, from July 1988 to February 1997, and from July 2000 until January 2007. She was first employed as a Payroll Assistant (Scale 1/2) , and had progressed to the level of Senior Payroll Officer (SO1) by 1996.

By 2005 Jane had overall responsibility for payroll administration for over 150 staff, and for supervising the work of two Payroll Assistants, both of whom she had trained on their arrival in the Payroll Section.

Mrs Close was a highly competent and reliable employee who coped well under pressure. Her attendance, time-keeping and general conduct were exemplary. She took organisational, procedural and technical changes in her stride and proved a competent and tactful supervisor of more junior staff. She was well liked by colleagues, and we were sorry to lose her.

P6.33.2 Reference: superficially good

Richard Lightfoot was first employed by this Borough from 1982 until 1985 as a yardman at our Crowley Road depot. From 1984 to 1989 he was employed as Assistant Caretaker at the John Russell School, and from 1990 to 2007 he was Resident Caretaker at St George's School. In his last post, he had sole responsibility for the cleaning of the school (a total of over 15,000 square feet), and he was also willing to undertake minor maintenance and repairs. We found him to be punctual and reliable, and his attendance record was good.[11]

11　Note what the reference omits: it says nothing of the fact that although regular and punctual, Mr Lightfoot was in his last two years all too often under the influence of alcohol, nor of the fact that he was dismissed for spraying the deputy headmistress with a fire-extinguisher.

'Final' and time-limited offers

6.34 The claimant's adviser should always treat the respondent's assertion that an offer is 'final' or 'non-negotiable' with a degree of scepticism. Respondents' advisers often describe their opening offer as 'final' and proceed to make several more 'final' offers.

6.35 Sometimes there are good reasons for an offer to be strictly time-limited. Barristers' fees, for example, often become payable at the point that the brief is delivered. Barristers need preparation time, so by three or four days before a hearing (or longer if the case is complex) the respondent's solicitor will be anxious to deliver the brief and let the barrister start preparing the case. Once this has happened, the respondent is committed to significant further costs and may well be unwilling to negotiate further: the money they might have been prepared to spend on a settlement has now been committed to legal costs.

6.36 If the respondent seeks to impose a tight time limit many weeks before the hearing, however, this can normally be taken with a pinch of salt: it may simply be an attempt to bounce the claimant into settling the case quickly, or even on inadequate advice. It is a good idea to meet the respondent's deadline for a response if possible, but if it is not possible – or not possible to take an adequately considered decision in the time – it will very rarely turn out that a day or so's delay several weeks before the hearing date causes the offer to be withdrawn.

Negotiating by letter

6.37 Negotiations frequently take place in a flurry of telephone calls in a short space of time, and only the final agreement is recorded in writing. It is often helpful, however, if the claimant fires an opening shot in negotiations by way of a letter setting out the strength (and sometimes admitted weaknesses) of the claim and attaching a schedule of loss.

6.38 The letter should make sense. There is no point drafting a schedule of loss showing a claim for £20,000 and writing a letter the gist of which is 'The claimant has a strong case worth £20,000 which he is willing to settle for £5,000.' If the claimant is willing to settle the claim for a quarter of its value, there has to be a reason why. If the letter fails to account for that, the respondent may conclude that the claimant knows he cannot prove his case, or has simply decided that he cannot face a hearing. There is a real sense in which a claimant needs an excuse to offer settlement at a substantial discount, if that is what he has decided to do. If the weaknesses of the case are self-evident, then there is no benefit in being coy. As so often, one eye needs to be kept on the risk of a costs application: if the claimant's letters are reasonable and proportionate, the risk of a successful costs application on the strength of the failure of negotiations will be much reduced.

6.39   There are two negotiation errors that are common among beginners. One is to make it obvious that the respondent is not expected to agree to the proposal, by ending the letter with something along the lines, 'I look forward to hearing from you with your next revised offer' or 'the claimant's proposal is of course negotiable and I look forward to hearing from you.' While it is not recommended that advisers should assert that an offer is 'final' if it is not, it is also self-defeating to make an offer and at the same time spell out that a lower offer is likely to find favour. For the same reason, it is futile to suggest a range of figures for settlement: indicating that the claimant would accept an offer 'in the range £10-£15,000' will not elicit the answer from the respondent, 'We'll make that £15,000, then, shall we?' The preferred result for the claimant, on making a settlement offer to the respondent, is that the respondent accepts the offer. The respondent will not accept the offer if it thinks settlement for less may be possible, so an offer letter should never make it obvious that that is the case.

Different methods of settling a claim

6.40   There are a number of ways that a claim once started can be disposed of before a hearing. Broadly, a claim may be withdrawn (either unconditionally or in return for some promise from the respondent), it may be settled by way of an ACAS conciliated agreement, or it may be settled by way of a compromise agreement drawn up in accordance with Employment Rights Act (ERA) 1996 s203. In addition, it may be dealt with by the tribunal in a manner agreed on by the parties. Each of these possibilities is considered below in turn.

Withdrawal

6.41   If for any reason the claimant decides not to pursue the claim, she can simply write to the tribunal to withdraw it. The effect of withdrawal is to bring proceedings to an end: see Procedure Rules r25(3).

P6.39 Letter opening negotiations

George Bean
Carrot & Marrow Solicitors
21 Lower St
Islington
London N12 3AB

20 August 2007

our ref NC 123456/2007
your ref GB/ar.6789

WITHOUT PREJUDICE

Dear Sir

Mr Matthew Pointer v Tailors of Gloucester Street

I enclose a schedule of loss in this case, which as you see shows a total claim of just over £10,000.

I have advised my client that his resignation under threat of dismissal for gross misconduct very clearly amounts, in law, to an actual dismissal. As he was denied a right of appeal against dismissal on the grounds that he had 'resigned,' the statutory disciplinary procedure was not complied with and his dismissal was unfair; again, there can be no serious doubt of this.

My client fully mitigated his loss within 11 weeks of his dismissal, so there can be no credible argument that he did not do enough to mitigate.

However, I have advised my client that he is vulnerable on contributory fault, and in the circumstances I have instructions to offer settlement for £5,000.

The conciliation period in this case has only a further week to run, so if the parties are to take advantages of the services of ACAS it would be helpful if you would take instructions on this offer as soon as you are able.

Yours faithfully

Natalie Cummings

6.42   A decision to withdraw a claim does need caution, however, because if the claimant takes that course it is possible that the respondent will make an application for its costs on the grounds that the claimant's conduct of the case has been unreasonable.[12] Withdrawal itself cannot be said to be unreasonable conduct such as to give the tribunal power to make an award of costs against the claimant, but – especially if the claim is withdrawn at a late stage – withdrawal may lead the tribunal to consider that the claimant has behaved unreasonably in failing to withdraw sooner. Claimants who are in serious doubt whether to proceed with their cases should be advised to make that decision as promptly as possible. If a last minute withdrawal is unavoidable, they should be ready with a good explanation for why that is so.

6.43   It will sometimes be advisable to seek an ACAS settlement of the case on the basis that the claimant withdraws in return for the respondent's undertaking not to make any application for costs. This is certainly helpful if the respondent has previously threatened a costs application; in other cases the benefit may need to be weighed carefully against the risk of prompting the respondent to consider an application that it otherwise might not have thought of. This decision will depend in part on the claimant's assessment of the quality of the advice the respondent is receiving: niche city employment firm Brisk & Wiley LLP will not overlook the possibility of applying for costs on withdrawal; Bluster & Bodge Employment Consultancy Ltd might.

6.44   Cases are sometimes settled by an exchange of correspondence, or a simple written agreement, in which the claimant promises to withdraw and the respondent promises to pay a sum of money, provide an agreed reference, etc. This is probably the most straightforward way of settling a case, and it is quite often used when settlement is reached on the day of the hearing. Otherwise it is surprisingly rare. Probably the reason for this is that it is widely known that an agreement to withdraw (or not to bring) an employment tribunal claim is not binding on the employee unless it is negotiated through ACAS or recorded in an agreement that conforms to the requirements of ERA 1996 s203 (a 'compromise agreement').

6.45   This is true, but it may have created a myth that goes further than the reality, and persuaded claimants and respondents that only a compromise agreement or an ACAS conciliated settlement is effective. Suppose the claimant promises to withdraw and the respondent promises to pay the claimant £5,000. The respondent pays up, but the

---

12 See chapter 11 below.

claimant then changes his mind and continues with the claim. In this situation, ERA 1996 s203 has the effect that notwithstanding his promise to withdraw, the claimant cannot be prevented from continuing his claim – although he will certainly have to give credit for the £5,000 received against any compensation he is ultimately awarded, and depending on the circumstances he could be at risk of a costs order if the tribunal thinks his conduct of the case has been unreasonable. This means that an informal agreement under which the respondent pays first and the claimant then withdraws is a bad idea from the respondent's point of view, because it gives the respondent no certainty that that is the end of the case. Claimants have nothing to fear from this, but respondents will normally – and understandably – be unwilling to settle a case in this manner.

6.46   If on the other hand the agreement is that the claimant withdraws the claim first, and the respondent then pays within a set period of withdrawal, there is no such risk for the respondent. For the claimant, there is the same degree of certainty as there would be under an ACAS settlement or a compromise agreement: the agreement is a contract, so if the respondent fails to perform its side of the bargain the contract can be enforced, like any other contract, in the county court. This is exactly the situation where the case is settled in this manner at the door of the tribunal.

ACAS conciliated settlement

6.47   The Advisory, Conciliation and Arbitration Service (ACAS) is a government agency that has the job of trying to broker a settlement in all employment tribunal cases. ACAS receives a copy of every claim to the tribunal. A conciliation officer will be assigned to the case and will write to the parties at an early stage to offer his services. The form on which ACAS records an agreement is called COT3.[13] Until October 2004, conciliation officers had a duty to act to promote a settlement throughout the proceedings.

6.48   Since 1 October 2004, there have been fixed conciliation periods during which the conciliation officer will have a duty to act. After the end of the conciliation period, there will only be a power to act.[14] In practice, ACAS will not act outside the conciliation period.

---

13 Generally pronounced 'cot 3'. The initials stand for Conciliation Officer of the Tribunal.

14 Fixed periods do not apply to discrimination or equal pay cases.

P6.46 Agreement to withdraw on terms

Carrot & Marrow Solicitors
24 Lower Street
Islington
London N12 3AB

17 January 2008

your ref GB/ar.6789
our ref NC 1234/2007

Dear Mr Bean

Andrew Tullet v The Big Shift Ltd ET/ 123456/07

As discussed just now, I should be grateful if you would sign and fax back to me the attached terms of settlement of this case.

Yours sincerely

Natalie Cummings

SETTLEMENT AGREEMENT

Andrew Tullet ('the claimant') and The Big Shift Ltd ('the respondent') have agreed as follows:

1. The claimant will by close of business on 18 January 2008 withdraw his complaint numbered 123456/07 of unfair dismissal and unauthorised deductions from wages from the tribunal.
2. On or before 30 January 2008 the respondent will pay to the claimant the sum of £6,750.
3. Each party will refrain from making or publishing any disparaging statement about the other, or any statement about the other calculated or intended to lower the other's standing or reputation with the public or in the eyes of any third party.
4. The fact of this agreement and its terms are confidential, save that either party may disclose them to his or its legal advisers or as required by law and the claimant may disclose them to members of his immediate family (that is, his wife, his parents, and his son).

Signed **Natalie Cummings**   Dated **17 January 2008**
for the claimant

Signed   Dated
for the respondent

Unfortunately, this means that by the time parties are at the point of settling the conciliation period has often ended and ACAS is unavailable.

6.49 The ACAS officer is a neutral go-between who will convey offers and counter-offers between the parties, but will not offer advice on the merits or value of the claim.[15] Most ACAS officers are friendly and pleasant to deal with, but it must be remembered that they are strictly impartial and will convey any information given to them to the respondent, so claimants and their advisers should never say anything to ACAS that they would not be prepared to say to the other side.

6.50 The ACAS officer's practical role can seem like little more than a post-box, but there are potential benefits for the claimant. First, ACAS offers a simple way of settling a case that is widely understood: the claimant will have no difficulty in persuading the respondent that a settlement achieved through ACAS is valid and binding. Secondly, in a case where feelings run high, using a neutral go-between is sometimes the only way of cooling the temperature sufficiently to negotiate at all. Thirdly, once ACAS notifies the tribunal that a settlement has been reached the tribunal will immediately take the case out of the list. Once the ACAS officer has confirmed that the case is settled – even if a settlement is reached after tribunal staff have gone home – the parties can be rest assured that the tribunal will be informed and the hearing will not take place. If the parties are negotiating at the last minute without the assistance of ACAS, they will not be able to get confirmation after hours that the case has been taken out of the list, so they may still need to attend.

6.51 If the parties approach ACAS after they have agreed a deal, the ACAS officer may refuse to become involved at the last minute, so if a COT3 settlement is desirable, the parties should approach the ACAS officer early in negotiations and keep in touch throughout. At the same time, the fact that negotiations are proceeding through ACAS does not prevent the parties from negotiating directly with each other when that is helpful.

6.52 As a rule, not much turns on whether a particular stage of the negotiations is conducted direct or through ACAS. Sometimes the psychology of negotiations is delicate, however, so the decision can be affected by a number of factors. The relationship with the respondent (especially if unrepresented) may be difficult, and the ACAS officer may be better able to keep tempers cool. Sometimes the claimant's adviser will wish to speak to the respondent's adviser direct to break a

15 ACAS officers do occasionally volunteer an opinion on these matters, but they are not legally qualified and it is not part of their job to do so.

deadlock, or to persuade him that a clause he is insisting on is unnecessary. Sometimes the claimant's adviser will simply wish to bring home to the respondent how strong the claim is: an adviser who genuinely feels very confident about a case may be able to convey that confidence, and undermine the respondent's, more effectively in a direct conversation than through an intermediary. On the other hand the claimant's adviser may be conscious of weaknesses in the case, and may prefer to keep the respondent's adviser at arm's-length in order to avoid letting that slip. Or the conciliation officer's telephone may simply be engaged at the point that the claimant's adviser wants to put a counter-offer and they will contact the respondent's adviser direct.

6.53   Once terms of settlement are agreed, the conciliation officer will record them on the COT3 form, which will be sent out to the parties for signature. It is important to note that the settlement is binding as soon as both parties have agreed – usually over the telephone – to the words that will appear on the COT3. If the claimant changes his mind between agreeing on the telephone and receiving the COT3, it is too late: the case is settled.

P6.53 COT3 wording – money and reference

The claimant is a school caretaker who has been dismissed after a clearly unfair procedure for being drunk at work and assaulting the head teacher.

The parties have agreed as follows:

1. The respondent will pay without admission of liability the sum of £3,500 (three thousand, five hundred pounds) to the claimant in full and final settlement of his complaint before the Employment Tribunal numbered 123456/07 and any other claim arising out of his contract of employment or its termination, provided that nothing in this agreement affects any claim the claimant may have in respect of accrued pension rights or personal injury. The respondent agrees to make the payment under this agreement within 21 days of receipt of copies of this agreement signed on behalf of the claimant.[16]

2. On any request by any third party for a reference for the claimant, the respondent will provide promptly and duly signed and dated on its headed notepaper the reference attached as Schedule to this

16 It is essential to agree a date for payment: an agreement to pay a sum of money but not on any particular date is certainly unsatisfactory and could be difficult to enforce.

agreement, and only that reference, provided that in the event of a request in the form of a telephone inquiry or questionnaire, the respondent will respond in a manner fully consistent with the contents of the Schedule hereto. At or before the time for payment agreed at clause (1) above, the respondent will provide to the claimant six copies of an open version of the agreed reference on company notepaper, duly signed and dated and headed 'To whom it may concern'.

3. Neither party will disclose to any third party (including the maker of any request for a reference for the claimant), save as required by law or to their respective legal advisers and in the case of the claimant his immediate family, the existence or content of this agreement.

SCHEDULE

[See reference for Richard Lightfoot at P6.33.2 above]

Compromise agreement

6.54   If the parties settle before the day of the hearing without using ACAS, the usual method is to draw up a compromise agreement that complies with the requirements of ERA 1996 s203. Section 203 requires an agreement in writing relating to the particular proceedings, which must identify an independent adviser who has advised the claimant on the effect of the agreement, and which must state that the conditions regulating compromise agreements under the ERA 1996 are satisfied. The adviser must be a qualified lawyer, or a person certified in writing by either a trade union or an advice centre as competent to give advice and authorised to do so. The adviser, whether a qualified lawyer or not, must be covered by insurance against claims in respect of negligent advice.[17]

6.55   Often the main reason for preferring to use ACAS rather than to enter into a compromise agreement will be that the respondent's adviser takes some persuading that the applicant's adviser, if unqualified, is a 'relevant independent adviser' for the purposes of s203. This is a legitimate concern for the respondent: if the claimant's adviser is not a relevant independent adviser, then the agreement will still be enforceable against the respondent, but will not prevent the claimant from continuing with the case. If the claimant is unrepresented, it is

---

17 Most advice centres and other organisations that provide free representation will have arrangements in place that are sufficient to meet these requirements in respect of their paid staff and their volunteers.

common for the respondent to agree to pay his legal costs of getting the necessary independent legal advice to make the agreement binding.[18]

6.56   A compromise agreement, like a COT3 agreement, is a contract which the claimant can enforce in the county court if the respondent does not comply with its terms.

6.57   The substance of a compromise agreement can be as simple or as complex as the parties require: it is perfectly possible to draft a short, simple compromise agreement that merely settles the case for a sum of money, or a sum of money and a reference. The example below demonstrates the formalities required for a compromise agreement, but its subject matter is unusual in that it is dealing with a point of principle.

DOCUMENT OUTLINE: Compromise agreement

identification of the parties

withdrawal of the claim

payment to the claimant and/or other terms as agreed

identification of the claimant's legal adviser or 'relevant independent adviser'

assertion that the agreement complies with the requirements of ERA 1996 s203

P6.57 Compromise agreement – dealing with a point of principle

COMPROMISE AGREEMENT

This agreement is made between Alice Fearon ('the claimant') and Naff Tat plc ('the respondent'). The claimant and the respondent agree as follows:

1. The claimant's complaint to the Employment Tribunal numbered 123456/06 against Naff Tat plc is withdrawn.

---

18   It is worth approaching the local law centre for this purpose: even if it has not been able to take on the case, it may be able to advise on a compromise agreement for a moderate fee paid by the employer. A fee in the region of £300–£500 would be typical.

2. The respondent affirms its commitment to the dignity of all its staff at work and undertakes to take the following steps to ensure and protect the dignity of its staff:

   (i) The respondent will within 14 days draw up a draft dignity at work policy dealing with personal privacy, sexual and racial harassment and any comparable mistreatment on grounds of sexual orientation, religion or disability, and submit the draft to the claimant for his approval. If the parties cannot agree within a further 28 days on a final draft of the policy, it will be finalised, taking the views of both parties into account, by Antonia Thwaite of the Humane Resources Consultancy Ltd. Once finalised the policy will be adopted by the respondent forthwith.

   (ii) The respondent undertakes to bring the dignity at work policy to the attention of all its staff within 14 days of its adoption, and to retain it in force for a period of three years without further revisions.

   (iii) The respondent will immediately institute a programme of equal opportunities training, to be provided by the Humane Resources Consultancy Ltd, for all managers of the grade P2 and above. Naff Tat plc will ensure that all such managers have attended a two-day course by 31 December 2007.

   (iv) The respondent will amend its disciplinary policy with immediate effect so that a manager who conducts a personal search of any staff member without specific grounds to suspect wrongdoing will be guilty of gross misconduct. It will bring this change to the attention of all its staff within 21 days of the date of this agreement.

3. On a mutually convenient date in June 2007 the Chairman and the Human Resources Director of the respondent will meet with the claimant and her legal adviser to review progress under this agreement.

4. The purpose of clauses 2 and 3 above are to mitigate the injury to feelings suffered by the claimant as a result of unlawful discrimination against her by the respondent. If these clauses are not fully complied with by 31 December 2007, the respondent will forthwith pay to the claimant the sum of £5,000 in compensation for her injury to feelings.[19]

---

19 The point of this is to head off any future dispute about what damage the claimant has actually suffered if the respondent fails to comply with those parts of the agreement that do not directly affect her. This too – compare para 6.18 above – could prove unenforceable as a penalty, although the aim is that it should be a valid 'liquidated damages' clause. For 'liquidated damages', see glossary.

5. The relevant independent adviser for the purposes of this agreement is Natalie Cummings of the North London Law Centre.[20]
6. The conditions regulating compromise agreements under the Employment Rights Act 1996 are satisfied.

SIGNED ....   DATED ....
FOR THE APPLICANT

SIGNED ....   DATED ....
FOR THE RESPONDENT

Consent order

6.58   If the parties can agree to the terms of an order that they would like the tribunal to make, then provided it has power to do so the tribunal will almost certainly be willing to make the agreed order. Tribunals only have the powers that they have been given by legislation, so they cannot – for example – order an employer to provide a reference in agreed terms even if both parties ask them to. If the parties' agreement is simply that the respondent admits liability and is to pay the claimant a certain sum of money, this can be embodied in a tribunal order without difficulty. It will be fairly rare that the respondent is willing to agree to this: more often, the respondent will be unwilling to admit liability and will wish the terms of any settlement to be confidential. The tribunal cannot order one party to pay the other a sum of money without finding that the paying party is liable.

6.59   If the parties wish to agree to terms that the tribunal does not have power to order, it is common to ask the tribunal to make what is known as a 'Tomlin' order.[21] This is an order staying the case for a set period while the parties give effect to their agreement. If the respondent defaults on the agreement, then the claimant can apply to the tribunal to have the case re-listed. If no such application is received by the tribunal within the period of the stay, the tribunal will dismiss the claim.

20 Paragraphs 5 and 6 are essential if the agreement is to be valid as a compromise agreement under the Employment Rights Act 1996. Many respondents will also wish the agreement to spell out that Ms Cummings is a 'relevant independent adviser' for the purposes of ERA 1996 s203(3)(c) and that there was in force when she gave the advice a contract of insurance covering the risk of a claim by the employee in respect of loss arising in consequence of the advice. These things must be so, but if they are not, a false assertion that they are does not validate the compromise agreement.
21 See glossary.

6.60   The practical difference between this and immediate dismissal on agreed terms is that if the respondent defaults, the claimant can choose between applying to the tribunal to hear the case or enforcing the agreement in the county court. In fact, it is rare that returning to the tribunal will be preferable to enforcing the agreement in the county court: the claimant would presumably not have entered into the settlement agreement unless he considered that it was more beneficial than having the case heard by the tribunal, and if that was so at the time the agreement was made, it will most likely still be so a week or so later when the respondent has failed to perform its side of the bargain.

6.61   Nevertheless, this does not mean that 'Tomlin' orders are useless. They have a psychological advantage in that the respondent knows that until it has paid the agreed sum (and performed any other part of the agreement), the tribunal case is not dead but only sleeping. The tribunal case was ready for hearing, and to bring it back to life the claimant has only to write to the tribunal: this is likely to seem more immediate to the respondent than the danger that it will be sued in the county court for breach of contract.

6.62   Occasionally tribunal chairmen express the view that they lack the power to make a 'Tomlin' order. This is mistaken: the tribunal has a wide power under rule 10 to determine its own procedure and to stay proceedings if it thinks fit, and there is no reason why it should not exercise that power for the purpose of facilitating settlement.[22] However, if the tribunal is determined not to make a 'Tomlin' order, then dismissal on agreed terms will normally be an adequate alternative.

P6.62 Consent order staying the case on agreed terms ('Tomlin order')

IN THE EMPLOYMENT TRIBUNAL   CASE NO. 123456/2006
LONDON CENTRAL

BETWEEN

JANE CLOSE

Claimant

and

THE LONDON BOROUGH OF HOLBORN

Respondent

draft

_____
ORDER
_____

The parties having agreed to the terms set out in the attached schedule

IT IS ORDERED BY CONSENT:

That all further proceedings in this claim be stayed until 31 January 2008 except for the purpose of carrying those terms into effect, both parties being free to apply to the tribunal to restore the claim on or before that date.

[SCHEDULE]

AGREEMENT

The parties have agreed as follows:

1. The respondent will pay to the claimant the sum of £7,500 in full and final settlement of her employment tribunal complaint numbered 123456/06, payment to be made within 14 days of receipt by the respondent of this agreement signed on behalf of the claimant.

22 Employment Tribunals (Constitution and Rules of Procedure) Regulations 2004 SI No 1861 Sch 1.

2. The respondent will supply to the claimant, in a letter duly signed and dated by Mark Bertram on the respondent's headed paper and promptly on request by any third party, the following reference:

[See reference for Jane Close at P6.33.1]

3. Any request in the form of a telephone call or a questionnaire will be answered by Mark Bertram and only by Mark Bertram in a manner consistent with the agreed reference set out under paragraph 2 above.

Signed ....   Dated ....
for claimant

Signed ....   Dated ....
for respondent

Settlement after partial victory

6.63   If the claimant wins on liability at the hearing, or wins part of his claim, the tribunal will then very often invite the parties to try to agree between themselves what the level of any award should be. Often it is beneficial for both parties to settle at this stage. If the claimant has been receiving social security benefits for part of the period that the award will cover, settlement avoids recoupment of those benefits.[23]

6.64   However, if the finding on liability only represents a partial win for the claimant, he should first think carefully about whether there is any prospect that he might wish to appeal the tribunal's decision. Settlement without thought for this possibility will be likely to make any future appeal impossible; but if the claimant insists that the terms of any settlement must keep open his right to appeal, then this may well make settlement impossible.

Example
Sufiya Halai of P2.17.2 and P2.31.3 was aggrieved by her employer's decision to stop paying her enhanced rates for weekend work. Suppose the dispute culminated in her resignation and claim to the employment tribunal, complaining of unauthorised deductions from pay and unfair constructive dismissal.

Contd

---

23   See ELAH 7 para 18.60.

> The hearing runs for a day and a half, and after lunch on the second day the tribunal announces its decision that Ms Halai has suffered unauthorised deductions and has been constructively dismissed, but that she contributed to her dismissal by 50% by not being prepared to negotiate about the enhanced pay. Ms Halai was out of work and receiving social security benefits for just over three months before finding another job, and there is no suggestion that she has failed to do enough to mitigate her loss. The tribunal asks the parties if they would like 20 minutes to discuss whether they can agree the amount of the award.
>
> Ms Halai is disappointed to be told that she is partly to blame for the loss of her job, but she knows that if the tribunal makes an award in respect of her lost earnings while she was unemployed she will lose the Job Seekers' Allowance she claimed during that period. She agrees to accept £2,400 in full and final settlement of her claim, and the tribunal duly records that 'terms of settlement having been agreed between the parties, the claimant's claim for a remedy is dismissed on withdrawal.'
>
> Ms Halai goes to see her adviser at the law centre and asks about appealing against the decision that she was partly to blame for her dismissal, and she is told that she has settled her claim for a remedy and there is now no possibility of an appeal: the case is closed.

6.65   If Ms Halai had seen this problem coming, she would have had various options, but she would not necessarily have been able to solve it. She could simply have told the tribunal and the respondent that she was not prepared to settle because she wanted to take advice about appealing the finding of contributory fault. If she had done that, then the tribunal would have made an award in her favour and she would have lost money through recoupment. She could have told the respondent that she was willing to settle, but only so long as it was an express term of the agreement that she reserved her right to appeal that finding of contributory fault. That would have been a rational enough position for her to take, but it might well have made it impossible to reach agreement. If the question of remedy was listed for a separate hearing (unlikely on these facts, but possible where extensive evidence and argument will be needed on remedy), she might have asked the tribunal to stay the remedy hearing until after her appeal against the finding of contributory fault.

Negotiation and costs

6.66 Respondents will often head settlement offers 'without prejudice save as to costs' and will threaten that, if the claimant does not accept the offer, they will rely on it, in support of an application for costs, as evidence of the claimant's unreasonable conduct. This echoes the practice in the ordinary civil courts, where costs will normally be ordered against a party who has won the case but failed to recover more than has been offered. However, the Employment Appeal Tribunal (EAT) has made it clear that this rule does not apply in the employment tribunals: the power to award costs only arises if a party has behaved unreasonably, and misjudging by a moderate margin the amount that the tribunal will award is not in itself unreasonable conduct.[24]

6.67 The claimant may be at a real risk of a costs order if he has no reasonable prospect of recovering more than has been offered: in other words, where the offer is equivalent to the most that the tribunal can be expected to award even if the claim is an unqualified success. This will be most likely in cases where the maximum value of the claim is modest, and will be less than the respondent's costs of fighting the case; or where the claimant's case is very strong and easily quantifiable.

6.68 A claimant who has received an offer of at this level should think carefully before refusing it because of the costs risk. There is authority that a claimant is entitled to continue with the case for the sake of a finding of liability, but if that is the claimant's concern it is advisable to make it clear to the respondent that an admission of liability would make the difference.[25] Similarly, the respondent's insistence on a confidentiality clause may be a legitimate sticking point for the claimant: again, if that is so, it should be made clear in writing to the respondent.

6.69 There is no reason why the claimant should not turn this tactic on the respondent in a suitable case. If the respondent's defence is misconceived and the amount that the claimant will recover is very clear (in an unfair dismissal case where the claimant's losses clearly exceed the maximum award for such cases, for example, or in a claim for statutory redundancy pay), the claimant can write to the respondent offering to settle for that amount and warning that the claimant may seek costs (or a preparation time order) if the offer is not accepted.

---

24 See *Kopel v Safeway Stores plc* [2003] IRLR 753, EAT.
25 *Telephone Information Services v Wilkinson* [1991] IRLR 148, EAT and P6.69.2 below.

P6.69.1 'Without prejudice save as to costs' settlement offer to respondent

The case is a complaint of automatically unfair dismissal for refusal to work on Sundays. It was not finished on the day of the hearing and has had to be listed for a further day some weeks later: the respondent's witnesses have finished giving their evidence but the claimant has yet to be heard. The claimant's adviser takes the view that the claim cannot now fail, but the claimant is anxious about giving evidence and wants to avoid completing the hearing if possible.

Carrot & Marrow Solicitors
24 Lower Street
Islington
London N12 3AB

6 April 2007

your ref GB/ar.6789
our ref NC 1234/2006

WITHOUT PREJUDICE SAVE AS TO COSTS

Dear Carrot & Marrow

Mr Pool v Savemore plc

In light of the evidence given by your client's witnesses at the hearing on 4 April, I invite you to consider urgently with your client whether your defence is misconceived.

Two of your client's three witnesses gave clear evidence that at the time of Mr Pool's dismissal they did not believe that he had any right to refuse Sunday work. One of them appeared to maintain this belief even at the hearing. Even more tellingly, Mr Harpar, who made the decision to dismiss my client, gave unequivocal evidence that the only reason for the dismissal was Mr Pool's refusal to work Saturday night shifts. As the Saturday night shift fell mainly on Sunday, your client's own evidence points conclusively to a dismissal for refusing Sunday work.

In the circumstances I take the view that persisting with the respondent's defence that Mr Pool was fairly dismissed for 'inflexibility' is unreasonable and/or misconceived: the only respect in which he was inflexible was his insistence on his right to refuse Sunday work.

Mr Pool's losses have been clearly quantified and are not open to any credible dispute. As you have seen from his statement and the bundle of applications and rejection letters that have been disclosed, he took immediate and vigorous action to mitigate his loss; and he secured a new job at slightly better pay than he was earning while employed by your client after only 15 weeks. I therefore have instructions to offer settlement of the case for the full sum claimed on his schedule of loss, failing which I will rely on this letter in an application to the tribunal for Mr Pool's whole costs, or alternatively his costs of preparing for and attending the resumed hearing.

Yours faithfully

Natalie Cummings

P6.69.2 Response to a 'without prejudice save as to costs' offer from the respondent

Mr Herbert has been dismissed because he refused to travel to the new location to which his employer moved its offices. He does not dispute the fairness of the dismissal, because his employer closed the office where he worked when they lost the lease, and they had no other job to offer him. The dispute is about whether he is entitled to redundancy pay, so the sum at stake is both modest and exactly quantifiable. The respondent has offered the whole sum claimed, and has threatened a costs application if the offer is rejected.

Carrot & Marrow Solicitors
24 Lower Street
Islington
London N12 3AB

10 January 2008

> your ref GB/ar.6789
> our ref NC 1234/2007

FAO George Bean

WITHOUT PREJUDICE SAVE AS TO COSTS

Dear Mr Bean

David Herbert v Supaclean Ltd

Thank you for your letter of 4 January.

I am afraid that your offer of settlement 'without admission of liability' is unacceptable to my client. The reason for this is that Mr Herbert is in negotiations with his bank over the effect of an insurance policy covering loan repayments in the event of his dismissal for redundancy. The bank has told him that if the tribunal finds that he was dismissed for redundancy, or if your client confirms in writing that this was the reason for his dismissal, his repayments will be covered for the agreed period. If the case is settled without an admission of liability, he will not have the benefit of his insurance. Depending on how long he is out of work, the insurance may be of considerably more value to him than the redundancy payment which is the subject of the claim.

In the circumstances I am instructed that unless your client is willing to admit liability, this claim cannot be settled even for payment of the full sum claimed.

The position my client takes on this cannot be characterised as unreasonable: he is entitled to a finding of liability, and there is a compelling practical reason why he should insist on that entitlement. In the circumstances I have advised him that there is no significant risk of a costs order against him.

Yours sincerely

Natalie Cummings

CHAPTER 7

Default judgment, case management discussions and pre-hearing reviews

Default Judgments

7.1   Where a response has been struck out, or was not presented, the tribunal has the power to make a default judgment.[1] A default judgment is a finding in favour of the claimant that is made without a hearing.

7.2   A default judgment appears tempting, because it offers victory without the difficulties of a hearing. In one sense this is true: a default judgment for £1,000 is much the same as a normal judgment for £1,000. It is binding on the respondent and can be enforced in the usual way.

7.3   Often, however, it is in the claimant's interest to proceed to a full hearing, because judgments from a hearing tend to be more secure than default judgments. Default judgments can be set aside on review if the tribunal considers it just and equitable to do so.[2] In practice default judgments are routinely set aside. Provided the respondent's explanation for not responding is not entirely fanciful, a review application will normally succeed. This means that a default judgment is relatively insecure, and is likely to be set aside if the respondent attempts to review it. This is surprisingly common. Respondents frequently fail to respond until a judgment is made, apparently because they fail to recognise the consequences until a finding against them is made. If the Respondent gets a second chance by successfully reviewing a default judgment against it, it is likely to be more strongly motivated to defend itself effectively than if it had been allowed take part from the outset: it has had the benefit of a demonstration of the risk it runs.[3]

7.4   The tribunal is less likely to revisit a case where there has been a full hearing and evidence has been heard. Since a respondent who has not presented a response will not be able to take part in the hearing, the prospects of success – unless the case is very weak – are strong. This means that it normally better to avoid a default judgment, if possible, in order to obtain a judgment that will be easier to defend against review.

---

1   Rule 8.
2   Rule 33.
3   The same insight is the reason why 'mock' examinations are helpful.

Different types of hearing

7.5 Hearings divide into four different types:

- case management discussions;
- pre-hearing reviews;
- substantive hearings;
- review hearings.

7.6 Case management discussions are held where the tribunal thinks that a meeting to discuss procedural and organisational aspects of the case will be useful. Pre-hearing reviews (PHRs) are hearings on a preliminary point. Preliminary points are issues that are vital to the case, but can be dealt with in isolation.

7.7 Substantive hearings deal with the legal or factual issues that will determine the case, and are discussed in chapter 9. Review hearings are occasionally held after the substantive hearing in order to give one party or the other the chance to attempt to persuade the tribunal to change its mind; they are discussed in chapter 9.

Case management discussions

7.8 Before the main hearing, the tribunal may think it necessary or desirable to hold a case management discussion. The tribunal can order this of its own motion, or on the application of one of the parties. There will almost always be a case management discussion in a discrimination case.

7.9 Case management discussions (CMDs) are heard by a chairman alone, and they are oral hearings to deal with the kinds of questions often dealt with by a chairman in correspondence. These are questions like:[4]

- whether or not a party should be permitted to amend the claim or the response;
- whether a hearing date should be postponed;
- whether orders should be made for disclosure of specific documents or written answers to questions;
- when witness statements should be exchanged;

---

4 See Employment Tribunals Rules of Procedure rule 10(2) for a longer – but not exhaustive – list of the orders that can be made at this stage.

- who should be responsible for preparing the bundle and when this should be done;
- whether expert evidence is to be permitted;
- what are the issues for the main hearing.

7.10 For once the 'plain English' of the rules reflects the reality quite well: these hearings can feel more like a discussion about what arrangements will be most convenient rather than a formal hearing. Often there is little or nothing that is seriously contentious at a case management discussion, and it is not at all uncommon for the parties to agree the issues and suitable directions before the hearing starts and propose them, jointly, to the chairman.

7.11 When push comes to shove, however (and it quite often does), the chairman is in control and can impose his view. Although often uncontentious and co-operative, a case management discussion can also be the forum for a serious dispute between the parties with far-reaching consequences for the final outcome of the case. It is important to be aware of which issues are likely to be fought over, and to be ready with arguments on any that are. Matters of timing, for example, or who is to be responsible for the preparation of hearing bundles, will usually be able to be agreed without much difficulty. Disputes about whether a particular document or class of documents should be disclosed by the respondent may be hotly contested, on the other hand.[5] Any significant amendment to the claim or response may be strongly opposed by the other party. An application for costs may be made at a case management discussion, and this too will almost always be strongly contested.

7.12 It is always a good idea to draw up, and if possible agree with the other side, an agenda for a case management discussion. This focuses the parties' (and the chairman's) minds on what needs to be considered, and helps with preparation for the hearing. Rule 10(2) can be used as a check-list for the questions that may arise in addition to the clarification of the questions for the main hearing.[6]

7.13 A proposed list of issues for the main hearing is a good idea, as is a set of proposed directions. Occasionally it will even be appropriate to prepare a skeleton argument for a directions hearing. Skeleton arguments may be desirable at this stage if there is a serious dispute about

---

5 As a rule of thumb, the more vigorously the respondent defends its right not to disclose a document, the more important it will be to the claimant to get hold of it if possible.

6 Of the Employment Tribunals Rules of Procedure 2004 (found at SI No 1861 Sch 1).

whether or not a particular document in the possession of one party or the other is privileged, for example, or whether proceedings should be stayed pending the outcome of a related appeal or other proceedings.

P7.13.1 Agenda for case management discussion

IN THE EMPLOYMENT TRIBUNAL   Case No 123456/2007

Ground floor, Victory House
30-34 Kingsway
London
WC2B 6EX

BETWEEN

SAIFUR RAHMAN

Claimant

and

SAINT JULIAN'S HOSPITAL NHS TRUST

Respondent

AGENDA FOR CASE
MANAGEMENT DISCUSSION
14 DECEMBER 2007

1. Clarification of issues for the main hearing.
2. Claimant's application to amend the claim.
3. Respondent's application to amend its response.
4. Claimant's application for an order for disclosure of all communications between personnel and management relating to the disciplinary proceedings.[7]
5. Witness statements.
6. Hearing bundle.
7. Listing.

---

7 This might need a short skeleton argument if the respondent argues that the material is covered by litigation privilege.

P7.13.2 List of issues and suggested directions for case management discussion

IN THE EMPLOYMENT TRIBUNAL   Case No 123456/2007
LONDON CENTRAL
BETWEEN

SAIFUR RAHMAN

Claimant

and

SAINT JULIAN'S HOSPITAL NHS TRUST

Respondent

PROPOSED LIST OF ISSUES
AND DIRECTIONS

Limitation
1. Was it reasonably practicable for SR to present his complaint by 3 September 2007?
2. If not, did he present it within such further time as was reasonable in all the circumstances?

Unfair dismissal
3. Did SR make a protected disclosure in informing the Chief Executive of the Trust of his concerns about what Sister Winston had said on 7 May 2007?
4. If so, was the fact that he had made a protected disclosure the reason or a significant part of the reason for SR's dismissal?
5. If not, what was the reason for SR's dismissal?
6. Was that an admissible reason for dismissal?
7. If so, was the dismissal (a) substantively fair; (b) procedurally fair?
8. If SR's dismissal was unfair, what loss has he suffered because of his dismissal?

Wrongful dismissal

9. Was SR guilty of gross misconduct?[8]

Suggested directions

- Updated schedule of loss to be provided by claimant on or before 6 January 2008.
- Hearing to be listed for three days.[9]
- Witness statements to be exchanged 28 days before the hearing.
- Index to hearing bundle to be agreed between the parties 14 days before the hearing.
- Bundle to be compiled and copied by the claimant, and one copy to be provided to the respondent seven days before the hearing.

Pre-hearing reviews

7.14   Unlike case management discussions, pre-hearing reviews (PHR) often involve the final resolution of some part of the case. Unlike the main substantive hearings, they normally deal with a single preliminary issue. However if the case is not dismissed at the PHR, it is normal for case management issues to be dismissed as well.

7.15   The claimant will not normally need to decide whether she wants a PHR. If a case contains certain preliminary issues a PHR is likely to be listed as a matter of course. Preliminary issues likely to result in a PHR include:

- Was the claim brought in time?
- Was the claimant an employee?
- Was the claimant disabled?
- Did the claimant comply with an applicable grievance procedure?

8   The respondent's position is that he was dismissed without notice for gross misconduct. It follows that the only issue on wrongful dismissal is whether or not he was guilty of gross misconduct. Note that here the question is not what the employer reasonably believed, but what actually happened. In light of Mr Rahman's future career plans, it could be very important to him to have the tribunal come to a conclusion on this – even though his damages for wrongful dismissal will be limited to his net pay for the duration of his contractual notice period – because a dismissal for gross misconduct in the circumstances alleged could have him placed on a register of persons prohibited from working with vulnerable adults.

9   See paras 8.3–8.7 below.

7.16 There is no requirement that the tribunal must notify the parties in advance of the questions it intends to deal with at a PHR. The notice of hearing should indicate what they intend to consider. Unfortunately, tribunals often list a PHR 'to consider matters generally'. This is an unhelpful phrase that gives little clue as to what documents or arguments they need to prepare and what evidence if any they need to call. It is suggested that any party in receipt of notice of a PHR 'to consider matters generally' should write to the tribunal for clarification. This is one occasion when a letter will be more productive that a telephone call, since the tribunal staff will not know what the Chairman who decided on the PHR had in mind.

7.17 Pre-hearing reviews will normally be heard by a chairman sitting alone. If either party requests a full tribunal 10 days or more before the hearing, and a chairman considers that 'substantive issues of fact' are likely to be considered at the pre-hearing review, then the chairman may order that the pre-hearing review should be heard by a chairman. If the claimant thinks there is a danger that a significant preliminary issue will be decided at the pre-hearing review, then he or she should usually request that it be heard by a full tribunal. The same letter might usefully seek some clarity about what will be decided at the review.

P7.17 Letter requesting that a pre-hearing review should be heard by a full tribunal

The Regional Secretary
London Central Employment Tribunal
19–29 Woburn Place
London WC1X 0LU

> my ref MR/ir.123
> your ref 123456/06

FAX ONLY 020 7273 8686

6 December 2007

Dear Madam

Gilbert Rutledge v Dick Whittington Newsagent Ltd

Thank you for your letter of 3 December giving notice of a pre-hearing review in this case on 11 January 2008.

I should be grateful if you would let me know whether it is intended that any substantive issues should be considered at the pre-hearing review. Specifically, it has been alleged by the respondent that the tribunal lacks jurisdiction because (a) the claimant's claim was presented out of time; and (b) that the claimant was not a worker for the purposes of the Working Time Regulations.

If it is intended to deal with either of these issues, I request that the review should be conducted by a full tribunal. This will assist the tribunal in dealing with the proceedings efficiently and fairly because it is undesirable that substantive issues of fact on which the claimant's entitlement to bring proceedings rests should be determined by a Chairman sitting alone.[10]

This letter is copied to the respondent. The respondent should note that if it objects to the application, it must write to the tribunal within seven days of receiving this letter, or before the date of the hearing (whichever date is the earlier) explaining the reasons for its objection, and should copy that letter to me. Rule 11 of the procedure rules has been complied with in relation to this application.[11]

Yours faithfully

Malcolm Rhodes

7.18   The main reason for pre-hearing reviews is pragmatic. It is often more efficient to deal with preliminary matters separately. It simplifies hearings by reducing the number of issues each hearing has to deal with. More importantly, it can dispose of cases without the need for long hearings if they do not survive the PHR. This should not be seen by

---

10 Rule 11(3) of the Procedure Rules requires a statement of 'how the application will assist the chairman or tribunal in dealing with the case efficiently and fairly' to be included in every interlocutory application. The provision is ill-judged, and inevitably invites bland and formulaic treatment. This statement or something very like it will be adequate for most if not all amendment applications.

11 This quotes rule 11(4)(b). The rule is unsatisfactory, because it is not clear whether the alternative date to 'within seven days of receiving' the letter is merely 'before the hearing' or 'seven days before the hearing'. However, the party applying for an order cannot be faulted for giving the respondent ambiguous instructions if the ambiguity is the ambiguity of the rules themselves.

claimants as an entirely bad thing. If you are going to lose your case, it may be preferable to lose it early in the process, after a short hearing, than later, after a long and gruelling battle.

7.19   The widespread use of PHRs also affects settlement negotiations. If there is a chance that a potentially expensive case can be knocked out, respondents are reluctant to settle until after the PHR. The flip side of this is that victory in a PHR often gives momentum to the claimant and encourages the respondent to settle.

7.20   The decision to hold a pre-hearing review will usually be made by the tribunal, after it was identified a preliminary issue from the pleadings, or because the respondent requests one. There is, however, nothing to stop a claimant making a similar application in a suitable case.

P7.20 Letter requesting a pre-hearing review

The Regional Secretary
London Central Employment Tribunal
Victory House, Kingsway

my ref NC/ir.123
your ref 123456/06

FAX ONLY 020 7273 8686

15 January 2007

Dear Madam

Monica Bannon v Easy Peasy Driving School Ltd

I should be grateful if you would put before a Chairman my request for a pre-hearing review in this case to consider the following question:

> *Should the respondent should be required to pay a deposit as a condition of being permitted to pursue its contention that the tribunal lacks jurisdiction to consider the claim on the grounds that the claimant is not an employee of the respondent's?*

The claim is one of sex discrimination involving serious allegations of sexual harassment over a substantial period. The respondent's contention that Ms Bannon cannot bring a complaint against it because she is not an employee has no reasonable prospect of success. It is clear on the face of Ms Bannon's contract with the respondent that she is engaged as a 'self-employed driving instructor,' but that she is under a contract 'personally to do ... work' for the respondent and is therefore within the extended definition of an employee for the purposes of the Sex Discrimination Act 1975. The respondent's argument appears to rest on a failure to grasp that this definition has a wider scope than the common law definition of an employee.

A pre-hearing review on this question will assist the tribunal in dealing efficiently and fairly with the case because the respondent has not to date engaged with the substantive allegations, relying solely on its insistence that Ms Bannon is not an employee. A clear indication from the Tribunal that the respondent is mistaken in this belief may permit the parties to focus on the real issues on which the case will be decided, and possibly also facilitate negotiations.

Ms Bannon is unfortunately unlikely to be well enough to attend a hearing and give evidence for two to three months, so a preliminary hearing on this issue in the near future is unlikely to be practicable. Please refer to the attached report from Ms Bannon's consultant.

This letter is copied to the respondent. The respondent should note that if it objects to the application, it must write to the tribunal within seven days of receiving this letter, or before the date of the hearing (whichever date is the earlier) explaining the reasons for its objection, and should copy that letter to me. Rule 11 of the procedure rules has been complied with in relation to this application.

Yours faithfully

Natalie Cummings

7.21   The other tactical use a claimant may make of the procedure is in response to a threat of costs. This may be particularly powerful in the hands of an unrepresented claimant.

> **Example**
> Suppose the respondent has said that the case is misconceived and threatened to apply for costs of up to £10,000 if it is not withdrawn.[12] The claimant does not believe his case is misconceived, but is not a lawyer and has not been able to get any legal advice on the strength of his claim. He cannot possibly afford to lose £10,000, so he is extremely worried by the threat. He therefore writes to the tribunal enclosing a copy of the respondent's letter and proposes a pre-hearing review, so that he can, in effect, get the tribunal's preliminary advice on the strength of his claim.

7.22   Letters making a threat of this nature are sometimes headed 'without prejudice save as to costs' and this could give rise to objections from the respondent, or even the tribunal itself, that the letter should not be shown to the tribunal before the hearing. There are two possible answers to this. The first is that if the letter is nothing more than a threat that if the claimant does not withdraw the claim the respondent will apply for costs, then it is not a genuine attempt at negotiation: this means that it is not entitled to the benefit of the 'without prejudice' rule in the first place. If that argument is not accepted, it can still be argued that the question that the tribunal is invited to determine at a PHR is whether the claimant should be required to pay a deposit against a possible future costs order. It follows from that that the PHR is 'as to costs' and is therefore a hearing at which a letter headed 'without prejudice save as to costs' can properly be produced.[13]

12   This is often the form in which the threat is made by respondents, but it is important to note that it is only the limit on what the tribunal can assess itself. It is not an absolute limit on the costs that can be ordered: the tribunal can order a detailed assessment of a party's whole costs – without limit – in the county court.

13   If the tribunal finds these arguments unconvincing it may send the respondent's 'without prejudice save as to costs' letter back to the claimant on the grounds that it is not something that can properly be retained on the tribunal file and should not be seen by the tribunal that decides the case. No harm will have been done.

CHAPTER 8

Approaching the main hearing

Fixing the date

8.1   The tribunal will sometimes – but not always – invite the parties to list their unavailable dates before assigning a hearing date (usually referred to as 'listing'). If this is done, the claimant's adviser should take care to provide unavailable dates for the claimant, any witnesses, and (assuming he intends to represent the client at the hearing) himself. If unavailable dates are given in advance, then provided they are not too extensive they will rarely, if ever, be questioned by the tribunal. Voluntary sector or volunteer representatives sometimes doubt whether it is permissible to take their own convenience into account, so it is worth spelling out that it is: many Free Representation Unit volunteers, for example, are still students, and should not feel shy to give as 'unavailable' dates on which they have exams to sit, or imminent exams or assessments to prepare for.

8.2   This is also the moment to tell the tribunal if you think its time estimate is wrong. This is important because cases are listed for a set number of days, and if the case is not completed in the allotted time the tribunal will not be able to continue on consecutive days: it will be necessary to find another date, often several months ahead, when all three members of the tribunal, the parties, their representatives and any remaining witnesses can be present. This is very undesirable: the tribunal's recollection of the evidence will fade, and depending on the order in which the evidence is given the tribunal may be left with strong and immediate recollections of the respondent's evidence as against distant and incomplete memories of the claimant's.

Estimating the length of the hearing

8.3   That said, estimating the length of hearing is an inexact process even for experienced practitioners. Much depends on the way the witnesses answer questions, and the way the chairman runs the hearing. The following factors have to be considered:

- The subject-matter of the case. If it is about a single event – a dismissal for gross misconduct, for example, or a failure to promote or appoint – then it will be shorter than a complaint that a course of conduct over a long period was discriminatory, or that a whole series of different acts added up to a fundamental breach of contract.

- The amount of relevant documentation. If there is a great volume of paper that the tribunal will need to read, and that the witnesses will need to answer questions on, then the hearing will take longer than if the bundle is only 30 or 40 pages long.
- The number of witnesses. This is relevant, but it is less important than it may seem at first sight. The factor that makes most of the difference is how long and complicated a story the witnesses have to tell, not how many of them there are.
- The length of witness statements.
- Whether any of the evidence will have to be taken through an interpreter. If so, the estimate for that witness's evidence needs to be doubled at least.

8.4   Most wages or contract claims are finished in a day or less. A straightforward unfair dismissal claim where the reason given is redundancy or gross misconduct will not usually take more than two days. Discrimination claims tend to take longer, although they can sometimes be finished in a day if the facts are simple and the complaint does not involve the telling of a long story.[1]

8.5   For more substantial claims, an approximate picture can be built up by considering each witness in turn. Witnesses will normally be asked to read their statements aloud before cross-examination begins. Witnesses will vary of course, but a speed of about 160 words per minute is probably a fair rule of thumb.[2] The reading of the statements will often need to pause while the tribunal is taken to documents mentioned in the statement and invited to read them. Once the witness has finished his evidence in chief, time will be taken for cross-examination, questions from the tribunal and re-examination.

1 For example, 'failure to appoint' cases tend to be much more straightforward than other discrimination cases because there is no story to tell about the previous relationship between the parties.
2 Varying between about 130 wpm for a slow reader and 190 wpm at the fastest: see Tauroza and Allison, 'Speech rates in British English', *Applied Linguistics* 1990 (11) 1, 90-105, OUP.

> **Example**
> The statement for Mr Rahman of P5.28.1 is 2,606 words long. Assuming he will read it at 160 wpm, that will take about 16 minutes. He mentions a number of documents in his statement, each of which the tribunal will probably want to read. Most of them are short: say 30 seconds each for the 6 letters, and a minute each for the 3 nurses' statements.[3] That gives Mr Rahman 20 minutes to complete his evidence in chief, assuming there are no supplementary questions.
>
> Cross-examination of Mr Rahman will occupy the longest portion of his evidence. The respondent will probably want 1-2 hours to cross-examine him on a statement of this length referring to this number of documents. The more relevant documents there are, and the more detailed they are, the longer the time that will have to be allotted to cross-examination.

8.6 Asking witnesses to read their statements aloud can be quite helpful in short cases: it allows the witness to settle in to giving his evidence with an undemanding task, and reminds everyone what he says in chief before cross-examination begins. However, if statements are long it can become a significant waste of time. Mr Rahman's statement is fairly short at 2,606 words. A statement running to 10,000 words will probably take more than an hour to read aloud even without pauses for documents. Longer statements are by no means rare. At this level, the authors suggest asking the tribunal (at the CMD) to list an initial day for the tribunal to read the statements and key documents. The parties should be able to agree a list of key documents between them.

8.7 If something changes that affects the likely length of the hearing after it has been listed, it is important to draw the fact to the tribunal's attention as soon as possible.

---

3 As this is an unfair dismissal case the respondent will have given its evidence first, so it can be assumed that the tribunal will already have read the notes of the disciplinary hearing by this time.

Postponement requests

8.8   Once the case is listed, the tribunal is likely to be less accepting of reasons given for unavailability than it would have been if they had been
drawn to its attention in advance. If the parties have not been invited
to give their unavailable dates, then a prompt request for a postponement on the grounds that the claimant, a witness or the representative
is unavailable will probably be granted, at least for the first time. The
more previous postponements there have been, and the closer to the
hearing a postponement request comes, the harder the tribunal is
likely to look at the reasons before granting it. If it is essential to
request a postponement close to the hearing, or after the case has
been previously postponed, the request should deal carefully with the
reasons why the need could not have been foreseen earlier, and why it
is essential that that witness – or that particular adviser – should be able
to be present.

8.9   Where the problem is with the representative's availability, a
claimant relying on free advice has a slight advantage. Tribunals will be
reluctant to postpone a case because of the unforeseen unavailability
of the respondent's counsel or solicitor: they will take the view that
there are plenty of barristers and solicitors in the world and the respondent can choose another. The same cannot be said of free representation: demand greatly outstrips supply, and a claimant whose law centre
adviser or FRU representative, for example, is unavailable on the day
of the hearing is unlikely to have any other options. This was recognised
by the EAT in *Yearwood v Royal Mail*.[4]

8.10   If an application for postponement is opposed by the other party, or
is made at short notice, the party applying should be ready to provide
evidence of the need for it – including medical evidence if the reason
for the request is illness. A medical certificate simply signing the
claimant off work for a period is likely to be insufficient, so the GP
(or other medical adviser) should be asked to deal specifically with
whether the claimant is well enough to attend a hearing – see *Andreou
v Lord Chancellor's Department*.[5]

---

4   EAT/843/97; May 1998 *Legal Action* 15; reproduced at appendix A below.
5   [2002] IRLR 728, CA. See also *Teinaz v London Borough of Wandsworth* [2002]
IRLR 721; ICR 1471, CA.

P8.10 Application for postponement – illness of representative

The Regional Secretary
London Central Employment Tribunal
Ground floor, Victory House
30-34 Kingsway
London
WC2B 6EX

your ref 123456/06
my ref JS/ir.321

FAX ONLY 020 7273 8686

22 May 2007

VERY URGENT PLEASE: HEARING TOMORROW

Dear Madam

Ngosi Nbuka v Ambience plc

I am afraid it is necessary for me to make an urgent application for a postponement of this hearing, listed for three days from tomorrow.

I have just heard that Natalie Cummings, who has conduct of this case for Ms Nbuka and was intending to represent her at the hearing, has been taken into hospital today with suspected appendicitis. Ms Cummings was off work yesterday, but had put her symptoms down to a 'tummy bug' and had expected to be able to return today. I understand that an operation is scheduled for tomorrow morning.

The case raises complicated issues of discrimination law and there is a substantial volume of documentation. Ms Cummings is one of two employment lawyers employed by the Law Centre, and there is no-one who can represent Ms Nbuka in her place. Moreover the papers are currently with Ms Cummings as she took them home to work on over the weekend. Ms Nbuka herself has not of course made any preparations to represent herself, and cannot reasonably be expected to be able to do so adequately between now and tomorrow.

For these reasons I suggest that it is strongly in the interests of the efficient and fair disposal of the case that the hearing should be postponed.

This letter is copied to the respondent. The respondent should note that if it objects to the application, it must write to the tribunal today explaining the reasons for its objection, and should copy that letter to me.[6] **Rule 11 of the procedure rules has been complied with in relation to this application.**[7]

Yours faithfully

Jennifer Selscombe

8.11   For an application as urgent as this, it is a sensible precaution to telephone the tribunal 10 or 15 minutes after sending the fax to check that it has arrived and is legible, and ask the clerk to make sure that it goes before a chairman at the earliest opportunity.[8]

The bundle

8.12   Once both sides have disclosed all their relevant documents, it will be necessary to agree the content of a hearing bundle. This is something that the parties or their advisers should normally be able to handle co-operatively, although occasionally there may be a dispute about whether a document that one side says is privileged should be included.[9] Agreement that a particular document should be included in the bundle does not amount to agreement that the document is genuine. If one side doubts the authenticity of a document it is prudent to make that doubt clear but agreeing that since the other side wants to refer the tribunal to it, it should be included in the bundle.

8.13   There are differing views about whose job it is to prepare the bundle, but this will rarely, if ever, be worth a serious battle. It is in the interests of both sides that it should be competently done in good time before the hearing. If the respondents are represented by solicitors

---

6   The usual instruction to write to the tribunal seven days before the hearing is meaningless here, so the standard paragraph is adapted.

7   Employment Tribunals (Constitution and Rules of Procedure) Regulations 2004 SI No 1861 Sch 1.

8   This is a request to a member of tribunal staff to go out of his way to help, so charm – and a willingness to explain the problem – is in order.

9   See glossary and paras 4.29–4.36 above.

who seem to know what they are about, it is probably worthwhile trying to charm them into doing it. If the respondents are incompetently represented, the consequence of persuading them to do it may be an incomplete bundle, in random order and with crucial pages either missing or illegible, and the claimant's copy not provided until the day of the hearing. The benefit of a clear well-organised bundle which the claimant's adviser has had a couple of days to decorate with highlighters, notes and sticky notes before the hearing is well worth the price of some quality time with the photocopier. It is for the same reason that respondents' solicitors will often be willing to take on the job: they will want it done properly, and in good time, and they may not trust the claimant or his advisers on either point.

P8.13 Letter proposing a joint bundle

George Bean
Carrot & Marrow Solicitors
24 Lower Street
London N12 3AB

my ref NC/1234/06
your ref CB/fc. 1234

5 January 2007

Dear Mr Bean

Yasmin Khan v First Call Cleaning Services Ltd 123456/2006

I enclose a draft index for a joint bundle of documents. I suggest that we can leave out all but a short extract of the company handbook, as indicated, and I do not think that it will be necessary to refer to more than one payslip as they are the same in the relevant respects. Please let me know if you disagree, or if there are any other documents that you would wish to see included.

The Law Centre is a small charity and has no secretarial back-up, so it would be very helpful if you would be willing to arrange for the bundle to be compiled and copied.

I will compile a short separate bundle of documents relevant to my client's efforts to find work after his dismissal, and the expenses he incurred in doing so. I do not imagine that you will have any documents that you wish to add to this bundle, but please let me know if I am wrong in this.

Yours sincerely

Natalie Cummings

The content of the bundle

8.14   The bundle should be limited to the documents that one side or the other wishes the tribunal to read and should not be any longer than necessary. 'For completeness' is an inadequate reason to include any document: if there is no better reason, it should be left out. In particular, documents should not be included in the bundle just because they have been disclosed by one party or the other. There will rarely be any need to include much of the pre-hearing correspondence between the parties or their advisers. Long documents – such as company handbooks, redundancy and redeployment policies, etc – should, if possible, be reduced to a short relevant extract instead of being included whole.[10] Repetitive documents – such as time-sheets, rotas, payslips – will sometimes need to be included at length if they need to be considered in detail, but often a representative sample will do.   ·

8.15   Preparing bundles is a tedious and time-consuming task, but it is important. Conducting hearings is demanding and stressful at the best of times. An ill-organised bundle adds considerably to the stress and difficulty, and is liable to annoy the tribunal as well.

8.16   There is a surprisingly large number of ways to get a bundle wrong.[11] Common mistakes include:

- Including irrelevant documents;
- Leaving out relevant documents;
- Random or erratic page numbering;[12]

---

10 It is helpful to include the title page and contents list (if any) at the beginning of the extract so that the tribunal can see what it is an extract of.
11 All of the errors listed below are drawn from life.
12 Page numbering should begin 1, 2, 3 ... and continue in the same vein.

- Including only half of double-sided documents;
- Double sided copying;
- Page numbers in different places on the page;
- Illegible pages;
- Eccentric page order;
- Hole punching different ways up;
- Broken ring binders;[13]
- Inaccurate index.

8.17 The importance of including all relevant material, while leaving out the irrelevant, means it is unwise to delegate compilation of the bundle to someone who does not properly understand the case. This is more often done by the respondents' representatives: the bundle is compiled by a trainee or paralegal who lacks the confidence to make judgments about what is and what is not relevant and includes everything in sight 'just in case'. The result is a bundle running to many hundreds of pages, only a dozen or so of which the tribunal is actually asked to read at the hearing.

8.18 The conventional order for the bundle is the claim and response first (plus questionnaires, requests for additional information and responses, etc), followed by other dated documents in chronological order (starting with the earliest), followed by any undated documents. It is probably helpful to understand a distinction between the two main categories of papers here. The ET1 and ET3, questionnaires, responses etc are, in effect, the paper record of the proceedings. The other documents are the paper record of the events that are the subject of the proceedings.

8.19 There are good reasons for this conventional order:

- It allows someone to pick up the bundle and understand the case by reading it from beginning to end. They start with the pleadings, which summarise what each side says happened, and then proceed to the documentary record of events. Trying to understand a case by reading through a bundle of emails, letters, payslips, appraisal records etc. without knowing what the central complaint is would be difficult if not impossible.

---

13 Normally as a result of overloading.

- Cross-examination tends to proceed chronologically. It is more convenient for the witness, advocate and tribunal if reference to documents moves smoothly through the bundle rather than jumping about.[14]
- Documents are much easier to find within a chronological bundle.[15]

8.20   Dividing documents by type is almost always a mistake. E-mail correspondence often suffers from this: it is apparently tempting to place it all at the back of the bundle under an index heading called 'miscellaneous e-mails' or similar, rather than putting each e-mail in its proper chronological place. It is obvious how this could make compiling the bundle easier, but it is a temptation that should be resisted: it makes conducting the hearing much harder.

8.21   Witness statements should not be included in the bundle, because the witnesses will need to be able to be referred to different pages in the bundle while their statement is open in front of them.

8.22   Bundles should always be paginated throughout in numerical sequence: each page, rather than each document, should be given a number. If it is necessary to add documents after the bundle has been compiled, they should be inserted in their logical place and given a number and a letter – so, for example, a four page document inserted between pages 23 and 24 should be numbered 23a, 23b, 23c and 23d. The index should be altered to show the insertion.

---

14   This is particularly important if the bundle consists of more than one volume.

15   This is important for everyone. Sometimes in the course of cross-examination a witness will give an answer that you know or believe to be inconsistent with a document that you have seen. If you remember the existence of the document, you probably remember roughly where in the story it occurs. If the bundle is in chronological order, then even if you do not remember the page number, you can probably find it and ask the witness to explain it without holding your cross-examination up too long. If the bundle is in random order or this document is out of its chronological place, it will be much harder to find. Similarly, your own witness may wish to deny a suggestion made to her in cross-examination and may know, for instance, that he wrote or received an email that proves her point.

P8.22 Index to bundle of documents – unfair dismissal

IN THE EMPLOYMENT TRIBUNAL   Case No 123456/2006
LONDON CENTRAL

BETWEEN

YASMIN KHAN

Claimant

and

FIRST CALL CLEANING SERVICES LIMITED

Respondent

---

*draft/*AGREED BUNDLE OF DOCUMENTS

Date	Description	Page

Statement of case

Documents

Bundles for specific purposes

8.23   Sometimes it will be necessary to prepare separate bundles for specific purposes. For example, there may be a preliminary hearing on a question about whether the claimant had sufficient continuous service to complain of unfair dismissal, or whether the complaint was presented in time. In that case, the tribunal will much prefer to have a bundle restricted to documents (sometimes very few documents) relevant to that issue only. It will often be more convenient to make a separate bundle of documents relevant to remedies, including mitigation of loss – especially if the mitigation bundle is extensive – and provide it to the tribunal only after there has been a decision in the claimant's favour on liability. Unless the tribunal has indicated before the hearing that it will consider remedies at a separate hearing, however, the remedy bundle should always be ready for the main hearing day in case it is needed. If there is to be a costs application, it is helpful to make a separate bundle of documents relevant to that – normally correspondence between the parties, and possibly attendance notes recording telephone conversations.

8.24   In the following example, because the costs application depended on a long course of unreasonable conduct by the respondent, almost all of which took the form either of correspondence or failure to answer correspondence, it was convenient to draw up a document that doubled as a bundle index and a chronology. The detail of this is not interesting, so only a short sample of the documents is shown.

P8.24 Combined index and chronology for strike-out application

IN THE EMPLOYMENT TRIBUNAL   Case No 123456/2004
LONDON CENTRAL

·BETWEEN

ANNE COOPER

Claimant

and

THE BIG OFFICE SUPPLIERS LTD

Respondent

COMBINED INDEX AND CHRONOLOGY
FOR STRIKE OUT APPLICATION

Date	Description	Page
17 Jan 07	A's Claim Form (ET1)	1
18 Feb 07	R's Response Form (ET3)	3
26 Apr 07	Directions hearing–	7
	• order for additional information of ET1 by 24 May 2007	
	• order for amended ET3 by 14 June 07	
	• other directions, substantive hearing 29/30 August 07	
28 May 07	A's additional information	10
30 May 07	Letter R/A refusing to provide amended ET3 until more detailed particulars of ET1	11
30 May 07	Letter R/ET: requesting A's claim to be struck out for failure to comply adequately with order for further particulars	12

Getting ready for the hearing

8.25   Final preparation for the hearing can be divided into two main categories: preparing the documents and preparing the advocacy. In practice, there is a great deal of overlap, since good tribunal advocacy is built knowing and understanding the relevant documents.

8.26   All advocates prepare differently, and only experience will tell you how you best prepare. The following rules of thumb may be helpful.

The big three documents

8.27   Before a tribunal claim begins three sets of documents should always be ready.[16] These are:

- Agreed bundle;
- Witness statements;
- List of issues.

The absence of any of these is likely to cause serious problems at the hearing.

Bundles and witness statements

8.28   Ideally, by the time final preparations are being made for the hearing, these will have already have been finalised. If they have not, strenuous efforts are in order. It is almost impossible to conduct a tribunal hearing sensibly without them and the tribunal is likely to be angry if they are not ready.

16 A schedule of loss should have been produced some time before the hearing began; see paras 10.37–10.38.

8.29   Even if you have them ready, it is still useful to run a final check that they are complete and you have sufficient copies.[17] Avoid, if at all possible, significant last-minute photocopying.[18]

List of issues

8.30   A list of issues is simply a list of the questions of fact and law that the tribunal will need to answer to decide the case.

8.31   Unlike the bundle of documents and the witness statements, the absence of a list of issues will not usually surprise or upset the tribunal. And few representatives leave a hearing feeling they would have won if only they had thought to write the issues down.

8.32   Despite this, a list of issues is vital, and the lack of such a list regularly loses cases. The point is that creating such a list focuses the mind on what you are trying to achieve and how. It is surprisingly easy to be unclear about this. It is easy to say that a dismissal is unfair and many litigants will be able to say something about why it is unfair. This, however, is a long way from stating precisely what the tribunal is being asked to resolve. Without a sufficiently clear idea of what the issues are, tribunal advocacy is very difficult.

8.33   This also means that it is not necessary to write up the issues formally and present them to the tribunal. A list on the back of an envelope will do much the same job. Formal lists of issues are, however, extremely useful in complex cases. Without an agreed list, in a difficult case, it is easy for the tribunal and the parties to lose track of the issues. A formal list, discussed at the beginning of the hearing, also prevents latter argument over precisely what the case is about.

8.34   One danger to presenting a formal list of issues is that is should cover what you want to argue. It will not be open to a claimant to complain that the tribunal has failed to make a decision on a certain key question if the claimant offered the tribunal a list of issues that did not include that question.

8.35   If a formal list of issues is to be prepared, it is sensible to do so in advance of the hearing so that it can be agreed by the other side.

---

17 Assuming that your client and the respondent have already had copies, you will need your copy, three for the tribunal and one for the witness table.

18 Photocopiers are especially susceptible to Murphy's law in these circumstances.

P8.35.1 Informal list of issues

1. What was Mr Blunt's weekly net wage?

2. Was Mr Blunt paid for his work between 2 and 13 April 2007?

3. If so, how much?

P8.35.2 Formal list of issues

IN THE EMPLOYMENT TRIBUNAL   Case No 123456/2006
LONDON CENTRAL

BETWEEN

PAULINE PHELPS

Claimant

and

SHARPE, GENTLEMAN & CO SOLICITORS

Respondent

Constructive Dismissal

1. Did the respondent breach the term of trust and confidence by:

    (a) refusing to consider the claimant's suggestion that she might work full-time for Ms Grey
    (b) refusing, on 21 August 2006 to consider moving the claimant to work in a different room despite her evident distress
    (c) failing to reply to her letter of 17 February 2007 from her GP
    (d) requiring her on 1 March 2007 to provide reception cover on a rota?

2. Was the claimant's resignation on 10 May 2007 in response to a breach of the term of trust and confidence?

3. Did the claimant affirm her contract by remaining in employment between 1 March 2007 and 10 May 2007?

Disability Discrimination

4. Was the claimant disabled between July 2006 and May 2007?

5. Did the following provisions, criteria or practices adopted by the respondent put the claimant at a substantive disadvantage compared with people who were not disabled:

> (a) the requirement from August 2006 that she work as a pool secretary instead of a specific fee-earner or fee-earners
> (b) the requirement from August 2006 that the claimant work a open-plan office
> (c) the requirement that she provide reception cover on a rota from March 2007?

6. Would it have been a reasonable adjustment for the respondent to:

> (a) Assign the claimant to a specific fee-earner or fee-earners?
> (b) Provide an alternative to the open-plan office?
> (c) Remove the claimant from the receptionist pool?

Miscellaneous documents

8.36   As well as the big three, there are many documents that it might be necessary or helpful to prepare. Like the list of issues, these are often as helpful to prepare as they are to have.

8.37   It would be impossible to draw up an exhaustive list of these kinds of documents to draft in a case: every case is different, and one of the aims of this book is to encourage users not to assume that case preparation will always follow the same course, and to be prepared to think flexibly about what might be needed in the particular circumstances.

8.38   With that reservation, there are some kinds of documents that are often but not always needed. Some will be ordered by the tribunal in some cases. In many cases it will be helpful to agree the contents with the respondent, but if that is impossible, the next best thing will be to go to the hearing armed with a draft. If the claimant is well prepared with a draft chronology, for example, and the respondent has not, then the respondent is likely to come under pressure from the tribunal to agree the claimant's draft. The following is a list of some of the main possibilities.

Chronology

8.39   The tribunal will almost certainly be helped by a chronology – that is, a list of the main events in the case in date order, showing their dates – if the parties have time to prepare it. If the story is so long and complicated that a full chronology runs to several pages, it will probably be helpful to prepare a one-page outline chronology in addition.

8.40   Preparing a chronology is an extremely good way of getting to grips with a difficult and complicated case. Many lawyers produce one as a matter of course for just this reason. For the same reason any kind offers from the other side to prepare a neutral chronology for agreement should be treated with suspicion: the party that has done this piece of work is likely to be at an advantage in general familiarity with the case.

Cast list

8.41   If there are a lot of different individuals involved in the story, a list of them showing briefly how they fit into the picture will assist.

List of essential reading

8.42   If the case is particularly document-heavy, then it is a good idea to agree a list of the most important documents for the tribunal to read at the beginning of the hearing, and to invite them to set aside a day or half a day for this purpose.

Glossary

8.43   If the tribunal will have to understand technical terms, or if the story involves a large number of organisations or departments familiarly referred to by their initials, the tribunal will be helped by a glossary.

Organogram

8.44   If the employer's organisational structure is at all important, a diagram showing this structure (often called an 'organogram') will be useful.

Observing a hearing

8.45 When it comes to preparing to present the case, a good first step for anyone who is not familiar with tribunals is to observe a case (or time permitting, several) before their own comes on for hearing. Lawyers often speak of tribunal hearings as 'informal.' They might seem so to anyone accustomed to appearing in the Chancery Division of the High Court, but for many claimants, the tribunal hearing will be the most formal meeting they have ever taken part in. Being cross-examined, in particular, can be stressful and intimidating. Observing another case will at least take the edge of complete unfamiliarity off proceedings.

8.46 Tribunal hearings are normally public: anyone can go and sit at the back at (almost) any hearing for as much or as little of the hearing as they wish. Tribunal clerks or chairmen do occasionally quiz those present about who they are and what their role is. A claimant who wishes to observe a case should not be put off by this, and should not be made to feel that they have to identify, explain or justify themselves if they do not want to. It should be perfectly adequate to say 'I am a member of the public and I want to watch the tribunal doing its work', or similar.

Examination in chief

8.47 Since most witnesses give their evidence by way of a written witness statement, there should not normally be too much to do in the way of examination-in-chief. Supplementary questions may be needed for one or both of two purposes: to fill gaps in the witness statement as drafted, and to respond to points made for the first time in the other side's witness statements.[19] If more than minimal examination-in-chief is needed, it is advisable to have a list of prepared questions, and to have found out what your witnesses' answers to them are in advance.[20] This is where 'leading questions' will be frowned on.[21]

---

19 See also para 5.11.
20 You cannot properly tell your witness what to say see paras 5.29–5.36 above but there is no obligation to ask a question unless you think the answer assists you.
21 See glossary above.

Cross-examination

8.48   Cross-examination will normally require much more detailed preparation. This is probably the most difficult job that the claimant or his
adviser has to do.

8.49   The assumption underlying cross-examination is that the best way
of discovering the facts is to give each side a chance to attack the other
side's evidence. The point of cross-examination is to get evidence from
the other sides witness that will help your case.

8.50   Cross-examination may be either constructive or destructive. Constructive cross-examination aims to get statements from witnesses on
the other side which the tribunal will accept as true, but which help your
case. For example, if a claimant has been dismissed for ill health, constructive cross-examination may include getting her manager to confirm that, prior to her illness, she had been a good employee. If a
claimant has been dismissed for misconduct, it may be useful to get a
HR manager to admit that prior to the incident he had a clean disciplinary record. These are not things that the witnesses are likely to
deny, especially if they are clear on the face of the documents, but,
understandably, neither are they things that are likely to emphasise
on their own.

8.51   Destructive cross-examination consists of questions aimed at undermining the witness's story: showing his evidence to be mistaken or
untruthful. For example, if a supervisor gives evidence of a particular
incident, which the claimant denies, destructive cross-examination
would attempt to show that it was unlikely that the incident took place.
If the dismissing officer says that he dismissed on grounds of redundancy, destructive cross-examination might aim to show that he actually dismissed because of racial prejudice.

8.52   The aim of all cross-examination is to persuade the tribunal to find
in your favour. Claimants are often disappointed that respondent witnesses rarely admit to having been untruthful and continue to insist on
their version of events even after the holes in their story have been
pointed out. This is to be expected: by the time a witness gives his evidence, he has either decided to lie or, far more likely, convinced himself that his version of events is true. If cross-examination has shown
that the respondent's evidence is inconsistent with the documents in
ways their witnesses cannot coherently explain, the claimant is likely
to win the day.

Putting your case

8.53 Many tribunals and practitioners will say that one purpose of cross-examination is to put your case to the other side's witnesses. This is a throw-back to the days before witness statements, when witnesses for one side would only have the chance to comment on the other side's evidence if that evidence was put to them in cross-examination. Suppose Mr Sneath, the claimant, was going to say in his evidence that Mrs Blewitt, the personnel manager, gave him a thumbs down sign the day before the disciplinary hearing and said 'I hope you've got good lawyers because you're going to need them.' Mrs Blewitt gives her evidence first. If witness statements have not been exchanged before the hearing, Mrs Blewitt does not know what Mr Sneath is going to say. The tribunal will want to hear what she says to his allegation – does she admit it or deny it, and if she denies it does she do so convincingly? So if there have been no witness statements, Mrs Blewitt must be asked: 'You gave Mr Sneath a thumbs down sign the day before the hearing didn't you?' and 'and then you said "I hope you've got good lawyers, etc"?' Otherwise she will never get a chance to comment on Mr Sneath's evidence.

8.54 Lawyers are conservative by nature, and it is still conventional – even though witness statements are now almost universal in employment tribunal proceedings – to put the case to the opposing witnesses. Tribunals will still sometimes refuse to take account of evidence for one side that has not been put to the other side's witnesses.[22] Although there is no longer a practical need for this exercise, therefore, it is still advisable to ensure that every disputed allegation by the claimant is put to the relevant witness or witnesses on the other side. This can feel very artificial: the result is likely to be a series of questions of the form:

Q: 'You did ABC didn't you?'
A: 'No.'
Q: 'And then you said DEF?'
A: 'No.'
Q: 'The claimant did not do GHI as you say, did he?'
A: 'Yes he did.'

---

22 This must be wrong if a witness statement containing the evidence in question was given to the other party before the hearing. A claimant whose case has been severely impeded by the tribunal's refusal to take part of his evidence into account for this reason should consider appealing.

Q: 'The truth was you said JKL wasn't it?'
A: 'Nope.'

8.55   This is a wearying performance for everyone, but until the Employment Appeal Tribunal rules that the practice is redundant it is necessary.[23]

Preparing to cross-examine

8.56   Cross-examination needs to be carefully prepared. That is not to say that it is ever possible to stick to a rigid list of prepared questions; but the strategy needs to be thought out in advance and lists of probable questions and areas to cover are essential.[24] It is a difficult skill that only improves with practice, but preparation can make up to some degree for inexperience.

8.57   The most important thing is to be thoroughly familiar with all the statements on both sides, and with all the relevant documents. In some ways preparing for a hearing is like revising for an exam: it is necessary to know the material well enough to realise at once in the course of the hearing when a witness has said something that is inconsistent with his own statement, or with the statement of another witness, or with one of the documents in the bundle. If you are going to want to take a witness to a particular document in the bundle, then it is sensible to put a sticky note on that page of the bundle, highlight the relevant passage, and cross-reference your cross-examination notes to the page number.

8.58   In case you stray widely from your list of questions, it is also helpful to have a summary check-list of the key areas to cover with each witness and to remember to look at it before ending the cross-examination. In the heat of the moment – and especially if one part of the cross-examination went either particularly well or particularly badly – it is all too easy to forget to cover a whole topic. For an adviser, it is sensible to take a moment to check with the claimant that there is nothing he

---

23   There is some support for the view that it is not in the decision of the EAT in *Network Rail Infrastructure Ltd v Griffiths-Henry* [2006] IRLR 865.

24   Barristers and solicitors are often discouraged in the course of their training from preparing lists of questions. The thinking behind this seems to be that a list of questions can lead to a flat delivery and, worse, to ignoring what the witness actually says in favour of moving mechanically on to the next question. The authors take the view that although these are real risks, the benefits of detailed preparation outweigh them. It is, however, necessary to be conscious of the need for flexibility and responsiveness.

thinks you should have asked that you did not.[25] A claimant acting in person should similarly be allowed to confer briefly with a friend or relative accompanying them.

What questions should you ask?

8.59   Often there will be deliberate ambiguities in a statement that need to be teased out. Sometimes there will be inconsistencies between one part of the statement and another, or between this witness's evidence and that of one of the respondent's other witnesses. Sometimes there will be documentary evidence that contradicts what the witness says. Sometimes the statement will have been drafted by a lawyer who has been too keen to put the 'right' words into the witness's mouth, and the witness when asked will simply contradict her own statement.

8.60   Some rules of thumb may be helpful. Leading questions are usually preferable: the aim is to take the witness where you want him or her to go by asking a series of questions to which there is only one possible answer. It is a good idea to start with easy, non-threatening questions. If the representative is going to give a witness a particularly hard time on one issue, it is better to save that to the end: otherwise the witness is likely to be defensive and unforthcoming from the start. The order in which questions on a particular issue are asked can be crucial. The key is often to predict what the witness will think is the 'right' answer, and then ask the questions in an order that makes use of that.

Example 1

Suppose the witness to be cross-examined is the manager who decided to dismiss the claimant. The reason given for the dismissal was that the claimant was believed to have been responsible (accidentally) for starting a damaging fire. The claimant believes that the fire was a convenient excuse, and the real reason for his dismissal was that he had been complaining about changes in the way he was paid. His representative has noticed that the date on the fire service report implicating the claimant is after the date of the dismissal letter. This is damaging for the

---

25   A long conversation will be frowned on by the tribunal, but a brief exchange should certainly be permitted. It is worth emphasising the need to take a little time at this point: the process is stressful, and the tribunal may have been pressing for speed, but there is still nothing wrong with a couple of minutes' silence while the claimant checks through his notes before confirming that the cross-examination is finished.

respondent, because it tends to support the claimant's belief that the fire was not the real reason for his dismissal – but it is not necessarily fatal and the manager may be able to explain it away.

What follows is a pair of demonstrations, with comments in italics, of how the cross-examination might go, one effective and the other very much less so:

Wrong

Q: Please turn to the fire report on page 24. What is the date on it? *The witness has no scope to hedge – the date is there in black and white.*

Q: Now turn to the dismissal letter on page 21. What is the date on that? *Again, there is only one possible answer, and already the witness will see the point that is about to be made and be starting to think about how he can deal with it.*

Q: Why didn't you wait until you had seen the fire service report before deciding to dismiss the claimant? *This is the witness's opportunity for damage limitation. He has not damaged his credibility by lying because he has been given no opportunity to do so.*

Right

Q: This was an important decision wasn't it? *The only possible answer to this is 'yes'.*

Q: Did you make sure you had all relevant information before you took it? *Here too there is an obvious 'right' answer and 99 in 100 witnesses will give it.*

Q: There was a fire service investigation into the cause of the fire wasn't there? *There is no point denying this: the witness will almost certainly know that the report is in the bundle.*

Q: The point of that was to establish the cause of the fire? *There is not much point denying that either.*

Q: Did you take the fire service report into account before you decided to dismiss? *Now the witness is in a tight place. He has just confirmed that he took into account all relevant information. He is now being asked about a piece of highly and obviously relevant information that he did not take into account. With luck, he may forget in the heat of the moment that the report post-dates the dismissal letter, and give the 'right' answer – 'Yes, of course I did'. If he does, the trap can be sprung:*

Q: Turn to the dismissal letter – what is the date on it?

Q: Turn to the fire report – what is the date on that?

Q: So your answer just now that you read the fire report before you decided to dismiss was not true, was it? *Even if the witness was too canny to lie, he is still much worse placed having claimed to have taken all relevant information into account and then being forced to admit that this was not the case than he would be if simply challenged directly about the sequence of events as in the first example.*

Example 2

The witness is a manager who claims to have been unaware that the claimant, whom she appointed, was disabled at the time she dismissed him for poor performance. In the papers there are two probationary appraisals, conducted by the manager, that say that the claimant was trying his best and was responsive to feedback. The job is not a difficult one, and on paper the claimant is over-qualified for it. The manager says that she knew the claimant was dyslexic, but did not think it was serious enough to amount to a disability for the purposes of the Disability Discrimination Act 1995.

Wrong

Q: You knew Derek was dyslexic didn't you? *This much is uncontroversial.*

Q: You knew he was intelligent enough to get a first class degree in history? *The witness is given the opportunity to wriggle with something like 'I interview a lot of new staff – I did not remember his exact qualifications.'*

Q: So if he was underachieving in this junior role it must have been because of his dyslexia? *This is an open invitation to the witness to think of some other plausible reason – 'No – I thought he was over-qualified for the role and not very well motivated.' She can be challenged on her own assessment in his probationary reviews that he was doing his best, but now she knows where the questioning is going she may say that this was an over-generous assessment in an attempt to motivate him.*

Right

Q: You appointed Derek? *There is no reason why she should deny this.*

Q: You read his CV? *Reading his CV before appointing him was obviously the right thing to do, so 9 out of 10 personnel managers will say 'yes' even if they have no specific memory of having done so.*

Q: So you knew he had a first class degree? *This is hard to deny – the CV is there in the bundle, and she has just admitted to having read it.*

Q: You did not require a graduate at all in this role? *She is unlikely to deny this – she knows that the person specification is in the bundle.*

Q: You conducted the two probationary reviews? *Again, she cannot sensibly deny this.*

Q: Did you conduct them fairly and accurately to the best of your ability? *Again, there is only one answer to this.*

Q: So you stand by your assessment that Derek was doing his best? *Now she is in a place where it is difficult for her to deny this too.*

Q: And that he was responsive to feedback? *Similarly.*

Q: But he was under-performing so badly that you had to dismiss him? *She has to say yes to this because it is at the heart of her case.*

Q: You knew he was dyslexic? *In this context, the question is going somewhere.*

Q: Given that you knew Derek was able and doing his best, that was the obvious explanation for his difficulties wasn't it? *All the likely alternative explanations have been ruled out, so it is difficult for the witness to deny this now.*

P8.60 Check-list for cross-examination

The witness to be cross-examined, P, is a manager who decided to dismiss the claimant, who is disabled, for poor performance. The claimant, N, was the highest-earning salesperson in his department before a spell of severe back pain. He complains of disability discrimination. A full set of cross-examination notes would be much more detailed; this is an outline of the main topics N wishes to cover in cross-examination.

P's knowledge of disability:

- knew of back problems on appointment
- knew it was serious at least by 7 October 2003

Performance during probationary period
Reason for performance issues – back pain[26]
Knowledge of prognosis[27]
Specific requests for adjustments:

- request for different working hours
- request to work part of the week at home
- request for ergonomic assessment of workplace
- request for 'Access to Work' assessment

Reasonableness of adjustments:

- size of department
- departmental sales figures – recent Group award
- claimant's performance before back problems
- cost of ergonomic assessment
- nil cost of 'Access to Work' assessment

Submissions

8.61 As well as presenting evidence to the tribunal the parties will have the opportunity to make submissions. This is their opportunity to persuade the tribunal that their view of the evidence is the right one. This is less important than it might appear. By the time submissions are made, the tribunal should have a good idea of what the parties will say. If they do not, it is normally because the issues were not properly established or the cross-examination was poor.

8.62 This is not to say that cases are not won through convincing submissions, only that many more are won by good cross-examination (or lost by bad cross-examination). Submissions should still be prepared, and the majority of the work should be done before the hearing begins.

---

26 N wishes to establish that he was dismissed for a reason relating to his disability.

27 This is relevant because P says dismissal was justified even if discrimination. N wishes to make him admit that he had not bothered to find out what the prognosis was, and if he had, he would have learned that N's consultant believed that he would be back to full productivity within a short time.

8.63   Submissions may be oral or in writing. Written submission are not compulsory and will not be expected unless the case is complicated. Preparing them is a very similar task in either case, although if you are going to hand the tribunal a set of written submissions you should prepare a finished document in sentences and paragraphs, whereas if you are going to deliver your submissions orally, your preparation may take the form of some scribbled notes. The tribunal will normally expect that the parties will make oral submissions at the end of the hearing.

8.64   Although written submissions are not compulsory it is normally a good idea to prepare them if time allows. By making both oral and written submissions you give yourself two chances to influence the tribunal. And the process of writing submissions is another excellent way of preparing yourself for tribunal.

8.65   Where a skeleton argument is needed, the rules say it should be prepared and sent to the tribunal and the other side at least seven days before the hearing.[28] This rule is ill-considered: a skeleton argument on a point of law can be provided before the hearing begins, but written submissions dealing with the evidence cannot usefully be drafted until after the evidence has been heard. Fortunately rule 14(6) gives tribunals power to consider representations submitted later if they consider it appropriate – in other words, to ignore rule 14(5) whenever they like. Tribunals exercise this power freely. Written submissions tend to be helpful – at the very least because they save the tribunal the trouble of taking detailed notes of submissions – and tribunals are slow to refuse what is in effect an offer of assistance from the parties' representatives.

8.66   Claimants should therefore, where appropriate, draft written submissions during the course of the hearing, and present them at the end either alongside or instead of oral submissions. It is prudent to have a first draft ready for the start of the hearing, but it is to be expected that much of the work will need to be done after the witnesses have given their evidence and been cross-examined: late nights between consecutive hearing days will often be unavoidable.

8.67   The likelihood is that the tribunal will accept written submissions offered on the last day of the hearing, but if not that does not mean that the work in preparing them has been wasted. They will still be very useful as a memory aid for the representative making oral submissions, and they may also prove useful if there is any subsequent dispute

---

28 Employment Tribunal Rules 14(5).

in relation to an appeal about whether a particular point was made at first instance.

8.68   The best way of approaching the writing of written submissions is to start with the list of issues. For each issue, write down the answer you would like the tribunal to come to and then explain why it should.

P8.68 Skeleton argument–redundancy claim

IN THE EMPLOYMENT TRIBUNAL   Case No 123456/2007
LONDON CENTRAL

BETWEEN

MARGARET ROCHDALE

Claimant

and

GEORGE FABLE LIMITED

Respondent

SKELETON ARGUMENT

Introduction

1. George Fable Limited is an estate agents' business which until November 2006 was split between two offices, one at premises called Marchmont House in Camden Town, and the other in Kentish Town. Mrs Rochdale was employed by the respondent as a part-time book-keeper at its Camden office from 25 October 1999 until 10 November 2006. Her contract of employment provided by clause 7.3 that she could be required to work 'anywhere in England and Wales.' She lives less than five minutes' walk from Marchmont House.

2. The respondent owns Marchmont House, where until November 2006 it used the ground floor for its estate agents' business and let the first and second floors to a tenant. In April 2006, the respondent received an offer from its tenant at Marchmont House for a lease of the whole building. The respondent considered that the offer was advantageous, and decided to expand its Kentish Town office and relocate its Camden Town operations to Kentish Town in order to take advantage of the offer.

3. The respondent announced the proposed move to all the March-mont House staff at a meeting on 5 May 2006. Trevor English, the respondent's Managing Director, told them that the move was not yet a certainty, but was likely to take effect in September or October 2004. He invited staff to contact him if they had any questions or concerns about the move.

4. It is common ground that it would have taken Mrs Rochdale about 25 minutes to walk to the new office from her home, and a comparable time (including waiting time) if she travelled by bus.

5. On 12 May 2006, Mrs Rochdale wrote to Mr English about the move. Her letter said:

> I am afraid that because of the situation with my Mother I will not be able to move to the new office. Please let me know what your intentions are in relation to my employment.

6. Mrs Rochdale's mother is in her late eighties and very frail, and it is common ground that Mr English was aware both of this, and of the fact that it was Mrs Rochdale's habit to go home every lunchtime to give her mother her lunch. He was also aware that her mother would also occasionally call her home during the working day to attend to minor domestic emergencies. He had always been tolerant of this as Mrs Rochdale was a conscientious worker and always made up the time lost.

7. Mr English's reply to Mrs Rochdale's letter of 12 May 2006 indicated that he was sorry that she had decided to resign, but that he understood her reasons. Mrs Rochdale wrote back to say that she was not proposing to resign but that she wanted to know if he was proposing to make her redundant. There were several further exchanges of correspondence in which Mr English insisted that he was not dismissing Mrs Rochdale, and therefore no question of redundancy arose, and Mrs Rochdale insisted that she had no wish to resign.

8. On 31 August, Mr English held a further meeting with staff at which he announced that the Camden Office would close on Friday 10 November 2006, and staff should report for duty at the Kentish Town office on Monday 13 November.

9. On Friday 10 November, Mr English gave Mrs Rochdale an envelope containing her P45, showing her leaving date as 10 November. She was paid up to that date.

The issues

10. Mrs Rochdale has complained to the tribunal of wrongful dismissal and failure to pay statutory redundancy pay. The respondent has contended that she was not dismissed, but that if she was she is not entitled to a redundancy payment because she has unreasonably refused an offer of suitable alternative employment.

11. The issues for the tribunal to decide are:
    (i)   Was Mrs Rochdale dismissed, or did she resign?
    (ii) If she was dismissed,
          (a) on what date was she given notice of dismissal?
          (b) was her dismissal wholly or mainly attributable to the fact that their employer had ceased or intended to cease to carry on the business for the purposes of which she was employed in the place where she was employed?
    (iii) If she was dismissed for redundancy, did she receive an offer of suitable alternative employment?
    (iv) If she received an offer of suitable alternative employment, did she unreasonably refuse it?

Argument for the claimant

(i) Resignation or dismissal

12. Mrs Rochdale expressly stated on several occasions that she did not intend to resign and that she was willing to continue working at Marchmont House. Her statement in her letter of 12 May that she would not be able to work at the new office was not capable of being a resignation because it was not certain or unequivocal. It did not state a definite intention to cease her employment, nor did it state a date on which her employment would terminate. It was clearly implicit that if the move did not take place, Mrs Rochdale would be content to continue to work at Marchmont House. For similar reasons, none of Mrs Rochdale's subsequent letters is capable of being construed as a resignation.

13. The first occasion on which either party took any step that unequivocally indicated that her employment was to terminate was the respondent's act in giving Mrs Rochdale her P45 on Friday 10 November.

14. Moreover, the termination of her employment was brought about by the respondent's closure of the claimant's workplace, which was determined on by the respondent for its own purposes. The claimant made it clear at an early stage, before the move was a certainty, that one of the consequences of the move would be the termination

of her employment. The respondent went on to take the step that it knew would terminate Mrs Rochdale's employment.

(ii)(a) Date of dismissal

15. It is submitted that Mrs Rochdale was dismissed without notice on 10 November when she was given her P45. Until that date, the respondent continued to insist that it was not dismissing her. Dismissal must be unequivocal, and certain as to the date on which it takes effect. Despite Mrs Rochdale's repeated requests for clarification, the respondent had not previously told her on what date her employment would terminate.

(ii)(b) Reason for dismissal

16. It is submitted that it is clear that the reason for Mrs Rochdale's dismissal was the respondent's closure of her workplace. By section 139(1) of the Employment Rights Act 1996:

> ... an employee who is dismissed shall be taken to be dismissed by reason of redundancy if the dismissal is wholly or mainly attributable to —
>> (a) the fact that his employer has ceased or intends to cease —
>>> (i) to carry on the business for the purposes of which the employee was employed by him, or
>>> (ii) to carry on that business in the place where the employee was so employed.

17. The respondent intended to cease carrying on business from Marchmont House where Mrs Rochdale worked, and this was the reason for the termination of her employment. The fact that her contract of employment contained a mobility clause is neither here nor there: the place where she was in fact employed was the Camden office — see *High Table v Horst* [1997] IRLR 513 and *Bass Leisure v Thomas* [1994] IRLR 104.

(iii) Was Mrs Rochdale offered suitable alternative employment?

18. It is conceded that it was made clear to Mrs Rochdale that the same job was available for her at the new location if she was willing to relocate, and that this constituted an implicit offer of suitable alternative employment.

(iv) Did Mrs Rochdale unreasonably refuse the Respondent's offer of alternative employment?

19. It is well established that the question whether an employee's refusal of alternative employment was unreasonable is subjective and should take account of her relevant personal circumstances, and the burden is on the employer to show that the decision was unreasonable. Mrs Rochdale had compelling personal reasons for her decision not to go to work at the new office, and she cannot be said to have acted unreasonably in insisting that she needed to be available for her mother at very short notice. Moreover, her decision is conclusively demonstrated to have been reasonable by the fact that she succeeded in securing similar employment at a slightly higher salary five minutes' walk from her home only four weeks after her dismissal.

Conclusion

20. The Tribunal is invited to find that Mrs Rochdale was dismissed without notice on 10 November 2006, and to award her:
    (i) damages for wrongful dismissal; and
    (ii) redundancy pay.

Natalie Cummings

11 April 2007

The main or substantive hearing

9.36   What can go wrong at the hearing?

The respondent comes to the hearing with a large pile of documents that you have not seen before • The respondent makes new allegations at the hearing that the claimant was not previously aware of but could refute given time • Someone fails to turn up • The tribunal is not prepared to go ahead • One of your witness appears, under cross-examination, to be untruthful • The chairman treats the claimant with evident hostility • The chairman refuses to permit the claimant to cross-examine in an important area • The chairman imposes strict time-limits on cross-examination or submissions • The claimant forgets to ask one of the respondent's witnesses about a crucial topic

Arriving at tribunal

9.1   Obviously it is important to be on time. Tribunals have busy schedules, and arriving late will always start things off on the wrong foot. This means that it is wise to make sure that you know exactly how to get to the tribunal and have considered anything (parking, train times, etc) that might effect your journey.

9.2   It is also sensible to aim to arrive between half an hour and an hour early. As well as allowing for delays, this allows you to get settled and take a few deep breaths before the tribunal starts. It also allows for a talk with the other side, which is useful for sorting out any outstanding practical details, exchanging or agreeing chronologies or lists of issues, etc. It is also frequently time needed for settlement negotiations.

9.3   It is worth having a checklist of what you will need to take to the tribunal. It is embarrassing to arrive to argue a pensions case, requiring a good deal of financial calculation, only to discover that you left your calculator at home.

Make sure you have:

- your own marked copy of the bundle of documents (see para 8.12);
- four clean copies of the bundle: three for the tribunal and one for the witness table;
- at least six copies of each witness statement: one for the representative, three for the tribunal, one for the witness table and at least one for the use of the public;
- a copy of any relevant legislation (ideally the current edition of *Butterworths Employment Handbook*, which the tribunal will have);
- five copies any authorities (i.e. copies of previously decided cases) relied on: one for the representative, three for the tribunal, one for the respondent's representative;
- notebooks, post-its, pens and highlighters;
- a calculator;
- a diary (for agreeing future hearing dates).

The hearing room

9.4   Hearing rooms vary in size, but they are laid out in a conventional way. The tribunal members sit facing the rest of the room, usually on a slightly raised platform, behind a long desk. There will be desks facing them at the front of the room for the parties and/or their representatives, with room for at least two people to sit on each side.

The claimant and her representative (if any) sit on the right hand side of the room facing the tribunal, and the respondents and their representative sit on the left. There are usually one or two rows of chairs behind the parties for members of the public and the Press, etc. Between the parties desks and the tribunal there is a table and chair for the witness who is giving evidence at any given time; opposite that on the other side of the room, there may be a table for a member of tribunal staff. If the parties are represented, it is usual for the representatives to sit on the inside of their respective desks, with their clients nearer the walls. This is because there may be occasions when the representatives need to speak to each other in the course of the hearing.

Formalities

9.5   The chairman and members of the tribunal are addressed 'Madam' or 'Sir' as appropriate.[1] Everyone remains seated, except witnesses while they are being sworn. While a witness is being sworn, everyone else in the room should remain still and silent: some tribunals will be very much annoyed if there is any fidgeting with papers or whispering during this solemnity. Barristers sometimes refer to their opponents as 'my learned friend' in the hearing. Traditionally, only barristers are allowed to have learned friends: anyone else using the expression may cause a slight wince. 'My colleague' or just 'Miss Fanshawe' is preferable in any event.

The shape of the hearing

9.6   Employment tribunals have a wide power to regulate their own procedure, but there is a conventional order in which hearings are usually taken. As so often, this appears nowhere in the employment tribunal rules, but is a practice drawn from the ordinary courts. Tribunal chairmen are encouraged now to introduce themselves and their wing members and start either by stating what they consider the issues to be or by asking the parties to clarify what they think the issues are. Then, unless either party has any preliminary application to make (for an adjournment, for example, or for the other party's claim or response to

---

1   It is a good idea to get this right.

be struck out), the hearing will normally proceed as follows:

either

    Claimant calls her first witnesses
    Respondent cross-examines
    Claimant calls her second witness
    Respondent cross-examines
    ... and so on until all the claimant's witnesses have given evidence
    Respondent calls its first witnesses
    Claimant cross-examines
    Respondent calls its second witness
    Claimant cross-examines
    ... and so on until all the respondent's witnesses have given evidence
    Respondent makes closing submissions
    Claimant makes closing submissions

or

    Respondent calls its first witness
    Claimant cross-examines
    Respondent calls its second witness
    Claimant cross-examines
    ...
    Claimant calls her first witness
    Respondent cross-examines
    Claimant calls her second witness
    Respondent cross-examines
    ...
    Claimant makes closing submissions
    Respondent makes closing submissions

9.7   The choice between these two possibilities usually – but not invariably – depends on which side has something to prove first. In a discrimination case, the claimant cannot succeed without showing discrimination, so the claimant calls her witnesses first. In an unfair dismissal case (if dismissal is admitted), the employer has to start by showing that it had an acceptable reason for the dismissal – if it fails, the dismissal was unfair without further argument. So in that case, the employer starts. In a constructive dismissal case, the claimant has to start by showing that she was dismissed, so the claimant starts. Chairmen do not always follow these rules, so it is important to be prepared.

9.8   Often there are cases where it is hard to say exactly how this rule should apply – for example, where the claimant is complaining of both unfair dismissal and discrimination. It is not worth getting bogged down in this question. It is worthwhile for the claimant to know the conventions, so that whoever starts, she knows what is likely to happen next and is not taken by surprise. However, in a long case particularly, it is important not to place to much reliance on a prediction about the order in which the tribunal will take the case.

Example

In case about sex discrimination and unfair dismissal, suppose the claimant takes the view that the main complaint is sex discrimination and she will therefore give her evidence first. The case is listed for five days, and she estimates that her own evidence (with cross examination) will take at least a day and a half. The respondent is calling four witnesses, one of them being the decision-maker and clearly its main witness. The claimant expects her evidence will therefore take up the first day and a half of the hearing. By day 1 of the hearing she has started but not finished preparing to cross-examine the respondent's main witness, and she has no cross examination notes at all for the respondent's other three witnesses.

The tribunal decides that as the case is about dismissal, it wants to hear from the respondent first. The respondent decides to call its minor witnesses first so that they can be released at the end of day 1.

This sequence of events is a serious blow to the claimant, who was not expecting to cross-examine these witnesses until day 3 at least and has not yet begun her preparation to do so. If she applies for an adjournment on this basis, she is most unlikely to get it. Even if she does, she may be ordered to pay the respondent's costs thrown away by the adjournment. On the other hand, if the hearing is not adjourned, she has to cross-examine 'cold'.

Opening statements

9.9   Occasionally one party or the other wishes to make an opening statement to the tribunal before the evidence begins. This is very much the exception rather than the rule, and tribunals will often be resistant to the suggestion. The claimant should certainly not feel that an opening statement is expected. The purpose of an opening statement, if it is made, will be to ensure that the tribunal knows what the issues are that it will have to decide, focus its attention on what it should be looking for in the evidence, and give it a framework for understanding what it hears.[2] Long opening statements will normally be strongly discouraged.

Reading time for the tribunal

9.10   Tribunals do not routinely read bundles of documents and witness statements before the beginning of the hearing. In a complicated case involving a lot of documents, it will often be helpful to ask the tribunal to spend an hour or so – or longer if necessary – at the start of the hearing reading the witness statements and the most important documents, so that by the time the oral evidence begins they know what the case is about. If the case is long enough to justify it – probably six or seven days at least – the pre-reading may take a whole day. If that is likely, it is sensible to try to agree this with the other party and the tribunal at a directions hearing, or in correspondence before the hearing starts. Otherwise everyone will turn up on the first day of the hearing only to be sent away until the next day while the tribunal does its homework.

Claimants with special needs

9.11   The tribunal should be willing to adjust its practices to take account of the special needs of parties. Indeed, it has a duty to make reasonable adjustments to those with disabilities. If any adjustments are needed, a request should be made in writing, or at a case management discussion. The following is a list of the kinds of adjustments that might be requested, but claimants should be ready to ask for whatever meets their own specific needs:

- sign language interpreters;[3]
- rest breaks;[4]

---

2   Normally a list of issues will do this job adequately.
3   The tribunal service will pay the interpreters' reasonable fees.
4   For example, for a claimant who has difficulty concentrating for a long period.

- to be given extra time to take notes;
- to have a friend or support worker sit by them when they give evidence;[5]
- opportunity to get up and move around;[6]
- additional hearing days (where other arrangements mean the hearing will be slower than usual);
- modified lighting;[7]
- to be allowed to use a Braille machine or laptop with speech output;
- to be accompanied by a guide dog or other assistance animal;
- a less formal physical environment – for example, to have the hearing with the tribunal members and parties sitting around a large table instead of in a normal hearing room;
- to have repetitive or hostile questioning strictly controlled, or questions relayed through the chairman;[8]
- to have the use of a microphone and amplification when they give their evidence.

9.12   If the tribunal does not grant a request, it is possible to appeal to the EAT. Such an appeal should be approached cautiously, since it is likely to delay proceedings and, regardless of the outcome, may influence the tribunal negatively.

Taking notes at the hearing

9.13   It is important for claimants to take good notes of the employment tribunal proceedings for two reasons. The first is to assist with the conduct of the hearing itself: it may be necessary to put to a witness something that she has said earlier, or to refer to what a witness said under cross-examination in closing submissions. The impact of this may be damaged or destroyed if the claimant does not have a reasonably accurate note of what was said. The second is that the evidence that was given at first instance may be important when it comes to an appeal.

---

5 For example, where the claimant is particularly intimidated by the process by reason of mental health problems or learning difficulties.
6 For example, for a claimant with back pain.
7 For example, for a claimant with a visual impairment.
8 This will be difficult, as cross-examination is very much the traditional method of testing the truthfulness of a witness. However, the request itself may serve to restrain the respondent's representative significantly: advocates will have their own preference not to be seen to bully a vulnerable witness.

9.14   Taking good notes while conducting a case in the employment tribunal is difficult. If the respondent is represented by a barrister, there will probably be someone from the respondent's solicitors at the hearing to take notes. The claimant may not be so lucky: voluntary sector advice agencies, in particular, will almost never be able to spare two lawyers to attend a hearing. If there is a representative, she should aim to take notes of the most important things that are said, but priority obviously has to be given to conducting the proceedings, not recording them. Taking good notes of your own cross-examination is almost impossible. The claimant herself may be able to take good notes, but is likely to be very preoccupied, so if possible it is better to have a friend, relative or colleague present for this purpose.

9.15   It is worthwhile giving some thought to this before the hearing. An adviser who is going to rely on someone who is not used to taking notes should make sure the note-taker has a suitable notebook and pens, and knows what it is most important for them to record. The task is tiring, especially for someone who is inexperienced, so it will often be sensible to ask the note-taker to take the best notes she possibly can of the claimant's cross-examination of the respondent's witnesses plus the answers to any additional questions from the tribunal, but otherwise only to write down anything she considers particularly important.

9.16   The respondent's legal team will sometimes turn up at the hearing with a laptop computer and ask for permission to take notes on that. This is the best way of getting a really accurate record of the course of the hearing, because a good typist can type considerably faster than most people can write longhand, and it is potentially in both parties' interests that full notes of the evidence should be made. If this arises, it is suggested that the claimant should propose that permission should be given on condition that the respondent undertakes (a) to take complete notes of the proceedings (that is, not merely taking notes of what they think is helpful to their side) and (b) to make their notes of the hearing available to the claimant, unedited, immediately after the end of each hearing day. This could be done by e-mailing or faxing each day's notes to the claimant on return to the office.

9.17   This way both sides will benefit from the convenience of full notes of the evidence, and if there is any appeal, both sides will be saved the expense and inconvenience of trying to agree the notes many weeks or even months after the hearing. It would be extremely unlikely for the respondent's representatives to attempt to doctor the notes in any way under these circumstances, but if the claimant did have any concern about the accuracy of notes made and provided in this way, she should be sure to raise that with the respondent immediately. Neither party's notes of the hearing are privileged.[9]

Evidence

Some definitions: evidence in chief, cross-examination, re-examination and leading questions

9.18   Three technical terms are needed first. Evidence in chief is the evidence given by a witness in her own statement or under questioning by the advocate on her side; examination in chief is asking questions of one's own witness. Cross-examination is the questioning of a witness by the other party's advocate. After a witness has been cross-examined, the party who called her is entitled to put further questions, called re-examination.

9.19   Leading questions are questions that indicate the expected answer: 'Did Mr Smith then hit you on the head with a blue ring binder?' is a leading question, and the addition of the words 'or not?' on the end does not alter that. 'What happened next?' is not. Leading questions are strongly discouraged in examination-in-chief and re-examination, because the impact of a witness meekly agreeing with statements formulated by the lawyer or her own side is very much less than impact of an account given in her own words. In cross-examination, leading questions are essential, and will not be discouraged: for example 'You did not look at the claimant's personnel file at all before you decided to dismiss him, did you?'

9.20   It is worth noting that none of these terms is defined or used in the employment tribunal rules of procedure: they are concepts borrowed from the ordinary criminal and civil courts. They are widely used in the employment tribunals nevertheless, and they are such fundamental concepts for trained lawyers that tribunals will often seem oblivious to the fact that they may be new to parties acting in person or to inexperienced lay advisers.

---

9 *Lambert v Home* [1914] 3 KB 86; and for the meaning of privilege see glossary and para 4.29 above.

Calling your own witnesses

9.21 Although witness statements will normally be read, replacing examination in chief, a representative will be expected to introduce her witnesses and get them started.

9.22 Start by saying something like:

> 'My first [/next] witness is Mr Smith. Mr Smith would you come to the witness table?'

9.23 Mr Smith will then be sworn and seated at the witness table. There is no set way of beginning, but the following is fairly typical:

> 'Please look at p34 of the bundle of statements, is this your witness statement?'

> 'Please turn to p 38, is that your signature?'

> 'Is this statement true to the best of your knowledge and belief'

> 'Please turn back to p34 and begin reading at paragraph 1.'

9.24 If the witness refers to in her statement to documents that you want the tribunal to read, ask the witness to pause when she gets to that part of her statement. 'Would you pause there a moment and turn to page *n* of the bundle? Is this the letter [/report /etc.] you have just referred to?' If the tribunal has already been given a reading list and has read the document, the witness can resume. If not, suggest that the tribunal takes a few minutes to read it now.

9.25 If the tribunal allows them, additional questions can either be asked at the end or by breaking in while the statement is being read.

9.26 When your own witness is being cross-examined, do not interrupt unless it is essential. It is possible to object to a question or line of questions, but it is rarely prudent to do so. The chairman should intervene if she considers that the line of questioning irrelevant or that the manner of the questioning is inappropriate. If she has not done so of her own accord, that probably means that she considers the questions proper.[10] If it is really necessary to intervene, apologise

---

10 Nevertheless, if you think your witness is being asked irrelevant questions purely to harass her, or is being seriously bullied, but the chairman is doing nothing to restrain this, then it is right to intervene. Catching the Chairman's eye may be enough, it is certainly worth trying first.

for the interruption and ask the Chairman to restrain the line of questioning.[11]

Cross-examination

9.27   It is worth remembering that the aim of cross-examination is not to batter the witness into submission, but to convince the tribunal. The tone of the questions should be firm, but polite. Anything savouring of courtroom drama should be avoided. Cross-examination needs to be carefully prepared: see paras 8.44–9.60.

9.28   In a case with multiple claimants or respondents, all parties will have an opportunity to cross-examine all the other parties' witnesses. In practice, one party will normally end up doing most of the cross-examination.

Re-examination

9.29   Once a witness has been cross-examined, the other side has the opportunity to re-examine. Re-examination must relate to the cross-examination, and as for examination-in-chief, leading questions are firmly discouraged.

9.30   The best general advice on re-examination is 'Don't.' It will rarely help and may do harm. If you think that part of your witness's evidence has been damaged under cross-examination, asking further questions on the same subject will often merely emphasise the point. Only re-examine if you are reasonably confident that the witness has previously given an apparently misleading or inconsistent answer simply because she failed to understand the question properly; and that you can give her an opportunity to repair the damage without leading.

---

11   A shout of 'Objection!' can be relied on to go down badly.

Example

Your client was summarily dismissed on 21 June 2007 for smoking at work two days earlier. In cross-examination, he faced the following line of questioning:

Q: You were aware of the Respondent's policy that smoking would be treated as gross misconduct?

A: No, I had never heard of it.

Q: An email addressed to 'staff@prissco.co.uk' would reach you?

A: Yes.

Q: And presumably if you received an email from Dave Smart you would read it?

A: Of course.

Q: Especially if it was marked 'important announcement'.

A: Yes.

Q: Turn to page 217 of the bundle. [This is an email from Dave Smart addressed to staff@prissco.co.uk headed 'important announcement' and announcing the policy] What is the date on it?

A: 9/3/07

Q: So the policy was announced three months before you were dismissed, but you ignored it?

A: I've never seen this email before.

Q: You have already agreed that an email addressed to 'staff@prissco.co.uk' would reach you, but now you say that this particular email didn't reach you?

A: I don't understand it why this didn't reach me, but I never saw it.

Your client has been made to look quite bad at this point. He is denying knowledge of something that, on the face of it, he was told in clear terms only a few months before the dismissal. What you have noticed in the course of this exchange, however, is that Dave Smart's emails tend to be dated, American fashion, 'mm/dd/yy' instead of 'dd/mm/yy'. This means that the date on this email is in fact 3 September 2007, after the dismissal, rather than 9 March 2007. It did not reach your client for the simple reason that at the time it was sent, he was no longer employed by Prissco.

This is the kind of damage you probably can repair (provided the witness is moderately quick-witted) in re-examination:

Q: Please turn to page 217. You were asked whether you had received this at the time, and said that you had not.[12] Would you turn to page 346? What is this?

A: Dave Smart's email asking me to the disciplinary hearing on 21 June.

Q: What is the date on it?

A: 6/19/07 that's odd. Oh I suppose it must be 19 June 07. I think Dave's emails were always dated like that.

Q: Would you turn back to page 217 when do you think this email was sent?

A: I'd say 3 September 2007.

Note that this is achieved without leading. If you just ask 'Dave's emails always showed the date American style, starting with the month, didn't they? So the date on the email at page 217 is 3 September not 9 March?' you have led your witness shamelessly.

Tribunal questions

9.31   The tribunal is also likely to ask the witnesses questions. Practice on this varies; some tribunals will break into the parties' questioning, others will wait to the end.

9.32   It is worth paying close attention to the tribunal members' questions: they can provide useful insights into how they are thinking and what they consider important.

---

12 This preamble is to let the witness and the tribunal know what area of his evidence you want to look at.

Submissions

9.33　After the witnesses have given their evidence, each side has an opportunity to make submissions to the tribunal: in other words, to make a speech to the tribunal seeking to persuade it to find one way or the other.

9.34　By this point the tribunal should already have a clear idea of what the case is about and what your claim is. Submissions are your opportunity to draw attention the best evidence in your favour, explain any weak points in your case and deal with any legal points that need to be addressed.

9.35　If the respondent's case has strong elements, or some evidence came out their way, it is best to deal with these points rather than ignoring them in the hope that they will go away.

What can go wrong at the hearing?

9.36　Hearings are unpredictable and all kinds of things can go wrong on the day. What follows is a list of some of the most common problems that can crop up, with suggestions as to how they might be handled.

The respondent comes to the hearing with a large pile of documents that you have not seen before.

9.37　This is fairly common. The claimant will have to make a fairly swift decision about how important the new documents are. It may be sufficient to ask the tribunal for a short break of 20 minutes to half an hour to enable the claimant to read the new documents and consider them. If they are particularly important, or the claimant will have difficulty in analysing them in a short time, then it may be necessary to ask the tribunal to adjourn the hearing to another day. If this is necessary, the claimant should consider making an application for a costs or preparation time order.[13]

9.38　Alternatively, the claimant may simply wish to ask the tribunal to exclude the new material from its consideration on the grounds that it should have been disclosed earlier. Either way, stress should be laid on the respondent's failure to comply properly with whatever order was previously made about disclosure of documents.

13　See para 11.4.

The respondent makes new allegations at the hearing that the claimant was not previously aware of but could refute given time.

9.39　This is a variation on the previous example. Again, if the new material is important enough, it may be necessary to request a postponement.

Someone fails to turn up

9.40　When the tribunal is due to start, representatives may find themselves without clients; clients may be missing their representative; or both may be looking for a witness. The only thing to be done in these circumstances is to try to find out what has happened and tell the clerk, who will inform the tribunal.

9.41　If there is substantial delay, the tribunal is likely to call the parties in to ask for an explanation. At this point, the tribunal will have three choices: wait for the missing individual to arrive; postpone the hearing or hear the case without them. The choice will depend on the circumstances and how much the tribunal knows.

9.42　If the missing person is on your side, your priority will normally be to avoid the case continuing without her. A claim where the claimant does not appear is unlikely to win. And a claimant finding herself without her anticipated representation at the last moment is unlikely to do her claim justice.

9.43　The best argument will always be a good reason for the failure to attend. If you have no information about this, all you can do is emphasise the prejudice to your client of allowing the hearing to go ahead. If the claimant has previously conducted the proceedings properly, point that out. Point out too that the only prejudice to the respondent is the inconvenience and expense of coming back another day; this is much less than the prejudice to the claimant in having the hearing go ahead without her evidence, and can if appropriate be compensated by costs.[14]

9.44　If you are the claimant and your representative has failed to turn up, you will almost certainly want to resist any suggestion that you should represent yourself. It is true that the tribunals are very used to hearing from unrepresented parties (and will help them, to a greater or lesser degree); but point out if necessary that it is one thing to appear as a litigant in person when you have had a chance to prepare. It is quite another to appear having relied on somebody else to represent you.

14　Do not expect the tribunal to be greatly impressed by the availability of costs, though: many claimants will be unable to pay costs even if an order is made against them.

9.45   If you are the one who has had problems reaching the tribunal it is important to let your client or representative as the case may be know as soon as possible. If you have difficulty reaching them, or are a litigant in person call the tribunal directly. This should be done as soon as it seems likely you will be late. It is better to ring early, saying that you might be late, then arrive on time, than to ring after the tribunal is already wondering where you are.

The tribunal is not prepared to go ahead

9.46   This is more common than it should be. Tribunal hearings are over-booked.[15] On any given day more cases are due to take place than there are tribunals to hear them. This is because many cases settle and so drop out of the list. The aim is to judge the number of hearings scheduled so that, on the day, just enough have settled to allow the others to be heard. Sometimes the tribunal guesses wrong and is caught short. If when you get to the tribunal it turns out that your case has not been allocated to a particular tribunal, it is described as 'floating': that is, waiting in case a tribunal becomes free to hear it in the course of the day.[16] Sometimes if you are unallocated you will get to start your case later in the day; if you are unlucky, you will wait around for half the day and then be sent home. This is frustrating and time-wasting for the parties, but there is nothing to be done about it. Occasionally the tribunal service will call the parties the day before the hearing to say that the hearing will not go ahead.

One of your witness appears, under cross-examination, to be untruthful

9.47   The best that can be done is to remain poker-faced, and then play down the importance of the witness or the particular piece of evidence in submissions. Representatives should resist the temptation to blame themselves when this happens. Much of what will happen at the tribunal is determined by the people concerned and the history of the case. Both were determined long before you got involved.

15 Like flights, though with more excuse.
16 Because another case has finished, or been settled.

The chairman treats the claimant with evident hostility

9.48   If this happens, accurate and complete note-taking becomes extremely important. If the chairman (or a member) of the tribunal says something that indicates hostility to the claimant, the claimant should write it down at once and, if she has anyone with him or her, ensure that they write it down as well.[17]

9.49   The claimant should consider whether to make an application for the chairman to remove him or herself from the case because of apparent bias. Obviously this is a tactic that has a high cost, and should not be used lightly. First and foremost, it will certainly antagonise the tribunal, so unless the tribunal grants the application it will make it more likely that the claimant loses the case. It is therefore a tactic that has more to do with laying the foundations for a subsequent appeal than with winning the case this time round. If granted, it will almost certainly – unless there happens to be another tribunal free to hear the case on the same day – necessitate an adjournment.

The chairman refuses to permit the claimant to cross-examine in an important area

9.50   The tribunal has a general power to control proceedings, and will sometimes restrain a particular line of cross-examination on the grounds that it is not relevant. It may be necessary to explain where the questions are heading or why they are relevant. Unfortunately this will sometimes lose what would have been a useful element of surprise. If the tribunal is determined to restrain a series of questions that the claimant regards as crucial, careful notes should be taken of this exchange in case it needs to form the basis of a subsequent appeal.

The chairman imposes strict time-limits on cross-examination or submissions

9.51   This is becoming more and more common with increasing pressure on tribunals to deal with cases quickly. Tribunals sometimes ask for estimates of how long each stage will take, and then hold parties to their estimates. This is particularly unfair in the case of an unrepresented claimant because it takes experience to estimate how long cross-examination will take. In any event, much depends on the

---

17   There is nothing wrong with turning briefly to the accompanying person and whispering: 'Please write that down' if this happens.

manner in which the witness answers questions: a witness who gives terse one-or two-word answers will finish her evidence much faster than a witness who tells a long rambling story in answer to each question. If the claimant feels that she is being seriously disadvantaged by time limits, she should put up a fight at the time: outline briefly what remains to be covered and why it is important. It may be helpful to refer the tribunal to Employment Tribunals (Constitution and Rules of Procedure) Regulations 2004 reg 3 and point out that the need to deal with cases justly comes first, and trumps (if necessary) the aim of dealing with them 'expeditiously'.[18]

The claimant forgets to ask one of the respondent's witnesses about a crucial topic

9.52   This is easily done. If the witness is still present, it should not be too difficult to remedy. The claimant should explain the omission to the tribunal, and ask for the witness to be recalled. Although the tribunal will not be best pleased, it should normally agree, especially if the claimant is a lay-person representing herself. If the witness was released on a previous day and is no longer attending the hearing, the tribunal is likely to be more reluctant, but if the omitted topic is important enough it may be necessary to make the request anyway. Thought should be given to whether this will extend proceedings enough to necessitate an extra hearing day: if it does, there will be a real risk of a costs order.

---

18 Legalese for 'quickly'.

Remedies[1]

---

1   This chapter owes a considerable debt to a paper on the same subject
   originally written by Tim Pitt-Payne and subsequently added to by Robin
   White and Katherine Newton for FRU training events.

Introduction

10.1 'Remedy' is the term used to describe the what the claimant gets if successful: most often a sum of money, although in some cases other remedies are available.

10.2 Although remedy is normally the last thing to be considered by the tribunal, it should be the among the first things to be considered by the claimant. No case should be begun without the claimant having formed a clear idea of what he wishes to achieve. This is easy to say, but difficult to do in practice.

10.3 This chapter is not intended to be a detailed account of the law relating to remedies: rather it aims to give guidance about how to approach the question of remedy and some tips on how to maximise compensation.[2] For simplicity, and because most claims relate to dismissal one way or another, the discussion here is mainly confined to dismissal.

What do you want?

10.4 People bring tribunal cases for many different reasons and to achieve very different things. And there is unlikely to be a single reason for bringing proceedings. Instead there will be complex mix of pragmatism – 'I need the money I haven't been paid' or 'I need to sort this out so I can get another job' – altruism – 'Nobody else is going to go through what I've been through' or 'I'm going to take a stand' and emotional – 'Those bastards!'.

10.5 It is important to identify these motives and the desired outcome, and to make a clear-eyed assessment of whether the desired outcome can in fact be achieved through the tribunal process.[3] To be useful this must be done at an early stage. Ideally, preparation for the tribunal process should work backwards, identifying the desired result first and then determining what needs to happen if it is to be achieved.

10.6 Advisers need to be particularly careful that they have understood their client's aims. Advisers have a tendency to focus on financial outcomes, because those are the most the most readily achievable, but

---

2 For accounts of the relevant law, see the relevant parts of ELAH 7, Harvey and Korn & Sethi, *Employment Tribunal Compensation* (3rd edn, OUP, 2005).

3 See also para 1.20 above.

that can miss the point badly. Sometimes the case is all about money, but it may be that what the client mainly wants is to retain a professional accreditation (or just get a reference) which they need to get another job, or to ensure that the terms of their mortgage insurance are met, or even to keep the security dog they have worked with for years.

10.7   Advisers also need to take care in managing their clients' expectations. The employment tribunal cases that hit the headlines tend to be high value claims. Most tribunal awards are for much more modest sums. If the only cases the claimant has read about have involved awards in the hundreds of thousands, that can cause them to overestimate significantly the award they are likely to receive.

10.8   Many claimants also want to 'clear their name' or rebuke their employer for their misdeeds, or humiliate their former manager in front of more senior managers. The last may sound like straight revenge, but it can serve a legitimate purpose. Managers wield a significant power over their subordinates, and it is salutary for them to learn that misuse of this power can lead to having to give a detailed public account of their actions under pointed cross-examination.[4] Aims of this kind need to be treated with caution, however, because the tribunal itself will have a more limited view of its own role.

10.9   Many claimants – and respondents too – have exaggerated expectations of the tribunal system. If you are an adviser, it is worth warning the claimant that the tribunal consists of three men and women who should have, between them, a reasonably wide experience of workplace disputes, and one at least of whom will know some employment law, but whose knowledge of the circumstances of this particular dispute will be limited to what they can glean from the papers and what the witnesses tell them. They have no special ability to detect untruthfulness in a witness or to compel a witness to tell the truth.[5]

---

4 This is probably part of the reason why some litigants seem to feel better for having been to tribunal even when they have lost.

5 In fact, they have no superpowers at all.

Recommendations and declarations

10.10   In discrimination cases, the tribunal may make a recommendation.[6] A recommendation is an instruction to a respondent to take action to remove or reduce the effect of the discrimination relating to the case. For example, in a sex discrimination claim relating to flexible working a tribunal might recommend that the respondent introduce a flexible working policy within six months.

10.11   There is no power to enforce recommendations, so the tribunal cannot force a respondent to act if they are determined not to, but failure to implement a recommendation may lead to an increased financial award.

10.12   The purpose of a recommendation is stated in the relevant sections as 'obviating or reducing the adverse effect on the complainant of any act of discrimination to which the complaint relates', but this should not be taken to limit the availability of recommendations to cases in which the claimant has remained in the employment of the respondent. Injury to feelings is one of the recognised kinds of adverse effect on a claimant, and a recommendation as to the former employer's future conduct is clearly capable of reducing the injury to the claimant's feelings.[7]

10.13   The potential of recommendations should not be overlooked. Often all the claimant wants out of a discrimination claim is financial compensation, but, particularly where feelings are seriously injured, recommendations can be powerful. Although the tribunal cannot enforce the recommendation, many employers (especially public sector employers) faced with a recommendation will make a real attempt to comply with it.

10.14   In addition to recommendations the tribunal may make declarations of various kinds, for example that the claimant has suffered discrimination as to the terms of his contract of employment or that a particular statutory right has been infringed.[8]

---

6 SDA 1975 s65(1)(c), RRA 1976 s56(1)(c), DDA 1995 s17A(2)(c), SOR 2003 reg 30(1)(c), RBR 2003 reg 30(1)(c).

7 An employment tribunal held otherwise in *Bayoomi v British Railways Board* [1981] IRLR 431, but this was a first instance decision and is not binding on another tribunal.

8 See, eg, ERA 1996 s11.

Reinstatement and re-engagement

10.15 In unfair dismissal cases the tribunal has the power to order reinstatement or reengagement.[9] Reinstatement is an order that the claimant be treated as if they were not dismissed. In effect the dismissal is cancelled. Re-engagement is an order that the claimant is given employment comparable to that from which he was dismissed 'or other suitable employment' on such terms as the tribunal decides. Re-engagement is the more flexible remedy: the tribunal can decide whether and if so to what extent to compensate the claimant for lost earnings, whether after re-engagement he should receive the same pay as he did before dismissal, where he should work, and so on.

10.16 The term 're-employment' does not appear in the Act but is commonly understood by employment lawyers to refer to reinstatement and re-engagement together.

10.17 Reinstatement and re-engagement were originally intended to be the primary remedies for unfair dismissal, but in practice such orders are rarely made and even more rarely complied with.[10] In the 2005–06 tribunal year only eight such orders were made. This meant that an order was made in only 0.1% of hearings.[11] The main reason for this is that by ERA s116 an employer can resist re-employment on the grounds that it is not practicable to comply, and tribunals are reluctant to make futile orders. The likelihood of an order for re-employment being complied with is strongly affected by the employer's attitude to it: if the employer is determined that re-employment will not work, then it almost certainly will not. Moreover, the time between dismissal and the tribunal hearing is now much longer than when these powers were created. Months or even years after a dismissal there will rarely be a realistic chance of the employee returning to work.

10.18 These difficulties tend to lead to re-employment being neglected by claimants and their advisers. Probably one part of the reason that it is so rare is that it is rarely sought with any real determination or expectation of success. This is a shame, because a re-employment order has some significant advantages and can – even where it is unlikely to

---

9 ERA 1996 s114–115

10 But keep reading: there are good reasons why claimants would do well to apply for them more often than they do.

11 Employment Tribunal Service Annual Report and Accounts 2005–2006.

lead the claimant actually to return to work – be a powerful tactical weapon in the hands of the claimant.

10.19   The main advantage of re-employment is that it can evade some of the consequences of the cap on compensation for unfair dismissal. A reinstatement order restores the employment as if the dismissal had never been, and full arrears of pay and other benefits – with no upper limit – have to be paid by the employer.[12] This sum still has to be paid if the reinstatement does not in fact take place. Hence if the employee's lost earnings up to the date of the hearing are likely to exceed the upper limit on compensation in force, it is worth trying for a re-employment order for the sake of enhanced compensation.

10.20   Pension rights may be a further compelling reason to try for re-employment. An employee, for example, who is dismissed on capability grounds when he should have been given early retirement on medical grounds may suffer a pension loss for which, by reason of the upper limit on the compensatory award, he cannot be properly compensated. Reinstatement may allow him to be medically retired and avoid that loss, even if he is not in fact fit to return to work. There is no reason why reinstatement should not be awarded for this purpose.

10.21   Employers are often very anxious about re-employment, so the threat to seek an order for reinstatement or re-engagement can provide them with a powerful incentive to settle.

10.22   Note the following points that may need to be made in applying for re-employment:

- There is no rule that the tribunal must not order re-employment if it is not practicable for the employer to comply with such an order. Practicability is just one of the factors that the tribunal must take into account. If the employer is to blame for the fact that re-employment is impracticable, it can sensibly be argued that the employer should not through its fault be permitted to bar the claimant from a remedy that is to his advantage, even if that advantage is confined to enhanced compensation.

- If the claimant wants to be reinstated merely in order to be medically retired, practicability is unlikely to be an issue: the employer is not in fact going to be called upon to find a role for him, nor will there be any need to re-establish a relationship of trust and confidence.

---

12 In the case of re-engagement the tribunal has a discretion about how much to award by way of arrears, but similarly the upper limit is lifted for the purpose.

- Contributory fault, too, is a factor that must be taken into account in deciding whether to order re-employment, but the tendency of tribunals (and advisers) to treat it as an outright bar is unfounded.
- Re-engagement is a sufficiently flexible remedy to permit the tribunal to take account of contributory fault. If it takes the view that the claimant was at fault and that fault contributed to his dismissal, but the decision to dismiss him was in fact unfair, then there is no reason why he should not be re-engaged with a disciplinary warning, or (if, for example, demotion would have been fair) in a lower-paid position.

10.23   As with recommendations there is no power to enforce re-employment orders, but failure to comply is likely to lead to an increased award.[13]

Awards of money

10.24   In many cases the only applicable remedy is an order that the employer pays the employee some money. Often the approach is compensatory: the aim is to put the claimant in the position he would be in (subject in some cases to an upper limit) if he had not suffered the wrong that he is complaining of. In other cases, there is a fixed award for breach of a specific statutory right that does not depend on proving any loss: for example, the award for failure to provide written reasons for dismissal is two weeks' pay.[14] Some of the kinds of claim with which employment tribunals deal lend themselves to straightforward arithmetic, some require a combination of arithmetic and fortune-telling, some are compensated by the award of more-or-less conventional sums, and some are compensated by sums fixed by the legislation. Detailed guidance on how to calculate compensation is beyond the scope of this book, but a few examples may help clarify the different approaches.[15]

13   See Korn & Sethi, para 3.41.
14   Subject to an upper limit on the amount of a week's pay for these purposes.
15   For the detail, Korn & Sethi, n2 above.

Example 1
Susan has been dismissed without notice in breach of contract from a job in which she took home £180 per week. Her contract entitled her to four weeks notice, and she did not get another job in that time, so her loss by reason of the breach of contract is four weeks' net pay.

Her damages for breach of contract are therefore:

£180 x 4 = £720

This is simple arithmetic.

Example **2**
Boris earned £200 for a 40 hour week for six weeks in late 2007. The minimum wage was £5.52 per hour during that period, so he was underpaid by 52 pence per hour. He complains of unauthorised deductions from wages and is awarded

£0.52 x 40 x 6 = £124.80

This too is simple arithmetic.

Example 3
Rob, who earned £500 per week, was summarily dismissed for gross misconduct when he squirted his supervisor with the fire extinguisher in the course of a heated argument about overtime. When he asked for written reasons for dismissal his supervisor said 'Fuck off out of here you idiot, what do you think you've been dismissed for?'

The tribunal awards Rob 2 x£310 = £620 for breach of his statutory right to written reasons for dismissal.

The award for breach of this right is two weeks' gross pay, subject to an upper limit on a 'week's pay' of £310. The award bears no relation to any loss suffered by reason of the breach: it is a fixed sum which the tribunal must award and may not vary.

Example 4

Hyacinth applied for a promotion worth an extra £2,375 per year after tax, but failed to get it on grounds of her race. She worked for a further six months after the appointment of a different candidate, and then left for another job with a different employer. In her new job she earns more than she would have if she had been promoted.

The tribunal considers that Hyacinth's financial loss attributable to the discrimination is limited to six months' lost increment and awards her

£2,375/2 = £1187.5 for lost earnings plus £7,000 for injury to feelings[16]

The figure for lost earnings is a matter of simple arithmetic. The question how much the injury to Hyacinth's feelings is 'worth' in financial terms is much more difficult: tribunals tend to pick a round figure that 'feels right' in the circumstances, although their feelings on the subject will be guided by previous decisions of the EAT and the Court of Appeal.[17]

Example 5

Hyacinth appeals to the EAT, complaining that the tribunal failed to give any consideration to her argument that if she had received the promotion she would have been in a stronger position to negotiate with her current employer, and would be earning more now. She says a more realistic estimate of her loss is another £2,000 per year for three years.

Very often tribunals are required to compare the claimant's situation as it is with his situation as it might have been had the discrimination (etc) not occurred. There can be a considerable element of guesswork involved.

---

16 Plus interest: for how to calculation of interest on a discrimination award, see ELAH 7 para 19.42.

17 See ELAH 7 para 19.16, Korn & Sethi para 17.31.

Evidence of loss

10.25   Where there is a claim for compensation, evidence of loss should be carefully prepared. The bulk of the claim will normally be for lost earnings. Here there are typically three main things to argue about: (i) what the claimant would have earned in the relevant period if he had not been dismissed; (ii) what the claimant has earned and/or will earn in the relevant period; and (iii) what is the relevant period.[18] In discrimination cases there will normally be some debate as well about the appropriate award for injury to feelings.

What the claimant would have earned

10.26   This can often be agreed between the parties: the claimant's entitlements are set out in his contract of employment. Sometimes there is argument about variable benefits: e.g. whether he would have received a pay rise if he had not been dismissed, or whether he would have benefited from a discretionary bonus, and if so, of how much. If there is disagreement on this, the statement (or if appropriate a separate remedy statement) should set out the grounds on which the claimant says he would received the higher figure. So for example, he might point out that he had received a pay rise of between 3% and 6% every April since he had worked for the employer; or say that although the bonus was expressed in his contract to be purely discretionary, in fact he and his colleagues had always received a bonus that was calculated as a proportion of their annual salary determined arithmetically by the performance of the department as a whole over the previous year. It may be necessary to request performance figures from the respondent in order to do this kind of calculation; it may also be relevant to request details of any pay rises awarded to other employees.

What the claimant has earned/will earn: mitigation

10.27   Where there is a claim for lost earnings, there is almost always also a duty to 'mitigate the loss' – that is, the employee who has been dismissed unfairly or as a result of unlawful discrimination may not retire at that point on the strength of his claim and seek to recover in full what he would have earned up to age 65: he must do his best to get another job.

---

18   For simplicity this section confines itself to the consequences of dismissal.

10.28   The tribunal will only order the respondent to compensate the claimant for losses reasonably incurred. If the tribunal believes that the claimant has failed to take reasonable steps to mitigate his loss, he will not be compensated for whatever element of his loss he could reasonably have avoided. This is often the most contentious aspect of the argument about remedy, and is worth careful attention.

Heading off criticism of efforts to mitigate

10.29   A claimant whose complaint is about the loss of his job should start to look for another job as soon as he reasonably can. If he is too ill, or too upset or depressed, to look for work straight away, he should see his doctor.

10.30   The claimant should aim to take at least one step towards finding alternative work every day, and should document his job-search minutely, including the following:

- make a note of every telephone call;
- keep a copy of every letter and completed application form;
- keep all rejection letters;
- make a note of each 'situations vacant' column checked;
- keep a copy or clipping of each advertisement responded to;
- print out details of any relevant website visited;
- print out all relevant e-mails sent or received;
- keep notes of any career advice sought or received;
- keep records of any expenses incurred in the job search – travel tickets, receipts for meals taken away from home, receipts for photocopying or printing.

10.31   The best situation for a claimant to be in at the time of the hearing is to have a small claim for lost earnings because he has by the time of the hearing got a better-paid job than before. If that is not achievable, the second best outcome is to have a lower-paid job. This tends to be regarded by tribunals as convincing evidence that a claimant is serious about mitigating his loss, so it will maximise his chances of securing compensation for a substantial period into the future.

10.32   The worst outcome is still to be looking for work at the time of the hearing. If the claimant is still unavoidably unemployed by the time of the hearing, he should come armed with a fat file of evidence of mitigation. Here, for once, sheer length and weight is a virtue: the aim is to deter the respondent from even attempting to argue that there has been insufficient effort to mitigate.[19] Most respondents faced with a credible 300 page mitigation bundle will decide to concentrate on other approaches to damage limitation.

What is the relevant period

10.33   This too is often contentious, particularly if the claimant is still out of work at the time of the hearing. The respondent will seek to persuade the tribunal that he has not tried hard enough, and it should not be held responsible for any lost earnings for more than, say, three or six months after the dismissal. The claimant's aim will be to persuade the tribunal that there are good reasons why his losses to date are unavoidable, and, if they are continuing, why they are likely to continue for a long time into the future. A good mitigation bundle is very helpful here: if the claimant can show that he has applied unsuccessfully for every reasonably suitable job that has been advertised within reasonable travelling distance from his home since dismissal, it will be very difficult for the employer to say that his continuing losses are his own fault.

10.34   Where the claimant says that ill-treatment by the employer damaged his health, and because of that he is still too ill to apply for work at all, or his illness means that he cannot realistically expect to secure work at his previous level, the tribunal is unlikely to accept this without supporting medical reports. Bear in mind that in an unfair dismissal case, although the claimant cannot claim for personal injury caused by the dismissal, illness caused by the dismissal or surrounding circumstances may provide the explanation for his failure to mitigate as quickly or as completely as might have been hoped. In such a case, if the respondent argues that there has been inadequate mitigation, medical evidence may be necessary.

Injury to feelings

10.35   If there is (as there usually will be) injury to feelings over and above the pure affront of having suffered discrimination, it is necessary to spell this out in evidence. Compensation for injury to feelings can only be recovered in discrimination cases. Something more than a bare assertion that the claimant was upset will be needed. It can be difficult to get this kind of information from claimants in a form in which it will convince the tribunal, either because their feelings are too painful to talk

---

19   That is not to say, of course, that irrelevant material should be included.

about easily, or because they are just not used to describing their emotions and the effects of their emotions.

10.36　　This is a tricky task, because it is important not to put words into the claimant's mouth or suggest 'right' answers to him; but at the same time, it may be necessary to be quite persistent if you are to tease out the real effects of the discrimination. Bear in mind that individual reactions to discrimination will differ widely, and not necessarily in proportion to the severity of the treatment. Some people will be angry, but basically able to brush the experience off; others will be profoundly upset; others will become significantly depressed.

Questions it can be helpful to ask include:

- how did it make you feel when [xyz] happened?
- what did you do?
- did you talk to anyone about it?
- were you tearful?
- how long did you spend crying?
- was that the only time it made you cry?
- how did you spend the next few days/weeks/months?
- did you go out?
- did you see friends?
- did it affect your relationship with your partner/spouse/family?
- did it affect your relationship with your friends?

If the upset caused by discrimination is severe, it can be helpful to have supporting evidence from a family member or friend. Where depression has resulted, medical evidence will be needed.[20]

The schedule of loss

10.37　　The claimant should quantify his loss as early as possible in proceedings. There are two main reasons for this. First, the earlier the respondent knows the size of the claim, the greater the chances of realistic negotiations: the respondent will be more inclined to settle before it has spent substantial sums of money on legal fees than after. Secondly, if the respondent knows at an early stage what its maximum risk is, it is better equipped to judge how much it should spend on defending the claim. If the claimant wishes to argue subsequently, in opposing a

20　For an example of evidence about injury to feelings, see paragraph 11 of
　　P5.28.2 above.

costs application, that the respondent's legal costs were disproportionate to the size of the claim, he will be far better placed if he quantified the claim at an early stage.

10.38   General guidance on how to quantify claims can be found at
chapters 18 and 19 of *Employment Law: an adviser's handbook* (7th edn).
Guidance on preparing schedules of loss can be found at para 20.99.

P10.38.1 Schedule of loss – unfair dismissal

IN THE EMPLOYMENT TRIBUNAL   Case No 123456/2007
LONDON CENTRAL

BETWEEN

JOSEPH CLARKSON

Claimant

and

NEW PIN CLEANING SERVICES LIMITED

Respondent

SCHEDULE OF LOSS

1. Compensation for unfair dismissal

   (a) Basic award[21]
       a week's pay: £193.60
       2 years' continuous employment
       age at EDT:[22] 64
       multiplier:[23] 3

       3 × £193.60 = £580.80

---

21 See generally ELAH 7 para 18.15.
22 Effective date of termination.
23 The multiplier is a figure derived from the claimant's age and length of
    service.

(b) Compensatory award[24]

> take home pay: £170 p/w
> 11 May 2007 to 28 October 2007
> 20 weeks = £3,400.00

> less
> 2 weeks' painting and decorating
> work @ £250 per week =
> £500.00

> loss of statutory rights[25] = £300.00

2. TUPE Regulation 11 award[26]

   13 weeks' pay @ £193.60 = £2,516.80

3. Section 13 unauthorised deductions[27]

   2 weeks' @ £170 = £340.00

   TOTAL = £6,637.60

24 See generally ELAH 7 para 18.24.
25 See ELAH 7 para 18.34.
26 An award to employees where the undertaking in which they are employed is transferred and the employer has not complied with the duty under the Transfer of Undertakings (Protection of Employees) Regulations 1981 to inform and consult employee representatives.
27 That is, unauthorised deductions from wages contrary to ERA 1996 s13. See generally ELAH 7, para 4.9.

P10.38.2 Schedule of loss – race discrimination

IN THE EMPLOYMENT TRIBUNAL   Case No 123456/2004
LONDON CENTRAL

BETWEEN

ABOSEDE OJO

Claimant

and

EAST LONDON RIGHTS SHOP

Respondent

SCHEDULE OF LOSS

Lost earnings

net pay in current job: £16,394.18 p/a = £315.28 p/w

net pay in job applied for: £21,352.18 p/a = £410.61 p/w

net weekly loss = £95.34

net loss from 12 September 2007

to hearing date on 6 February 2008: 21 weeks

21 × £95.34 = £2,002.14

travel expenses: £20.20 per week

21 × 20.20 = £424.20

Subtotal = £2426.34

interest @ 7% since mid-point date

10 November 2007

47p per day

$0.47 \times 89 = £41.83$

Injury to feelings

say £5,000.00

interest since 12 August 2007 @ 7%[28]

178 days @ 96p per day = £170.88

Total = £7,639.05

Enforcement

10.39 Unfortunately, respondents do not always pay tribunal awards without further action on the part of the claimant. The process of enforcement can be as difficult and as time consuming that the original claim. Ultimately, it may not be possible to recover the award at all. Claimant should not, however, be too discouraged. Often non-payment is the result of intertia and disinclination rather than either active avoidance or inability to pay.

10.40 Tribunal awards are payable as soon as the judgment is issued, but begin to accrue interest only after 42 days (which is also the period in which the respondent must start any appeal). Some respondents conclude that they have 42 days to pay. This is not the case.

10.41 The first step should be to send the respondent a copy of the tribunal's judgment as soon as it is received with a short covering letter; something to the effect: 'Please find enclosed a copy of the tribunal's Judgment of [date]. You will see that the tribunal has made an award of £x in my favour. I look forward to receiving your cheque shortly.'

---

28 See ETP 3 paras 20.8 and 20.9.

10.42   This is strictly redundant: the respondent should have received its own copy of the judgment at the same time the claimant did, but it does no harm and might head off a delay while the respondent insists that it has not seen the judgment. It also serves as an early indication that the claimant expects to receive the award, and is not going to go away without a fight if not paid.

10.43   If payment is not forthcoming within a couple of weeks of this, contact the respondent and request an explanation. A certain amount of polite but insistent prodding will often yield results. If promises of payment on a certain date are made but not honoured, telephone promptly on the day payment should have been received to ask what has happened.

10.44   How long this stage goes on depends largely on the claimant's patience, and also on whether there is any reason to think that the respondent is playing for time while it seeks to make enforcement impossible. The next step is enforcement proceedings.

10.45   First, give the respondent a final deadline in writing: write a letter warning that if payment is not received within a further short period (perhaps seven days), enforcement proceedings will be begun.

10.46   The tribunal has no enforcement powers. To be enforced, a tribunal judgment will need to be registered in the County Court. The claimant files a copy of the award together with form N322A at the County Court. The form is available from any county court, or from the Court Service website.[29] A fee is charged for registration, currently £35.[30] The fee will be added to the registered judgment, so once the award is registered the respondent will owe the original amount plus £35.

10.47   The judgment must be registered in the right court. County Courts cover a set geographical area and will not register judgments relating to cases from outside that area.[31] It is unclear whether it is the claimant or the respondent's address that determines the appropriate court and practice varies. The easiest way to check is to call the claimant's local court and ask if they will register the judgment and, if not, which is the appropriate court. Court addresses can be found through the court service website.[32]

---

29   www.hmcourts-service.gov.uk
30   Claimants receiving benefits may be exempt from the fee.
31   The consequences of attempting to register in the wrong court are not dire; one of the authors has had the embarrassing experience of having the form returned to him twice, before he hit on the right court.
32   www.hmcourts-service.gov.uk

10.48 Once a tribunal award is registered it becomes a County Court Judgment. This has two effects. First, the existence of a CCJ will sometimes convince a respondent to pay up. To many people a CCJ is real in a way that a tribunal judgment is not. CCJs also show up on credit checks and an outstanding CCJ can have grave effects on the credit-worthiness of an individual or company. Secondly, once a CCJ exists, it can be enforced in the same way as any other court judgments.

10.49 The County Court has a number of powers of enforcement:

Order to Obtain Information	Requiring the respondent to attend court to answer questions about his finances and ability to pay[33]
Warrant of Execution	Using bailiffs to recover goods which can be sold to cover the debt
Third Party Debt Order	Ordering somebody who owes the respondent money (in practice, usually their bank, which of course owes them money any time they have an account that is in credit) to pay the relevant amount of it to the claimant
Attachment of Earnings Order	Ordering the respondent's employer to pay a portion of his wages to the claimant
Charging Order	Securing the debt against land owned by the respondent

10.50 The Court will not pursue any of these options on its own. To use them the claimant will need to make further applications to the court. This will require further fees, which will also be added to the judgment debt.

10.51 A full discussion of enforcement proceedings is outside the scope of this book. Further information is available from the Court Service website and County Courts. Philip Tsamados has also written an

---

33 This will require the judgment to be registered in the respondent's local court. It can be transferred there if necessary, but if you anticipate that you might ask for an order to obtain information it is sensible to register it there to begin with.

excellent booklet on enforcing tribunal awards available from Central London Law Centre.[34]

Enforcement of settlement

10.52   To enforce a settlement a claimant will need to bring a civil case in the County Court. Although this sounds intimidating, the case will normally be straightforward, since all the claimant need to prove is that a settlement will be agreed, but the money has not been paid. This will create a CCJ and lead into the enforcement system described above.

Insolvency

10.53   Respondents frequently suggest that they are unable to pay because they are insolvent. Such statements should be taken with a pinch of salt. It is easy to check whether an individual or company has been made bankrupt of insolvent. Personal bankruptcies are registered with the Insolvency Service.[35] Companies House records will show a company's insolvency.[36] In each case, the information is available on the relevant agency's website.

10.54   If the employer is insolvent, some of the award may be recovered through the National Insurance Fund. This fund covers a limited amount of unpaid wages, notice pay, redundancy payments and the basic award in unfair dismissal. Details of the scheme and instructions for applying may be found on the Insolvency Service website. See also ELAH 7, para 18.69.

10.55   Further money may be recovered through the insolvency process, but employee debts are far down the list of creditors and claimants will rarely see much money once the other debts have been paid.

10.56   If the employer is not registered as insolvent, claimants should be reluctant to abandon enforcement proceedings unless convinced they will be fruitless. It is certainly sensible to ask searching questions about why – if the employer is insolvent – they are not registered as such.

10.57   One method that unscrupulous employers may use is to put one company into insolvency then create another company, which carries on much the same work. This is known as a Phoenix Company. This

---

34   www.londonlawcentre.org.uk/publications.html

35   www.insolvency.gov.uk

36   www.companieshouse.gov.uk

is a difficult tactic to counter. In theory, it may be possible to enforce against either the Directors or the new company, but in practice this is likely to require High Court litigation and a specialist legal team – resources that are unlikely to be available and whose cost is likely to dwarf the original award. Claimants should, however, considering informing Companies House and Revenue & Customs. Companies House may investigate the Directors' conduct. And Revenue & Customs may investigate whether tax evasion has occurred in the process.

CHAPTER 11

The decision; costs, correction and review

The decision

11.1   The decision may be given orally at the end of the hearing, or the tribunal may wish to take time to consider and write its decision, in which case the parties may be sent away not knowing who has won and who has lost. The latter is called 'reserving' its decision.

11.2   If the tribunal announces its decision and gives reasons at the hearing, it will send out a written judgment afterwards. The judgment will simply state which party has won, who has to pay what in compensation or costs, and may include a declaration (for example, that one party has discriminated against the other). The tribunal will not send out written reasons unless one of the parties requests them. A party wishing to appeal must have written reasons. It is suggested that unrepresented claimants who have lost their cases should always request written reasons in order to be able to think about (and get advice on) whether or not to appeal. Even if there is no question of an appeal, written reasons may make it easier to understand the result. The request can be made either at the hearing or within 14 days after the written judgment is sent out. If the claimant requests written reasons at the hearing, he or she should make an immediate note of having made that request.

11.3   If the tribunal reserves its decision, it will always send out written reasons for the decision. Reserved decisions are usually sent out within four to six weeks of the hearing. If a decision has not been received within about eight weeks of the hearing, it is worth making inquiries: occasionally the tribunal makes a mistake and sends reasons to one party but not the other, or to the wrong address, or records that it has sent out reasons when it has not; and of course there is always the possibility of a postal failure. Because of the strict time limits for appealing, if reasons have not been received it is important to find out promptly if the tribunal believes it has sent them.

Costs and preparation time orders

11.4   In certain limited circumstances the tribunal will order one party to reimburse the other's legal costs of fighting the case (this is a costs order) or to pay the other a sum of money to compensate for the time that they or their advisers have spent preparing the case (this is called a preparation time order).[1] Unlike the ordinary courts, employment tribunals do not as a matter of routine order the unsuccessful party to pay the successful party's costs. The tribunals' power to award costs is much more restricted.

11.5   The rules state that if the tribunal is satisfied that a party has 'acted vexatiously, abusively, disruptively or otherwise unreasonably, or the bringing or conducting of the proceedings by the paying party has been misconceived', then it shall consider making a costs or preparation time order.[2] In practice tribunals almost never consider such an order unless an application is made.

11.6   Applications are usually made, if at all, after the decision is announced, and are usually decided immediately.[3] This means that a claimant who intends to make a costs application, or who fears that a costs application may be made by the respondent, should go to the substantive hearing equipped with all the information that he or she needs to support or, as the case may be, resist the application.

When to apply for costs or a preparation time order

11.7   Before the 2004 rules came into force, the costs regime was heavily weighted in favour of parties – more often than not respondents – who were paying for legal representation: only costs actually incurred could be recovered. The introduction of preparation time orders does not completely redress the balance, but it is likely to have the effect that successful applications by claimants become more common.[4] It should be noted that a claimant can apply for a preparation time order in respect of time spent by legal advisers who have not charged any fees.

---

1 For brevity, the term 'costs' is used in this chapter to refer to both costs and preparation time orders except where it is necessary to distinguish between them.

2 Employment Tribunals Rules of Procedure 2004 r40.

3 This should not be regarded as an absolute rule. Occasionally unexpected additional hearing days may prejudice the claimant's ability to go on paying for representation. If this is the case, and the delay is clearly the fault of the respondent, a costs application should be made straight away. The tribunal should be told that if a costs order is not made the claimant may not be able to afford to be represented at the resumed hearing. This, of course, must not be said unless it is true.

4 Employment Tribunal Service statistics for 2004–05 and 2005–06 do not give figures for preparation time orders, so it is impossible to test this assumption.

11.8   A costs application can be made by the claimant whenever the respondent has acted unreasonably, etc, or where the respondent has caused a postponement or adjournment of the hearing. In general, the application will have a greater chance of success if the claimant has previously warned the respondent that he or she considers its conduct unreasonable and is contemplating a costs application, but sometimes there will be unreasonable conduct at the hearing which the claimant has not foreseen.

11.9   Typical grounds on which a costs application might be made against a respondent include:

- insistence on running a misconceived defence, for example, that the claimant was not an employee when she very clearly was, or that there had not been a TUPE transfer when it was clear that the undertaking in which the claimant was employed had retained its identity in the hands of the transferee, or that a claimant with a prosthetic leg did not have a disability for the purposes of the Disability Discrimination Act 1995;
- refusal to agree a realistic settlement proposal;[5]
- persistent failure to provide documents or information ordered by the tribunal, or to exchange witness statements when ordered;[6]
- production of a large volume of new documentation on the day of the hearing;
- excessive requests for disclosure, further information or written answers;
- making new allegations against the claimant on the day of the hearing;
- late amendment of its response;
- abusive letters or telephone calls or attempts to intimidate the claimant into dropping the claim;[7]
- attempts to intimidate the claimant's witnesses;
- unfounded allegations against the claimant, his or her advisers or the tribunal.[8]

---

5 But see para 6.66.

6 But do not expect the tribunal to be impressed by a short delay.

7 Note that in a discrimination case this may also be an act of discrimination by way of victimisation, and could found an additional claim.

8 It is particularly helpful if the respondent makes wild accusations of bias or unfair dealing against the tribunal, or otherwise shows a disrespectful attitude to the proceedings.

Arguing for a costs or preparation time order

11.10   Sometimes the conduct in question will be a single unreasonable act, but often it will be necessary to take the tribunal through a history of the communications between the parties in order to demonstrate that the respondent has been unreasonable. If that is the case it is prudent to collate a separate bundle of documents relevant to the costs application so that the tribunal can quickly and conveniently be shown the sequence of events. This is where a history of conspicuously patient and forbearing letters on the part of the claimant comes into its own: the unreasonableness of the respondent will be displayed to much better advantage against a background of consistent courtesy on the part of the claimant. Tribunals will often be reluctant to listen to lengthy complaints about the conduct of the proceedings, so it is unwise to embark on this kind of application unless there are good grounds for it. If there are, a degree of persistence may be needed.

11.11   The fact of unreasonable, etc, conduct by one party gives the tribunal power to make a costs order in favour of the other party. Once that fact is established, however, it does not follow that the tribunal must make a costs order. Tribunals quite often make this mistake, and as this is a basis on which a costs order could be challenged on appeal it is sensible for the party seeking costs to remind the tribunal that it has a discretion once it is persuaded that it has power to award costs.

11.12   Factors that can influence the tribunal in its exercise of discretion include:

- the seriousness of the unreasonable conduct relied on;
- the degree of inconvenience and/or expense caused to the claimant;
- warnings that the claimant has given the respondent about the possibility of a costs application;
- the conduct of the party seeking costs;[9]
- the means of either party.

11.13   When it comes to an argument that the respondent's defence was misconceived, the tribunal may suggest that unless it was clear on the papers that the defence was doomed, it cannot be said to have been misconceived. This is a mistake: the point is what the respondent knew or should have known. If the employer's response to the claim and witness statements look convincing, but its witnesses when they give evidence

---

9   The tribunal will be reluctant to award costs if it feels that there is significant blame on both sides.

simply do not back what has been put in their statements, then the defence may still have been misconceived: the employer after all had access to its own witnesses before the tribunal did, and should have made sure their statements reflected what they believed to be the truth.

Preparation time orders

11.14   Although the discretion whether to make a preparation time order is expressed in the same terms and is exercised in the same way as the discretion to make a costs order, there are some features of this power that are quite distinct.

11.15   First, it should be noted that unlike a costs order, a preparation time order cannot be made in respect of the time spent by a party or his or her adviser at the hearing itself. It is difficult to understand the policy behind this: often the consequence of unreasonable conduct is that a hearing is extended. A party who is paying for legal representation may be able to recover the cost of the additional day(s) in tribunal; but a party who is representing him or herself, or is represented by an unqualified adviser (whether or not for free) will not.

11.16   Secondly, preparation time orders do not reimburse the receiving party for money spent on the preparation of a case, but for the time spent at a fixed hourly rate.[10] This has two odd effects. The first is that a party who is paying for an unqualified representative at more than £27 per hour will recover less than he or she has spent. The second is that a party who is represented for free by an unqualified adviser will recover £27 per hour for his or her adviser's preparation time. The latter will be something of a windfall for the claimant.[11]

11.17   Free advice and representation can bring a further complication. A claimant represented by an unqualified adviser will in a suitable case be able to claim for that adviser's preparation time. A claimant represented for free by a qualified lawyer will, ironically, be in a weaker position. A preparation time order is only available to a party who has not been legally represented at the hearing (or at the time the case was determined, if it was determined without a hearing). So a claimant

---

10   £26 from 6 April 2006 and by a further £1 on each subsequent 6 April, so at the time of writing £27.

11   Who may well think it appropriate to pay any money received as a result of a preparation time order in respect of time spent by an adviser acting for free to the Citizens' Advice Bureau, law centre or other advice charity in question.

who has been legally represented for free throughout cannot claim a preparation time order. However, having been represented for free, he or she has incurred no costs – so there can be no costs order either.[12] Some examples may help.

Example 1

Ann pays a considerable sum of money for advice and assistance by a solicitor with the preparation of the case, but decides that the cost of representation at the hearing is prohibitive. She will not be legally represented at the hearing, so she will be limited to a preparation time order at £27 per hour. She will be able to be awarded this in respect of the time her solicitor has spent, but at an hourly rate much lower than any solicitor is likely to charge.

Example 2

Brian is represented for free by a solicitor from his local law centre. She appears for him at the hearing. Brian cannot claim for preparation time because he has been legally represented at the time the case was determined; he cannot claim for costs because he has not incurred any: his solicitor has acted for free.

Example 3

Chris is also represented for free by the same law centre solicitor. Because his case is listed on the same day as Brian's case, she refers him to the Free Representation Unit for representation. He is represented at the hearing by a law student. Chris, not having had legal representation at the hearing, will be able to claim preparation time. He can claim £27 per hour for all the time spent by his solicitor and his FRU representative in preparing the case, even though he has not had to pay anything for the services of either.

---

12 One possible way around this is by way of conditional fee agreement (CFA), under which the claimant becomes liable to pay for the services of the advice agency if, but only if, a costs order is made. It is arguable that this does not really give the tribunal jurisdiction to make a costs order, but some tribunals have made costs orders on this basis and since the sums involved have been modest the question has not yet been made the subject of an appeal.

The amount of a costs or preparation time order

11.18   A claimant seeking a costs or preparation time order should be ready to give the tribunal clear and credible information about the costs he or she has incurred or about the time that has been spent in preparing for the hearing. This should not present any particular difficulties for claimants who are paying for legal representation and have incurred actual legal costs, but claimants who are either representing them-selves or being represented for free are likely to have difficulty quantifying the time spent unless they and/or their advisers have kept a running note of this.

Resisting a costs or preparation time order

Misconceived ground

11.19   If the respondent applies for costs on the basis that the claim was misconceived, this will normally rely on the definition of misconceived as including 'having no reasonable prospect of success'. The claimant should argue that her claim was not misconceived unless at some point before the hearing she knew or should have known that her case had no reasonable prospect of success. The fact that the claim has failed is not enough: it needs to have been doomed to failure, and evidently so, before the tribunal should find that it was misconceived. It may be helpful to remind the tribunal that it would have been open to the respondent to invite the tribunal to list the case for a pre-hearing review and order the claimant to pay a deposit under rule 20 if it considered that the case was self-evidently hopeless. If the respondent did not do this, then its assertion now that the case was misconceived may be opportunistic.

Refusal of a settlement offer

11.20   If the respondent applies for costs on the strength of a previous offer of settlement headed 'without prejudice save as to costs', the claimant may be assisted by *Kopel v Safeway Stores plc* which makes it clear that claimants in the employment tribunal will not be penalised in costs merely for failing to do better after a hearing than they could have done by accepting an offer of settlement.[13] Failing to predict the tri-

13   [2003] IRLR 753.

bunal's award accurately should not be regarded as unreasonable in itself; refusing an offer of the maximum the tribunal could reasonably be expected to award may well be.

Postponement or adjournment

11.21 The power to award costs of a postponement or adjournment is confined to the cost of the additional work required by reason of the postponement or adjournment. A party resisting a costs order should take a sceptical view of the additional costs caused by a postponement: the obvious consequence of a postponement is that preparation for the hearing has been done early, but it does not necessarily follow that additional preparation has to be done. It is different of course if the case is adjourned after parties and lawyers have arrived at the hearing: then, inevitably, there will be additional costs.

The claimant's means

11.22 Tribunals have power to take the paying party's means into account when deciding whether and if so at what level to make a costs order.[14] It follows that claimants who think there is a significant risk of a costs order against them should go to the tribunal with evidence about their income and expenses.

The respondent's choice of representation

11.23 If the respondent argues before the hearing that the applicant's case is misconceived, and/or the applicant's total award cannot exceed a certain modest sum that is being offered by way of settlement, then a real question may arise whether it made sense for them to instruct solicitors at all. If the respondent has chosen to instruct City solicitors at £250 or £350 an hour and specialist counsel at £800 or £1,000 per hearing day on a case which, it says, never had any real chance of success, it can quite sensibly and properly be suggested by the claimant that the respondent's choice of legal adviser is disproportionate. The employment tribunals are after all designed to be accessible to lay people. If the respondent takes the view that a case had no reasonable prospect of success or was incapable of resulting in an award of more

---

14 Rules 41(2) and 45(3).

than £1,000 or so, then a fair question is: 'Why did you need a team of highly paid specialist lawyers? Why could a personnel officer not deal with this?'[15]

Changing the judgment

11.24   There are three ways that a judgment can be changed or altered after it has been sent out to the parties.

11.25   For minor clerical or uncontroversial arithmetic errors, a certificate of correction should be requested from the chairman who heard the case.[16] Curiously, there is no time limit for applying for a certificate of correction.

11.26   Where there is reason to ask the tribunal that decided the case to look again at its decision – because new evidence has become available, for example, or because one party was unaware of the date of the hearing – then an application should be made to the same tribunal to review its decision. Where the tribunal has made an error of law in coming to its decision, there is a right of appeal to the Employment Appeal Tribunal: see chapters 12 and 13 below.

Applying for a certificate of correction

11.27   All that is required is a letter to the tribunal explaining the error and making the request.

---

15   And if it took highly paid legal advisers to tell them that, the next question is, 'Why did your lawyers not advise you to dispense with their services at an early stage?'

16   Rule 37.

P11.27 Letter applying for a certificate of correction

The Regional Secretary
London Central Employment Tribunal
Ground floor, Victory House
30-34 Kingsway
London
WC2B 6EX

10 January 2008

Dear Madam

Rajiv Menon v Squeaky Cleaners Ltd

I should be grateful if you would put before Mr Ruby, who heard this case on 20-23 November 2007, my request for a certificate of correction. The judgment reads at paragraph 2 'the respondent is ordered to pay the claimant £57.65.' It is clear from the rest of the judgment and the reasons that the correct sum is £57,653.34. £10,000 is awarded for injury to feelings (see paragraph 46 of the written reasons) and £47,653.34 for lost earnings (see paragraph 49 of the written reasons).

Yours faithfully

Natalie Cummings

Applying for a review of a decision[17]

11.28 There are limited grounds on which it is possible to ask the tribunal to review certain kinds of decision – that is, to look again at the decision and decide whether to revoke or vary it. Judgments (the final outcome of the case or part of the case) or a decision not to accept a claim or a response can be reviewed. Case management orders cannot. Although the tribunal can, and from time to time does, make a new case management order that overrides the old one.

---

17 See also ETP3 19.9-19.41.

11.29   The grounds for review are set out at rule 34(3), and they are:

(a) the decision was wrongly made as a result of an administrative error;

(b) a party did not receive notice of the proceedings leading to the decision;

(c) the decision was made in the absence of a party;

(d) new evidence has become available since the conclusion of the hearing to which the decision relates, provided that its existence could not have been reasonably known of or foreseen at the time;

(e) the interests of justice require such a review.

11.30   When an application for review is received by the tribunal, the chairman who heard the case will decide whether or not to hold a review hearing. There will be no hearing if the chairman considers that there are no grounds for the decision to be reviewed, or that there is no reasonable prospect of the decision being varied or revoked.

11.31   If the chairman decides to grant a review hearing, the review will, if practicable, be heard by the original tribunal. It can be seen from this that a review is essentially a request to the same tribunal to think again about the case, so it will rarely be useful to apply for a review unless there is a real possibility that the tribunal might change its mind. Some examples of situations in which it might be sensible to apply for review are:

Example 1
The claimant did not receive notice of the hearing, and the case was dismissed in her absence. At a review application she would need to satisfy the tribunal that she genuinely did not receive the notice of hearing. That will be easiest if the tribunal's file shows that it was wrongly addressed, but a claimant in this position should not assume that she will be disbelieved if the problem is simply that some of her post went astray. If she does persuade the tribunal that she genuinely did not receive the notice of hearing, the tribunal should revoke its decision and list the case for a new hearing date.

Example 2
The claimant failed to attend the hearing, although he knew when it was, for urgent and compelling reasons. If the claimant did not explain his absence at the time, his reasons for that failure would have to be very compelling indeed. A serious accident

on the way to the tribunal should be sufficient, for example, or a call to attend hospital to be with a seriously injured spouse or child.

Example 3
The claimant was dismissed for redundancy. She argued at the hearing that there was no genuine redundancy situation, but her employer had not replaced her and the tribunal accepted that her post was redundant. A few days after the hearing she heard saw her old job advertised in the local paper. Here there is new evidence – which was not available at the time of the hearing – which gives the tribunal reason to reassess its conclusion that the redundancy was genuine.

Example 4
The claimant, who was unrepresented at the time, received a letter from the respondent's solicitors saying that his claim was misconceived and they would apply for costs of up to £10,000 against him. He withdrew his claim and it was subsequently dismissed by the tribunal on the respondent's application. A week or two later, the claimant was advised that his case had been strong and there were no grounds on which the respondent could have realistically applied for costs. This would be an application on the grounds that 'the interests of justice require such a review.' If the tribunal refused a review, that decision could be appealed. It is important to note here that the review application is a necessary first step, even if an appeal then follows. This is because the original decision dismissing the case on withdrawal cannot be said to be in any way in error: at the time it was made, it was the only sensible thing the tribunal could do. The only decision of the tribunal's that is open to attack by way of appeal is the refusal to review their original decision in light of new information.

11.32 An application for review must be made within 14 days of the date when the decision was sent to the parties. The application for review should spell out which of the grounds listed at rule 34 are relied upon. See overleaf.

P11.32 Application for review of a decision

The Regional Secretary
London Central Employment Tribunal
Ground floor, Victory House
30-34 Kingsway
London WC2B 6EX

17 November 2006

Dear Madam

Mike Allen v ADAL Ltd
I should be grateful if you would put before Mr Colt, who heard this case, my application for a review of the tribunal's decision of 9 October 2006 under rule 34 of the tribunal Rules of Procedure on the grounds that:

(i) new evidence has become available since the hearing which was not available, and could not have been foreseen, at the time of the hearing; and

(ii) the interests of justice require a review.

The claim was of unfair dismissal. The respondent had dismissed Mr Allen, giving redundancy as the reason and alleging a downturn in business that forced them to reduce their staff costs. Mr Allen alleged that his post was not genuinely redundant, and that the real reason for his dismissal was that there had been personal friction between him and his manager.

The tribunal's decision recorded that the evidence of a downturn in business was equivocal, but (at paragraph 24) that it was clear that the respondent had reduced its management team by one with a cost saving of some £57,000 per year. On the basis of this the tribunal accepted that there had been a genuine redundancy situation, and proceeded to find that Mr Allen's selection for redundancy had been fair.

On 12 November Mr Allen received anonymously in the post a copy of an advertisement in the Sutton Echo for an 'Engineering Process Manager.' I enclose a copy. The post appears to be Mr Allen's old job.
I suggest that in light of this new evidence there are grounds for a concern that the tribunal may have been materially misled by the respondent as to the reason for Mr Allen's dismissal.

Yours faithfully

Natalie Cummings

Review and appeal

11.33   If a decision contains an error of law it can be appealed. The process of appealing is dealt with in the next two chapters.

11.34   It is rarely, if ever, appropriate to raise errors of law by way of application for review. However, there will sometimes be borderline cases where it is difficult to decide whether to ask the tribunal to review its own decision, or to appeal the decision to the Employment Appeal Tribunal. In these cases, the best course is to do both, but to inform the EAT of the review application and ask it not to take any action on the appeal until the review has been determined. Alternatively a review application can be made at once and a decision on appeal postponed in the hope that the review application will be decided by the time the time for appealing expires. If this course is chosen, however, great care must be taken to ensure that the appeal deadline does not slip by before the review application is decided.

CHAPTER 12

Appealing to the EAT: preliminary matters and the notice of appeal

Introduction

12.1 A party that is dissatisfied with the decision of an employment tribunal may appeal, on a question of law only, to the Employment Appeal Tribunal (EAT). This chapter explains what kind of appeal the EAT will hear, how to go about starting an appeal, and what to do to prepare for the hearing. Chapter 13 deals with the hearing itself.

Terminology

12.2 The party who appeals to the Employment Appeal Tribunal (EAT) is technically known as the appellant, and the other party is the respondent (that is, the party who responds) to the appeal. This can get confusing, because the respondent to the appeal is not necessarily the same person as the respondent to the original claim: if the employer (who was the respondent at the employment tribunal) appeals to the EAT, the former employer is now the appellant and the employee becomes the respondent.[1] For this reason, the EAT usually prefers that in argument the parties should stick to the terms used before the employment tribunal and refer to the employee as the claimant and the employer as the respondent, even if the appeal is brought by the employer.

12.3 In a book of this nature (as opposed to in a particular case) it is sometimes necessary to generalise about what is required of those who are challenging the decision of the tribunal, and those who are seeking to uphold it, so that approach is not followed here. In this chapter, the term 'appellant' is used to refer to the party who is challenging the employment tribunal's decision, and the term 'respondent' to refer to the party (even if the employee) who is seeking to uphold the tribunal's decision. In the precedents, the parties are either referred to by name, or as 'the employee' and 'the employer' or 'the company', 'the hospital', etc.

---

1   The plot thickens again if the appeal is allowed, and the respondent to the appeal – that is, the claimant as was – appeals to the Court of Appeal. Then the claimant, who was the respondent at the EAT is now the appellant, and the respondent, who was the appellant at the EAT, is now the respondent again.

Public funding

12.4   It is important to note as a preliminary that public funding is available in theory for representation at appeals to the EAT. Claimants who are thinking of appealing and are not earning or are on a low wage may wish to consult a law centre or solicitors with a Legal Services Commission contract for employment work to find out whether they are eligible. However, the sums of money involved in employment cases are often too small to justify public funding even where the claimant is financially eligible, so many claimants will be on their own at this stage too. The Employment Appeal Tribunal is, like employment tribunals, very used to dealing with non-lawyers.

Free representation before the Employment Appeal Tribunal

12.5   The factors governing the availability of free representation operate differently at the level of the EAT than at first instance, and claimants who cannot afford to pay for representation will have a better chance of finding someone to act for free if they understand a certain amount about how this works.

12.6   There are two significant factors. The first is that appeals are normally much shorter than employment tribunal hearings. This is because, except in very unusual cases, no witnesses will be heard, and because the questions on which the EAT will hear an appeal are narrowly defined. Appeals only rarely last more than a day, and a large proportion will be completed in half a day or less. This also means that preparation for an EAT case is normally much lighter than for a first instance case: witnesses do not have to be interviewed, statements do not have to be prepared, documents do not have to be requested and disclosed, the hearing bundle will be much shorter and so on. This means that offering free representation on an appeal is less daunting in terms of work for the lawyer who makes the offer.[2]

2   Especially for someone who is acting for free in the sense that they themselves are doing the work for no pay – this is a distinction that may be lost on the client, who does not pay in either event, but it can be useful to be aware of it. A lawyer working full time for a legal charity that provides free representation is normally paid a salary. A lay adviser at a Citizens' Advice Bureau (CAB), a Free Representation Unit (FRU) volunteer or a barrister acting for no fee ('pro bono' as barristers and solicitors still call it) is giving his time for nothing, so the longer the case takes the more time he loses from paid work.

12.7   The other factor is double-edged. This is that appearances before the EAT, which is the next step up the legal hierarchy, tends to be regarded by representatives both as more interesting and more intimidating than appearing in the employment tribunals. Hearings are often presided over by High Court judges, and proceedings are superficially more formal. Some advisers who conduct cases routinely and skilfully in the employment tribunals simply lack the confidence to appear at the EAT and may be unwilling to take cases to appeal because they feel (although unqualified advisers are allowed to appear there and often do) that the EAT is the preserve of barristers and solicitors. The other side to this, however, is that many advocates will be more willing to take on appeals for free because they provide valuable – and comparatively rare – experience.

12.8   Both of these factors mean that a claimant who has failed to secure free representation at first instance from a local legal charity or other body should not assume for that reason that he will be refused help with an appeal. It is worth asking again at this stage, especially if the appeal raises a question that could be of general importance to other claimants in the future.

12.9   It is worth mentioning two specific sources of free representation at the EAT, both of which tend to find it easier to help at this stage than at first instance. One is the Free Representation Unit (FRU), and the other is the Bar Pro Bono Unit. Both organisations are London-based, and part of the reason they are more likely to be able to help with appeals is the simple geographical fact that the EAT for the whole of England and Wales has its hearings in London.

12.10   Claimants who live or work(ed) in greater London will often be able to be referred to FRU direct from their local Citizens Advice Bureau (CAB) or law centre. Claimants from outside London will have a harder task, but as the EAT in London deals with appeals from the whole of England and Wales, FRU will accept referrals on appeal for claimants from elsewhere in the country provided the referral comes from a registered FRU referral agency. The best bet for claimants outside London is to ask their local CAB to speak to FRU.

12.11   The Bar Pro Bono Unit applies more stringent tests than FRU on the question whether a client is able to afford to pay for representation, and on the merits of the case, so to maximise chances of an offer of representation it is sensible to make parallel applications to both organisations. Once an offer of representation from one has been accepted, the other should be informed immediately. Although FRU volunteers are mostly still in training and BPBU refers cases only to qualified barristers, FRU volunteers have the benefit of specialisation (and specialist support), whereas most junior barristers are generalists. Because of this, it is not possible to make reliable predictions about which organisation will provide a higher quality service. Neither FRU nor the BPBU can ever guarantee to provide representation for every case they accept: both are dependent on the availability of a suitable volunteer on the particular day.

12.12   A third source of free representation is called the Employment Lawyers Appeals Advice Scheme (ELAAS). This cannot be directly accessed by claimants and is not guaranteed, and for that reason should probably – although the quality of the representation is usually very high – be treated as a last resort. Where there is a preliminary hearing (as to which, see para 11.34 below), litigants who have no representative on record with the EAT as acting for them may be offered the assistance of an ELAAS adviser. The ELAAS adviser will be at the EAT on the day to advise and represent if appropriate. he will have had the papers a few days in advance, but will not be able to meet the client before the day of the hearing and will not be able to take on conduct of the case. If the case then goes forward to a full hearing, there should be an opportunity to be referred to FRU and/or the Bar Pro Bono Unit at this point also.

12.13   The greater availability of free representation in the EAT, compared with the tribunal, means that it can be a useful indicator of the strength of the appeal. At the tribunal level a failure to get free representation only means that there are many more cases than there is help available. At the EAT, if serious efforts have been made to find free representation without success, this is more likely to indicate that the appeal is not a strong one. There are certainly exceptions to the rule, but, in general, reasonably arguable EAT cases are easy to find representation for.[3]

---

3   This is particularly true of FRU, where the volunteers are at the beginning of their careers and eager to gain experience at this level.

The Employment Appeal Tribunal's composition and powers

12.14   The EAT is governed by the Employment Appeal Tribunal Rules 1993 as amended in 2001 and 2004.[4] An updated version of the rules is available on the EAT website.[5] A practice direction – giving more detailed instructions on how to run an appeal – was issued in December 2004. A copy of this will be sent to anyone who presents an appeal.[6] Again, it is a good idea for anyone embarking on an appeal to the EAT to take 20 minutes or so to read through the current rules and practice direction so as to have an idea, in broad outline, of how the process works and where to find specific powers.

12.15   The EAT is composed in a similar way to an employment tribunal, with a judge supported by two lay members, one with a background in the trade union movement and the other having management experience. The presiding judge will be either a circuit judge or a High Court judge with employment law experience.

What kind of appeal will the EAT hear?

12.16   Tribunals delivered judgments on approximately 40,000 claims in 2005–06.[7] This suggests that at least 40,000 parties were unhappy with tribunal decisions in this period. Yet only 555 cases reached full hearings in the EAT. This is because the right to appeal to the EAT is a narrow and limited one. It is not a right to challenge any part of the first decision that a party was unhappy with. Instead the EAT will hear appeals only on questions of law. To appeal, a party must identify an error of law. Unfortunately it is far from obvious what this means.

12.17   To understand what the EAT will and will not do, it is more helpful to understand why the EAT is confident that it knows best on certain kinds of questions, and why on others it has a strong inclination to defer to the employment tribunal. The point that disappointed claimants often find difficult to understand is that there is built in to the system an acceptance that tribunals will sometimes get the wrong answer, and

4   SI No 2854.
5   www.employmentappeals.gov.uk
6   It is also available on the EAT website.
7   Employment Tribunals Annual Report 2005–06.

this will not always be able to be corrected. Justice is not always done in the employment tribunals, any more than in any other court.

12.18   If there is a disagreement between the EAT and the employment tribunal about what the law is – what a certain provision in the legislation means, for example, or what is the effect of previous decisions of the EAT or higher courts – then the EAT will impose its own view. The law is to be found in legislation and law reports, and the EAT has equal access to these materials and, as the senior judicial body, can interpret them more authoritatively.

12.19   When it comes to deciding which witnesses are telling the truth, whether one party or another has acted fairly or reasonably, or exercising a discretion about what it is just to do in all the circumstances, however, the EAT is at a disadvantage. The employment tribunal has heard the witnesses give their evidence: it has observed their demeanour when they were questioned, it has heard their hesitations and their tone of voice, it has had various opportunities to judge their character. It also has access to a great wealth of nuance in the case that the EAT – which, except in very rare cases, does not hear witnesses at all, and will certainly not have heard all the evidence that the tribunal has heard – lacks. It will have built up, from hearing the evidence of countless employees, managers, personnel officers, etc, in other cases, a broad experience and 'feel' for how employers and employees behave and how it is reasonable to expect them to behave. It is altogether closer to the 'coal face' than the EAT.

12.20   For these reasons, the EAT approaches decisions of the employment tribunal in the latter category with great deference, and will not interfere unless they are very clearly wrong.

Perversity

12.21   To attack a finding of fact it will be necessary to show that there was no evidence at all to support the finding, or that the evidence was so thin and implausible that no reasonable tribunal could have accepted it.[8] To attack an inference or an exercise of discretion, it will need to be shown that no reasonable tribunal could have drawn that inference or exercised the discretion in that way: in other words, that the decision was 'perverse'.

---

8   It must be remembered that evidence includes what witnesses have said. A common error among non-lawyers is to say: 'So-and-so said such-and-such, but there was no evidence.' That a witness has said it is in itself evidence.

12.22   This is a tough test, and successful perversity appeals are rare. This is often hard for claimants to accept. The outcome that tends to make a claimant feel most aggrieved is having been disbelieved when he has told the truth. Losing on a legal technicality may well be less painful. Unfortunately it is the legal technicality that is likely to be appealable, and the tribunal's wrong assessment of the truthfulness of the witnesses that will not. Perversity appeals are unpopular with the EAT and very few of them succeed.

Bias appeals

12.23   The only ground of appeal less popular with the EAT than perversity is bias. This places two demands on the claimant or adviser. The first is to approach the question whether to appeal on grounds of bias with great caution. Bias should never be inferred simply from the result. If the claimant's reasoning amounts to 'They found against me when I was clearly right so they must have been biased', then an appeal on grounds of bias should not be attempted. More often, the claimant's perception that the tribunal was biased will be based on the tribunal's manner in conducting the hearing, subtle differences in the way the tribunal addressed counsel for the respondent and the claimant or his representative, hostile body language, signs of boredom or exasperation when the claimant was speaking and so on. These impressions may be compelling at the time, and they may in fact be justified. They are also an extremely difficult basis for an appeal: there will be no record of them, the tribunal and the respondent will almost certainly deny that anything was amiss. A detailed analysis of the tribunal's body language will be more likely to convince the EAT that the claimant is paranoid than that the tribunal was biased. It is almost never advisable to pursue an appeal on such grounds.

12.24   On the other hand, there will sometimes be real – and demonstrable – grounds to complain of bias, and here it will be necessary to face down the EAT's reluctance to entertain or allow an appeal on this basis. If the bias allegation is based on what a member of the tribunal said in the course of the hearing, then it will be very difficult to proceed unless either the other party or the tribunal, or both, agree what was said. This places an emphasis on note-taking at the hearing. If something is said that appears to indicate bias, the best course is to write it down and then immediately read back the note of what was said and ask the tribunal to confirm that the note is accurate; and to make a note too that that confirmation was received. This will make it very difficult for the tribunal or the other party to deny subsequently that the offending remark was made.

12.25   It will very rarely be possible to deduce bias from the decision itself, but tribunals do occasionally betray a fixed unwillingness to contemplate the possibility that a respondent witness could have lied simply because of his status or importance in the employer organisation. In these cases it may well be possible – and if it is possible, it will normally be preferable – to put the appeal on grounds of perversity, or failure adequately to explain the decision.

12.26   There are specific rules at paragraph 11 of the EAT Practice Direction 2004 as to the procedures that will be followed if an allegation of bias or other improper conduct of a hearing is to be made. Any claimant basing an appeal on such grounds must take care to follow these. There is a warning at paragraph 11.6.3 that unsuccessful pursuit of such an appeal may put the appellant at risk of an order for costs, but it should be remembered that the EAT's power to award costs is limited.

12.27   By rule 34A of the Employment Appeal Tribunal Rules 1993, the EAT may make a costs order where it appears that 'any proceedings brought by the paying party were unnecessary, improper or vexatious or misconceived or that there has been unreasonable delay or other unreasonable conduct in the bringing or conducting of proceedings by the paying party.' In practice the EAT rarely makes costs awards and they are rarely a serious risk except in bias cases. The EAT will see an accusation of bias as a serious allegation and one should not be made without evidence. However, it is not unreasonable or improper, without more, to bring an ultimately unsuccessful bias appeal.

Appeals on preliminary or procedural matters

12.28   It is not just final decisions of the employment tribunal that are open to appeal: sometimes the claimant may wish to appeal a decision of the tribunal on a preliminary point, or on procedural matters. The latter are often referred to as 'interlocutory' decisions, and an 'interlocutory appeal' is an appeal on this kind of matter. The following are some examples of each kind of decisions that a claimant might wish to appeal.

Preliminary substantive decisions[9]

12.29
- a decision that the claimant was not an employee and the tribunal therefore lacks jurisdiction;
- a decision that a complaint was not presented in time;
- a refusal to extend time for a complaint;
- a decision that the claimant does not have sufficient continuous service to complain of unfair dismissal;
- a decision that the claimant was not disabled within the meaning of the Disability Discrimination Act 1995.

12.30 These are all substantive decisions that can be appealed in the same way as final decisions after a full hearing. No special considerations apply to them, except that it is important that if any of these preliminary issues is heard first, and full hearing of some part of the claim follows some weeks or months later, any appeal against the preliminary decision must be started within 42 days of promulgation of that judgment.

Interlocutory decisions

12.31
- a refusal to permit the claimant to amend the claim;
- a decision to permit the respondent to present a late response;
- a decision to permit the respondent to amend the response;
- a refusal to postpone a hearing;[10]
- a refusal to order the respondent to provide written answers, further information or disclosure of particular documents;
- a refusal to make adjustments to arrangements for the hearing for the benefit of a disabled claimant;
- a refusal to order the attendance of a witness;
- a refusal to strike out the employer's response;
- a refusal to give a direction for expert evidence;

---

9 See glossary.
10 It will almost never be practicable to appeal a decision to postpone, partly because by the time the appeal is heard the original hearing date will be lost, and partly because a decision to postpone can be annoying for a claimant but will very rarely significantly damage his prospects of success; a refusal to postpone, on the other hand, may deprive a party of representation or of the evidence of a particular witness.

- a refusal to hear argument on a procedural application on a particular occasion;
- a decision to conduct a hearing in private, or not to.

12.32 These kinds of decisions are difficult to appeal because of the broad discretion that the tribunal has to manage the procedural aspects of the case. The EAT will not interfere just because it considers that it would have exercised any discretion differently: again, it will have to be persuaded that the tribunal's approach demonstrates an error of law.

12.33 There are three typical directions of attack on a decision of this nature. The first is that the tribunal did not accept that it had power to do what it was asked to do at all: here the ground of appeal is not that the tribunal exercised its discretion wrongly, but that it did not exercise it at all because it did not believe that it had a discretion to exercise. Suppose, for example, the claimant points out that there is a witness employed by the respondent who has highly relevant evidence and from whom the tribunal may wish to hear, and invites the tribunal to call the witness and make him or her available for cross-examination by either side. If the tribunal's response is that it considers that this will extend proceedings and it does not believe it is necessary or proportionate, it will be difficult to attack that decision on appeal. If, on the other hand, the tribunal's response is to say that it is for the parties to call witnesses and the tribunal has no power to do what has been asked, then this is a clear error of law and the tribunal has not exercised the discretion that it undoubtedly had.

12.34 The second and third kinds of attack are closely related. One is that the tribunal has exercised its discretion without taking account of all relevant considerations, and the other is that the tribunal's decision has been influenced by some irrelevant consideration. Suppose, for example, the claimant has requested a postponement because her law centre adviser is unable to attend on the day fixed for the hearing, and the tribunal explains its refusal to postpone on the basis that it is not usual to list cases to suit the availability of professional legal representatives. The claimant may found an appeal on the fact that the tribunal has failed to take into account the relevant consideration that he is not paying for her representation and therefore cannot necessarily substitute a different professional representative.[11]

12.35 For an example of a procedural decision based on an irrelevant consideration, suppose the tribunal decides to conduct a hearing in private because one of the respondent's witnesses is a high-ranking

11 See para 8.9 above.

public servant who will be cross-examined about allegations of serious misconduct against him. The status of the respondent's witnesses and the gravity of any allegations against them are both irrelevant to the question whether the hearing should take place in public, so the claimant will be able to attack this decision on the basis that an irrelevant matter has been taken into consideration by the tribunal.

Points not argued below

12.36   The EAT will not as a rule entertain arguments that were not put to the employment tribunal.[12] In situations where the new point would require additional findings of fact which the tribunal could have made if the point had been raised at first instance, the justice of this is apparent. If, for example, a complaint of constructive unfair dismissal succeeds, but on appeal the employer seeks to raise for the first time an allegation that the claimant had affirmed his contract by waiting several weeks after the breach before resigning, the EAT will rightly refuse to hear the appeal. If the employer had said earlier that the claimant had affirmed, the tribunal could have made findings on whether the delay amounted to affirmation in the circumstances. An appeal is not intended to give either party the chance to reformulate their case in the light of experience and then have a second and better-informed bite at the cherry. If on the other hand the tribunal simply makes a spontaneous error of law in the course of its decision against which the losing party did not think to give it specific warning, it is much harder to see why the decision should be immune from appeal.

12.37   The EAT's practice in this kind of situation is inconsistent. If the error is clear enough and does not arise from the appellant's failure to formulate his case properly, the question 'was this argued below?' may well be overlooked. The result is that it is often difficult even for experienced lawyers to predict in advance which appeals will fall foul of this rule and which will not.[13] This underlines, however, the usefulness of presenting the tribunal that hears the case at first instance with written submissions so that there can be no subsequent doubt about what points were taken then. It also means that parties must be careful that their written submissions cover all the relevant points.

12   See *Kumchyk v Derby City Council* [1978] ICR 1116.
13   A cynic might say that the rule is most accurately stated thus: the EAT does not entertain arguments that have not been put to the employment tribunal unless it feels like it.

Starting an appeal

12.38   The document that starts an appeal to the EAT is the notice of appeal. This must be received by the EAT within 42 days of the date when the written record of the decision, direction or order which is appealed was sent to the parties, together with the written record of the decision and written reasons for it and the original claim and response. It is essential that all of these documents are included with the notice of appeal: the EAT takes a rigorous approach to incomplete appeals, and an appeal from which one of the required documents has been omitted will not be accepted. If the missing document is provided even one day late the appeal will be deemed out of time.[14] If any documents are unavoidably missing, explain why.

12.39   It is preferable, if possible, to draft and send the skeleton argument at this stage. The reason for this is that the process of writing a skeleton argument will very often help the appellant to clarify the issues and the arguments in his own mind. The best way to find out whether an argument is convincing is to write it all down in order. If the appellant finds that by the time he has finished writing his skeleton, he has not even persuaded himself of the merit of a particular ground of appeal, there is probably not much in that ground and it will be best to drop it. On the other hand, in the process of writing down the argument for another ground, the appellant may realise that it is better put as two separate errors rather than one. Often the best way of approaching the task will be to start with the skeleton argument, and then edit the same document to create the (much shorter) notice of appeal.

12.40   This covering letter enclosing a notice of appeal is intended to double as a check-list for the documents that need to be included.

14   See *Gdynia America Shipping Lines Ltd v Chelminski* [2004] IRLR 725 and *Kanapathiar v Harrow LBC* [2003] IRLR 571.

P12.41 Covering letter enclosing an appeal to the EAT

The Registrar
Employment Appeal Tribunal
Audit House
58 Victoria Embankment
London EC4Y 0DS

Fax 020 7273 1045

13 September 2007

Dear Madam

Yasmin Creasey v Bristol Advocacy Project

I enclose the following:

☑ Notice of appeal

☑ Judgment of the employment tribunal

☑ Written reasons for the decision of the employment tribunal

☑ Claim form (ET1)

☑ Response (ET3)

Yours faithfully

Natalie Cummings

Drafting the notice of appeal

12.41 The standard form for an appeal to the EAT is to be found at the schedule to the EAT Rules or on the EAT website.[15] Unlike form ET1, it is a simple form that can easily be typed out. It looks like this:

15 www.employmentappeals.gov.uk

1. The appellant is *(name and address of appellant)*.
2. Any communication relating to this appeal may be sent to the appellant at *(appellant's address for service, including telephone number if any)*.
3. The appellant appeals from *(here give particulars of the decision of the employment tribunal from which the appeal is brought including the date)*.
4. The parties to the proceedings before the employment tribunal, other than the appellant, were *(names and addresses of other parties to the proceedings resulting in judgment, decision or order appealed from)*.
5. Copies of

    (a) the written record of the employment tribunal's judgment, decision or order and the written reasons of the employment tribunal;
    (b) the claim (ET1);
    (c) the response (ET3); and/or (where relevant)
    (d) an explanation as to why any of these documents are not included;

    are attached to this notice.

6. If the appellant has made an application to the employment tribunal for a review of its judgment or decision, copies of

    (a) the review application;
    (b) the judgment;
    (c) the written reasons of the employment tribunal in respect of that review application; and/or
    (d) a statement by or on behalf of the appellant, if such be the case, that a judgment is awaited;

    are attached to this notice. If any of these documents exist but cannot be included, then a written explanation must be given.

7. The grounds upon which this appeal is brought are that the employment tribunal erred in law in that *(here set out in paragraphs the various grounds of appeal)*.

12.42   Item 7 is the difficult part. The grounds of appeal should be carefully drafted: they will often be the first thing that the EAT judge will read, and the basis on which he decides whether or not the case can go ahead to a hearing. Sometimes it will be sufficient simply to put the error of law complained of in two or three concise sentences; in more complex cases it may be necessary to outline the factual background and summarise the tribunal's decision in order to put the errors alleged in context. Both approaches are illustrated here.

12.43   The most important single piece of advice that can be offered on drafting a notice of appeal is to keep it as focused as possible. Tribunals are far from perfect and they often make mistakes, but they rarely make a very large number of different mistakes in a single decision. Any temptation to 'pad' the notice of appeal by expressing what is essentially one ground of appeal in several different ways should be resisted. There is nothing wrong with a notice of appeal that complains of one error only. A rambling 10 page notice of appeal that complains of 14 separate counts of perversity will make an EAT judge feel tired from the outset. He is also likely to think that if the appeal has that many points, none of them is likely to be very good.

12.44   The notice of appeal should normally be a self-contained document that is sufficient, read on its own, to tell the EAT what the case was about, what the employment tribunal decided, and why the appellant says that that is wrong. The EAT judges may sometimes skim or even skip the claimant's account of the facts because they have started by reading the employment tribunal's decision which also sets out the facts. Nevertheless it is suggested that it is best to include it. Employment tribunal decisions vary greatly in quality, and sometimes the account of the facts will be unclear, inadequate or misleading.

12.45   Where the appellant sets out the factual background in the notice of appeal (or for that matter the skeleton argument), he should make it clear which assertions are uncontroversial and which are or were matters of dispute between the parties. If the notice of appeal is at all long, it is helpful to divide it into sections under different headings. However short it is, it should be divided into numbered paragraphs. Here as in any other kind of writing 'a paragraph per idea' is a good rule to follow. Long paragraphs that deal with several different subjects are very difficult to read.

P12.45.1 Short notice of appeal

IN THE EMPLOYMENT APPEAL TRIBUNAL   Case No EAT/
BETWEEN

MRS YASMIN CREASEY

Appellant

and

BRISTOL ADVOCACY PROJECT

Respondent

NOTICE OF APPEAL
---

1. The appellant is Mrs Yasmin Creasey.

2. Any communication relating to this appeal may be sent to the
    appellant at the North London Law Centre, 14 Border Street.
    Shoreditch, London EC2A 1AB, tel: 020 7123 1234.

3. The appellant appeals from the decision of the employment tribu-
    nal sitting at Bristol on 9 August 2004 to dismiss her complaint of sex
    discrimination.

4. The other party to the proceedings before the employment tribunal
    was the Bristol Advocacy Project, 14 Tavistock Rd, Clifton, Bristol.

5. A copy of the employment tribunal's judgment ~~or order~~ and of the
    written reasons or it, and of the claim and response, ~~direction or
    order~~ are attached to this notice.

6. The grounds upon which this appeal is brought are that the
    employment tribunal erred in law in that:
    (a) It failed to address the question of whether the abbreviation
        of the appellant's probationary period by reason of her
        absence on maternity leave constituted a detriment, and if so,
        whether this was a detriment to which the appellant was
        subjected on grounds of her sex.

(b) The appellant asks the Appeal Tribunal to find that the abbreviation of the appellant's probationary period by reason of her absence on maternity leave was a detriment to which she was subjected on grounds of her sex, and to remit the case to the same tribunal for a further remedy hearing on that element of her complaint.

Natalie Cummings
NORTH LONDON LAW CENTRE
13 September 2007

DOCUMENT OUTLINE: Long notice of appeal

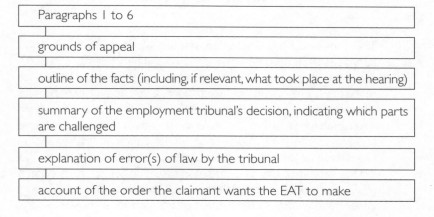

Paragraphs 1 to 6
grounds of appeal
outline of the facts (including, if relevant, what took place at the hearing)
summary of the employment tribunal's decision, indicating which parts are challenged
explanation of error(s) of law by the tribunal
account of the order the claimant wants the EAT to make

P12.45.2 Long notice of appeal

IN THE EMPLOYMENT APPEAL TRIBUNAL   Case No EAT/
BETWEEN

CLAUDIA CHAMPION

Appellant

and

MINISTRY OF TRUTH

Respondent

GROUNDS OF APPEAL

THE FACTS

1. The appellant, Miss Champion, started work in the Information Service in 1976, aged 16. Between 1976 and her resignation in 2003, she worked at various Information Units and Information Service offices in London and the South East. On 1 May 1997 she was appointed to a higher executive officer (HEO) role at the Guildford Area Manager's Office (AMO), which was housed in the same building as the Joint Information Unit's Office at Adshead Way, Guildford. The Joint Information Unit's Office employed an HEO, as did the separate AMO at Croydon. Information Service rules defined HEO as a 'mobile grade' with the result that Miss Champion could under her contract of employment be transferred to any suitable civil service post in the UK.

2. In June 2006, a reorganisation was announced in which the Croydon and Guildford AMOs would be merged at the Adshead Way site, and the Croydon AMO would close. The effect at HEO level was that three HEO posts (two at Adshead Way and one at Croydon) would be replaced by two HEOs at Adshead Way.

3. An Information Service manager, Mr James Petrie, was in general control of the reorganisation. Mr Petrie consulted affected staff about their preferred outcomes to the reorganisation, and Miss Champion reiterated her wish, which had previously been discussed with managers as a realistic medium-term career goal, to be appointed Manager of the Central London Information Unit. Because of this, Miss Champion was not appointed to either of the HEO posts in the

new structure. By September 2006 Miss Champion's existing post had disappeared without any decision having been taken about her future.

4. The question of Miss Champion's redeployment became the subject of dispute between her and the respondent, and the cause of distress to her, and on 13 September 2006 her General Practitioner signed her off work for 28 days with stress and depression. She did not return to work full time after that date.

5. Miss Champion met with Mr Petrie in October 2006. The parties are in dispute as to the content of this meeting, which is referred to below as 'the disputed meeting.' Specifically, Miss Champion says that by the end of the meeting, she had been offered no certainty of any substantive posts at any fixed time in the future. Mr Petrie says that she had been offered, and had refused, a vacant HEO post at the Guildford Strategic Information Centre.

6. Miss Champion raised a formal grievance about the manner in which the reorganisation had been handled, and resigned in April 2007 after the rejection of her appeal against the outcome of that grievance.

THE HEARING BEFORE THE EMPLOYMENT TRIBUNAL

7. Miss Champion's complaint to the tribunal focused on the respondent's treatment of her in failing to provide her with any certainty about her future when her job ceased to exist; and more specifically the respondent's failure to declare a redundancy and follow its own redundancy procedure. These same facts founded a complaint of constructive dismissal claims for damages for breach of contract and disability discrimination.

8. This appeal hinges on the treatment by the tribunal of the evidence given by Mr Petrie relating to the disputed meeting. Mr Petrie described the meeting in his witness statement, and referred to notes he had made. In his oral evidence given during the first three days of the hearing he was emphatic that he had made these notes on the same day shortly after the end of the meeting.

9. Between the third day of the hearing on 6 February and the fourth day on 29 April 2008, Miss Champion obtained an order for the disclosure of the statistics files associated with Mr Petrie's typed file-notes of the meeting. These appeared to show that the computer file in question had been created not on 19 October 2006, but at 10.17 am on 3 January 2007, not long after the first letter from Miss Champion's solicitors to the respondent.

10. Miss Champion's representative asked for Mr Petrie to be recalled to explain the discrepancy between this and his previous sworn evidence. However, when the chairman warned that there might be costs implications and the Respondent's counsel said that costs would be sought vigorously, he did not feel able to pursue the application.

THE DECISION

11. The tribunal made the following findings:

(i) Miss Champion's post had ceased to exist (page 12, para 3, [12]);

(ii) there was a vacant post at the Guildford Strategic Information Centre available for Miss Champion and (implicitly – page 11, para 8, [11]) she was aware of that;

(iii) the respondent had done its utmost to resolve Miss Champion's position despite her refusal to consider any possibility other than the Central London Information Unit Manager's post, so there was no breach of the trust and confidence term in the way they had handled the reorganisation (page 12, paras (10),(11), [12]);

(iv) Miss Champion had a disability for the purposes of the Disability Discrimination Act 1995 (page 9, para 18(2) [9]);

(v) but there was no discrimination because the failure to appoint her to a substantive post was attributable to 'the fixed attitude that she had adopted' (para 18(3), page 9, [9])

12. The decision did not address the conflict of evidence between Miss Champion and Mr Petrie as to the disputed meeting, nor did it allude to the doubt that had been cast on Mr Petrie's evidence or record any finding as to which account was accurate.

GROUNDS OF APPEAL

13. The tribunal erred in law in that:

(i) It failed to make a finding as to the content of the disputed meeting or to deal with the doubt cast on James Petrie's evidence as to the meeting. The appellant relies on *Anya v University of Oxford* [2001] EWCA Civ 405. The respondent's notice of appearance places the disputed meeting of October 2006 at the centre of its case and clearly identifies Mr Petrie as its key witness. The dispute as to the content of this meeting was central to the resolution of the case, and it was something on which the tribunal would have been obliged to express a view even if Miss Champion had not been able to produce the statistics file associated with Mr Petrie's alleged contemporaneous notes. The statistics file merely go to make the necessity for a finding on this point the more acute.

(ii) It failed to consider recalling Mr Petrie to explain his previous evidence in light of the statistics file. Rule 11(1) of the Employment Tribunals Rules of Procedure (Schedule 1 to the Employment Tribunals (Constitution and Rules of Procedure) Regulations 2001 SI No 1171) then in force provided, so far as is material:

> 'The tribunal shall make such enquiries of persons appearing before it and witnesses as it considers appropriate and shall otherwise conduct the hearing in such manner as it considers most appropriate for the clarification of the issues before it and generally to the just handling of the proceedings.'

14. When invited by Miss Champion's representative to recall Mr Petrie, the Chairman of the tribunal indicated that it was for the parties and not for the tribunal to call witnesses, and warned of possible costs consequences in insisting on recalling him. The appellant contends that the employment tribunal erred in failing to apprehend the tribunal's duty under rule 11(1) of the Rules of Procedure to make such inquiries as it considers appropriate for the clarification of the issues before it. Since the disputed evidence went to the heart of the case as put by both parties, and since serious doubt had been cast on Mr Petrie's evidence, it was incumbent on the tribunal at least to consider whether it should recall Mr Petrie of its own motion. Its insistence that it was for the parties to make an application to recall him if they wished to was a refusal to exercise a discretion that it undoubtedly had.

THE ORDER SOUGHT

15. The Appeal Tribunal will be respectfully invited to set aside the decision of the employment tribunal and remit the case for re-hearing by a differently constituted tribunal.

NATALIE CUMMINGS
NORTH LONDON LAW CENTRE
6 June 2008

The choice of order disposing of the appeal

12.46　The grounds of appeal should also specify what the claimant is asking the EAT to do.[16] This is something that requires careful thought at the outset.

12.47　　An appeal will rarely be a simple matter of win or lose: there will be various different ways in which the EAT could deal with the case. Sometimes the decision below will simply be reversed. Sometimes the EAT will hold that, contrary to the tribunal's decision, the complaint was justified – there has been discrimination, or an unauthorised deduction from pay, or unfair dismissal or whatever was the subject of the complaint – but will send the case back ('remit' it) to the tribunal for an assessment of the remedy. Sometimes the EAT will hold that the tribunal has approached one of its factual findings in the wrong way, or failed to make findings of fact that it needed to make. In that case it will almost always be necessary to remit the case to the same tribunal or a different one to make more findings of fact.[17]

12.48　　Losing an appeal outright is simpler of course: the EAT dismisses the appeal and the employment tribunal's decision or order stands.

12.49　　The range of options, and the kinds of factors that influence the EAT in deciding how to dispose of the appeal and whether to remit to the same or a different tribunal, are probably best understood in the context of some concrete examples.

> **Example 1**
> The claimant complains that she has been dismissed for using inappropriate language in the workplace. She says that male colleagues have spoken in the same way without being disciplined and she has suffered sex discrimination. Her employer's defence is that conventional standards of conduct are different for men and women, so what it has done is impose the same rule on both men and women, namely that they observe conventional standards of conduct. The tribunal accepts this argument and dismisses the claim. The claimant appeals.

16　See EAT Practice Direction 2004 para 2.4.
17　See paras 12.51–12.53 below for the choice between these options.

The EAT has no difficulty with this.[18] It holds that imposing different standards on men and women is sex discrimination and allows the appeal. However, the EAT does not hear witnesses, and the employment tribunal has made no findings about the losses that the claimant has suffered because it dismissed her claim. The EAT is not in a position to decide how much compensation to award, so it remits the case to a different tribunal to hear evidence on this and decide on the appropriate remedy.

Comment

The EAT could, here, have remitted the question of remedy to the same tribunal. The attack, superficially anyway, was only on the tribunal's understanding of how to apply the law rather than on the fairness of the hearing. The appellant may well fear that if the tribunal did not decide in her favour in the first place, its assessment of compensation may be adversely affected by its belief that she has not suffered a real injustice. In light of the decision in *Sinclair Roche & Temperley v Heard*, the EAT is unlikely to be willing to accommodate this fear expressly, but it may reach the same result by deciding that the original tribunal's handling of the case was 'wholly flawed' or 'completely mishandled'.[19] As the factual considerations affecting the remedy have probably not previously been explored, there is no duplication of effort in sending that question to a new tribunal.

Example 2

The claimant complains that he has been dismissed for refusing to work on Sundays. His employer says that the reason for the dismissal was his inflexibility. The tribunal accepts this, and the claimant appeals.

The EAT examines the tribunal's decision and holds that it is impossible to tell from the tribunal's decision whether the tribunal considered that the claimant was inflexible in any way other than in refusing, as was his right, to work on Sundays. The claimant must have been a shop or betting shop worker: see ERA 1996 s101. The EAT holds that if this was the only respect in

---

18 'Of course', it might be said; but see *Schmidt v Austicks Bookshops Ltd* [1978] ICR 85 for a closely analogous case.

19 [2004] IRLR 763, EAT.

which the claimant was inflexible, then his complaint must succeed, and remits the case to a different tribunal for consideration of whether, in light of this guidance, his dismissal was unfair.

Comment
The earlier decision contains within it the suggestion that the tribunal felt that the employee had been unreasonable, and had fundamentally misunderstood how the protection against compulsory Sunday working operates. Sending it back to the same tribunal is likely to leave the claimant with a doubt that he has had a fair hearing if the tribunal reaches the same result again. The claimant will have had to persuade the EAT that this outweighs the saving of costs and time that would be achieved by sending the case back to the same tribunal.

Example 3
The claimant complains of sexual harassment. The tribunal does not believe her complaint, and finds that none of the incidents she complains of actually took place. The respondent applies for costs on the grounds that bringing a claim to the tribunal that was based on lies was unreasonable. The tribunal agrees, and says in its decision: 'In the circumstances we consider we have no option but to award costs to the respondent.'

The claimant appeals, saying that even if the tribunal was persuaded that her conduct in bringing the case was unreasonable, it still had a discretion to exercise whether or not to award costs. The EAT agrees, and remits the case to the same tribunal so that it can exercise its discretion whether or not to award costs.

Comment
Here the claimant has won a very hollow victory. The question whether to award costs depends heavily on what happened in the course of the hearing, so it is very difficult to ask a different tribunal to exercise the discretion: it would not have any better access to the factual background than the EAT. The likely outcome is that the tribunal will make the same decision again, but this time it will tick all the right boxes on the way.

Example 4

The claimant is dismissed for fighting at work. She says it was a very lively workplace and the fight was a play-fight that got out of hand, and she complains of unfair dismissal. The tribunal says that the claimant's conduct was very reprehensible but that taking all the other factors into account it considers that a final warning would have been more appropriate.

The employer appeals, saying that the employment tribunal erred in substituting its own judgment for the employer's as to what penalty should have been imposed.[20] The EAT allows the appeal, and remits the case to a different tribunal for a complete rehearing.

Comment

Here the first tribunal took a wholly wrong approach to the question of fairness: the employer's complaint that it substituted its judgement for the employer's is clearly well-founded. For similar reasons to examples 1 and 2 it is preferable to send the case back to a different tribunal.

Example 5

The claimant is dismissed within a few weeks of starting work for a new employer when she insists on being paid the £25,000 per annum at which the job was advertised. She brings complaints under the Sex Discrimination Act 1975 and the Equal Pay Act 1970, the latter because the employer employs a man in an identical role and does pay him £25,000 per annum.

The tribunal finds the employer's evidence unsatisfactory and holds that the claimant was entitled to be paid the same as her male colleague.[21] It dismisses her sex discrimination complaint on the grounds that this simply duplicates her equal pay claim.

The claimant appeals, and the EAT finds that the tribunal has failed to deal with the question whether or not the claimant's dismissal was an act of sex discrimination. It remits the case to the original tribunal for findings on this.

---

20 See *Foley v Post Office* [2000] ICR 1283.
21 'Evidence unsatisfactory' is the standard judicial code for 'a pack of lies'.

Comment
Here it is clear that the original tribunal took a dislike to the claimant's employer and disbelieved his evidence, and the error was more a matter of oversight or misunderstanding of the claimant's case than a positive finding against her. The attack on the decision is not an attack on the fairness of the process and the claimant is probably very happy for the remaining question to go back to the same tribunal.

Example 6
When the claimant walks into the hearing room, the Chairman rolls his eyes heavenwards and says 'You again! You had better watch your step.' The claimant's previous complaint had been heard by the same chairman, who had disbelieved his evidence and awarded substantial costs against him. The claimant is again unsuccessful, and appeals to the EAT on grounds of bias.

The EAT finds that there was an appearance of bias and remits the case to a different tribunal for rehearing.

Comment
For obvious reasons, it would be impossible to remit a case to the same tribunal after a successful bias appeal.

Example 7
The claimant has complained of sex discrimination. Four weeks before the hearing, she seeks permission to amend her complaint to clarify that she is relying on both direct and indirect discrimination. The tribunal refuses permission on the grounds that a new claim is now out of time and there are no grounds on which it can properly extend time. The claimant appeals this decision to the EAT, which manages to hear the appeal within 10 days.[22]

---

22 This is not unrealistic: if there are real grounds for urgency – for instance on an interlocutory (see glossary) appeal where a hearing date is imminent – the EAT can move with startling speed. If you ask the EAT to expedite a hearing, you should be ready to work fast yourself: otherwise there is a danger of getting more than you bargained for.

> The EAT considers the claimant's formal claim, as originally presented, and takes the view that the allegations she has made there are sufficient to support an indirect discrimination claim. It holds that for this reason the question about time limits did not arise, so the tribunal approached the exercise of its discretion on a mistaken basis. The EAT considers that it has sufficient knowledge of all the relevant factors to allow it to exercise the discretion itself. It does so, and permits the amendment.
>
> *Comment*
> Often where the complaint on appeal is that the tribunal exercised a discretion wrongly, the appellant may prefer that the EAT should exercise the discretion itself rather than remit the case either to the same or a different tribunal. The EAT is likely to be willing to do this – particularly if there is a reason for urgency – if it feels that it has all the relevant facts at its disposal. Quite often both parties will prefer that the EAT should exercise the discretion itself, especially if neither has any way of predicting how the EAT is likely to exercise it.

12.50   It can be seen from these examples that there is a great variety of ways of disposing of a successful appeal, and the claimant should think carefully about what order he would wish the EAT to make if he wins his appeal. If it is the employer's appeal, the claimant will obviously prefer that it is dismissed, but he should still think about whether there is scope for limiting the damage if the employer wins by influencing the terms of the order the EAT makes.

12.51   Often an important consideration is whether the case goes back to the same, or a different, tribunal. For detailed guidance on this, see *Sinclair Roche & Temperley v Heard*.[23] If there has been a successful challenge to the fundamental fairness of the employment tribunal's process and the case is to be re-heard in its entirety, remission will almost always be to a different tribunal. If there has been some fairly technical failure by the tribunal in exercising a discretion that is liable to be influenced by the factual context, with which the original tribunal is already familiar, then the EAT may be more inclined to remit the case to the same tribunal. If there is a decision that fails by an oversight to

23 [2004] IRLR 763, EAT.

deal with one of the claimant's heads of claim, again the EAT will probably remit that matter to the same tribunal.

12.52   The claimant's tactical decision whether she wants the case remitted to the same or a different tribunal will probably depend in part at least on whether she feels that the original tribunal was fundamentally well-disposed to her case or not. The EAT's decision whether to remit the case to the same or a different tribunal may depend in part – although this will not be acknowledged – on whether it feels that the tribunal got the wrong answer, or got the right answer by the wrong route.

12.53   Often, but not always, the party appealing the decision will prefer that remission should be to a different tribunal, and the party resisting the appeal will prefer remission to the same tribunal. Example 5 is an exception to this.

Remission to the same tribunal for expanded reasons

12.54   One of the basic requirements of an employment tribunal's decision is that it must contain sufficient factual findings and reasoning to allow the parties to understand why they have won or lost. Failure to provide adequate reasons is therefore an error of law.[24]

12.55   The EAT has adopted the troubling practice of adjourning the appeal in cases of this sort and remitting the case to the same tribunal before the appeal is heard so that it can rewrite its decision: see *Burns v Consignia plc* (No 2).[25] This has been approved by the Court of Appeal in *Barke v Seetec*.[26] The theory is that if the tribunal has made a good decision but, by oversight, not made its reasoning clear, it should have a chance to do so.

12.56   The problem with this is that inadequate reasons tend to indicate inadequate reasoning by the tribunal: a tribunal that has not given sufficient reasons for its decision is unlikely to have gone through the necessary mental processes to justify the result it arrived at. A remission to enable the tribunal to improve on its reasons after it has arrived at its decision will not mean that the tribunal reconsiders the case – in other words it will not revisit the mental processes by which it arrived

---

24 *Meek v City of Birmingham District Council* [1987] IRLR 250, CA.
25 [2004] IRLR 425, EAT.
26 [2005] ICR 1373, [2005] IRLR 633.

at the result – but will instead simply act as an invitation to the tribunal to explain a process of reasoning by which it could properly have arrived at the result it did arrive at.

12.57 The practical result of this is that appeals based on inadequate reasoning by the tribunal will very often be futile, unless the reasoning is so inadequate that a referral for clarification is obviously inadequate.

Rejection of an appeal on the papers

12.58 Sometimes a judge at the EAT will read the notice of appeal and accompanying documents and form the view that the appeal discloses no reasonable grounds for bringing the appeal. In these cases, rule 3(7) of the EAT Rules of Procedure permits the EAT to reject the appeal without a hearing. It is important to be aware that this decision is not final: there is a right either to redraft and resubmit the notice of appeal within 28 days from the rejection, or (in effect) to request an oral hearing before a judge.

12.59 A claimant should only be deterred by rejection at this stage if he recognises that the appeal was really just an attack on legitimate findings of fact or an exercise of discretion. Claimants who believe that what they are complaining of is an error of law should persist. The EAT is rather too much inclined to reject appeals at this stage, and the decisions are not always fully considered. A case which looks hopeless on a quick read of the papers may look very different after a full argument.

12.60 A significant factor for unrepresented claimants is that if they request an oral hearing, they may be able to benefit from free representation at that hearing under the Employment Lawyers' Appeals Advice Scheme (ELAAS). This can be extremely valuable: the ELAAS advisers are experienced employment lawyers who may be able to focus the appeal on its one or two best points and dramatically improve its chances of success.

12.61 An oral hearing on a decision to reject an appeal on the papers is requested by writing to the Registrar to 'express dissatisfaction' with the reasons given by the judge or Registrar for rejecting the appeal. This letter can be very brief. It will do unrepresented appellants no harm to request ELAAS representation in the same letter.

P12.61 Letter expressing dissatisfaction with decision to reject the appeal on the papers

The Registrar
Employment Appeal Tribunal
Audit House
58 Victoria Embankment
London
EC4Y 0DS

3 November 2006

Dear Madam

Croke v Little Sprigs Nursery PA/123/05

Thank you for your letter of 18 October 2006. I am dissatisfied with the decision to reject my appeal at this stage, and I request an oral hearing.

I should be grateful for representation at the oral hearing under the ELAAS scheme if a representative is available.

Yours faithfully

Sharon Croke

Notes of oral evidence given at the original hearing

12.62   Sometimes it will be necessary for the purposes of an appeal to draw the EAT's attention to oral evidence that was given to the employment tribunal. Employment tribunal hearings are not tape-recorded or recorded by a shorthand writer, but the chairman has a duty to take notes of the evidence. These notes – written in longhand – are of widely variable quality and completeness. Some chairmen take nearly verbatim notes of the hearing (some slow proceedings right down to dictation speed for the purpose), some write down only what they consider important; some are accurate and others less so.

12.63   When it comes to a remitted hearing, it can be useful to get hold of portions of the other side's notes of the previous hearing, particularly if there is any risk that their evidence may change. Very often the respondent, having a full legal team, will have taken very good notes of the hearing: these can be useful on a remitted hearing. Notes of a hearing are not privileged and must be disclosed if relevant.[27]

When are notes of evidence needed?

12.64   Notes of evidence will normally be needed if the appeal is on grounds of perversity: if it is said that the tribunal made findings of fact for which there was no evidence at all, or made findings against the over-whelming weight of the evidence, the EAT will not be able to decide whether this is so unless it knows what evidence was given. If it is said that the tribunal has failed to resolve one of the key factual issues between the parties, notes of evidence may not be necessary if the relevant difference between what the claimant says and what the respondent says is clear from the witness statements. There may, however, have been an important factual issue that only emerged clearly in cross-examination. If that is so, then notes of those parts of the cross-examination will be needed.

12.65   Again, this will make more sense in the context of concrete examples. The examples used are those that appear at para 12.49 above.

> In example 1, there is no relevant dispute of fact between the parties: the employer says that the rule it applied was not discriminatory, the claimant says it was, but both sides agree what happened. This appeal can clearly be resolved without notes of evidence.
>
> In example 2, the respondent would probably have wanted the EAT to see notes of any evidence given about how the claimant was said to have been inflexible, in the hope of persuading the EAT that the tribunal had a legitimate basis for finding that the claimant had been inflexible in some way other than merely refusing to work on Sundays.

---

27 See *Lambert v Home* [1914] 3 KB 86 and para 4.36 above.

In examples 3 and 4, both appeals concern the complaint that the tribunal applied the wrong legal test. The test applied by the tribunal appears from its decision, so notes of evidence will not help the EAT decide this.

In example 5, whether or not notes of evidence are needed depends on how the respondent approaches the appeal. If the respondent says that the reason the tribunal did not deal with the sex discrimination issue is that the claimant did not give any evidence about it, the EAT may require notes of evidence in order to establish whether or not that is the case. If the respondent simply argues that as a matter of law the claimant cannot run an equal pay case and a sex discrimination case on the same facts, then notes of evidence will not be needed.

In example 6, notes of evidence will not be needed unless the claimant says that there is something in the way the tribunal has analysed the evidence that amplifies the impression of bias.

Getting hold of notes of evidence

12.66 The EAT Practice Direction directs:

> 7.1 An Appellant who considers that a point of law raised in the Notice of Appeal cannot be argued without reference to evidence given (or not given) at the Employment Tribunal, the nature and substance of which does not, or does not sufficiently appear from the Written Reasons, must ordinarily submit an application with the Notice of Appeal. The application is for the nature of such evidence (or lack of it) to be admitted, or if necessary for the relevant parts of the Chairman's notes of evidence to be produced. If such application is not so made, then it should be made:
>
> 7.1.1 if a PH is ordered, in the skeleton or written submissions lodged prior to such PH; or
>
> 7.1.2 if the case is listed for FH without a PH, then within 14 days of the seal date of the order so providing.

12.67 This is far from user-friendly. What it seems to mean is that if the appellant thinks that the notes of evidence will be needed, he should ask the EAT to give directions about them. The subsequent sub-paragraphs of paragraph 7 set out the procedure that the EAT will follow. The gist is that the EAT will ask the parties to try to agree a note of what evidence was given in the relevant respects. If they cannot agree then, provided the EAT considers that notes of evidence are necessary it will send a request for the chairman's notes to the tribunal. There is a warning about possible costs penalties if parties unreasonably request notes of evidence or unreasonably fail to co-operate in agreeing what evidence was given.

12.68   The procedure set out in the practice direction is cumbersome. It is not obvious why the EAT needs to get involved at all in negotiations between the parties with a view to agreeing notes of evidence until and unless they have broken down. However, the practice direction had better be followed, so it is suggested that a party who thinks that notes of evidence will be needed should add at the end of his notice of appeal an application for directions as to notes of evidence. The following example could follow on from paragraph 15 of P12.45.2 above.

P12.68 Application for directions as to notes of evidence

APPLICATION FOR DIRECTIONS
AS TO NOTES OF EVIDENCE

16. The claimant believes that it will be necessary for the just resolution of the appeal for the Appeal Tribunal to have sight of notes of the evidence given by Mr Petrie and Miss Champion as to the dates and content of the disputed meeting, and by Mr Petrie as to when and how his notes of the meeting were created.

17. This evidence is relevant to the central question in the appeal, namely whether the tribunal failed to resolve a key factual issue between the parties.

18. The witnesses whose evidence is relevant are Mr Petrie and Miss Champion.

19. The relevant evidence is any evidence relating to the content of the disputed meeting, or as to the time or manner of creation of Mr Petrie's notes of that meeting.

20. The claimant's notes of the relevant evidence are incomplete, but they are attached.

21. The claimant accordingly asks the Appeal Tribunal to direct that the parties should seek to agree notes of the relevant parts of the evidence, and, in default of such agreement, that the Chairman's notes should be requested.

Affidavits

12.69 Where there is a challenge to the way the hearing was conducted, and particularly if there is a complaint of bias, it will often be necessary for the claimant and/or her adviser to make a sworn statement about what took place at the hearing. This form of sworn statement is called an affidavit. An affidavit can be drafted by anyone, but it has to be sworn in the presence of a solicitor. Any high street firm of solicitors or law centre is likely to be able to provide a solicitor to administer an oath at short notice, usually for a fee of around £10. Once the statement is drafted, it should be taken by the person making it to a solicitor and sworn.

P12.69 Affidavit in support of a bias appeal

Sworn by José Corujo on 6 November 2006
This is the 1st affidavit
filed on behalf of the claimant by this deponent
on .... November 2006

IN THE EMPLOYMENT APPEAL TRIBUNAL   Case No
EAT/1234/06
BETWEEN

JOSÉ CORUJO

Appellant

and

SOUTHERN TRAINS PLC

Respondent

I, José Corujo, of 14 Marlborough Court, Mitcham Lane, Croydon, Surrey CR0 4BZ make oath and say as follows:

1. My complaint of unfair dismissal was heard at the London South employment tribunal on 3 and 4 April 2006. The presiding Chairman was Mr Marks.
2. When I walked in to the hearing room, Mr Marks raised his eyes heavenwards and said, 'You again! You had better watch your step this time.'

3. Mr Marks was the Chairman who heard a previous complaint I had made against Southern Trains in July 2005. He had not believed my evidence, and he had awarded £4,000 costs against me because he said that I had made up all my evidence.
4. I was very shaken when Mr Marks said this. I thought I had no chance of a fair hearing before him. I told him that I did not think it was fair that he was hearing this case because he was biased against me. He said 'You had a very fair hearing from me last time. Let's get on with the case.'
5. The hearing went very badly for me. When I was speaking Mr Marks glared at me, sighed heavily and interrupted me constantly. When I was giving my evidence he asked a lot of very hostile questions. He did not ask the respondent's witnesses any questions at all, and he listened and took notes without interrupting when their counsel was speaking.

Sworn at   in the   )
County of   )
this   day of   2006   )

Before me

Officer of a Court, appointed by the Judge to take Affidavits

Responding to an appeal

12.70   If the claimant is successful – wholly or in part – before the employment tribunal, the employer may appeal.

12.71   In a case that is listed for a preliminary hearing, the respondent to the appeal is sent the notice of appeal before the preliminary hearing and invited to make 'concise written submissions' on the notice of appeal with a view to showing that the appeal has no reasonable prospect of success. These submissions can follow a very similar format to a skeleton argument, but it is important that they should be concise. The point is to demonstrate that there is really nothing to argue about, so long and detailed argument is likely to demonstrate the exact opposite.

The respondent's answer

12.72   The form for this, like the form for a notice of appeal, is very straightforward, and can be downloaded from the EAT website.

12.73   Drafting the respondent's answer is often very easy, requiring nothing more than a statement that the respondent intends to resist the appeal on the grounds given in the tribunal's decision. There is need for some thought at this stage, however. Two decisions need to be made. The first is whether, if the employment tribunal's reasoning is defective, there is any alternative basis on which the result can be supported. The second is whether the respondent should put forward a cross-appeal.

12.74   To decide whether to put forward an alternative argument in support of the tribunal's decision, the question the respondent to the appeal should ask is this: supposing the attack made by the appellant on the decision is well-founded, can I say that given the tribunal's findings of fact (or the facts that are agreed to be common ground), this result was inevitable anyway? If the answer to this is yes, then an alternative basis can be put forward for the tribunal's decision.

12.75   However, there is a tactical aspect to this decision. Putting forward an alternative basis for the tribunal's decision does make it look as if the respondent to the appeal fears that that the decision as it stands is weak and needs bolstering. For this reason, additional grounds for the tribunal's decision should be used where the tribunal has missed the point, or set out a weak basis for its decision when there was a much stronger basis available to it. Additional grounds weaker than those relied on by the tribunal should never be thrown in as a make-weight if what is set out in the decision is the best argument for result reached by the tribunal.

P12.75 Respondent's notice

The facts of this appeal are taken from example 4 at para 12.49 above: Ms Loop was dismissed for fighting at work. The tribunal's decision that 'taking all the other factors into account a final warning would have been more appropriate' flies in the face of established authority and is indefensible. However, elsewhere in its decision the tribunal has accepted Ms Loop's evidence that play fights at this workplace were common, sometimes involving senior management and always condoned by them. In the circumstances, she says, in this workplace it was impossible to characterise such behaviour as gross misconduct and therefore unfair to dismiss her summarily for a first offence.

IN THE EMPLOYMENT APPEAL TRIBUNAL   EAT/1234/07

BETWEEN

PAMELA LOOP

Appellant

and

ADSARUS CREATIVE LTD

Respondent

RESPONDENT'S ANSWER

1. The respondent is Pamela Loop.
2. Any communication relating to this appeal may be sent to the respondent at the North London Law Centre, 43 Holloway Lane, London N19 5BQ
3. The respondent intends to resist the appeal of ADSARUS Creative Limited.
4. The grounds on which the respondent will rely are ~~the grounds relied upon by the Employment Tribunal for making the decision or order appealed from and~~ the following grounds:[28]

    (i) The employment tribunal found (at paragraphs 13 and 14) that the respondent's conduct was indistinguishable from conduct that was regularly engaged in by colleagues working at the

---

28   This is an extreme case, where there is simply nothing to be said in defence of the grounds given by the tribunal. Normally the respondent will rely on the reasons given by the tribunal plus additional grounds if necessary.

appellant's London Road premises and condoned by senior management. It follows from this that it was not open to the appellant to characterise what she had done as misconduct, and still less so to characterise it as gross misconduct.

(ii) In the circumstances, the tribunal's decision that the appellant's decision to dismiss the respondent was unfair was an inevitable consequence of the findings of fact it had made (and which are not challenged by the appellant) at paragraphs 13 and 14 and should stand.

5. ~~The Respondent cross-appeals from~~
6. ~~The Respondent's grounds of appeal are~~

NATALIE CUMMINGS
NORTH LONDON LAW CENTRE

Cross-appeals

12.76   A cross-appeal is an appeal – in reply to the main appeal – by the respondent to the main appeal. If both parties are aggrieved by the decision, it may simply be a matter of timing who is the appellant and who is the respondent.

12.77   A respondent who wishes to cross-appeal must decide whether he wishes to cross-appeal in any event, or only if the main appeal is successful. Sometimes the cross-appeal simply will not arise unless the main appeal is successful. This too will make much more sense in the context of some examples.

> **Example 1**
> Suppose Saifur Rahman of P3.11.2 and P5.28.1 wins his case. The tribunal finds that he has been unfairly dismissed and awards him compensation. However, by the time of the hearing he has decided to study full-time for a nursing degree, and the tribunal decides that he has not done enough to mitigate his loss and awards him no compensation past the point at which his nursing course started.
>
> Mr Rahman and the Hospital are both aggrieved by this outcome. Mr Rahman says that his decision to study to be a nurse was entirely reasonable in the circumstances, and the tribunal wrongly approached the question of mitigation as if he had to

prove that he had done enough.[29] The Hospital says that having found that Sister Winston had invented her allegation against Mr Rahman, the tribunal wrongly inferred that he had been dismissed for making a protected disclosure without making any findings of fact about what motivated the disciplinary panel to dismiss him.

Alternative (a)
The Hospital asks its lawyers to advise on appeal, but decides against as Mr Rahman's compensation is less than the amount it would cost to do so. Mr Rahman appeals the decision on mitigation, at which point the Hospital realises that if he wins his appeal, it may face a much larger compensation award. It therefore decides to cross-appeal the finding of liability. Here Mr Rahman is the appellant, the Hospital is the respondent, and the Hospital's appeal is a cross-appeal. The Hospital decides to make its cross-appeal conditional: it is not worthwhile going through a rehearing on liability just to escape paying Mr Rahman the modest compensation awarded by the original tribunal, but if Mr Rahman wins his appeal and opens up the possibility of much larger award, then it wants to have the chance of defeating the claim outright.

Alternative (b)
Mr Rahman is disappointed with the amount of compensation he is awarded, but he decides that he does not have time, now he is studying, to conduct an appeal himself and he cannot afford to pay for representation. He decides not to appeal. Meanwhile the Hospital has decided that this is a matter of principle, and it lodges its notice of appeal. When Mr Rahman realises that he will have to argue a case in the EAT anyway in order to hold onto his award of compensation, he thinks he might as well appeal the decision on mitigation while he is about it, so he cross-appeals on the mitigation point. This time the Hospital is the appellant and it is Mr Rahman, respondent to the main appeal, who has cross-appealed. Mr Rahman decides to make his cross-appeal unconditional: if the Hospital loses its appeal, he would prefer to avoid a further hearing before the employment tribunal to

---

29 This is wrong but it is a mistake tribunals make from time to time. See *Wilding v British Telecom* [2002] IRLR 524, CA.

reassess his compensation, but he thinks that if he wins his cross-appeal the Hospital will probably offer him some more money to settle the case.

Example 2
Suppose that on Mrs Rochdale's claim for redundancy pay the tribunal finds that Mrs Rochdale has been dismissed for redundancy but has unreasonably refused an offer of suitable alternative employment so she is not entitled to redundancy pay.[30] Mrs Rochdale appeals the finding that her refusal of alternative employment was unreasonable. The employer does not agree that it dismissed Mrs Rochdale at all, or that, if it did, the reason was redundancy, but neither finding matters to the employer if the tribunal's decision on the last point stands. The employer therefore makes its cross-appeal conditional: it only wants the EAT to decide it if Mrs Rochdale wins her appeal.

P12.77 Respondent's answer and cross-appeal

This is Mr Rahman's cross appeal in example 1, alternative (b) above.

IN THE EMPLOYMENT APPEAL TRIBUNAL   EAT/ 1234/2007

BETWEEN

SAINT JULIAN'S HOSPITAL NHS TRUST

Appellant

and
SAIFUR RAHMAN

Respondent

RESPONDENT'S ANSWER

1. The respondent is Saifur Rahman.
2. Any communication relating to this appeal may be sent to the respondent at the North London Law Centre, 43 Holloway Lane, London N19 5BQ.

---

30 See P8.68 above.

3. The respondent intends to resist the appeal of Saint Julian's Hospital NHS Trust.

4. The grounds on which the respondent will rely are the grounds relied upon by the Employment Tribunal for making the decision or order appealed ~~from and the following grounds~~:

5. The respondent cross-appeals from the tribunal's decision of 11 February 2008 that he should not be compensated for any financial loss after the commencement of his full-time nursing course in October 2008.

6. The respondent's grounds of appeal are:

(i) That the tribunal erred in imposing on the respondent the burden of showing that he has sufficiently mitigated his loss. The correct test is to inquire whether the employer has demonstrated on the balance of probabilities that the employee has failed to mitigate his loss: see *Wilding v British Telecom* [2002] IRLR 524.

(ii) In light of the tribunal's finding at paragraph 27 that the respondent has been unfortunate in failing to find alternative work despite vigorous efforts to mitigate his loss up to September 2004, its finding that he was unreasonable in deciding to enter full-time education as a student nurse from October 2004 was perverse in the sense that it was a finding that no reasonable tribunal properly directing itself on the facts already found could have reached.

Order sought

(iii) The respondent respectfully invites the Appeal Tribunal to allow the cross-appeal and remit the case for a re-hearing limited to the question of what further compensation he should be awarded for the period from 1 October 2008.

Natalie Cummings
NORTH LONDON LAW CENTRE
5 May 2008

The EAT hearing and after

13.38   Getting an appeal allowed by consent

P13.39.1 Letter to the EAT requesting that an appeal be allowed by consent

P13.39.2 Draft order of the EAT dismissing an appeal by consent

13.40   Further appeals

13.42   Funding an appeal to the Court of Appeal

The Practice Direction

13.1　Detailed guidance for parties to appeals in the EAT is set out in the EAT Practice Direction of July 2004, which can be downloaded from the EAT website at www.employmentappeals.gov.uk. Much of what follows is a summary of that guidance, but the Practice Direction itself is essential reading for anyone taking or responding to an EAT appeal.

The appeal bundle

13.2　Collating the appeal bundles is the appellant's job. The task is likely to be less onerous than putting together the bundle for the original hearing as the EAT's task is restricted compared to the employment tribunal's. The documents required for an appeal are listed in the EAT Practice Direction 2004 at para 6.2, and they are as follows:

1. Judgment or order appealed from and written reasons.
2. Sealed Notice of appeal.
3. Respondent's answer or submissions for a preliminary hearing.
4. Formal claim (plus any additional information or written answers, that is, any information provided in response to the respondent's requests, but not including documentary evidence).
5. Response (plus any additional information or written answers).
6. Questionnaire and replies (if the case is a discrimination case).
7. Relevant decisions and orders of the employment tribunal (that is, any decisions or orders other than the one appealed that are necessary to allow the EAT to understand the background to the appeal).
8. Relevant orders of the EAT (and here it is probably wise to assume that all the EAT's orders in the case are relevant).
9. Affidavits and employment tribunal comments (if any).
10. Any other relevant documents (including extracts from the bundle before the employment tribunal, and any necessary notes of the oral evidence that the tribunal heard, either as agreed by the parties or as recorded by the chairman).

13.3　The bundle should be compiled in this order. Like a bundle for the employment tribunal, it should be page-numbered throughout, and it should have an 'index' page at the front listing what is in it and where it is to be found.[1] If there are more than a hundred pages in all, the

---

1　See P8.22.

appellant should speak to the EAT clerk to discuss whether two bundles are necessary.[2] It is helpful (but not essential) to add 10 numbered tabs, so that the bundle is divided into the sections shown above.

The skeleton argument

13.4   EAT judges periodically complain that 'skeletons' are too inclined to turn into fleshy corpses. It is understandable that a busy judge wanting to get to the heart of a lot of appeals in a short time should have a strong preference for a concise document, and it is certainly inadvisable to submit a rambling or repetitive skeleton argument. At the same time it should be remembered that the parties to the appeal have a different agenda from the judge's. They want to win the case more than they want to help the judge deal with it quickly.

13.5   Unlike the employment tribunals, the EAT judges do read the documents in the case before the hearing starts. Often they will have a formidable command of the detail of the case by the time of the hearing. Some judges will listen patiently to advocates, and will genuinely not make up their minds until they have heard oral argument from both sides. Others will be difficult to shift once they have read the papers and formed a preliminary view. Some simply take in information and argument better through their eyes than their ears.

13.6   These factors mean that parties to appeals do well to take warnings against long skeleton arguments with a pinch of salt. The skeleton argument should make all the main points that the party wishes to make, and should refer to any case law that the claimant wishes to refer to in argument. It should be a self-contained document that, read alone, is capable of persuading a judge that he or she knows what the case is about and what the right answer is. It is helpful to set out in the body of the skeleton argument any legislation relied on, and to indicate (and often quote) the relevant paragraphs of any case law. The standard advice on skeleton arguments is that the advocate should aim to write the judgment for the judge. This can be taken too literally, but it is a useful guide to the right style and tone, which should be calm and measured.

2   The clerk will be a specific member of staff at the EAT who is normally assigned to the case throughout. He or she is identified by the initials shown at the end of the EAT case number: for example if the clerk is Pamela Clarke, the case number will be along the lines EAT/1234/07/PC. The EAT clerks are mostly friendly and helpful. They cannot give advice on the law, but they are a useful source of guidance on administrative matters.

13.7   The skeleton argument should be sent to the EAT at least three weeks before a full hearing, or 10 days before a preliminary hearing.[3] These deadlines should be met if at all possible, but if a late skeleton argument is presented with an apology and a reasonable excuse the consequence will rarely be worse than a growl from the judge. The most important thing is to give the judge and members of the EAT a chance to read the skeleton argument in advance, so if all else fails a skeleton argument lodged three or four working days before the hearing will normally be enough to head off a postponement and costs.[4] The appellant's skeleton should be accompanied by a chronology.[5]

13.8   Skeleton arguments will vary widely with the needs of the particular case, so the following document outline is just a suggestion for one way that the skeleton could be laid out.

DOCUMENT OUTLINE: Skeleton argument

factual background

main issues in dispute

[summary of the course of the hearing if relevant]

summary of the tribunal's main findings, indicating which are accepted and which are challenged

summary of the relevant law

argument

conclusion/order sought

3 Practice Direction para 13.
4 These comments are not intended to encourage parties to be relaxed about the deadlines in the EAT Practice Direction and the EAT rules: they are intended to be observed, and judges can be expected to be irritated if they are not. Irritating the judge is invariably a bad start. On the other hand, a party who is unavoidably late with a skeleton argument can be reassured that provided the excuse is reasonable the sky is unlikely to fall.
5 Practice Direction para 13.

P13.8 Skeleton argument

IN THE EMPLOYMENT APPEAL TRIBUNAL   EAT/1234/07

BETWEEN

CANDICE THOMAS

Appellant

and

THE SOUTHWEST ECHO LIMITED

Respondent

<u>SKELETON ARGUMENT</u>

INTRODUCTION

1. The appellant, Mrs Thomas, was employed by the respondent's predecessor from 17 July 1995 as area controller for the distribution of newspapers in the area of Exeter. Initially she worked mainly from home, visiting her employer's office once a week.

2. In September 2003, the respondent took over the undertaking in which Mrs Thomas worked. The respondent reorganised its business in November 2004. After the reorganisation, Mrs Thomas was required to attend the respondent's office every weekday afternoon. She accepted this variation in her conditions of employment.

3. By a letter dated 5 September 2005, the respondent informed Mrs Thomas of further changes to her work. From 19 September 2005, she was to spend most of her working time on visits to newsagents and others. Mrs Thomas was extremely unhappy with this proposed change, but agreed to co-operate while she tried to resolve the situation.

4. Mrs Thomas invoked the respondent's grievance procedure in relation her new working conditions. The procedure ran its course, and her appeal to the respondent's managing director was finally rejected by his letter of 13 February 2006. She had a further meeting with her line manager on 2 March 2006, but after discussing the financial implications with her husband, resigned by a letter dated 4 March 2006.

THE CLAIM AND THE TRIBUNAL'S DECISION

5. Mrs Thomas complained of unfair constructive dismissal. Her claim was heard on 1 and 2 August 2007, and the tribunal promulgated written reasons for its judgment on 2 October 2007.

6. The tribunal held that in imposing the changes of September 2005 on Mrs Thomas, the respondent had committed a fundamental breach of her contract of employment, and that having made her dissatisfaction with the changes clear, invoked the grievance procedure and waited until its conclusion, she had not affirmed her contract. This finding has not been challenged by the respondent.

7. However, the tribunal held (at paragraphs 19 and 20 of its decision) that Mrs Thomas had affirmed her contract by continuing to work for the three weeks between her receipt of the respondent's letter of 12 February 2004 rejecting her grievance and her resignation on 4 March 2006.

ARGUMENT FOR THE APPELLANT

(i) Requirement to act reasonably

8. The relevant portions of paragraphs 19 and 20 of the tribunal's decision read as follows:

> 'Although the period of three weeks between say 13 February and 4 March 2006 is not by itself very long, the Tribunal took into account the fact that the claimant had had several months to consider the effect on her of the new working arrangements imposed in September 2005. It would be unreasonable for her not to have contemplated, during this period, the situation she would be in were her grievance to be dismissed in the end.
>
> The Tribunal accepted the claimant's evidence that the decision to resign was a big decision for her and that she needed to discuss the matter with her husband. But again, this could reasonably have been done over the previous months.'

9. There is no requirement for an employee faced with a fundamental breach of her contract of employment to act reasonably. She may resign and complain of constructive dismissal provided only that she is at the time of her resignation entitled to accept the repudiation. She retains this entitlement unless she has meanwhile affirmed her contract.

10. Affirmation of a contract is not to be inferred from delay alone, and the innocent party is not bound to accept the repudiation within a reasonable or any other time: see *WE Cox Toner (International) Ltd v Crook* [1981] ICR 823, 828E-829A. It follows that the tribunal's view that Mrs Thomas could reasonably have made a provisional decision as to how to respond to her employer's rejection of her grievance during the period that the grievance was under consideration was not a relevant factor or one that the tribunal was entitled to take into account. In doing so, the tribunal in effect imposed on Mrs Thomas a duty to act reasonably in response to her employer's fundamental breach of contract, and then imposed a harsh standard when judging whether or not she had acted reasonably.

(ii) Failure to consider what was communicated by conduct

11. The facts of Mrs Thomas's case are superficially similar to the facts of *WE Cox Toner v Crook*, and it is submitted that the tribunal was led by the similarity into the error of failing to give independent consideration to the question of what Mrs Thomas's actions between receipt of the managing director's letter of 12 February and her resignation on 4 March would have communicated to her employer.

12. In *WE Cox Toner v Crook*, the employee was a senior employee who had demanded a retraction of certain allegations against him by way of a letter from his solicitors indicating that he regarded the allegations as a fundamental breach of his contract and would treat himself as constructively dismissed if they were not withdrawn. The Employment Appeal Tribunal considered that the employee's delay of a month, during which he continued to work, after the employer's reply refusing to retract the allegations amounted to an affirmation of the contract. It is clear from the judgment that the EAT considered the critical factor to be the question of what the employee's action would have communicated to the employer:

> 'When ... despite their refusal to withdraw the allegation, he continues to work ... for a month thereafter, viewed from the angle of the employers, it must have appeared that he had decided not to resign but to continue in the employment.'

13. The tribunal proceeded as if bound by this to find that a similar period of delay after the final rejection of her grievance must in Mrs Thomas's case also be read as constituting affirmation. The tribunal's failure to direct itself to the question of what her conduct between 13 or 14 February and 4 March 2006 would have communicated to

her employer is a fundamental error in their approach. Mrs Thomas had not, as Mr Crook had, previously threatened through solicitors to resign if her grievance was not resolved, and had not therefore laid the foundation for the respondent to draw the conclusion that she must have changed her mind from so short a delay as three weeks.

14. In the absence of any finding as to what Mrs Thomas's actions between 13 February and 4 March 2004 would have communicated to her employer, it is submitted that the employment tribunal's decision cannot stand.

ORDER SOUGHT

15. The appellant respectfully asks the Appeal Tribunal to set aside the decision of the tribunal and remit the case to the same tribunal for re-hearing on the correct basis of the question whether by her silence between 13 and 3 March 2004 the appellant had affirmed her contract of employment on the correct basis, and if she did not, whether she was unfairly dismissed.[6]

Natalie Cummings
NORTH LONDON LAW CENTRE
26 September 2006

Bundles of authorities

13.9 'Authorities' here means the material used by the parties to persuade the EAT that their statement of the law is correct. The main appeal bundle will be composed of material that is specific to the particular case: the decision in that case, the claim form and response, extracts from the hearing bundle before the employment tribunal, etc. The authorities bundle will normally contain reports of other decided cases of the EAT or higher courts and may also include extracts from the relevant legislation, extracts from textbooks or legal journal articles, etc.

---

6 The tactical decision to ask for remission to the same tribunal could have been taken the other way: much will depend on the atmosphere of the original hearing. Here the rest of the tribunal's decision suggests that it had not taken a dislike to Mrs Thomas and had found her evidence credible, and only found against her because it felt bound to do so.

13.10   Paragraph 14 of the EAT Practice Direction gives instructions for the citation of authorities.

13.11   The EAT should be sent three copies of a complete bundle of all authorities relied on. The bundle of authorities should be agreed with the other party if possible so that all the authorities that either side is relying on are contained in a single bundle. Strictly speaking this is the appellant's job, but if the appellant is unrepresented or represented by a small organisation that does not have easy access to all the necessary materials it is worth trying to charm the respondent's representative into taking on the task. Ideally, the specific passages relied upon in the authorities should be sidelined (that is, a vertical line should be added in the margin beside the passages relied on) so that the EAT can quickly and easily find the relevant parts.

13.12   Cases should be listed first in date order, then any legislation, and finally any other materials. Extensive reference to authority is not encouraged. It will be fairly rare that a case can be argued in the EAT with no reference at all to authority, but if there is only one relevant previous case then the authorities bundle should contain only that case.

13.13   Lawyers specialising in employment law form a fairly small sub-group of the legal profession, and most EAT judges will have appeared in their time as advocates before the EAT. Because of this, there is a real chance that the presiding judge at the EAT will have taken part either as judge or as advocate in one or more of the cases on which the parties rely as authorities. It is a good idea to check whether this is so once the hearing list has appeared on the EAT website (this will normally be by the Friday afternoon of the week before the hearing), in order to pick up any available clues as to the judge's likely direction of approach. If the judge today was on the losing side in the case that you rely on, it will be prudent to tread carefully. Assertions that the result in that case was 'obvious' or 'inevitable', for instance, are unlikely to go down well. Even more tact will be called for if today's judge presided in the case you say was wrongly decided or seek to distinguish.[7] If the other party is in that position, being aware of it in advance may provide opportunities to increase their discomfort.

---

7 See para 1.35 above.

P13.13 Index to bundle of authorities

This example is of a substantial authorities bundle that was required for a complex argument, but it should not be regarded as typical. More often only two or three cases will be needed, and no other authorities. The EAT will have a copy of Butterworths Employment Law Handbook, so there is no need to include legislation unless it is not contained in that book.

IN THE EMPLOYMENT APPEAL TRIBUNAL   Case No
EAT/1234/07

BETWEEN

THE STATE OF RURITANIA

Appellant

and

MR STEVEN NEWTON

Respondent

INDEX TO JOINT BUNDLE OF AUTHORITIES

CASES

Preliminary hearings

13.14   If the EAT cannot decide on the papers whether there is enough in the appeal to justify a full hearing, it will list the case for a preliminary hearing. Preliminary hearings take place before a full EAT, and skeleton arguments are required as for full hearings. Employment Lawyers Appeals Advice Scheme (ELAAS) representation may be available for an unrepresented appellant.[8] Preliminary hearings can take anything from a few minutes to an hour or so. The purpose, from the appellant's point of view, is to persuade the EAT that there is a reasonably arguable case.

13.15   As so often, the theory is one thing and the practice is another. Some EAT judges have a tendency to hear the whole appeal at the preliminary hearing, and may dismiss it not because it is not reasonably arguable but because, having heard it fully argued, they do not think it is well-founded. For this reason an appellant whose case is listed for a preliminary hearing should be as well prepared for the preliminary hearing as he or she would be for the full hearing, and ready, in effect, to argue the case in full at this stage if necessary.

13.16   When it comes to authorities for a preliminary hearing, appellants are in something of a bind. If the preliminary hearing is conducted only as an inquiry into whether the case is reasonably arguable, authorities will rarely be necessary, and some judges will be irritated by a full skeleton argument making extensive reference to authority at this stage. On the other hand, an appellant appearing before a different variety of judge may find him or herself faced with a series of pointed questions about the effect on the appeal of previous decided cases. The best advice is probably not to cite authorities extensively in the skeleton argument for a preliminary hearing, but to go to the hearing armed with copies of all the relevant authorities (and having read them carefully) in case it turns out that the judge wishes to discuss them.

13.17   Skeleton arguments for preliminary hearings should be lodged at the EAT not less than 10 days before the hearing. The appellant's skeleton argument should be accompanied by a chronology listing the main relevant events in date order.[9]

---

8   See para 12.12 above.
9   Practice Direction 2004 para 13.4.

Rule 3(10) hearings

13.18 A rule 3(10) hearing is the hearing before a judge sitting above that takes place if an appellant objects to the rejection of the appeal on the papers: see para 12.58. Similar comments apply to rule 3(10) hearings as to preliminary hearings: it is prudent to attend ready to argue the case in full.

The hearing

13.19 At the EAT, like the employment tribunal, the form of address for the members of the tribunal is 'Madam' or 'Sir' as appropriate.[10]

13.20 Unlike in employment tribunal hearings, parties or advocates stand to address the court. It is conventional to pause at the door and bow in the general direction of the presiding judge if leaving or entering the room while the court is sitting.[11] Everyone in the hearing room stands when the judge and members enter or leave the room: this will be difficult to forget because an usher will say loudly 'Court rise!' at the appropriate moment.

13.21 Often there will be several cases listed in each court for a 10.30 start. They will not all start at 10.30 of course, but the EAT may not always take them in the order in which they appear on the list, so it is necessary to attend promptly at the time given. An usher (curiously, ushers at the EAT wear a black robe, although no-one else does) will tell the parties when they need to go into court for their case, but this does not mean that the other parties and/or their representatives are not allowed in until called. It is a good idea for parties who are not called on first to sit at the back of the court for the hearing or hearings before theirs (or at least for part of them) to get an idea how this judge runs things. Hearings are normally public, and it is perfectly acceptable to enter or leave quietly while the hearing is going on. An usher will come to the waiting-room to call the parties to the hearing room in time for their hearing.

---

10 Barristers appearing at the EAT sometimes get this wrong and address the judge 'my Lord'. This is probably because the same judge was sitting a week or so previously in the High Court, where this is the correct form of address. When they sit in the EAT, however, 'Madam' or 'Sir' is correct.

11 A nod will do; anyone who finds this either embarrassing or objectionable can omit it without adverse consequences.

13.22   In the EAT, there will almost never be witnesses, so the hearing follows a simpler pattern than hearings in the employment tribunals. Normally the appellant will be expected to make his or her submissions first, followed by the respondent. The appellant will then have the opportunity to reply briefly to any points made by the respondent with which he or she has not already dealt. The EAT will then either adjourn to consider its decision, to be given the same day; or it may reserve its judgment, which means that it will not finalise the decision that day but will take some time over it (typically a few weeks) and hand it down on a date to be announced.

13.23   Occasionally the EAT will decide not to call on one side or the other to make any submissions at all. If this happens, it should not be taken as a slight or resisted: it is unequivocal good news. If the respondent to the appeal is not called upon, it means that the EAT has listened to the appellant's arguments and is not persuaded by them; the respondent need not add anything to persuade the court to dismiss the appeal. If, contrary to the usual rule, the respondent is asked to speak first, it almost certainly means that the EAT thinks that the appeal is strong and wishes to hear first from the party it considers has the harder task. If it happens this way around, then the decision not to call upon the appellant is bound to be provisional: if the respondent makes more headway than the EAT had expected, and having heard the respondent's arguments the court is inclined after all to dismiss the appeal, the appellant will certainly be called upon before a final decision is made.

Advocacy before the EAT

13.24   Presenting a case before the EAT feels very different from advocacy at the employment tribunal. In some ways it is easier. The issues are clearly defined in advance, each side has read the other's skeleton argument, the bundle is probably much shorter, and witnesses – the biggest wild-card in any hearing – are mercifully absent. Law students will be comfortingly reminded of 'mooting'.[12]

13.25   On the other hand, the legal argument itself is likely to be more focused and more difficult.

13.26   A representative who has submitted a fully reasoned skeleton argument may be at a loss to know what exactly to say on the day of the

---

12 A game of formal legal argument, in a mock appeal court setting, that law students play.

hearing. The judge and wing members will not want to hear the skeleton read aloud: they will almost certainly have read it themselves before the hearing begins. Much will depend on the style of the presiding judge. Some will say 'Yes, Miss Campbell?' and then wait in silence until you have finished speaking, giving no clue what is going on in their minds. Others will go straight to what they think is your weakest point and ask difficult and pointed questions about it. Some will even start by announcing their own 'provisional' view, which – though it can be discouraging – at least gives you a clear idea of what you are up against. The representative needs to be ready for any of these approaches, or anything in between. It is helpful to have a prepared speech that picks up and develops the points made in the skeleton argument – adding illustrations or analogies, for example, or going into a more detailed analysis of the cases cited, or drawing attention to the underlying merits – but it is also essential to be ready to abandon the script and simply deal with what the judge or wing member indicates is troubling her.

13.27   The judge's task is to understand the submissions made by the parties or their advocates, and then to decide whether to accept or reject them. The advocate's task is to make her submissions as lucidly and persuasively as possible. Often the result is a lively debate between the presiding judge and an advocate. This is useful insofar as it helps the judge to understand exactly what points the advocate is making in order to be able to adjudicate on them. Sometimes, however, it becomes an attempt by the judge to persuade the advocate to see – and admit – the flaw in his or her case. Judges, after all, have almost always been advocates themselves for many years, and many still like to win arguments.

13.28   This can place the advocate in a difficult position. Occasionally it is prudent to give ground and admit that part of the argument originally put forward is not well-founded, but as a rule the advocate should resist making important concessions even under significant pressure from the judge, since any concession made before the EAT will be very difficult to withdraw for the purposes of a further appeal.

13.29   This is easy advice to give, less so to follow. Judges are, as a rule, clever and determined individuals who are used to calling the shots, and they are authority figures in an environment where the people around them are more than averagely respectful of authority. Judges – like everyone else – should be treated with respect in the sense of courtesy, and the additional formality that is conventional in court is not in itself objectionable. At the same time, they should not be allowed to muscle in on the advocate's own decisions about how to run the case in the interests of her client. If an extended wrangle is developing after it is clear that the judge has understood the submission and is not persuaded by it, a formula along these lines can be useful: 'You have had my submissions on that question and I have nothing to add to them. The next point I wish to make is ...'

13.30   The point to remember – even if the judge appears to have forgotten it – is that the judge's task is to decide the case, not to persuade one side or the other to concede it.

Judgments

13.31   In most cases the EAT will retire for a time after submissions have been completed to consider their decision, and will then announce it orally, with reasons, on the same day. The judgment is tape-recorded, but a transcript will not be made unless requested by one of the parties or ordered by the EAT.[13] It is usually prudent to request a transcript as it is difficult to take a full note if the judge gives oral judgment at normal speaking speed, and it is at the least unsatisfactory for parties to realise after it is too late that they did not properly understand the reasons for the decision. A transcript will be needed if there is to be any further appeal. A transcript can be requested once the judge has finished giving judgment, or in writing within 14 days of the hearing.

13.32   If the EAT thinks that the case is difficult, or it does not have time to finalise its decision on the same day, it will reserve its judgment. In that case the parties will be given a few days' notice of the date when the judgment will be handed down. Sometimes they will get a draft judgment – which is strictly confidential – to check for minor factual or drafting errors a day or so before it is handed down.

13.33   Whether or not a written judgment is provided, the EAT will always issue an order: this is a short document, normally only one page long, that says very briefly how the appeal is disposed of without giving reasons.

---

13   The EAT will normally only do this if it considers that the judgment contains guidance that could be important for other cases, or if the appeal is allowed and the case is remitted to an employment tribunal. In the latter case, the employment tribunal will need a transcript of the judgment so that it understands what it is required to decide.

Costs

13.34   If judgment is given on the day, either party may wish to make an application for costs. The relevant rules are at 34A–D of the EAT Rules and at paragraph 19 of the EAT Practice Direction. If an application for costs at the hearing is contemplated, it is usually a good idea to notify the other party of the fact before the hearing. The EAT's power to award costs is similar to that of the employment tribunal, and costs are still very rare. The application should only be made if there are strong grounds for it. A party applying for costs should go to the hearing with several copies of a schedule showing what costs have been incurred and how.

13.35   Parties who have paid for legal representation can claim the costs they have incurred. Parties acting for themselves can claim payment for the time they have reasonably spent preparing the case in one of two ways. The detailed provisions are at EAT Rules para 34D, but broadly parties can claim either a fixed rate of £27 per hour, or for the amount that they can prove they have lost 'for the time reasonably spent on doing the work'. In other words, parties can claim for the loss of money they would have earned in the time they have reasonably spent preparing the case, or if they cannot prove any such loss, then they can claim £27 per hour.[14] It would seem to be open to a party representing him or herself who earns less than £27 per hour to choose not to prove his or her actual loss, but to claim the £27 hourly rate instead.

---

14 On the face of it there is no limit on the amount that can be claimed for actual lost earnings, although the EAT could be expected to look very closely.

P13.35 Letter to the respondent warning of an intention to apply for costs

This is a letter written on behalf of the appellant in example 1 at para 12.49 above. She says that her appeal is so strong that the respondent should concede it.

Mr G Marrow
Carrot & Marrow Solicitors
21 Lower St
Islington
London N12 3AB

5 November 2007

Dear Mr Marrow

Fiona Cameron v The Old Fashioned Tailor Ltd EAT/1234/07/PC

Your client's evidence was clear, as recorded in the employment tribunal's decision in this case, that the company believed that it was entitled to impose different standards of workplace behaviour on men and women, and that it did so. Specifically, the tribunal found (at paragraph 14) that Ms Cameron was dismissed for using language that the company would have and did tolerate in male employees.

Ms Cameron's appeal is bound to succeed, as your client has admitted discriminating against her on grounds of her sex. Please consider urgently with your client whether they should agree that the appeal should be allowed and the case be remitted to a different tribunal to consider remedy.

If the appeal is not conceded, I have instructions to make an application for costs at the hearing.

Yours sincerely

Natalie Cummings

Withdrawing or settling an appeal

13.36 Appeal cases are settled more rarely than first instance cases, but it can still be fruitful to negotiate at this stage. It is slightly more complicated withdrawing or settling a case that has been appealed to the EAT than a case that is pending before an employment tribunal: the permission of the EAT is required to withdraw an appeal, and it is not sufficient simply to write to the EAT indicating the wish to withdraw.[15]

13.37 If the appellant wishes to withdraw, then, a letter must be written to the EAT signed by both parties asking for permission to withdraw the appeal and enclosing a draft order also signed by both parties. It is difficult to imagine circumstances in which this application would be refused.

P13.37.1 Letter to the EAT seeking permission to withdraw an appeal

The Registrar
Employment Appeal Tribunal
Audit House
58 Victoria Embankment
London EC4Y 0DS

FAX ONLY 020 7273 1045

5 November 2007

Dear Madam

Harriet Sharpe v Fencemarket plc EAT/1234/07/PC

The parties having agreed terms of settlement in this case, both parties request that the appeal should be dismissed on withdrawal.

We attach a draft order to that effect.

Yours faithfully

Natalie Cummings   George Marrow
for the claimant/appellant   for the respondent

15 See Practice Direction para 15.

P13.37.2 Draft order of the EAT dismissing an appeal by consent

EMPLOYMENT APPEAL TRIBUNAL

BEFORE   Appeal No EAT/1234/07/PC

IN THE MATTER of an Appeal under section 21(1) of the Employment Tribunals Act 1996 from the decision of an Employment Tribunal sitting at Reading and entered in the Register on the 30th day of July 2007

BETWEEN

HARRIET SHARPE

Appellant

and
FENCEMARKET PLC

Respondent

DRAFT ORDER

UPON THE APPLICATION of the appellant and the respondent by letter dated 5 November 2007

AND BY CONSENT

AND UPON consideration of the aforesaid application

IT IS HEREBY ORDERED that leave be granted for the appeal to be withdrawn and the said appeal is thereby dismissed.

DATED _____

To: North London Law Centre for the appellant
Carrot & Marrow Solicitors for the respondent
The Secretary, Central Office of Employment Tribunals, England and Wales
Case No 123456/07[16]

---

16 This case number should be the original employment tribunal case number, not the EAT case number.

Getting an appeal allowed by consent

13.38   This is less straightforward, because even if the parties are unanimous that the employment tribunal's decision is wrong, that is no guarantee that the EAT will agree. The parties themselves cannot set aside the employment tribunal's order or remit the case to the tribunal for a rehearing: only the EAT can do that.

13.39   However, if the parties are agreed as to the order the tribunal should make, they should write a letter to the EAT attaching a draft order and either explaining in the body of the letter or in a skeleton argument signed by both sides why the appeal should be allowed on the terms suggested. The EAT may list the case for a hearing at which one or both parties can seek to persuade them to dispose of the case as requested, but if the employment tribunal's error of law is clear, a persuasive skeleton argument submitted with the letter and draft order may be sufficient to head off a hearing.

P13.39.1 Letter to the EAT requesting that an appeal be allowed by consent

Natalie Cummings' letter to the respondent threatening a costs application if the appeal is not conceded has had the desired effect, and the parties are now agreed that sex discrimination did occur and the only live question is how much compensation Ms Cameron should receive.

The Registrar
Employment Appeal Tribunal
Audit House
58 Victoria Embankment
London EC4Y 0DS

FAX ONLY 020 7273 1045

5 November 2007

Dear Madam

Fiona Cameron v The Old Fashioned Tailor Ltd EAT/1234/07/PC

The parties are agreed that the tribunal erred in failing to find, in light of the respondent's own clear evidence that it dismissed Ms Cameron for conduct that it would have tolerated in a male employee (as to which see in particular paragraph 14 of the tribunal's decision) that the respondent discriminated against Ms Cameron by dismissing her.

Both parties request that the appeal should be allowed and the case remitted to a fresh tribunal for a hearing as to remedy. We attach a draft order to that effect.

Yours faithfully

Natalie Cummings   George Marrow
for the claimant/appellant   for the respondent

P13.39.2 Draft order of the EAT allowing an appeal by consent

EMPLOYMENT APPEAL TRIBUNAL

BEFORE [   ]¹⁷   Appeal No EAT/1234/07/PC

IN THE MATTER of an Appeal under section 21(1) of the Employment Tribunals Act 1996 from the decision of an Employment Tribunal sitting at Reading and entered in the Register on the 30th day of July 2007

BETWEEN

FIONA CAMERON

Appellant

and

THE OLD FASHIONED TAILOR LTD

Respondent

DRAFT ORDER

---

17 This should be left blank. The order will almost certainly be made by the Registrar, but it could go to a judge.

UPON THE APPLICATION of the Appellant and the Respondent by letter dated 5 November 2007

AND BY CONSENT

AND UPON consideration of the aforesaid application

IT IS HEREBY ORDERED that the appeal is allowed and the case is remitted to a fresh tribunal for consideration of remedy only.

DATED _____

To: North London Law Centre for the appellant
Carrot & Marrow Solicitors for the respondent
The Secretary, Central Office of Employment Tribunals, England and Wales
(Case no. 123456/07)[18]

Further appeals

13.40 Appeal from the EAT is to the Court of Appeal (or in Scotland to the Court of Session). Permission must be sought from the EAT when the decision is handed down, or from the Court of Appeal within 14 days of that date. Note that the Practice Direction is misleading on this point. The PD says, at paragraph 21.1, that an application to the Court of Appeal for permission must be made 'within 14 days of the sealed order'. However, the Civil Procedure Rules (Part 52.4) require an application to be made within 14 days 'after the date of the decision' unless the lower court (in this context, the EAT) directs otherwise. The order may be sealed a day or so after the decision is made, but time runs from the date when the decision was made – that is, the day of the hearing, or where judgment is reserved, the day judgment is handed down. It could be argued that 'such period as may be directed by the lower court' in CPR 52.4 gives the EAT power to give a direction by way of a PD that overrides the period set out in CPR 52.4 in relation to all appeals from the EAT, but there is no certainty that that argument would be accepted. If it is important for the appellant to have an extra day or two in which to apply to the Court of Appeal for permission

18 This should be the original ET case number.

(and it often will be), the safer course is to ask the judge at the hearing for a specific direction that time run from the date on which the order was sealed, or to make the same request in writing to the Registrar as soon as the order is received. It will probably be necessary to point to the apparent conflict between the CPR and the PD, and to ask for a specific direction for the avoidance of any doubt.

13.41   Making an application to the Court of Appeal for permission to appeal is a cumbersome and time-consuming process and the time in which it must be done is short.[19] Parties should therefore give some thought, before the hearing at the EAT, to the question whether or not they will want to appeal further if unsuccessful. Funding is likely to be difficult, but parties should not delay an application for permission until the funding problem has been solved: this is unlikely to be an acceptable excuse for a late application.

Funding an appeal to the Court of Appeal

13.42   Appeals to the Court of Appeal raise difficult – and often insuperable – practical problems for parties without much money. If there has been public funding for the first appeal, it may be worth an application for public funding for a further appeal, but this will normally be much more difficult. Only a solicitor or an advice agency that has a contract with the Legal Services Commission can help.

13.43   If public funding is not available, then if the would-be appellant either has an offer of free representation, or is considering representing himself at the Court of Appeal, the main obstacle will be the risk of having to pay the other side's costs if the further appeal fails. Costs orders in the employment tribunal and the EAT are rare, and are generally only made against a party who has in some way behaved badly. The situation is very different in the Court of Appeal, where the normal rule – subject to fairly rare exceptions – is that costs are ordered against the losing party. Costs for even a short hearing in the Court of Appeal can run to many thousands of pounds, and the risk of losing the case and having to pay this is usually prohibitive. If the employer loses the case at the EAT but then decides to appeal to the Court of Appeal, this fear can even force a claimant who has been successful so far not to oppose the appeal.

19 Guidance on this is beyond the scope of this book: see CPR 52 and the accompanying Practice Direction; and *Employment Court Practice* (Sweet & Maxwell, 2007), Chapter 8.

13.44　　　There are various approaches to this problem that can be tried, and sometimes one of them will work. None has much chance unless the case is in some sense a test case: that is, a case that is likely to determine the rights of a lot of other people as well as the claimant him- or herself.

13.45　　　The simplest of the available techniques is to persuade the other party to promise not to make an application for costs. This sounds optimistic, but if it is the employer who wishes to appeal further because the decision at the EAT sets what the employer regards as a dangerous precedent, it can work: in this event, the employer wants the case properly argued on both sides so that the precedent set by the Court of Appeal is final and authoritative.

13.46　　　If the other party will not agree this voluntarily, then if there are reasons why it is clear that a costs order against the employee would be unfair whatever the outcome, the EAT or the Court of Appeal may be persuaded to grant permission only on condition that there will be no costs against the employee in any event. If, for example, the employer's appeal only arises because the employer behaved badly and got its response struck out at first instance, it might be said that – even if there is reason to ask whether the striking out order was excessive – there would be no question of an appeal at all if the employer had conducted its case properly.

13.47　　　If it is not possible to head off any threat of a costs application from the outset, the other approach is to look for backing from a body that will underwrite the risk of a costs order and/or fund the appeal in its entirety. If the case is one of discrimination, it may be worth approaching the Commission for Equality and Human Rights, although it is not yet clear how much litigation the new Commission will support.[20] At best, it is unlikely to support any case unless it is expected to have a wide public significance. The claimant's trade union may be approached, but a trade union that has not supported a case at first instance will rarely be willing to back an appeal to the Court of Appeal: persuading it to do so will probably depend on persuading it that a previous decision not to back the case was a mistake.

13.48　　　If no single body is willing to underwrite the risk, if the point is sufficiently important it may be possible to put together a consortium of bodies each of which will agree to pay a proportion of the costs if the

---

20　At the time of writing the Commission is due to replace the Equal Opportunities Commission, the Commission for Racial Equality and the Disability Rights Commission from 1 October 2007.

appeal is unsuccessful: for example, trade unions, pressure groups, charities, or advice umbrella organisations. If the case is important enough, this may be worth a try, but it will take luck, good contacts, strong powers of persuasion and a great deal of telephone time.

APPENDICES

Yearwood v Royal Mail

YEARWOOD

Appellant

V

ROYAL MAIL AND OTHERS

Respondents

EAT/843/97
Morison P, Messrs Jackson and Warman
11 July 1997

MR JUSTICE MORISON (PRESIDENT):

This is an interlocutory appeal, that is, it is an appeal against a refusal of an Industrial Tribunal Chairman to adjourn a case which is due to take place on 14 July 1997. It is a case in which there are allegations of race discrimination involving Royal Mail and three named individuals.

The circumstances in which the application for an adjournment came to be made are that the Applicant in this case, Mr Yearwood, presented his IT1 dated 3 February 1997, naming in paragraph 3, a Jenny Sabastion of the Wellingborough District Racial Equality Council as a representative. That organisation is a charity and is not in receipt of substantial funds. They provide legal assistance in race discrimination cases in their area. They are engaged on behalf of another applicant in a case in the Leicester Industrial Tribunal. The case has gone part-heard and was adjourned and re-listed for hearing on 14 July.

On 6 June, after the part-heard case had been listed for hearing, the organisation received formal notification from the Bedford Industrial Tribunal that Mr Yearwood's case was listed for hearing on 14 July. Promptly they wrote to the Bedford Industrial Tribunal requesting a postponement. The request was refused. They also wrote to the Leicester Industrial Tribunal on 12 June asking for the part-heard case to be re-listed. Not surprisingly, the Leicester Tribunal told the organisation that it would be better if they renewed their application to Bedford, because 'priority is given to part-heard claims'. Accordingly, further applications were made to the Bedford Industrial

Tribunal who have refused them subject to any decision, of course, that we make in this matter.

These questions, that is, whether cases should be adjourned or not in the interests of justice, are very difficult to determine and we have considerable sympathy with the attitude which has been taken by the distinguished Chairman in this case.

There are many good reasons for holding parties to a commitment which has been made. When the date was originally fixed for this case I think it was at a time when the organisation thought that they would be available.

Furthermore, the Respondents to the complaint have an interest in having their case heard and determined, particularly where individuals have been named as Respondent, as has happened in this case. Justice delayed is, as we know, justice denied, and we can understand the learned Chairman taking the attitude he did. But that said, this seems to us to be a listing crisis of the sort which is capable of causing injustice.

Had the organisation to which I have referred been a professional firm of Solicitors, there could be no doubt that it would have been the right decision to have refused an adjournment and to require Mr Yearwood to obtain alternative legal services, or the services of a different partner within the same firm. But organisations such as the one in question do, in our experience, provide useful assistance to the community which they serve, and we are mindful of the difficulties which listing problems can genuinely cause them. They have in our judgment, acted properly and promptly in this matter.

There is no particular prejudice which the Respondents are able to identify if the appeal were to be allowed, although they do point out that the three individuals do not work in the same place and have been organised to attend on 14 July, but that said, there is no further particular injustice which they can legitimately point to, if we were to accede to the appeal.

Not without some difficulty, we have arrived at the conclusions that the interests of justice require that this case should be adjourned. If it is not, Mr Yearwood would have to appear on 14 July without representation to ask for an adjournment; we imagine that, in those circumstances, the Tribunal would be likely to accede to his request. If that were to happen, then the inconvenience to the witnesses would be much greater than if we were to accede to the appeal. If, on the other hand, he turned up unrepresented on 14 July, and an application for adjournment was refused, we can well understand how he might feel at a disadvantage in proceeding with complaints of unlawful discrimination, which are serious complaints to make and to have tried. It seems to us, in general, that it is important that this type of case in particular should be heard after the parties have had a fair opportunity to prepare for the hearing before the Industrial Tribunal.

Therefore, with difficulty, we have on balance been prepared to accede to this appeal. Although for technical reasons we are forced to say that the refusal of the adjournment was, in our judgment, so unreasonable as to be worthy of our interfering with it, we would like to make it quite clear that we are not unappreciative of the reasons which must have lain behind the attitude which has been taken by the Chairman in this case.

For these reasons we feel obliged to allow this appeal and to order that the case be adjourned from 14 July.

Useful organisations

Advisory, Conciliation and Arbitration Service (ACAS)

ACAS national

Brandon House
180 Borough High Street
London SE1 1LW
Tel: 020 7210 3613
Website: www.acas.org.uk

ACAS Helpline:
08457 47 47 47
08456 06 16 00 (textphone)

Equality Direct (confidential advice service for small businesses in equality):
08456 00 34 44

Advisory Service (formerly Race and Equality Advisory Service):
08457 47 47 47

ACAS Equality Service (for small to medium businesses in Yorkshire & Humber only):
0113 205 3854
equalityservices@acas.org.uk

Regional offices

East of England
Acas House
Kempson Way
Suffolk Business Park
Bury St Edmunds
Suffolk IP32 7AR
Tel: 01284 774 500

London
Euston Tower
286 Euston Road
London NW1 3JJ
Tel: 020 7396 0022

Midlands (East)
Lancaster House
10 Sherwood House
Nottingham NG7 6JE
Tel: 0115 985 8253

Midlands (West)
Warwick House
6 Highfield Road
Edgbaston
Birmingham B15 3ED
Tel: 0121 456 5434

North East
Cross House
Westgate Road
Newcastle upon Tyne NE1 4XX
Tel: 0191 269 6000

North West (Liverpool)
Pavilion 1
The Matchworks
Speke Road
Speke
Liverpool L19 2PH
Tel: 0151 728 5600

North West (Manchester)
Commercial Union House
2–10 Albert Square
Manchester M60 8AD
Tel: 0161 833 8500

Scotland
151 West George Street
Glasgow G2 7JJ
Tel: 0141 248 1400

South West
The Waterfront
Welshback
Bristol BS1 4SB
Tel: 0117 906 5200

South East (Kent)
Suites 3-5, Business Centre
1-7 Commercial Road
Paddock Wood
Kent TN12 6EN
Tel: 01892 837 273

South East (Hampshire)
Cygnus House
Ground Floor
Waterfront Business Park
Fleet
Hampshire GU51 3QT
Tel: 01252 816 650

Wales
3 Purbeck House
Lambourne Crescent
Llanishen
Cardiff CF14 5GJ
Tel: 029 2076 2636

Yorkshire & Humber
The Cube
123 Albion Street
Leeds LS2 8ER
Tel: 0113 205 3800

Central Arbitration Committee

Third Floor
PO Box 51547
London SE1 1ZG
Tel: 020 7904 2301
Fax: 020 7904 2301
E-mail: enquiries@cac.gov.uk
Website: www.cac.gov.uk

Certification Officer

Brandon House
180 Borough High Street
London SE1 1LW
Tel: 020 7210 3734
Fax: 020 7210 3612
E-mail: info@certoffice.org
Website: www.certoffice.org

Citizens Advice

Myddleton House
115-123 Pentonville Road
London N1 9LZ
Tel: 020 7833 2181 (admin only)
Fax: 020 7833 4371 (admin only)
Website: www.citizensadvice.org.uk (for details of regional offices)
www.adviceguide.org.uk (for practical, reliable, up-to-date
information including frequently asked questions in English, Welsh,
Bengali, Gujarati, Punjabi, Urdu and Chinese on a wide range of topics
and factsheets to download. Information is continuously reviewed by
advisers and covers England, Northern Ireland, Scotland and Wales.)

Community Legal Services

Website: www.clsdirect.org.uk

Department for Business, Enterprise and Regulatory Reform (formerly DTI)

Website: www.berr.gov.uk

Legal Services Commission

85 Gray's Inn Road
London WC1X 8TX
Tel: 020 7759 0000
Website: www.legalservices.gov.uk

Legal Services Commission (Northern Ireland)

2nd Floor
Waterfront Plaza
8 Laganbank Road
Mays Meadow
Belfast BT1 3BN
Tel: 028 9024 6441
Fax: 028 9040 8990
Website: www.nilsc.org.uk

See below for Scottish Legal Aid Board

Scottish Legal Aid Board

44 Drumsheugh Gardens
Edinburgh EH3 7SW
Tel: 0131 226 7061
Fa: 0131 225 5195
Website: www.slab.org.uk

Trades Union Congress

Congress House
Great Russell Street
London WC1 3LW
Tel: 020 7636 4030
Fax: 020 636 0632
Website: www.tuc.org.uk

Employment Appeal Tribunal

London

Audit House
58 Victoria Embankment
London EC4Y 0DS
Tel: 020 7273 1040
Fax: 020 7273 1045
Email: londoneat@tribunals.gsi.gov.uk
Website: www.employmentappeals.gov.uk

Edinburgh

52 Melville Street
Edinburgh EH3 7HF
Tel: 0131 225 3963
Fax: 0131 220 6694
Email: edinburgheat@tribunals.gsi.gov.uk
Website: www.employmentappeals.gov.uk

Employment Tribunals

General enquiries

Tel: 0845 795 9775
Minicom: 0845 757 3722
Fax: 020 7273 8686

Aberdeen
Mezzanine Floor
Atholl House
84–88 Guild Street
Aberdeen AB11 6LT
Tel: 01224 593137
Fax: 01224 593138

Ashford
1st Floor Ashford House
County Square Shopping Centre
Ashford
Kent TN23 1YB
Tel: 01233 621346
Fax: 01233 624423

Bedford
8–10 Howard Street
Bedford MK40 3HS
Tel: 01234 351306
Fax: 01234 352315

Birmingham
1st Floor Phoenix House
1/3 Newhall Street
Birmingham B3 3NH
Tel: 0121 236 6051
Fax: 0121 236 6029

Brighton (hearing centre)
St James House
New England Street
Brighton BN1 4GQ
Tel: 01273 571488
Fax: 01273 623645

Bristol
The Crescent Centre
Temple Back
Bristol BS1 6EZ
Tel: 0117 929 8261
Fax: 0117 925 3452

Bury St Edmunds
100 Southgate Street
Bury St Edmunds
Suffolk IP33 2AQ
Tel: 01284 762171
Fax: 01284 706064

Norwich (hearing centre)
Elliot House
30 Ber Street
Tel/Fax: as for Bury St Edmunds

Cardiff
2nd Floor Caradog House
1–6 St Andrews Place
Cardiff CF10 3BE
Tel: 029 2067 8100
Fax: 029 2022 5906

Carlisle (hearing centre)
1st Floor Stockhund House
Castle Street
Carlisle
Cumbria
Tel/Fax: as for Newcastle

Dundee
13 Albert Square
Dundee DD1 1DD
Tel: 01382 221578
Fax: 01382 227136

Edinburgh
54–56 Melville Street
Edinburgh EH3 7HF
Tel: 0131 226 5584
Fax: 0131 220 6847

Exeter
2nd Floor Keble House
Southernhay Gardens
Exeter EX1 1NT
Tel: 01392 279665
Fax: 01392 430063

Hull (hearing centre)
Wilberforce Court
Alfred Gelder Street
Hull HU1 1YR
Tel/Fax: as for Leeds

Leeds
4th Floor City Exchange
11 Albion Street
Leeds LS1 5ES
Tel: 0113 245 9741
Fax: 0113 242 8843

Leicester
Kings Court
5A New WalkPier Head
Leicester LE1 6TE
Tel: 0116 255 0099
Fax: 0116 255 6099

Liverpool
1st Floor Cunard Building
Liverpool L3 1TS
Tel: 0151 236 9397
Fax: 0151 231 1484

London Central
19–29 Woburn Place
London WC1H 0LU
Tel: 020 7273 8575
Fax: 020 7273 8686

London South
Montague Court
101 London Road
Croydon CR0 2RF
Tel: 020 8667 9131
Fax: 020 8649 9470

Manchester
Alexandra House
14–22 The Parsonage
Manchester M3 2JA
Tel: 0161 833 0581
Fax: 0161 832 0249

Newcastle
Quayside House
110 Quayside
Newcastle upon Tyne NE1 3DX
Tel: 0191 260 6900
Fax: 0191 222 1680

Nottingham
3rd Floor Byron House
2A Maid Marian Way
Nottingham NG1 6HS
Tel: 0115 947 5701
Fax: 0115 950 7612

Reading
5th Floor 30–31 Friar Street
Reading RG1 1DY
Tel: 0118 959 4917
Fax: 0118 956 8066

Sheffield
14 East Parade
Sheffield S1 2ET
Tel: 0114 276 0348
Fax: 0114 276 2551

Shrewsbury
Prospect House
Belle Vue Road
Shrewsbury SY3 7AR
Tel: 01743 358341
Fax: 01743 244186

Southampton
3rd Floor Duke's Keep
Marsh Lane
Southampton SO14 3EX
Tel: 023 8071 6400
Fax: 023 8063 5506

Stratford
44 The Broadway
Stratford
London E15 1XH
Tel: 020 8221 0921
Fax: 020 8221 0398

Thornaby (hearing centre)
Part Ground Floor
Christine House
4 Sorbonne Close
Thornaby-on-Tees
Cleveland TS17 6DA
Tel/Fax: as for Newcastle

Watford
3rd Floor
Radius House
521 Clarendon Road
Watford
Herts WD1 1HU
Tel: 01923 281750
Fax: 01923 281781

LEGAL REPRESENTATION

Bar Pro Bono Unit

289–293 High Holborn
London WC1V 7HZ
Website: www.barprobono.org.uk

Free Representation Unit

6th Floor
289–293 High Holborn
London WC1V 7HZ
Tel: 0207 611 9555
E-mail: admin@freerepresentationunit.org.uk
Website: www.freerepresentationunit.org.uk

Law Centres Federation

293–299 Kentish Town Road
London NW5 2TJ
Tel: 020 7428 4400
Fax: 020 7428 4401
E-mail: info@lawcentres.org.uk
Website: www.lawcentres.org.uk

LawWorks (formerly Solicitors Pro Bono Group)

10–13 Lovat Lane
 London, EC3R 8DN
Tel 0207 929 5601
Fax 0207929 5722
Website: www.lawworks.org.uk

SPECIALIST CHARITIES

Andrea Adams Trust
(bullying)

Hova House
1 Hova Villas
Hove
East Sussex BN3 3DH
Tel: 01273 704 900
Fax: 01273 704 900
E-Mail:
mail@andreaadamstrust.org
Website:
www.andreaadamstrust.org

Age Concern England

Astral House
1268 London Road
London SW16 4ER
Tel: 020 8765 7200
Freephone information:
0800 00 99 66
Website: www.ace.org.uk

Mind
(mental health)

15–19 Broadway
London E15 4BQ
Tel: 020 8519 2122
Fax: 020 8522 1725
E-mail: contact@mind.org.uk
Website: ww.mind.org.uk

MindinfoLine

Mind
PO Box 277
ManchesterM60 3XN
Tel: 0845 766 0163
E-mail: info@mind.org.uk

Mind Cymru

3rd Floor
Quebec House
Castlebridge
5–19 Cowbridge Road East
Cardiff CF11 9AB
Tel: 029 2039 5123
Fax: 029 2034 6585

Public Concern at Work
(whistleblowing)

Suite 301
16 Baldwins Gardens
London EC1N 7RJ
Tel: 020 7404 6609
Fax: 020 7404 609
E-mail: Enquires:
whistle@pcaw.co.uk
Helpline: helpline@pcaw.co.uk
Services: services@pcaw.co.uk

RNIB

Royal National Institute of Blind
People
105 Judd Street
London
WC1H 9NE
Tel: 020 7388 1266
Helpline: 0845 766 9999
Fax: 020 7388 2034
Website: www.rnib.org.uk

RNID

19–23 Featherstone Street
London EC1Y 8SL
Tel: 020 7296 8000
Textphone: 020 7296 8001
Fax: 020 7296 8199

Freephone information:
Tel: 0808 808 0123
Textphone: 0808 808 9000
SMS: 0780 000 0360
E-mail:
informationline@rnid.org.uk
Website: www.rnid.org.uk

Terrence Higgins Trust

314–320 Gray's Inn Road
London WC1X 8DP
Tel: 020 7812 1600
Fax: 020 7812 1601
E-mail: info@tht.org.uk
Website: www.tht.org.uk

Stonewall
(equality and justice for lesbians, gay men and bi-sexuals)

England

Tower Building
York Road
London SE1 7NX
Tel: 020 7593 1850
Fax: 020 7593 1877
Minicom: 020 7633 0759
E-mail: info@stonewall.org.uk
Website: www.stonewall.org.uk

Scotland

9 Howe Street
Edinburgh EH3 6TE
Scotland
Telephone: 0131 557 3679
E-mail: info@stonewallscot-
land.org.uk
Website: www.stonewall.org.uk

Wales

3rd Floor, Transport House
1 Cathedral Road
Cardiff CF11 9SB
Tel: 029 2023 7744
Fax: 029 2064 1079
E-mail:
cymru@stonewall.org.uk
Website: www.stonewall.org.uk

The Greenhouse
1 Trevelyan Terrace
High Street
Bangor
Gwynedd LL57 1AX
Tel: 01248 370 082
E-mail:
jenny.porter@stonewall.org.uk
Website: www.stonewall.org.uk

Index

Note: P = Precedent